TAFFANEL

Taffanel

⇥ GENIUS OF THE FLUTE ⇤

Edward Blakeman

UNIVERSITY PRESS

2005

OXFORD

UNIVERSITY PRESS

Oxford University Press, Inc., publishes works that further
Oxford University's objective of excellence
in research, scholarship, and education.

Oxford   New York
Auckland   Cape Town   Dar es Salaam   Hong Kong   Karachi
Kuala Lumpur   Madrid   Melbourne   Mexico City   Nairobi
New Delhi   Shanghai   Taipei   Toronto

With offices in
Argentina   Austria   Brazil   Chile   Czech Republic   France   Greece
Guatemala   Hungary   Italy   Japan   Poland   Portugal   Singapore
South Korea   Switzerland   Thailand   Turkey   Ukraine   Vietnam

Published by Oxford University Press, Inc.
198 Madison Avenue, New York, New York 10016
www.oup.com

Library of Congress Cataloging-in-Publication Data
Blakeman, Edward.
Taffanel : genius of the flute / Edward Blakeman.
p.   cm.
Includes bibliographical references and index.
ISBN-13 978-0-19-517098-6; 978-0-19-517099-3 (pbk.)
ISBN 0-19-517098-9; 0-19-517099-7 (pbk.)
1. Taffanel, Claude Paul, 1844–1908.   2. Flute players—France—Biography.   I. Title.
ML419.T14B53 2005
788.3'2'092—dc22   2004012891

Printed in the United States of America

for Helen and Laura

and for Jeanne Samaran, without whom . . .

If every book tells a story, then there is also a story behind every book. This one began on a summer afternoon in Paris in 1980. I had just arrived there to begin a research project on French flute music, when a chance conversation in the Bibliothèque nationale led me to the Conservatoire, where Paul Taffanel's granddaughter, Jeanne Samaran, was a librarian. We talked, and she asked if I could return the next day. When I did, I found the desk in her office piled high with material collected by Taffanel—letters, papers, photographs, and so on.

From that moment, Paris became the magical place it has remained for me ever since: the place where over the years I have traced the footsteps of this remarkable man who played such a significant role in the history of the flute and French music during the heady years of the *belle époque* at the end of the nineteenth century and beginning of the twentieth. His was the Paris completely rebuilt by Baron Haussmann, with broad boulevards and brand-new department stores; the Paris that hosted five international exhibitions during his lifetime; the Paris of the Impressionists and Symbolists; of Maupassant, Zola, and Proust; of Bizet, Massenet, and Debussy.

Paul Taffanel's world was defined essentially by one word: progress. It ebbed and flowed politically—alongside growing prosperity there was unrest, anarchy, the scandal of Panama, the Dreyfus Affair—but in science and the arts all was discovery. He was born in 1844, the same year as Sarah Bernhardt and Paul Verlaine. Alexandre Dumas wrote *The Three Musketeers* that year, and the first telegraph link was established between Paris and Rouen. Taffanel's life spanned a revolution and a war with Prussia, the expansion of the railways, the development of photography, the invention of electricity, and the building of the Eiffel Tower. When he was born there were horse-drawn carriages; by the time he died there were motorcars. His life ended in 1908 as the first images were being sent by telephone cable, the first tourist coaches were heading for the Alps, and a new word, *cubism*, was being coined. It was the year that Messiaen was born, that Ravel was composing his *Mother Goose* suite, and Saint-Saëns was devising the first film music.

I began my research by cataloging the fascinating archive of *Papiers Paul Taffanel* that had been passed down through the family but only rarely consulted, and it formed the primary source for a Ph.D. thesis. This book is based on that thesis and quotes extensively from the *Papiers*, with the gracious permission of Jeanne Samaran and Béatrice and Bruno Dugas-Viallis. It also includes new information that has come to light over the past decade, and I have taken the opportunity to explore in more detail Taffanel the man as well as the musician.

Along the way I have been fortunate to receive assistance, advice, and permission to use material, from many people and institutions. I am profoundly grateful to them all:

To the Centre national de la recherche scientifique, and the British Council, who awarded me three scholarships in Paris; the Royal Northern College of Music, Manchester, who appointed me the first Ida Carroll Research Fellow; and the University of Birmingham, where I submitted my thesis. In particular to Nigel Fortune, John Manduell, Roger Nichols, Robert Orledge, Jan Smaczny, Colin Timms, Trevor Wye, Christopher Yates, and the late Ida Carroll.

To the Bibliothèque nationale, the Bibliothèque de l'Opéra, the Archives nationales, the Château-Musée de Dieppe, and Duke University Library. In particular to Jean-Claude Avisseau, Pierre Bazin, Martine Kahane, Jacqueline Magnien, Catherine Massip, and Jean-Michel Nectoux.

To Oxford University Press, and especially to Kim Robinson, Eve Bachrach, and Gwen Colvin.

In France, my particular thanks to Michel Debost, Béatrice and Bruno Dugas-Viallis, Bernard Duplaix, Ghylaine Durteste, Joël-Marie Fauquet, Yves Gérard, Jacqueline Labbé, Marcel Nussy-Saint-Saëns, Danièle Pistone, Yvette Poiré-Gaubert, Dominique Taffanel, Derek and Edna Ullmann, and Denis Verroust. In England, to William Bennett, Simon Hunt, Denis McCaldin, and Michael Wood. In America, to Nancy Andrew, Tula Giannini, Blanche Moyse, Louis Moyse, John Solum, and Nancy Toff.

I remember with gratitude the late Francis Bayer, Fernand Caratgé, Gaston Crunelle, Charlotte Lacome d'Estalenx, Madeleine Hennebains, Robert Hériché, Alain Marion, Marcel Moyse, Pierre Paubon, René Le Roy, Jacqueline Rabaud, Claude Taffanel, and Annette Thiollier. I was also privileged to benefit from the insight of the late Charles Samaran, eminent historian, former director of the Archives de France, and son-in-law of Paul Taffanel.

My greatest debt of all is to Jeanne Samaran. Her constant support, friendship, and generosity have made this project not only possible, but also deeply rewarding.

⇥ CONTENTS ⇤

➤ TAFFANEL ◄

On 17 September 1896 a young American boy posted a letter. It was addressed simply to:

Mons. Taffanel
Flautist
Paris
France

Amazingly, it arrived. Someone in the Paris postal service was able to supply the precise address—8 avenue Gourgaud—and scribble it on the envelope. Fame indeed!

By that date, the day after his fifty-second birthday, Paul Taffanel was a renowned public figure: not only professor of flute at the Paris Conservatoire but also chief conductor of both the Opéra and the Société des concerts du Conservatoire. As both flutist and conductor he had recently taken part in the golden jubilee concert of his great friend Camille Saint-Saëns. In particular, he had played the piece that for so many years he had made his own: Saint-Saëns's lyrical *Romance* for flute.

> He played as only he can play, with a voice which seems not to come from an instrument, which is not even of this world . . . a sigh, a fleeting breath across the night, a long drawn phrase which Tamino and his magic flute would have envied, then a short intermezzo, some capricious decoration, a cadenza from a supernatural bird, and a return to the languorous, contemplative line . . . playing like this is akin to an act of creation.[1]

How frustrating, therefore, that no recordings of Taffanel's playing have ever come to light. What did he actually sound like, this diminutive Frenchman who single-handedly re-created the art of flute playing? That was what the young American wanted to know, among other things:

Honorable Sir,

I am 12 years old and play the flute. I am trying to collect old and new postage stamps. I take the liberty to ask you for some from old letters, papers, etc. The old [*sic*] the stamps are the better, any kind from any country, U.S. stamps included will be thankfully received. I have studied the flute for 4 years. My father is a violinist and teacher. I have heard a great deal about you. I wish I could hear you play.

Most respectfully,

Noel Paul Bartley

562, Main Street
Buffalo, New York

There were many, however, who did hear Taffanel play and who wrote about it. Even Taffanel himself left some indication of why he has since been dubbed "the father of modern flute playing." That is what this book sets out to explore, as well as looking briefly at his eventful second career as a conductor. As for Paul Taffanel the man, whose character will also emerge from these pages, we can safely assume that Noel Paul Bartley received a very large packet of stamps!

CHAPTER I

Early Life

Bordeaux is, indisputably, the most beautiful town in France.
—STENDHAL, *MÉMOIRES D'UN TOURISTE* (1838)

Legend has it that all the branches of the Taffanel family stem from seven brothers who lived in the Midi region of France in the eighteenth century. Certainly the family can be traced back three generations before Paul Taffanel to a brother and sister, Antoine and Anne.[1] Antoine Taffanel, who came from Port-de-Peine in the Lot, had a son Bernard who married Anne's daughter (his first cousin) Magdeleine Nadouze on 12 February 1797. They had at least three children: a daughter, Joanni, and two sons, Emile and Simon-Jules. Magdeleine died sometime before 1839, but Bernard lived on for another ten years, so Paul Taffanel as a very young boy may have had some recollections of his paternal grandfather.

Taffanel's father, christened Simon-Jules but always known just as Jules, was born on 3 May 1812. At the age of twenty-two he joined the army and for the next four years was a "fusilier-musician" in the 50th Infantry Regiment based at Bourbon. His instruction manual names his profession as *luthier*—instrument maker. On 23 May 1839 he married Anne Bossière, born on 20 April 1814, who came from a Bordeaux family of leather tanners. Anne was the second of four children, with a sister, Marie, and two brothers: Jérôme, who continued the family business in Bordeaux, and Jean-Jules, who had moved to Paris. After their marriage, Jules and Anne Taffanel settled into a house owned by her parents at 24 rue Huguerie in Bordeaux near the Grand Théâtre and city center, and it was here that Paul Taffanel was born.

In later life he recorded the precise details of his birth in his *Notes biographiques*—a small black notebook he kept, charting the main events of his life (see fig. 1): "16 September 1844 (Monday 7 o'clock) morning."[2] His birth

5

certificate gave his name as Claude-Paul (Claude was his maternal grandfather's name), but he was usually known as just Paul.[3] He was the second of three children. His elder sister, Jeanne Fanelly, was born on 24 March 1840, and his younger brother, Henri Jérôme, on 25 March 1857. Jeanne died in Bordeaux at the age of thirteen, but the date and place of Henri's death are unknown. He was the black sheep of the family and estranged from them in later life.

By 1844 Jules Taffanel was well established in Bordeaux. In addition to his work as an instrument maker and repairer, he played in the orchestras of various theaters, notably the Grand Théâtre, where his earliest contract in 1838 names him as a bassoonist. Later contracts describe him as first trumpet and solo cornet, a position that he held for fifteen years. According to Paul Taffanel, "he could play every instrument."[4] He was also in demand as a teacher, and during the 1840s was conductor of the Bordeaux Garde nationale. His name featured prominently on a list of musicians in 1845 published in a spirited defense of music in Bordeaux, and he proudly kept a letter from the Duc and Duchesse de Montpensier the following year congratulating him on the consistently high standard of the military music.[5]

In those final years of Louis Philippe's "July Monarchy," Bordeaux was still a busy commercial port and city, even though the period of its greatest importance was past. It had been extensively rebuilt on elegant and spacious lines during the prosperous eighteenth century, but the Napoleonic Wars had depressed the sea trade and Bordeaux had never entirely recovered. The novelist Stendhal gave a vivid description of life there just a few years before Taffanel's birth in his *Mémoires d'un touriste*. He visited Bordeaux in the spring of 1838 and particularly noted how proud the Bordelais were of their Grand Théâtre, which he considered "horribly ugly." He concluded, however: "I like the inhabitants of Bordeaux, and their very epicurean lifestyle which is miles removed from the sly and ambitious hypocrisy of Paris."[6]

First Lessons and Concerts

Paul Taffanel showed an early interest in music, and when he was seven his father began to instruct him in solfège (the rudiments of music) and gave him lessons on three instruments: flute, violin, and piano. The young boy immediately showed a marked preference for the flute, so violin lessons were abandoned. Piano lessons were continued with a local teacher named Joseph Schad, a German musician who had settled in Bordeaux in 1847 after a modest concert career that included a period as an organist and as a professor at the Geneva Conservatoire. Schad had quickly assumed a significant role in Bordeaux musical life, and the historian François Fétis observed that his "pupils and his contacts ensured his good standing in artistic circles."[7] He was also something of a composer, to the evident surprise of the music critic of a local newspaper who marvelled that "it's possible to be a pianist and a man of taste!" He had to concede that "Monsieur Schad is one of those rare composer-pianists who knows the respect due to the old masters; his *Te Deum* is at once a delightful work and an excellent object lesson."[8] So Taffanel no doubt received a solid musical grounding as well as technical training on the piano from Joseph Schad. It stood him in good stead throughout his career. In particular, he always maintained that a knowledge of the piano was indispensable for any aspiring conductor.[9]

Exactly what type of flute Taffanel began lessons on is unknown. A receipt for keys and other accessories for an eight-keyed flute, signed "Lauriol" and dated 27 May 1850, is included among his father's papers, so it is possible that he made Taffanel's first flute. Decades later, when Jules Taffanel gave the young Philippe Gaubert his first flute lessons, he was described as using "the same old-fashioned instrument that had formerly served his own son."[10] But Paul Taffanel evidently changed to the Boehm flute from quite early on. The earliest surviving photograph shows Taffanel and his father both holding Boehm-system wooden flutes (see fig. 2). Jules has a conical-bore 1832 model, and Paul a cylindrical 1847 model—a state-of-the-art instrument, the definitive result of Theobold Boehm's years of scientific research into flute design and acoustics.

The choice of a Boehm system flute may have owed something to Paul Guercy, a local "distinguished amateur."[11] Guercy was a friend of Louis Dorus, the first flute at the Paris Opéra and the Société des concerts du Conservatoire, and he had learned the flute from Dorus's former professor at the Paris Conservatoire, Joseph Guillou, himself a former student of François Devienne, a player and composer who was one of the very first professors of flute at the Conservatoire at its foundation in 1793. Nothing else is known of Guercy except that having heard Paul Taffanel play he "took a liking to the boy, gave him some valuable advice and recommended him to Dorus."[12]

Taffanel could even have learned the flute using Dorus's 1845 revised and expanded edition of Devienne's popular *Nouvelle méthode pour la flûte* (originally published in 1795), which was dedicated to Paul Guercy. Certainly he always professed a high regard for Devienne and the continuing usefulness of his method, despite all the radical changes in flute construction: "Even in modern method books, exercises by this old master undeniably live on. They were absolutely perfect for training flute players, have never been surpassed, and have been taken up by successive specialist writers."[13]

Taffanel's *Notes biographiques* give only cryptic details of his first concert appearance: "August ( ) 1854 Concert Bains du 'Mail' La Rochelle (La Sirène)." The precise date in August 1854 is unknown and there were no reviews of the performance. However, two local newspapers did report the engagement of a

7

number of musicians to play for a series of *soirées dansantes* at La Rochelle, a coastal port some miles north of Bordeaux. These took place three times a week (Tuesday, Thursday, and Sunday) from 29 August to the end of the season at a seaside establishment called the Bains du Mer de Mail. "M. Taffanel, 1st cornet Solo" is named among the musicians, and elsewhere Jules Taffanel is also credited as the conductor of these concerts (earlier that year he had conducted the orchestra for a similar ball at the Grand Théâtre).[14] So it would have been easy for him to include an item played by his son in one of the programs.

The La Rochelle soirées were a great success. It was therefore decided to add an extra chamber concert so that such "excellent musicians" could be appreciated as solo performers.[15] The piece that Paul Taffanel refers to as "La Sirène" was the popular *Caprice de concert*, op. 12 by the Hungarian flutist-composer Adolph Terschak. It exists with orchestral or piano accompaniment, so Taffanel could have played it either at one of the *soirées dansantes*, as an interlude between dance numbers, or at the chamber concert.

Taffanel's first appearance that did attract a press review took place on Thursday, 22 January 1857 at 8 P.M. It was at a charity concert at the Salle Franklin in Bordeaux, combined with an annual lottery organized by the Société de Saint-Vincent de Paul in aid of the poor. The program, published in the *Mémorial bordelais* on the day of the concert, included two operatic fantasias for flute and piano to be played by Paul Taffanel (the pianist was unnamed): the *Fantaisie* on *Niobé* by Jean Rémusat, a popular concert flutist and native of Bordeaux, and the *Fantaisie* on *Norma* by Giulio Briccialdi, an Italian virtuoso who had given flute recitals all over Europe in the 1840s.

The following day *Le Courrier de la Gironde* listed the winning lottery numbers and the wide variety of prizes donated—and reported that the evening did not finish until after midnight! *L'Indicateur de Bordeaux* for 24 January added that the hall was packed, and commented: "We listened with inexpressible pleasure to the young Taffanel, a child of ten [*sic*], who played the flute with the most remarkable talent and command. This young man has the makings of a great artist."

One other concert that year may have been important for the young Paul Taffanel. On 10 June the composer Camille Saint-Saëns visited Bordeaux to conduct the first performance there of his symphony *Urbs Roma* which had won first prize in a competition sponsored by the Société Saint-Cécile.[16] Perhaps this was Taffanel's first experience of Saint-Saëns's music and he may even have been introduced to the composer. Saint-Saëns was Taffanel's elder by almost a decade, but they were later to become colleagues and close friends. Saint-Saëns greatly admired Taffanel's playing, and Taffanel never ceased to champion Saint-Saëns's music.

The Move to Paris

Events now moved fast for the young Paul Taffanel. Acting on the advice of Paul Guercy, and furnished with a letter of recommendation to Louis Dorus, his father decided to take him to Paris. Taffanel recorded in his *Notes biographiques*: "Feb 1858 left the Pension Méneuvriez / 13 March arrived in Paris / 14 May first lesson with Dorus."

The Pension Méneuvriez in Bordeaux was a respected Catholic boys' elementary school located at 4 impasse de Gourgue. The street no longer exists, but it was in the area of the present cours Victor Hugo, about a mile away from Taffanel's home. It was a fee-paying school with 133 pupils, run by a married lay teacher and three assistants. The official reports for 1855 and 1856 pay tribute to "a devoted teacher" and "a school run with care, diligence and conscientiousness, achieving excellent results."[17] So although Paul Taffanel's schooling was interrupted at the age of thirteen, he would already have received an excellent grounding that helped him later to continue broadening his own general education. All his life he was to remain an avid reader and collector of books on many subjects.

From the few documents that have survived from this period, it is clear that Jules Taffanel uprooted his entire family. He raised a loan by mortgaging his house in Bordeaux, and they stayed in Paris first with Jules Bossière, Anne Taffanel's brother. Within a few weeks they were installed in their own apartment at 47 avenue des Ternes, in the eighteenth arrondissement, where they remained until sometime in the early 1860s, when they moved to the rue St. Denis (third arrondissement). In 1867 they moved again, to a third-floor apartment at 1 passage du Désir (tenth arrondissement), where Anne Taffanel died the following year. Then, with the outbreak of the Franco-Prussian War in 1870, Jules Taffanel returned to Bordeaux. He moved back to Paris, however, later in his life, and died there in 1890. He is buried in the family grave in the famous Père Lachaise Cemetery.

It is not clear exactly what occupation Jules Taffanel took up in Paris in 1858. Various receipts for machinery suggest that he may have returned to instrument making and repairing. He would no doubt have augmented this income with some teaching, and maybe with some playing. He obviously had great faith in his son's ability and a shrewd understanding that the best musical training could be found only in Paris. It says much for his determination, therefore, that he was willing to abandon his own secure position in Bordeaux to further his son's chances of a career. That early photograph of father and son tells the story, as a solemn little boy, under the protective arm of his proudly confident father, gazes into the camera—and the future—with his flute held before him.

Paris, Dorus, and the Boehm Flute

"As the world now is, Paris forms the culminating point: all other cities are simply stations along the way. It is the heart of modern civilisation."[18] Wagner is here remembering Paris as he first knew it in the early 1840s. In the intervening years, social and musical life had become even more brilliant under the "upstart empire" of Napoleon III, who had proclaimed himself emperor in a daring coup d'état in 1852.[19] When Paul Taffanel arrived in March 1858, the fortunes of France were at their height and the prevailing tone was brash and materialistic. Paris itself was undergoing a physical renewal, as the medieval city with its labyrinth of small streets gave way to the broad boulevards in an almost complete rebuilding development engineered by Baron Haussmann, prefect of the Seine. Musical and artistic renewal would take longer to achieve, however, although on one level a thriving café society was springing up alongside Haussmann's boulevards.

Until the 1860s, music in Paris remained almost exclusively the province of the elite, and for most people it was synonymous with opera or operetta. There were seasons of orchestral and chamber music concerts (notably the Société des concerts du Conservatoire), but they were mainly restricted to private subscribers at the Conservatoire and at the Salles Erard and Pleyel. For musicians, this was essentially insecure, freelance employment, and their basic livelihood was earned in the numerous theater orchestras. The most prestigious of these were the government-subsidized Opéra and Opéra-comique, where the players' jobs were protected and pensioned.

Music at court was summed up succinctly by the contemporary violinist Eugène Sauzey as "frivolous in church, official and superficial in the concert hall," in marked contrast to the refined era of King Louis Philippe.[20] Princesse Mathilde, cousin of the emperor, stood virtually alone as a cultured patron of the arts and leader of a brilliant salon, and Sauzey and Dorus were both involved in her concerts at court in the early 1860s. The general situation, especially regarding opera, was surveyed by the music critic Paul Scudo: "Music, like all the other arts, seems to have arrived at a point of exhaustion, existing only with known formulas and old ideas."[21] But he did note some diversity and originality, in particular a rise of interest in instrumental music—something that would prove a great advantage to an aspiring young flute player.

On arrival in Paris, Paul Taffanel was welcomed by Louis Dorus "with open arms."[22] The Dorus family was originally of Dutch origin, and a certain Theodorus Vansteenkiste had adopted the final letters of his Christian name as his surname in the early eighteenth century on settling in France.[23] Louis Dorus, born Vincent-Joseph Vansteenkiste at Valenciennes on 1 March 1813, was the younger brother of the singer Juliette Dorus-Gras, with whom he made his first public concert appearance in 1826, the year of his *deuxième prix* (a second prize for flute playing) at the Paris Conservatoire. His father was a flutist in the Valenciennes theater orchestra and conductor of the Garde nationale. Dorus studied at the Conservatoire from the age of ten with Joseph Guillou and won a *premier prix* in 1828. He then spent several years in the orchestra of the Théâtre des Variétés before joining the Opéra in 1834, becoming first flute the following year and remaining there until 1866. He was also first flute of the Société des concerts from 1839 to 1868 and appeared frequently as a soloist with the orchestra. So highly regarded was he that when he finally decided to retire for health reasons, he had to write a second letter of resignation before the Société would finally let him go.[24]

Dorus was a founding member of the Association des artistes musiciens (the musician's union) in 1843, and a member of the "Musique de l'Empereur" from 1853. He was professor of flute at the Conservatoire for eight years from 1860 and was created a Chevalier of the Légion d'honneur in 1866. He married in 1836 and had three children: Emile, Juliette, and Henriette. Juliette became a singer and married the cellist Hippolyte Rabaud. Their son, Henri, was a conductor and composer, and eventually director of the Conservatoire after the First World War. Unfortunately, little tangible evidence survives of Dorus's life and career, just a couple of photographs (see fig. 3), a collapsible wooden music stand that he used when teaching, a small bust of him in the reserve collection of the Musée Carnavalet in Paris, and three autographed letters and two pages of manuscript music in the music department of the Bibliothèque nationale.

A Louis Lot flute belonging to Dorus that was donated to the Musée du Conservatoire has since disappeared—which is particularly ironic as Dorus was a key figure in the acceptance of the Boehm flute in France. According to Fétis, he changed to the first, conical version of the flute in 1833: "Convinced by then of the superiority of Boehm's improved flute as regards its low notes, intonation, ease of playing in all keys and because it made possible the performance of many trills formerly well nigh impossible, Monsieur Dorus did not hesitate to start practising it."[25] Between 1837 and 1839 he even went into semiretirement to practice the Boehm flute, and in 1838 he patented a closed G-sharp mechanism for it. When the second, cylindrical version of the instrument appeared in 1847, Dorus was the first to adopt it. By this time he had become a friend of Boehm, who dedicated his brochure *De la fabrication et des derniers perfectionnements des flûtes* (1848) to Dorus, and also two pieces of music: *Fantaisie sur des thèmes suisses*, op. 24 (1845), and Larghetto, op. 35 (1857).

Boehm mentioned Dorus in several letters to the English flutist Walter Stewart Broadwood (of the firm of piano makers): "Dorus, who played always on wood, plays since 1855 silver flutes; and as he does it, his colleagues and pupils all do the same." Referring to German players, Boehm declared: "There is not one like Dorus or de Vroÿe [another contemporary French player], if I speak of perfection on every respect." And again: "As to fine taste, I consider Dorus and de Vroÿe as first; as to tone, Ott, Kruger and several others are superior."[26]

All in all, Dorus comes across as an excellent and cultivated musician, and as a modest man. He was not averse to appearing as a flute soloist playing fashionable sets of brilliant variations, but he much preferred to be involved in chamber music. Contemporary reports made much of his partnership with his sister. They often performed Lebrun's *Le Rossignol* together, but the frequent references in reviews to their "nightingale"-like agility were accompanied by other recurring descriptions of Dorus's playing that paint a rather different picture from that of the usual virtuoso flutists of his time: "warm and mellow playing . . . he sings so well . . . never such soft, such sweet tones . . . a smooth and delightful singing manner . . . so poised, so well tuned, so delightful . . . in tones both mellow, brilliant and sweet."[27] In an age dominated by a flute virtuosity determined to emulate the pyrotechnics of the violin—Paganini was the archetypal model—he quite clearly stood apart: "Dorus knows how to make the new instrument easy both for players of the old flute and for beginners. Every day at the Opéra you can admire the purity of his tone, and especially the extraordinary accuracy of his intonation."[28]

In 1844 the *Revue et gazette musicale* waxed lyrical after hearing Dorus as a soloist at the Salle Herz: "What grace, what purity, what fineness there is in his playing! In the end you could not describe this delightful flutist better than to say that he sings like his sister on his instrument, in other words he combines the most delightful musical sensibility with the purest musical style."[29] In the year of Taffanel's birth, that was prophetic of the shape of things to come, and it is interesting to note that Dorus appeared in Bordeaux with great success as a soloist that same year: "You would not have believed that anything could be as fresh, as smooth, as wonderful as the myriad sparkling and limpid caprices that showered from his resonant instrument: it was the stuff of miracles."[30]

It is significant that Dorus fitted somewhat uneasily into the established mold of flutist-composer. Fétis lists a series of transcriptions prepared in association with the pianist Herz, but the only original pieces that have ever come to light are a brief, unaccompanied and untitled variation for solo flute, and a simple, twenty-four bar accompanied melody copied in a presentation book and inscribed "Warm wishes to Monsieur A. de Beauchesne from L. Dorus, 1 August 1846."[31] This graceful *feuillet d'album* features the luminous upper-register notes of the flute in a particularly effective way, like a beautiful soprano voice. But Dorus seems never to have busied himself with the usual flutist's calling cards of brilliant fantasias and sets of virtuoso variations.

Instead, Dorus was deeply committed to serious chamber music. In 1847 he founded a concert series called the Société de musique classique. Nine players were involved—a mixture of winds and strings—and the repertoire included works by composers such as Beethoven, Weber, Hummel, Reicha, and Farrenc. The first season of six concerts began on 28 November, and the series continued for the next two years, though interrupted by the 1848 Revolution. The final concert was on 3 May 1849, after which there were no more mentions in the musical press.[32] However, Dorus's own chamber-playing activities continued to increase with a wide variety of other musicians such as Saint-Saëns (as pianist), the singer Pauline Viardot, and the cellist Charles Lebouc. He also frequented the soirées of the composer Rossini, where he was involved in the notable first performance of Saint-Saëns's *Tarentelle* for flute, clarinet, and piano. Rossini was keen to get the young Saint-Saëns a fair hearing and so he pretended to pass the piece off as his own, only revealing the true composer after he was showered with praise by his guests.[33]

Dorus's last recorded appearance, some years after his official retirement, was also in chamber music and it was a family affair. On 11 March 1877 he replaced Taffanel in a performance of Weber's Trio for flute, cello, and piano with Hippolyte and Juliette Rabaud. "He still has the same beautiful sound," reported the *Revue et gazette musicale*, "the same agile technique and vital sensibility as before. It seems that Monsieur Dorus has only retired to make way for younger players."[34] Taffanel himself commented to Firmin Brossa, one of Dorus's former students: "you would not have believed with what fervor and what technical polish he acquitted himself on this occasion."[35]

Lessons with Dorus

Nothing has survived to give any detailed information about Taffanel's life in the months after he first arrived in Paris in March 1858. He was aged thirteen, living with his family, and he presumably had regular flute lessons, with maybe some other schooling, and spent much time practising and perfecting his flute technique. Even the method and content of Dorus's teaching is unclear. His only published work, *L'Etude de la nouvelle flûte*, gives few clues. An essentially practical method, it contains little text and gives the impression that Dorus expected much to be left to the discretion of the individual teacher. There are no directions on musical interpretation, nor on the continuing development of tone—two elements that were so clearly to mark the style of the French flute school in the future.

As for the repertoire Dorus taught Taffanel, it is likely to have included the traditional fantasias and airs-with-variations to develop technique, but given Dorus's other interests, he no doubt searched farther afield, notably into the forgotten eighteenth-century repertoire. Along with the works by Boehm and Jean-Louis Tulou that Dorus played at the Société des concerts, there was a "flute solo by Mozart" as early as 1852.[36] He is likely to have passed on such discoveries to Taffanel, who would have begun from quite early on to glimpse something of the wider musical world in which Dorus moved.

Taffanel studied privately with Dorus for almost two years, and when Dorus was appointed professor of flute at the Paris Conservatoire, in January 1860, he arranged for Taffanel to join his class. It was an auspicious moment, marking the final triumph of the Boehm flute in France. Dorus imposed it immediately at the Conservatoire, and it soon became the standard instrument for all professional players. There had been an attempt twenty years earlier to have the Boehm flute adopted by the Paris Conservatoire authorities, but it had failed. It was spearheaded by the flutist Victor Coche with the assistance of Dorus and Paul Camus. Coche had requested that a new class for the Boehm flute be created, with himself as professor, and accordingly a trial of the new instrument was arranged on 23 January 1840. But the jury, led by the director of the Conservatoire, Luigi Cherubini, and including fellow composer Jacques Halévy and the conductor François Habeneck, had voted against the adoption of the new flute "for the present." They considered that "the sound of the old flute is more in tune and more pleasant," and that the new flute "has not yet been perfected."[37]

It was a victory for the Conservatoire professor Jean-Louis Tulou, and he scored again in 1851 with the adoption of his *Méthode* as the official instruction book for the Conservatoire. It was written for the old flute and was openly dismissive of the Boehm system.[38] But Coche, undaunted, tried again in a letter of 10 April 1857 to the director, Daniel Auber, anticipating the retirement of Tulou and openly canvassing to be appointed as his successor.[39] Ironically, he had been a pupil of Tulou and received a Conservatoire *premier prix* in his class in 1831. But the bombastic Coche, who always described himself as "the only one to have introduced the new system (Boehm flute) in France," appears to have had few supporters. Contemporary sources make no mention of his playing, and he was never a member of the orchestras of the Opéra or the Société des concerts. So although the Boehm flute was well established in France by 1860, and it was clearly time to adopt it at the Conservatoire, Dorus was the most admired player and the obvious choice. As for Tulou, in his resignation letter of 1 October 1859, he observed: "I am retiring with the satisfaction of having bravely done my duty."[40]

Tulou was by all accounts an amiable but eccentric man, the epitome of the virtuoso player-composer, and much given to fierce prejudices. His ardent republicanism had cost him the Conservatoire professorship in 1819, during the reign of Louis XVIII, and he had had to wait another ten years until a change of government and the retirement of Joseph Guillou. Tulou himself had been a pupil of Johann Wunderlich at the Conservatoire, gaining a *premier prix* in 1801. He was appointed first flute at the Opéra in 1814, resigned in 1822 (succeeded by Guillou), and was reinstated in 1826. He was a founding member of the Société des concerts in 1828. He was a prolific composer of all sorts of flute music, in a style that, along with his *Méthode*, stands indeed as the last bastion of the pre-Boehm virtuoso aesthetic.

But Dorus pointed a new way forward for the flute in France, and his role as mentor to Taffanel cannot be too strongly stressed. Taffanel would win a *premier prix* at the Conservatoire after only a few months, but the prelude to this was the intensive period spent studying privately with Dorus. He also went on attending Dorus's Conservatoire class, probably as an assistant, long after he had officially graduated. Indeed he stayed in close contact with Dorus and continued to consult him throughout his career. In later years there were regular family holidays spent at Dorus's home at Etretat on the Normandy coast. It must therefore have been with a heavy heart that Taffanel made an entry in his *Notes biographiques* for 1896: "11 June. Etretat. Funeral of Dorus."

→ CHAPTER 2 ←

The Conservatoire and After

I loved its dilapidation, its total absence of modernity, its air of
bygone days . . . especially I loved the memories of my own musical
education which was shaped in that absurd and venerable edifice.
— CAMILLE SAINT-SAËNS, *ÉCOLE BUISSONNIÈRE* (1913)

The Paris Conservatoire as Saint-Saëns remembered it from his student
days in the late 1840s was essentially the same when Taffanel arrived a
decade or so later. Its foundation dated from 1795, in the aftermath of the
French Revolution, when it had the joint aims of training singers for the Paris
Opéra and military musicians for the army. The general scope had widened
considerably by 1860, but the fundamental distinction between military and
civil students still remained, although they were not segregated. The Conservatoire on its original site at the intersection of the faubourg Poissonnière and
the rue Bergère in the ninth arrondissement was chiefly noted for the superb
acoustics of its concert hall—the venue for the annual examinations and the
home of the orchestra of the Société des concerts du Conservatoire. The composer Daniel Auber had been appointed director in 1842, and he continued
amiably but firmly to protect its traditions from the onslaughts of modernity.

The Conservatoire personnel in 1859–60 totaled 790. Alongside the director there were seven administrative staff, sixty-eight professors, fourteen
répétiteurs, and eleven general employees. Male students numbered 326 and
female students 228, with a further seventy-one evening-class students and
sixty-four *auditeurs*—students allowed to observe lessons.[1] All the lessons were
given in classes (there was no individual tuition), and for most instruments
there was just one class. The number of students in the flute class varied from
time to time but was generally around twelve. Entry to the class was by competitive audition in October of each year, depending on the number of va-
cancies available—often only two or three. In February and June there were
preliminary examinations that served both as a record of general progress and

as a means of establishing each student's eligibility to compete in the annual public examinations—the *concours*—held each July.

At the *concours*, a set piece was prescribed for each instrument, along with a piece of accompanied sight-reading. A jury of internal and external examiners, chaired by the director, could award a first or second prize, or first or second certificate of merit (*accessit*) to each candidate. The word *prize* in this context denoted the result of competition against a required standard, as well as between individual students. It was therefore possible for more than one *premier prix* to be awarded in the same year, or on occasion for it to be withheld altogether. The acquisition of a *premier prix* marked a student's graduation from the Conservatoire and was an important qualification for a successful musical career.

Within this well-established framework Louis Dorus worked his quiet revolution for the Boehm flute. He held his first flute class at 2 P.M. on 5 January 1860—the date that Taffanel registered as a student.[2] From then on, the classes took place three times per week, on Tuesday, Thursday, and Saturday, each one lasting for two hours. Although Taffanel was only fifteen, he was not actually the youngest flute student—there were three fourteen-year-olds—but apart from him only two others would have notable careers. Paul Génin graduated in 1861 and went on to become first flute at the Théâtre-Italien and with the Concerts Colonne, and a virtuoso player-composer in the old style. Auguste Cantié graduated in 1863, also became first flute at the Théâtre-Italien and at the Opéra-comique, and was also something of a composer.

The 1860 preliminary examination was held on 15 June, and Dorus allowed himself some special pleading at the end of his report: "N.B. Most of these students, having changed instruments and having been in a very big class, need to be treated very leniently."[3] By Taffanel's name he wrote: "A good musician, has perfect technical command of his instrument. Very good in every respect. He may compete." Five others were also allowed to proceed to the *concours* that year, and maybe as a tribute to his predecessor, Dorus chose Tulou's Fifth Concerto, op. 37 as the competition piece. It was a work he himself had played at the Société des concerts back in 1844.

The flute *concours* took place in the Conservatoire great hall on Monday 30 July, and a detailed account of the proceedings was written up in the official examination ledger. The jury was chaired by the director and included three Conservatoire professors—René Baillot, Antoine Elwart, and François Bazin, and three external musicians—Frédéric Duvernoy, Georges Kastner (a musicologist and author of a flute method published in 1844), and the flutist Louis-Antoine Brunot, who had gained a *premier prix* in 1838 and was first flute at the Opéra-comique: "a first class flute player, a student of Tulou, who had spirited away from his eminent master the secret of how to enchant and astonish both at the same time."[4] At the time of the Boehm flute trial at the Conservatoire, Brunot is credited with having "abandoned the new flute after studying it," but it is quite possible that he may later have reconsidered after the advent of Boehm's second model of flute in 1847 and its increasing adoption by professional players.[5]

Taffanel played fourth out of the six contestants, and the jury retired to vote in the traditional manner laid down by government decree:

> Monsieur le Président posed the following question: Are there grounds for awarding a *premier prix*? A unanimous yes. The vote for the *premier prix*? Monsieur Taffanel obtained eight votes, Monsieur Thorpe one vote. Consequently, Monsieur le Président announced that the *premier prix* was awarded to Monsieur Taffanel.[6]

In an article reporting on the *concours*, the *Revue et gazette musicale* noted this award to Taffanel at such a young age and commented on the advent of Dorus and the Boehm flute at the Conservatoire, and the "excellent style" of his students.[7]

Louis Lot had just been appointed official supplier of flutes to the Conservatoire, no doubt on the advice of Dorus, and Taffanel was presented at the prize-giving on 4 August with a new nickel silver instrument. His name and the date were engraved on the barrel of the body joint: "Conservatoire Impl de Musique / 1er Prix / décerné à P. Taffanel / 1860." Taffanel subsequently replaced that instrument, but he kept the engraved barrel and played on Louis Lot flutes throughout his career. Indeed these beautifully handcrafted instruments have remained the equivalent of Stradivarius violins for French flutists ever since.[8] Louis Lot's account book records the purchase of a solid silver flute, number 439, by Paul Taffanel on 4 February 1860—so he would already have had a new instrument for the *concours*—and he also bought a separate silver headjoint with a gold lip-plate (the number is not known) that year on 10 November. In January 1861, Lot carried out extensive repairs to Taffanel's silver flute and also to a wooden one. Then in 1864 Taffanel bought a wooden piccolo from Lot, number 839, and subsequently at least two more flutes (the Lot archives are not complete), numbers 2104 in 1875, and 4452 in 1888.[9] Louis Dorus bought number 600 in 1861 and later gave it to Taffanel (precisely when is not known). This is the instrument Taffanel is holding in the photographs taken circa 1906 (see fig. 24). It is a Boehm 1847 model flute in silver with a gold chimney and lip-plate, C foot, and Dorus G-sharp mechanism. Delicately made, it is very responsive and sonorous in tone.

Further Study at the Conservatoire

In anticipation of his *premier prix*, and presumably on Dorus's recommendation, Taffanel had joined the Association des artistes musiciens.[10] But he continued other Conservatoire studies after his graduation from the flute class, and he seems to have been under either the personal or the state patronage of Comte Emilien de Nieuwerkerke during this time. Nieuwerkerke was the minister for the arts throughout the Second Empire, and in the Conservatoire registers for 1861 and 1862 his name and address appear next to Taffanel's, with a note to apply to him, presumably for fees.[11]

At the beginning of the new academic year in October 1860, aged sixteen, Taffanel enrolled in Henri Reber's harmony class. Once again he was fortunate in his choice of teacher. Reber, born in 1807, had been a pianist and flutist in his youth and a Conservatoire composition student of Lesueur and Reicha. He was appointed professor of harmony in 1851 and elected to the Institut de France in 1853, succeeding Georges Onslow. Reber went on to become professor of composition in 1862, on the death of Halévy, and inspector of the regional branches of the Conservatoire in 1871.[12]

Taffanel joined Reber's class at the time Reber was completing his *Traité d'harmonie*. "The most perfect work . . . its rare combination of superb conciseness and absolute clarity make it a true masterpiece," declared Saint-Saëns, who succeeded Reber at the Institut in 1880, adding that Reber's "inclinations were those of the past, the delightful urbanity of his manner and style recalled bygone days."[13] Reber was not a prolific composer—some songs, a little chamber music, four symphonies—and the man and his music were one and the same: elegant, refined, somewhat austere and otherworldly. The only flute piece by Reber to have come to light is a lyrical *Rêverie* with piano accompaniment, arranged by him from a movement of his Orchestral Suite, op. 31 (1878).[14] The education Taffanel received from Reber was no doubt as distinctive, as rigorous, and as serious as his flute studies with Dorus. Debts to both teachers were later acknowledged with musical dedications: the *Grande fantaisie sur "Mignon"* (1874) to Dorus, and the prize-winning Wind Quintet (1876) to Reber.

Reber's harmony class was held on the same days as Dorus's flute class, but in the morning. There were seven students, including notably Jules Massenet, two years older than Taffanel, who had joined in January 1860 after gaining a *premier prix* for piano in the previous year's *concours*. Massenet's *Souvenirs*, like those of Saint-Saëns, paint a vivid picture of daily life at the Conservatoire at that time, and Taffanel later remembered that Massenet actually gave him his first harmony lesson—it was quite usual for a more senior member of the class partly to instruct a junior.[15]

Reber's reports reflected Taffanel's steady progress: "Intelligent and hardworking . . . very studious and intelligent . . . very conscientious and intelligent."[16] Unfortunately, before Taffanel could take his *premier prix*, Reber was appointed professor of composition, and the harmony class passed to Antoine-Louis Clapisson, the composer of numerous light operettas and *chansons*. He and Taffanel obviously did not see eye to eye, as Clapisson's verdict on the June 1862 examinations demonstrated: "Taffanel. Quite satisfied with his work, *when he works.*"[17] But Taffanel's was not the only personality clash with Clapisson: his registers abound in names of students that are crossed out. Nevertheless, at the *concours* on 6 July Taffanel was awarded a *premier prix* by five to four on the second round of voting. There were eleven entrants, and the test comprised two four-part harmony exercises set by the composer François Le Borne, one with the bass given and one with the treble.[18]

Having gained the harmony prize, Taffanel was free to leave Clapisson's class and rejoin Reber in his new composition class (twice a week for two hours on Wedneday and Saturday mornings), where the first hurdle was the examination in counterpoint and fugue. In the *concours* of 12 July 1863, Taffanel gained the lowest award (*troisième accessit*) while Massenet, now in Ambroise Thomas's composition class, carried off a *premier prix* and immediately followed it with the prestigious Prix de Rome scholarship for composition. Taffanel did not compete the next year, but on 9 July 1865 he also gained a *premier prix* for fugue (with the voting five to four against his fellow student Covin). The test was a four-part vocal fugue on a theme set by Auber, with a choice of one or two countersubjects. Taffanel then remained in Reber's class until the register noted: "canceled 19 November 1867."[19] Maybe he had been encouraged to compete for the Prix de Rome, but a choice had to be made, and by then the demands of his flute-playing career were becoming increasingly insistent.

Starting a Career

According to the critic Paul Scudo, the Paris musical scene that the young Paul Taffanel emerged into was largely moribund. In a series of sharp vignettes, published in three annual volumes between 1860 and 1862, Scudo pronounced on its activities. The Opéra was "unworthy" of its art, and of its position in "the capital of the civilized world." Hidebound by bureaucracy, it was merely an official showplace, "a pedestal for illustrious mediocrity." The Opéra-comique could be the most successful of the Paris theaters if only it was run by "men whose intelligence matched their enthusiasm," and if only there was a return to the traditional repertoire with good singers and proper productions, instead of trivialities like Clapisson's *Trois Nicolas*! In 1860 Scudo praised the Théâtre-Italien as an "adornment" of Parisian life, vitally necessary to maintain the taste for true vocal music, with Italy still the most abundant source of that art. At the same time, the Théâtre-Lyrique was undoubtedly the most enterprising house in terms of repertoire "for lovers of good music," especially by Weber and Mozart. But Scudo lamented that both houses declined during the next two years.

Meanwhile, although he had little praise for the "conservative" Société des concerts du Conservatoire, Scudo did applaud the considerable increase in the number of other orchestral concerts and noted the general development of a taste for serious chamber music: "The fantasy-ists, the composers of musical twaddle and trendy variations, have been sent packing from the brave company of those who pride themselves on enjoying and understanding the art that elevates the spirit and delights the heart."[20]

Nevertheless, there was still money to be made from playing fantasies in the fashionable salons, and the most coveted positions for a young flute player to aim at remained the orchestras of the Opéra and Opéra-comique, and the Société des concerts. Taffanel noted the date of his first professional appearance in Paris as 3 February 1861. It was at a concert at the Salle Herz playing in the orchestra of the Société des jeunes artistes conducted by Jules Pasdeloup.[21] The mixed program began and ended with overtures by Auber—*Le Vampire* and *La Muette de Portici*. In between there was the Wedding March and Chorus from Wagner's *Lohengrin*, Beethoven's Symphony no. 6, and an *Allegro de Concert* for violin and orchestra composed and played by the Italian virtuoso Antonio Bazzini.

Pasdeloup had founded the Jeunes artistes in 1852 (he was then in his early thirties) with the aim of giving talented youngsters, usually recent Conservatoire graduates, an opportunity to study the orchestral masterworks and perform new music. The Jeunes artistes comprised an orchestra of sixty-two players and a choir of forty voices, and they gave six concerts each winter season. The musicians were paid equally, the proceeds of the ticket sales divided after expenses had been deducted.[22] Scudo was critical of Pasdeloup, particularly his exaggerated, pantomime gestures, but he praised the efforts of his "valiant little troop of players" and declared that the Jeunes artistes were "younger, keener and less exclusive in their choice of works" than the Société des concerts.[23] Pasdeloup also had some powerful friends, among them Baron Haussmann, architect of the new Paris, who arranged for the Jeunes artistes to perform in the vast indoor arena of the Cirque d'Hiver (also known as the Cirque Napoléon) in the working-class district of the third arrondissement. Each Sunday afternoon the circus briefly moved out and the orchestra moved in for two hours, and then the circus returned in time to stage an evening performance. Pasdeloup now cleverly decided to change the name of his orchestra to the Concerts populaires, and, as Baron Haussmann put it, "the lower classes became acquainted with the immortal works of Haydn, Mozart, Beethoven, Mendelssohn and of Wagner."[24]

Taffanel, aged just seventeen, became second flute in the orchestra. The first flute—though hardly a "young" artist—was Louis-Antoine Brunot, born in 1820, who had been on the Conservatoire jury for Taffanel's first prize. Also in the orchestra were two other wind players who would later feature in Taffanel's chamber ensembles—the Société classique and Société des instruments à vent: the clarinetist Arthur Grisez and the bassoonist Jean Espaignet. The concerts were an immediate success, and the Cirque d'Hiver, with cheap seats for five thousand, became the popular alternative Sunday afternoon venue for those who could not get a subscription seat at the Conservatoire. Sixty concerts were given in the first three seasons, and Taffanel remained in the orchestra until 1866, when he joined the rival Société des concerts.

The year 1861 also marked Taffanel's first recorded appearance as a soloist in chamber music. On 31 March the *Revue et gazette musicale* praised the performance by the pianist Marie Mongin at a recent soirée, "very skillfully assisted by the cellist A. Marx and the flutist Taffanel."[25] The work they played was the Trio, op. 45 for flute, cello, and piano by Louise Farrenc. As a debut piece, Farrenc's Trio could hardly have been bettered. It offered great scope for display—particularly in some of the high register writing—but it was essentially a serious and substantial chamber work in direct line of descent from Weber's impressive Trio for the same instruments. And as Marie Mongin was a student of Farrenc, and the Trio, composed in 1857, was first performed by Dorus and dedicated to him, it seems likely that Taffanel's appearance was arranged by his attentive teacher.

In April of the following year the musical press noted Dorus himself appearing in public with Taffanel. The occasion was a concert at the Salle Herz featuring his daughter Juliette, and Dorus took the opportunity to include what was just described as "a duo by Doppler" with Taffanel.[26] This could have been any one of a series of lyrical and virtuoso works for two flutes and piano by the contemporary Austrian player-composer Franz Doppler in collaboration with his brother, Karl. It would have been a brilliant vehicle for Dorus to display his star student.

Taffanel noted this concert alongside another important event in 1862: his appointment as third flute in the orchestra of the Opéra-comique on 1 May.[27] Once again he encountered Brunot as first flute, with Victor Petiton as second. Little is known about Petiton except that, unlike Brunot, he seems to have adopted the Boehm flute at the time of the Conservatoire trial.[28] Sitting in the pit orchestra night after night, Taffanel would soon have heard a wide range of singers—good, bad, and indifferent—and gotten to know a huge number of light operas. The new sensation that year was Félicien David's exotic *Lalla-Roukh*, which ran to sixty performances, and there were forty-three other operas in repertory, the most popular being Boieldieu's *La Dame blanche* (56 performances), Monsigny's *Rose et Colas* (48), Auber's *Le Domino noir* (28), Grétry's *Zémir et Azore* (27), and Adam's *Le Postillion de Longjumeau* (27).[29]

Flute and Voice

But whatever was happening at the Opéra-comique, the singing that meant the most to Taffanel that year could be heard only at the Théâtre-Italien. The year 1862 marked the Paris debut of the young soprano Adelina Patti—just a year older than Taffanel, she was born in 1843—and after a long build-up in the press she finally appeared in Bellini's *La Sonnambula* on 16 November. It was the first of many performances in Paris during the next four decades. Whether Taffanel attended that premiere or not, he certainly soon became aware of what he called "that incomparable voice." He later recalled: "in times past I often went to the Théâtre des Italiens, and I must say that for me she was an invaluable model of sound production and limpid tone."[30] Saint-Saëns was similarly impressed with Patti: "pretty, lithe and gracious, with a voice that was fresh and pure, more than pure, clear as spring water, as crystal! . . . I always much loved Patti's talent because of its amazing simplicity . . . just the music itself with a voice of gold."[31] And among the many enthusiastic reviews in 1862, the *Revue et gazette musicale* particularly focused on the originality and naturalness of Patti: "The vocal quality is pure and open, its production is remarkably easy . . . she sings by instinct, because she has what no teacher or school could give her: she is a singer much more by nature than by education."[32]

Patti's example was crucial for Taffanel. It pointed a clear way forward for the flute as an expressive "voice," and, as time went on, the press reviews would reflect a similar picture of naturalness, ease, and purity of sound in his own playing. It is interesting to note, therefore, the publication that same year of Jean Rémusat's *Méthode* for flute. It had an unusually extensive explanatory text illuminating the challenges faced by players in the period of transition between the old and the new flutes. It was a message that Taffanel would have been familiar with from his studies with Dorus. Rémusat lamented that the "gentle flute" of the previous century had become debased, its gracefulness and expression reduced to musical gymnastics. Tone quality had also suffered, "and as that is to a flutist what the voice is to a singer, it is vital, by serious work on the embouchure, to achieve a good and beautiful sound."[33]

Meanwhile, Taffanel went on broadening his experience as a soloist, playing in various charity concerts. In March 1863 he appeared once again with Dorus, and with the celebrated singer Pauline Viardot. April saw him playing a Demersseman solo in a special concert at the Opéra-comique, and in December the press reported that "Mademoiselle Marie Sax, the famous artiste, and a young flute player, Monsieur Taffanel" had joined forces with several local musicians in the northern town of Arras.[34]

For musical recreation, Taffanel met up with three other flutists to play quartets at the Paris home of Eugène Walckiers around this time.[35] Walckiers, born in 1793, had been a student of Tulou, and although he never changed from the old eight-keyed flute, he was sympathetic to the Boehm instrument. He had published a particularly thorough *Méthode* in 1829, and he was something of a composer—like Berlioz, he had studied with Antonin Reicha at the Conservatoire. The English flutist Richard Rockstro praised Walckiers's flute duets, trios, and quartets as "exceedingly imaginative, occasionally rather eccentric, yet always elegant, charming and scholarly"—which appears to have been also an apt description of the man.[36] Taffanel and Walckiers were joined for these quartet sessions by two of Taffanel's slightly older contemporaries: Firmin Brossa and Johannes Donjon, both born in the same year, 1839. Brossa was a student of Dorus, and in 1870 he would move to England to become first flute of the Hallé Orchestra, and professor at the Royal Manchester College of Music on its foundation in 1893. Johannes Donjon, a Tulou student, remained in Paris and later became Taffanel's colleague at the Opéra and the Société des concerts. Together, the four of them embodied the state of flux that the art of flute playing was in, as a new musical world was poised to take over from the old. And maybe the seventy-year-old Walckiers could sense how bright the future would be for the flute in the imaginative hands of the nineteen-year-old Taffanel.

➳ CHAPTER 3 ↢

Advances and Retreats

I am not a composer for Paris . . . I want art in whatever form
it is manifest, not entertainment, artifice, and the system.
—GIUSEPPE VERDI, LETTER TO CAMILLE
DU LOCLE (7 DECEMBER 1869)

The Société des concerts is impervious to sympathy, to frailty, to
all the feelings which often guide humanity; nothing diverts
it from its path, nothing deflects it from its goal.
—CAMILLE SAINT-SAËNS, *HARMONIE ET MÉLODIE* (1885)

Verdi dubbed the Paris Opéra the "grande boutique," and Saint-Saëns
called the Société des concerts du Conservatoire the "sanctuaire."[1] Both
neatly summed up the attitudes of Parisian society in the 1860s, when music
as a consumer luxury coexisted with music as a cultural icon.

The Opéra, moving between thirteen buildings on twelve sites since its
foundation in 1670, had always been located in the most fashionable area of
Paris. In 1864 it occupied the Salle Le Peletier at the intersection of the present rue Rossini and rue Drouot in the ninth arrondissement. Here it was indeed surrounded by a complex of smart boutiques, and as a world within a
world—"a paradise of Mahommed on earth"—it supported an equally complex society of singers, dancers, musicians, artists, entrepreneurs, *claqueurs*,
Jockey Club members, ticket touts, and others. Grand opera was indispensable
to Parisian society: an art, a business, and an entertainment, ruled over by a director who was appointed by the government.[2]

Just as indispensable to fashionable society was the Société des concerts.
Since its foundation in 1828, by the conductor François Habeneck, the subscription tickets had been much sought after and often handed down within
families through successive generations. The concerts took place each year in
a fortnightly winter series on Sunday afternoons in the Grande Salle des concerts at the Conservatoire. The director of the Conservatoire was president of
the Society, and the orchestra and chorus were made up of professors and former graduates. The orchestra numbered approximately ninety musicians and
the chorus seventy voices. The repertoire had been circumspect from the out-

set, earning the Conservatoire the nickname "the home of Beethoven," and the Society became ever more dignified and insular with the arrival of Pasdeloup's popular Sunday concerts and other similar enterprises.[3]

The Opéra Orchestra

The Salle Le Peletier opened its doors to Paul Taffanel on 1 May 1864: "Opéra. Supernumerary. (Messieurs Dorus, Altès and Leplus)" was the entry in his *Notes biographiques*. He became an officially registered extra player, called on to augment the numbers for particular productions and to substitute during the absences of any of the three full-time flutists. All three were required for premieres and the first few performances of an opera, but after that usually only two would play. Consequently a system of rotation was devised, and the work was shared between them. The way it worked in practice can be seen in the records Taffanel later kept for part of 1871 and 1876. These show that while the players had their official positions of principal, second, and third flutes, on occasions any of the three might end up playing the first flute part.[4]

The prestigious Opéra orchestra (definitely a step up from the Opéra-comique) numbered about ninety-five players.[5] Dorus was the principal flute, and once again he may have had some influence in Taffanel's advancement, although there hardly needed to be any special favors, as Taffanel's reputation was steadily growing. The second flute was Henri Altès, with whom Taffanel was to have an uneasy relationship. Without Altès, the succession of Dorus's playing and teaching positions would have passed naturally to Taffanel. But Altès, born in 1826, and a former student of Tulou at the Conservatoire (*premier prix* 1842), was sufficiently senior to Taffanel to take precedence. Taffanel therefore had to wait to follow him into the first flute positions at the Société des concerts (1869) and the Opéra (1876), and finally the flute professorship at the Conservatoire (1893).

Altès has been immortalized in Degas's painting in the Musée d'Orsay, *Les Musiciens de l'orchestre*, which depicts him, among others, playing in the pit orchestra at the Opéra. Degas worked on it in 1868–9, just as Altès was succeeding Dorus as professor at the Conservatoire, and he also painted a sensitive portrait in profile of Altès, now in the Metropolitan Museum, New York.[6] Altès belonged firmly to the old virtuoso tradition, although he did adopt the Boehm flute, purchasing a Louis Lot (no. 476) in 1860.[7] He appeared from time to time as a soloist, usually in one of his own bravura *fantaisies* or *solos de concours*, but his career was made mainly as an orchestral player and a teacher. His flute pieces were soon forgotten, but his three-volume *Méthode*, published in 1880, is still used in France and valued for its methodical approach. Altès had a younger brother, Ernest (with whom he is sometimes confused), who was a violinist and conductor at the Opéra and the Société des concerts.

The third flute, Ludovic Leplus, was a son-in-law of François Habeneck, the founder of the Société des concerts. Born in 1807, he had joined the Opéra orchestra in 1848 as third flute and was now approaching his retirement. Back in 1840 he had been listed among the five most important flute players in Paris—alongside Tulou, Drouet, Camus, and Dorus—and described as one of those who had "abandoned the new flute after trying it out."[8]

In the summer of 1864 Dorus requested a three-month leave of absence from the Opéra orchestra, and on the recommendation of the conductor, George Hainl, to the director, Emile Perrin, Taffanel stood in for him. The repertoire he would have played that year was dominated by works from four big operatic names: *Moses in Egypt* by Rossini was the favorite, with twenty-eight performances, followed by his *William Tell*, Meyerbeer's *Les Huguenots*, Donizetti's *La Favorite*, and Verdi's *Il Trovatore* (given in a French version as *Le Trouvère*). Auber and Halévy also figured, with *La Muette de Portici* and *La Juive*, and popular among the ballets was *Giselle* by Adam.[9]

Taffanel's starting salary at the Opéra was a mere 100 francs per month, but this rose dramatically to 2250 francs in April 1866 when he was appointed second flute, replacing Altès, who had succeeded Dorus as first flute. By this time Taffanel also had the security of being registered with the Opéra pension fund. His salary later increased to 2700 francs in September 1875 and 3300 francs the following September when he in turn succeeded Altès as first flute.[10]

When Leplus retired in August 1866, Johannes Donjon became the new third flute. Donjon (as noted in the previous chapter) had been a Tulou student (*premier prix* 1856) and like Taffanel had spent some time in the orchestra of the Opéra-comique. He had also adopted the Boehm flute.[11] The two men became firm friends, and in 1887 Donjon dedicated his *Rêverie* for flute and piano to Taffanel—a gently reflective piece, indicative of a new style of playing and writing for the instrument.

The Conservatoire Orchestra

Taffanel began to make the move from the Cirque d'Hiver to the Salle du Conservatoire in 1865. He entered in his *Notes biographiques*: "29 October. Société des concerts. Aspirant actif," and "Concert Populaires (final year)." An *aspirant* was literally a young hopeful, usually a Conservatoire graduate, serving a term of probation as an extra player while waiting to be elected to a permanent position in the orchestra. The voting to admit Taffanel and several other candidates took place at a meeting of the committee of the Society on 17 October, and Taffanel became first piccolo.[12] Dorus and Altès were the first and second flutes, and George Hainl was the conductor, so Taffanel was reinforcing relationships already in place at the Opéra.

The first concert he could have played in would not have been until 4 January 1866, as the Society began its winter series late that season. It had just moved into the newly refurbished Salle du Conservatoire, which now had more comfortable seats, but fewer of them. Consequently, from the beginning of the following season, the subscribers were divided into two lists, for alternate Sundays, and from then on each of the seven concerts was repeated. The program for the inaugural concert on 4 January was quite untypical in featuring music only by living French composers: an overture by Dubois, a one-act comedy *Les Rivaulx d'eux-mêmes* by Pigault-Lebrun, and a cantata *Renaud dans les jardins d'Armide* by Lenepveu. It showed the new direction in which Hainl, appointed in January 1864, was trying to point the Society in its main series. During his conductorship he encouraged French composers such as Berlioz, Gounod, Franck, and Saint-Saëns and introduced various other works new to the Society by Haydn, Mendelssohn, Schumann, Meyerbeer, and even Wagner. Hainl therefore brought a breath of fresh air to the programs, to match the new decor of the auditorium, but not everyone was impressed: when Edouard Deldevez was appointed as Hainl's successor in 1872, the critic Arthur Dandelot regretted that he had not been elected instead of him some years earlier. He concluded somewhat dryly that Hainl was "a very good musician, but he belonged more in the theater than in the concert hall."[13]

Taffanel served a longish apprenticeship as an *aspirant* to the orchestra, but he was finally elected a *sociétaire* (a full member) at a committee meeting on 15 October 1867.

Solo Opportunities

Taffanel's first significant solo appearance in chamber music seems to have gone unreported by the musical press. It was on 26 February 1864 and he entered it in his *Notes biographiques* as "Concert Saint-Saëns (Bach Sonata. Meyerbeer was present)." Although the location of the concert and precisely which Bach sonata are not recorded, this is both the first conclusive mention of Saint-Saëns and the earliest evidence that Taffanel was following Dorus's lead in seeking out earlier and more serious repertoire for the flute. For the moment, however, the opportunities for playing such novelties were limited in Parisian musical circles. The more usual sort of opening for a flutist was the concert Taffanel gave on 16 April with the Italian singer Fanny Gordosa, sponsored by the writer Alexandre Dumas, author of *The Count of Monte-Cristo*. This time the press was there: "Gordosa, ranging from the solemn to the beguiling, wrestled victoriously with Monsieur Taffanel's flute in a delightful piece by Fischietti entitled 'The Singer and the Nightingale'."[14]

Early nineteenth-century Italian and French vocal music abounded in song-bird arias with obbligato flute parts, and they remained popular in Parisian musical salons. The instrument was therefore already associated with the female voice, but only in a superficial way, just as the sentiments and acrobatics of the music were only superficial. The fundamental identification of the flute with vocal tone and voice production, which was inspiring Taffanel through the artistry of Adelina Patti, was quite different, and it must have received a considerable impulse that year from a brief contact he had with her. His *Notes biographiques* includes the entry: "27 August. Havre. Etretat. concert Alkan (Patti)." Once again the details are tantalizingly sketchy, but according to the musical press, Patti was en route for the Birmingham Festival and she stopped off for two concerts with the tenor Barigli, first in Boulogne, then in Le Havre. The program included an aria from Meyerbeer's opera *L'Etoile du Nord*, with two obbligato flutes, and while the players (two local musicians) were named for the Boulogne performance, no names were given for Le Havre. But Dorus's holiday house at Etretat was not far from Le Havre, so it may be that Taffanel became involved in the concert while he was visiting him.[15]

As his career began to develop, Taffanel made more frequent entries in his *Notes biographiques*. There were concerts at Versailles, Troyes, and at the Pré Catalan, the fashionable Parisian nightspot in the Bois du Boulogne. He was also a member of the band of the Garde nationale, and he began to teach private flute students. A list of five names appears for the first time in 1864: do Canto, Roux, Rousselot, Varnali, and Letord. His most public solo appearance that year was at Pasdeloup's Concerts populaires on Christmas Day. In the middle of a mixed program of orchestral works by Mendelssohn, Beethoven, Haydn, Weber, and Wagner, he played the *Fantaisie* on Louis Niedermeyer's opera *Marie Stuart* by the English composer Robert Sidney Pratten. This was a popular, virtuoso set of variations dedicated to Walter Stewart Broadwood, whose connection to Boehm and Dorus has already been noted (see chapter 1). The audience was delighted, and the critics praised the "great talent" of "Monsieur Taffanel, a most skilful virtuoso . . . this brilliant soloist was lengthily and justly applauded."[16]

However, the smooth progress of Taffanel's career was briefly threatened early in 1865 by a call-up for national service. He noted that his name was picked by lottery on 24 March, but by 23 May he was discharged on medical grounds. It may have been that he was either not tall enough, or his sight was not good enough—his passport later described him as one meter, sixty-three centimeters (five feet, four inches) and short-sighted.[17] But he made good use of the reprieve with more solo and chamber music concerts that year than ever before: at least twelve in Paris, and one each in Lille, Amiens, and Bordeaux.

In Lille on 28 January, Taffanel was paid 250 francs for playing the *Fantaisie* on Donizetti's *La Fille du régiment* by Giulio Briccialdi, and once again Pratten's *Fantaisie* on *Marie Stuart*.[18] His fee compares with 1200 francs for a solo appearance by the singer Marie Sasse that same year, so a flute player still had quite a way to go to equal a singer! Taffanel then took the same two fantasias to Bordeaux in April—a triumphant first return to play in his native city. His compatriot Edouard Colonne also returned as a violin soloist in this concert with the Cercle philharmonique, a society modeled on the Paris Société des concerts. Both the audience and the local press were amazed by Taffanel: "Without doubt he is one of the best flutists we have ever heard . . . this artist gets around his instrument with a lightness, a clarity and a rapidity that are truly phenomenal . . . purity of tone, technique and expression are all combined . . . there was rapturous applause all evening."[19]

The year 1865 seems also to have been the first year that Taffanel played in public a *fantaisie* of his own composition, although in less than ideal circumstances. *Le Ménestrel* reported that at a private matinée Taffanel's accompanist had to transpose the manuscript piano part at sight when he discovered that the instrument was tuned differently from the flute![20] The piece was described as an air and variations on Donizetti's *La Fille du régiment*, and the following year when Taffanel returned to Lille, the printed program credited him as the composer of a set of variations for flute "on a German theme."[21] Neither piece has survived, but evidently Taffanel's first published *Grande fantaisie sur "Mignon," opéra d'Ambroise Thomas* (1874) was by no means his first composition in this genre.

Incidentally, tuning problems with the piano were an occupational hazard for players traveling around the salon circuit:

> One day, Taffanel and Charles Turban had to play at Mme D's . . . Saint-Saëns's *Tarentelle* for flute and clarinet, when they realised that the piano was actually tuned a semitone below normal pitch. Nothing could be done; only a Conservatoire graduate from the accompaniment class could have saved them from embarrassment by transposing a semitone higher. "Very sorry, dear Madame," said Taffanel, "we cannot play, your piano is much too low!" "Too low! I'll soon sort that out," cried the good Mme D . . . "Jean! Go quickly, and find me the crystal risers to put under the legs."[22]

Daily Life in 1866 and 1867

While Baron Haussmann was ripping up the old Paris and laying down the new, and Napoleon III's empire began more and more to resemble the madcap Gérolstein of Offenbach's latest operetta, Paul Taffanel kept a daily record of his activities for a period of nineteen months from 22 January 1866 to 25 August 1867.[23] Exactly why he began and finished on those dates is not clear. The last few pages are more sketchy and less carefully written than the others, so maybe he became tired of the idea or too busy to continue. Equally likely, there may originally have been more pages of this particular journal, and even ones for earlier or later years, which have since been lost.

Instead of using a conventional diary, or a notebook like the one for his *Notes biographiques,* Taffanel made a collection of loose, folded sheets of writing paper on which he recorded in outline the details of his professional and private life. He laid out the information in tabulated form, with columns for the date, daytime activities, lessons, and the Société des concerts, and evening activities. All the entries are abbreviated, with single words, surnames, and only the occasional brief comment.

Taffanel was twenty-one when he began this *Journal professionel* and the picture emerges in its pages of a busy, well-organized young musician, working most days of the year—he only managed to join the rest of the family for a couple of days in Dieppe on their July holiday. The single entry "ennui"— boredom—in the first week on 24 January 1866 only serves to highlight how extraordinarily full and fulfilling the rest of Taffanel's life was at this time. His major commitment was the orchestra of the Opéra, and he recorded the title of the opera for every evening he played, along with the initial *D* or *A* indicating whether Dorus or Altès had been the first flute. He proudly noted 12 May 1866 as "the first evening that I played first flute" (see fig. 4). The opera was Mozart's *Don Giovanni.* Rehearsals and concerts of the Société des concerts are also recorded during the winter season, and there are an ever increasing number of salon and chamber music concerts, with further occasional excursions as a soloist to other towns in France.

Several times each month Taffanel was required to rehearse and perform with the band of the Garde nationale, often for official occasions. Meanwhile, part of most days was taken up with teaching—the names of students, with dates and numbers of lessons, are meticulously noted—and with his own flute practice and composition studies (he was still a member of Reber's class at the Conservatoire). From time to time, Taffanel visited the flute maker Louis Lot to order and collect instruments for his students, and he regularly attended and assisted with Dorus's flute class at the Conservatoire. There are also references to "research," indicating that all the while he was expanding his knowledge of the flute and its repertoire.

A few family details are included, with frequent mentions of lunching or dining with the Bossières, Taffanel's relatives on his mother's side. The year 1867 was also when Taffanel moved with his parents and younger brother from the rue St. Denis to 1 passage du Désir, on the corner of the boulevard de Strasbourg in the tenth arrondissement (not far from what is now the Gare de l'Est). He also had several short periods of ill health, including bad toothache in July 1866 and a boil on his lower lip that prevented him from playing at the Opéra in December.[24] Among Taffanel's other papers is a card from the official dentist to the Paris Opéra, and he is known to have had lip and dental problems later in his career—he mentions them in letters to Johannes Donjon in 1888 and to Joachim Andersen in 1895, when he refers cryptically to "a weakness of the lips" that once jeopardized his flute playing—but it may be that these problems troubled him from quite early on.[25]

Colleagues and friends cited in the *Journal* include some little-known names like the violinist Jules Willaume and the oboist Félix Berthélemy, alongside significant figures on the Paris musical scene like the violinists Georges Jacobi and Pablo de Sarasate, flute players Eugène Walckiers and Paul-Agricole Génin, cellist Charles Lebouc, composer Louise Farrenc, and, of course, Saint-Saëns. Incidentally, Berthélemy collaborated with Demersseman on a *Duo brillant sur Guillaume Tell* for flute, oboe, and piano, which Taffanel no doubt also played with Berthélemy, and which he is recorded as having played with the oboist Raoul Triébert at the Société académique des Enfants d'Apollon in May 1870.[26] There are just a few hints in the *Journal* about Taffanel's interests and leisure activities away from the flute, with references to bookshops—among the few books of Taffanel's that have survived is a biography of the great tenor Adolphe Nourrit, published in Paris in 1867—libraries, occasional walks, regular dinner engagements with friends, and visits to various cafés.

From 1 April 1867 Parisians and thousands of foreign visitors flocked to the *Exposition universelle* that occupied a vast site on the Champ-de-Mars (where the Eiffel Tower now stands). The Exhibition played host to countries from around the world, but chiefly glorified the achievements of a brashly self-confident France. Sacheverell Sitwell memorably called the Exhibition "the apotheosis of the Empire . . . the painted ceiling of that gilded time," which catches the hectic party mood of a society that had no idea how close it was to destruction.[27] Taffanel was a regular visitor to the Exhibition and he took part in various of the official musical events that involved the Opéra and Société des concerts. Among the displays were musical instruments from all the chief makers. The critic Adolphe de Pontécoulant was mainly unimpressed—there seemed to him to be little there of any originality—but he did note two instruments exhibited by Theobald Boehm (a wooden concert flute and a nickel silver alto flute), and he had high praise for the flutes of Louis Lot: "finished to such a high standard that it really seemed as though the jeweller's art had been applied to the instrument maker's."[28]

Whatever else it may have been, Taffanel's *Journal professionel* was evidently a practical aide-mémoire, with additional names, dates, and numerical calculations on the reverse of some pages. Most intriguing is the reverse of the page for the week of 22 July 1867, where he made two pencil sketches of a hot-air balloon—the one belonging to the photographer Nadar that caused such a stir at the Exhibition, and that was painted by Manet.[29]

Among the many events Taffanel recorded in the *Journal,* one more is worth noting: the death of Jules Demersseman from tuberculosis on 1 December 1866, aged only thirty-three. Taffanel seems to have regarded him with a mixture of admiration and amusement. Years later, an American student of Taffanel's, Lancelot Bayly, remembered him reminiscing:

> Regarding Demersseman's performance, it was not of the highest artis- tic excellence. This is all the more remarkable from the fact that he was a student of the poetical Tulou, who had a decided predilection for lazy dreaming, and a perfect horror of display in any form . . . But if Demersseman's performance be condemned from a strictly musical point of view, from a Parisian popular concert audience it wrung howls of enthusiasm. The musical afternoons of Pasdeloup at the Cirque d'Hiver were many times enlivened by the "Oberon" Fantasia played magnificently by its versatile and eccentric author . . . Demersseman was display, and display was Demersseman.[30]

The reference to Tulou is striking, and unusual, in picking up on the "po- etical" quality of his playing. Whereas most contemporary commentators were predominantly taken with Tulou's virtuosity, Taffanel was more aware of, and attracted to, Tulou's intrinsic musicality. At some point, maybe from Tulou himself or from Dorus, Taffanel acquired a small oil portrait of Tulou that he kept throughout his life—a final link to the nineteenth-century virtuoso world of the flute. Taffanel also thought well enough of Demersseman's *Six- ième solo de concert,* op. 82 to set it for the Conservatoire flute *concours* in 1896 and 1900.

A Significant Year

The year 1868 opened with a personal loss for Paul Taffanel: the death of his mother at their home in Paris on 18 January. She was only fifty-four. The fu- neral took place two days later in the nearby Church of St. Laurent. This was also the year that Dorus retired from the last of his professional commitments. He had already left the Opéra orchestra two years earlier, and now he resigned from his professorship at the Conservatoire and from his position as first flute at the Société des concerts. Henri Altès succeeded him in both appointments, and Taffanel became second flute at the Société des concerts on 3 November.

In his letter of 30 October to Daniel Auber, director of the Conservatoire, Dorus explained: "My health no longer allows me to devote to my teaching all the meticulous care that you have the right to expect from me. I have struggled on for absolutely as long as I can, but I have no strength left." Auber replied, thanking Dorus for "your skill and devotion to the best interests of your students" and wrote to the minister for the arts recommending Altès, as he had already "stood in" for Dorus.[31] If that was the case, then it can only have been on rare occasions when Taffanel was unavailable, but presumably Auber would have found it unthinkable to appoint a mere twenty-four-year-old to such a prestigious position.

The following year, however, Altès broke with the Société des concerts on a point of honor over the expulsion of the singer Adolphe Lebaron, at the Annual General Meeting in January 1869. Various other members who resigned with Altès later retracted, but Altès was adamant, and in a letter of 22 May to the committee he declared that "my commitments do not allow me to devote the necessary time to the activities of our dear Society." The committee felt obliged to accept his resignation but postponed the decision about a new first flute until October. Meanwhile they elected Altès an honorary member by an almost unanimous vote, with one (unnamed) member against. Then finally, at a meeting on 19 October, they announced that "Monsieur Taffanel is unanimously elected first flute." Donjon became the second flute, and Edouard Lafleurance became the third, in a vote of eight to one against August Cantié.[32] Lafleurance, like Taffanel, was a native of Bordeaux. Born in 1836, he studied at the Conservatoire with Tulou, gained his *premier prix* in 1854, and was also appointed third flute at the Opéra on Altès's retirement. His nephew, Léopold, would later become a private student of Taffanel's in the 1880s.[33]

The earliest of the documents that have survived in Taffanel's collection of material on the flute date from this same year, 1868: a series of eight unsigned magazine articles on the instrument's history from antiquity to the present time. The final article expands the subject matter with some timely comments on the aesthetics of playing:

> The capabilities of the flute are in large part responsible for the vulgarity, monotony and disagreeable nature of the playing of certain virtuosi who, lacking all taste, abuse their technical knowledge in trying to produce cascades of notes rather than musical sounds, and end up like conjurers who appeal more to the eyes than to the ears.

> However, when treated properly, the flute is a beautiful instrument . . . its middle range has great softness, a resonant and persuasive smoothness, and its low notes have a moving nobility, a velvety quality, a mysterious sadness which is unequalled. If one would seek an idea of the true role of the flute . . . it is in the admirable orchestral parts of Gluck and Weber, to name only two, that one should look.[34]

Taffanel made a note in the margin of this final article to research a particular source quoted from the French physicist Félix Savart—further indication that his interest in the flute was by no means confined just to playing it.

The year 1868 also saw the beginnings of a new aspect of Taffanel's career. The music publisher Colombier invited him to arrange the flute parts for a series of "six very easy duos" called *Souvenirs du Théâtre-Italien*. The originals were for violin and piano, arranged by the leader of the Société des concerts, Charles Dancla, and the piano score retained the violin version but enclosed a separate flute part by Taffanel that differed in various ways from the one for violin.[35]

The repertoire of the Théâtre-Italien was also tellingly evoked in 1868 by the critic Guy de Charnacé, who published a study of Adelina Patti. He was very critical of many aspects of Patti's style and stagecraft, but for the sheer sound of her voice he had only praise:

> Nothing could be softer, cooler, smoother and at the same time brighter than this voice, as pure as the clearest spring water. Its notes are always full, round and in tune, at least when she doesn't try to make it more powerful than it naturally is. A tone just like rock crystal is the commanding quality of this voice, and the singer owes the major part of her success to it.[36]

De Charnacé goes on to observe that as Patti matures, she cultivates not only the virtuosity of her singing—he cites the mad scene with the flute obbligato in Donizetti's *Lucia di Lammermoor*—but also "nurtures the *andantes* and guarantees the greatest pleasure to lovers of the unaffected."[37] Given Taffanel's admiration for Patti, it is revealing to compare de Charnacé's verdict on Taffanel's own playing. It was delivered many years later in a letter he addressed to "the perfect flutist" from "an old, retired critic":

> I have a theory that certain artists draw from their instruments a particular quality of tone, so that they cannot be mistaken for anyone else. There could be a flutist of comparable virtuosity to Taffanel, but never one who sounded like him. I don't mean just in terms of the style of playing, but in the essence of the sound itself.[38]

"The sound itself" sums up a major part of Taffanel's aesthetic of the flute, and by 1868 the Paris musical press was well aware of the special nature of his playing: "Taffanel, whose fine skill as a flutist is today in all its maturity" . . . "Taffanel, the most distinguished flutist" . . . "Taffanel, the foremost flutist of our time."[39] Incidentally, the only mention of Altès appearing as a soloist during this period—with the singer Christine Nilsson, in the aria from Donizetti's *Lucia*—makes no comment on his playing, and there are virtually no references to other flute players.[40]

What is striking from the reviews at this time is Taffanel's involvement in a wide range of chamber music with the most respected Paris musicians. It is also clear that he was making a conscious effort to broaden the flute repertoire with more serious works, reviving the old (Schubert's Introduction and Variations, and trios by Beethoven and Weber) and championing the new — a Nocturne by Henri Fissot, and the Trio and Sextet by Louise Farrenc.[41] His fame also continued to spread beyond Paris. He appeared, for example, in Grenoble and Niort, and in Rouen for the unveiling of a monument to Louis Bouilhet, the poet and dramatist friend of Flaubert.[42]

The End of an Era

The year 1869 brought Taffanel recognition of a particularly tangible kind from a fellow player, Jules Herman, who was professor at the Lille Conservatoire and flutist in the orchestra of the Concerts du Cercle du nord. Taffanel had appeared with the orchestra in 1865 and 1866, and Herman now inscribed his *Introduction et variations sur "Le Carnaval de Venise,"* op. 23 for flute and piano "to his friend Monsieur Paul Taffanel." It is the earliest example that has so far come to light of a published piece dedicated to Taffanel.[43] Typical of its time — old-fashioned bravura display on a well-known warhorse of a theme — it is almost a metaphor for the Second Empire itself. Taffanel certainly accepted playing such pieces, but an invoice dated 10 August that year from the Paris branch of the publishers Peters Edition tells a parallel story.[44] It records the sale to Taffanel of three sonatas by the German composer Ferdinand Ries, a student of Beethoven. Taffanel was searching for a different kind of flute music, and he was evidently a regular customer as he received a discount of a third off the original price.

The invoice gives Taffanel's address as 31 rue de Constantinople (near the Gare St. Lazare in the eighth arrondissement), where he had moved with his father and brother in April 1870, and where they continued to live until January 1872. But the various family papers relating to this address show a gap between March and October 1871, the period of the internal political upheaval of the Commune, which followed the humiliating French defeat in the war with Prussia and the dreadful privations of the Siege of Paris. The emperor Napoleon III declared war on Prussia on 19 July 1870 and was defeated at Sedan on 1 September. On 4 September a Government of National Defense was proclaimed, but two weeks later the Prussians began the Siege of Paris, which continued until an armistice was negotiated in late January 1871. A new Assembly was then elected on 8 February, but rebellion broke out in the middle of March. The Commune then ruled from 28 March until it was finally suppressed on 28 May, when a more secure government of France resumed under the newly proclaimed, democratic Third Republic.[45]

After artistic life returned to normal, the critic Arthur Pougin contributed a series of articles to Le Ménestrel in which he named Taffanel among the musicians who remained in Paris during the five months of the Siege, and who took part in the Sunday evening concerts at the Opéra, which had been closed for theatrical performances since September.[46] The concerts came to an end on 12 March 1871. There was to have been one on 19 March, but the day before, a rebellious wing of Garde nationale troops led a bloody revolt against the new French administration of Adolphe Thiers and established the Commune. The Opéra was commandeered for patriotic performances, a new director, Eugène Garnier, was appointed, and a gala announced for 20 May. A further announcement postponed it for two days, but on the 21st the army moved in and overthrew the Commune. Some sense of order was restored by the first days of June, and the Opéra reopened on the 12th with a new director, Olivier Halanzier, and a performance of extracts from Auber's La Muette de Portici.

Life was terribly hard for musicians during this period. Playing and teaching came to a virtual halt, and it is likely that Taffanel served in the Garde nationale in the defense of Paris during the Siege. Pougin notes that many musicians left Paris between March and June 1871 (the period of the Commune), and this seems to have been when Taffanel and his family returned to Bordeaux. A letter from Taffanel on 31 July to the new director of the Opéra takes up the story:

> Having been in Bordeaux during these last events, when the situation was most critical for artists and when the Opéra had ceased to function, I found it necessary to sign a contract with the Casino at Trouville. Now the Opéra has reopened and I find myself in the awkward position of being in breach of one or other of my commitments, as I have been salaried to the Opéra for the past seven years.
>
> On learning of the reopening of the Opéra under your direction, I immediately consulted my closest colleagues, Messieurs Altès and Donjon, who *have been* and *continue* to fulfil the contract as if I was present. Unfortunately a hitch has suddenly occurred . . .[47]

Taffanel goes on to explain that his name has been deleted by mistake from the payroll, and therefore Altès and Donjon have not been reimbursed for their extra work. He implores the new director to reinstate him and undertakes to return to Paris in a month's time when his contract in Trouville comes to an end.

At first glance it would seem a straightforward situation to resolve. However, in the top left-hand corner of the letter there is a pencil annotation:

"Monsieur Altès refuses." It seems that Altès made an attempt to block Taffanel's reappointment. Fortunately he did not succeed, and the letter also has the word *reinstated* scribbled across the first page. Early in September *Le Ménestrel* reported a recent concert at Trouville that included "a flute solo by Taffanel," and he returned to Paris soon after, ready to pick up the threads of his former life and play a leading role in postwar musical developments.[48] A photograph taken around this time, in his mid-twenties, shows him once again looking confidently into the future (see fig. 5).

CHAPTER 4

New Beginnings

In 1870 no one had a lighter heritage to bear than
French musicians . . . curious to think how
musically feeble France was then!
—ROMAIN ROLLAND, *MUSICIENS D'AUJOURD'HUI* (1908)

The name of a composer on a concert billing who was both French
and living was guaranteed to put the world to flight.
—CAMILLE SAINT-SAËNS, *HARMONIE ET MÉLODIE* (1885)

For the sake of effect and a good story, both Rolland and Saint-Saëns exaggerated the prewar musical situation in France. However, the political upheaval of 1870–71 undoubtedly engendered a new musical nationalism and seriousness of artistic purpose in the emerging Third Republic. On 25 February 1871, in the immediate aftermath of the Siege of Paris, Saint-Saëns, Romain Bussine, and a few other like-minded musicians founded the Société nationale de musique. Its motto, *Ars gallica*, proclaimed the intention to foster the composition and performance of French symphonic and chamber music.

The minutes of the first meeting registered the presence of César Franck, Ernest Guiraud, Camille Saint-Saëns, Jules Massenet, Jules Garcin, Gabriel Fauré, Henri Duparc, Théodore Dubois, Paul Taffanel, and Romain Bussine.[1] Saint-Saëns, Taffanel, and Bussine were appointed to devise the rules of the Society. At the fourth meeting, on 17 March, a committee of six members was elected, headed by Bussine, with Taffanel as assistant treasurer, but the meetings were suspended from the middle of April to the end of October, during the Commune and its aftermath. By that later date Taffanel had left the committee, along with the composer Georges Bizet, although no reason is documented. The minutes merely note that letters have been sent to both musicians and that an election was held for new committee members "following the resignations of Monsieur Bizet and Monsieur Taffanel."

Whatever the reasons—maybe Taffanel's temporary move away from Paris and the uncertainty of his continuing career (see chapter 3)—they did not prevent him from appearing in the Society's concerts. The first two of these did not require a flute, so Taffanel played for the first time at the third concert, on

23 December. He appeared another eleven times up to 1891, after which he largely abandoned his solo career in favor of conducting. The list below gives the number of each Société nationale concert at which Taffanel appeared, with the date, the work(s) he played, and the other performers involved. An asterisk denotes an advertised first performance.[2]

Concert	Date	Composer	Work and Performers
3	23.12.71	Widor	*Sérénade* for violin, cello, flute, organ, and piano: Lamoureux, Tolbecque, Taffanel, Fauré, Widor
4	13.01.72	Saint-Saëns	*Tarentelle* for flute, clarinet, and piano: Taffanel, Turban, Saint-Saëns.
		Grandval	Suite for flute and piano: Taffanel, Saint-Saëns.
9	23.03.72	Grandval	Suite for flute and piano: Taffanel, Saint-Saëns.
10	06.04.72	Saint-Saëns	*Romance for flute and piano: Taffanel, Saint-Saëns.
13	18.05.72	Saint-Saëns	*Romance* for flute and piano: Taffanel, Saint-Saëns.
		Saint-Saëns	*Tarentelle* for flute, clarinet, and piano: Taffanel, Turban, Saint-Saëns.
28	27.12.73	Saint-Saëns	*Romance* for flute and piano: Taffanel, Saint-Saëns.
		Grandval	*Villanelle* for piano with flute accompaniment: Grandval, Taffanel.
78	16.03.78	Diémer	*Sérénade for voice, flute, and piano: Valdec, Taffanel, Diémer.
		Grandval	*Suite* for flute and piano: Taffanel, unnamed pianist.
156	18.04.85	Bernard	*Romance for flute and orchestra: Taffanel, cond. Bernard.
170	05.03.87	Chausson	*Hébé* for voice, two flutes, alto flute, harp, and string quartet: Storm, Taffanel, Lefèbvre,

			Lafleurance, Laudou, Rémy Quartet.
		Bériot	Sonata, op. 64 for flute and piano: Taffanel, Bériot.
		d'Indy	*Suite in D for 2 flutes, trumpet, and strings: Taffanel, Lefèbvre, Teste, Rémy Quartet.
		Grieg arr. Blanc	*Three Lieder for two flutes, alto flute, harp and string quartet: Taffanel, Lefèbvre, Lafleurance, Laudou, Rémy Quartet.
184	14.04.88	Durand	*Romance for flute and piano: Taffanel, Diémer.
		Bruneau	*Pièce for flute and harp: Taffanel, Hasselmans.
199	01.02.90	Lefèbvre	*Pièces (Barcarolle—Scherzo mélancolique) for flute and piano: Taffanel, Lefèbvre.
		Lambert	Hymnis for voice, flute, and piano: Depère, Taffanel, unnamed pianist.
213	04.04.91	Fournier	*Allegro for flute and piano: Taffanel, Diémer.
		Grandval	*Valse mélancolique for flute and harp: Taffanel, Hasselmans.

The gaps between these concerts, particularly between numbers 28, 78, and 156, were only rarely filled by other flute players. Those who did appear were Amédée de Vroye, who took Taffanel's place in concert no. 29 on 10 January 1874, playing the same program as in no. 28; a Monsieur Sartorelli, who also played Saint-Saëns's *Romance* and de Grandval's *Villanelle* on 9 February 1884; Alfred Lefèbvre (listed above in no. 170), who played the obbligato in Saint-Saëns's song *Viens, une flûte* on 8 January 1886; Marcel Gennaro, who played in a Suite for violin, flute, and piano by Eugène Meurant on 5 April 1890; and finally Adolphe Hennebains, who played Charles Bordes's *Suite basque* and a Bach sonata on 10 January 1891. Taffanel was therefore clearly the preferred player—so much so that Ernest Chausson, secretary of the Society in 1887, had to return a manuscript to Alfred Bruneau: "Regarding the *Romance* for flute, are you hoping that Taffanel will play it?" he wrote. "No doubt yes, and that's understandable. Unfortunately it will have to wait . . . ," and

Chausson explained there was already a concert organized for 5 March with four pieces in which Taffanel would play and it would be impossible to add a fifth![3] At the same time, the limited range of composers' names on the preceding list also demonstrates that the flute was only gradually being absorbed into the mainstream of French chamber music.

The Société classique

On his return to Paris in the autumn of 1871, Taffanel began to keep a log of his activities in the small black notebook that also contained his *Notes biographiques*.[4] First came a list of rehearsals and concerts of the Société des concerts; then details of the Opéra, including which works were performed and who played flute in the orchestra; then his teaching commitments, with three flute students at the Collège Chaptal and two at the Institution Figuiera. Each of these lists stops after only a few weeks, and there is also an incomplete inventory of the music that Taffanel owned: six flute sonatas by Bach; the Serenade by Beethoven; Beethoven's Violin Concerto, Violin Sonatas, and two *Romances*; a flute and piano arrangement of the Adagio from Beethoven's Wind Septet; and a flute and piano arrangement of Boccherini's Minuet. The list then breaks off at the name of the composer Boehm, but it is enough, with the Beethoven entries, to demonstrate that Taffanel's interests were already broader than just the flute.

Apart from an entry, "16 Jan. 1st concert 'Société classique,'" in his *Notes biographiques* for 1872, Taffanel kept no record of this important new enterprise. In November 1871 *Le Ménestrel* reported that a new society had just been created "with the aim of performing the main works for strings and wind by the great composers."[5] Completing a quintet of wind players with Taffanel were Théophile Lalliet (oboe), Arthur Grisez (clarinet), Jean-Baptiste Mohr (horn), and Jean Espaignet (bassoon). The string quartet was led by the violinist Jules Armingaud, with Edouard Lalo (violin), Joseph Mas (viola), and Léon Jacquart (cello). Added to this basic ensemble was a roster of well-known pianists the Society could call on as required: Marie Bedel, Elie Delaborde, Alphonse Duvernoy, Henri Fissot, Alfred Jaëll, Ernst Lubeck, Aglaé Massart, Caroline Montigny-Rémaury, Camille Saint-Saëns, Wilhelmine Szarvady, and Léonide Viguier. There are immediate parallels here with the Société de musique classique (also an amalgam of strings and winds) with which Dorus was involved between 1847 and 1849. Once again, perhaps his influence may be seen helping to focus and direct Taffanel's ideas.

The *Revue et gazette musicale* followed the new society with sustained interest, and it is possible to reconstruct most of the programs from its preview and review pages, with some additional information from *Le Ménestrel*. The repertoire played is listed in appendix 4. The first concert took place at the Salle Erard at 8:30 P.M. on Tuesday 16 January 1872. Incidentally, that was a busy month for Taffanel as he moved apartments once again, a mile or so northeast to 19 rue Clauzel in the ninth arrondissement. The mix of works in the first concert was characteristic: the Spohr Nonet for wind and strings, Beethoven's String Quintet, op. 29 (the extra player was not named), Mendelssohn's Cello Sonata, op. 45, and the Weber Trio for flute, cello, and piano. The Scherzo of the Weber was encored: "a real triumph for M. Taffanel," commented *Le Ménestrel*. "In short, an admirable debut for this society which can make a real contribution to the art of music by popularizing hitherto unknown works. There was a musical gap in Paris between string quartets and orchestral concerts: that gap is filled."[6] The *Revue et gazette musicale* added that the musicians rendered even the "merely workmanlike" Spohr Nonet "truly interesting . . . their playing was absolute perfection. Consummate musicians, first-rate virtuosi, together they achieved marvellous results."[7]

The Société classique established a pattern of six Tuesday evening concerts at the Salle Erard between January and March/April each year. The programs displayed a good balance of classical, romantic, and modern works and were received with great success for four seasons. Then after 1875 they ceased abruptly. No reason was given and there was even an attempt by Armingaud and Jacquard to organize an additional concert in March 1876, but a sudden extra rehearsal call at the Opéra prevented all the wind players except the clarinetist Grisez from appearing.[8]

On the face of it there seems no reason why the Société classique should have disbanded. It had carved a particular niche for itself in Parisian musical life: "a perfect ensemble . . . an authentic style . . . an undisputed authority which it enjoys among musicians and audiences alike."[9] During its four years, the strings presented many of the standard chamber works, including the always popular ones with piano, while Taffanel and his colleagues were able to revive a neglected repertoire of wind works by Bach, Handel, Beethoven, and Mozart. Meanwhile, five modern composers—Alexis de Castillon, Eugène Chaine, Léon Gastinel, Edouard Lalo, and Jules Massenet—were encouraged to write new pieces for wind and strings. By 1875 the wind players had performed works by nineteen different composers.

However, Armingaud and his quartet were at least a generation older than Taffanel and his wind colleagues, most of whom had been young professionals together in Pasdeloup's orchestra in the early 1860s. The Société de quatuors Armingaud et Jacquard was also long established, having played together regularly in Paris from 1856 to 1868.[10] Maybe Taffanel questioned the continuation of a society where the strings and winds were unequal. Wind players just did not have the same background of chamber ensemble playing, and perhaps never would while they continued to be dependent on the strings. Ironically, this must have been most apparent to Taffanel in the performances of the new works for wind and strings that were being written for the society. This is touched on by Hugues Imbert when he writes that Taffanel "understood what benefit there would be for wind players in perfecting their skill if they got together to perform works specially written for them, without the aid of the strings."[11] The Société classique had been a useful experiment, but it could not be considered an end in itself. So it was only a matter of time, and more thought, before Taffanel's dissatisfaction with the situation resulted in the founding of an exclusively wind chamber music society in 1879. And to make the point about independence, maybe it is significant that of the new works for wind and strings written for the Société classique, only Lalo's *Andantino et intermezzo* (in a revised form entitled *Aubade*) was ever played at the later Société des instruments à vent, despite the duplication of much of the other repertoire. Lalo's piece, which had to be encored at its premiere, was also the only one to be published.

Saint-Saëns's Romance and Other New Works

The Société classique was by no means the only chamber music organization with which Taffanel played during the early 1870s. He was almost always the chosen flutist when pianists or singers wanted to add some variety to their recital programs, and he appeared regularly in the more structured series of chamber concerts given by the violinist Georges Jacobi, the pianist Louis Diémer, and the cellist Charles Lebouc. He also appeared often with Saint-Saëns, although Saint-Saëns's *Romance*, composed in March 1871 for flute and orchestra or piano, was actually dedicated to another flutist, Amedée de Vroye (mentioned earlier), a former student of Victor Coche, now first flute of the Théâtre-Lyrique and the Musique de la Garde. Nevertheless, Taffanel gave the public premiere, partnered by Saint-Saëns, at the Société nationale on 6 April 1872.[12]

The *Romance* is a slight piece, but bewitchingly atmospheric. It spins an expressive line with the direct, unsentimental appeal of a lyrical *mélodie*. Given Taffanel's admiration for the music of Saint-Saëns, it must have seemed the perfect vehicle for communicating a new approach to flute playing. Taffanel, like Patti, wanted to make his audiences aware of the beauties of the Andante.

The flutist Fernand Caratgé remembered being introduced to the elderly Saint-Saëns decades later in 1920. "You are a student of Gaubert," said Saint-Saëns. "Good! But if only you had heard Taffanel . . . " and he immediately went to the piano and made Caratgé play the *Romance* with him.[13] Taffanel thought so highly of the piece that he offered it, in its orchestral version, for consideration by the committee of the Société des concerts, but there is no record of the *Romance* being performed by the Society.[14] It crops up, however, time and time again in reviews of chamber concerts: "the lovely *Romance* for flute by C. Saint-Saëns, ravishingly interpreted by M. Taffanel."[15] In fact Taffanel played it more often than any other recital piece.

Another new solo piece was added to Taffanel's repertoire in 1872, and this time it was dedicated to him: a Suite for flute and piano signed "Madame C de Grandval." The vicomtesse Clémence de Grandval was a member of the aristocracy, and she was also a pianist and a composition student of Saint-Saëns. Her Suite, compared with the works that were yet to be written for Taffanel, is not very significant musically, but it was the first direct response to Taffanel's particular style of flute playing. The five movements—Prélude, Scherzo, Menuet, *Romance*, and Final—follow eighteenth-century models, and the style is altogether more intimate than the usual flute *fantaisies* and variations. Taffanel played it twice with Saint-Saëns at the Société nationale (see above) and regularly in other concerts throughout the 1870s. Vincent d'Indy was at the first performance at the Société nationale (the first time he had visited the Society), and he wrote to a cousin about "a suite for flute and piano admirably played by Taffanel, but only the 3rd movement was any good, all the rest was very *trying and not succeeding*. I quite forgot to say that the composer was Mme. de Grandval, who was there with her husband who must have been bored."[16]

At the Société classique in 1873 one critic thought both of the last two movements were "full of delightful and ingenious details," and later that year another critic congratulated Saint-Saëns and Taffanel on playing the whole Suite "with unparalleled finesse and perfection."[17] The *Révue et gazette musicale* passed further judgement in 1878, praising the Prélude—"a real pearl"— but declaring the other movements did not quite live up to it. In short, the whole work was "too long, and despite the high quality of the performance the audience's attention was visibly wandering."[18]

In his *Notes biographiques* Taffanel singled out two particular concerts in 1872. Both were charity events: one in January at Amiens, the other in May at Villers-Cotterêts. The Amiens concert was for the Société philharmonique in aid of war orphans, and Taffanel himself arranged the Villers-Cotterêts concert as a benefit for the widow of his friend and colleague the violinist Jules Willaume, who had died in January 1871. This concert was notable for including Gabriel Fauré among the players, as piano accompanist.[19]

But from the point of view of Taffanel's development as a flutist, two concerts at the end of the year were more significant. Both involved performances of music from the flute's distant past. At the Société des concerts on 8 and 15 December Taffanel played the solo from Gluck's *Orphée*—the *Scène au champs Elysées*, now usually known as the *Dance of the Blessed Spirits*. Maybe this was a countersuggestion from the committee to his request to play the Saint-Saëns *Romance*. One critic described Taffanel's playing as "very stylish" and "beguil-

ingly expressive," while another jokingly instructed readers to forget Offenbach, whose *Orpheus in the Underworld* was at that time a better-known bur-
lesque on the same subject, and instead take note of "Gluck's calmly glowing
genius, and the sublime flute cantilena."[20] Once again Vincent d'Indy was in
the audience, this time overwhelmed by both the music and the performance:

> It is impossible to imagine anything more beautiful in its simplicity
> than that sublime, d minor flute melody (which Taffanel, moreover,
> played with a perfection worthy of Gluck), that song which begins
> with a sigh and gradually elevates the most inexpressive instrument to
> the absolute heights of passion, it's awesome![21]

Everyone agreed that Taffanel had scored a new and notable success, and
it soon became another of the pieces with which he was closely linked. He and
Philippe Gaubert eventually included it in their *Méthode* as an exercise in style
and interpretation (see chapter 12). A few days later Taffanel repeated the
Gluck solo at one of Lebouc's concerts, along with three pieces from Rameau's
Pièces de clavecin en concert: "La Livri," "L'Indiscrète," and "La Timide." This
time, as well as the now customary praise for his playing, there was a perceptive analysis of it:

> M. Taffanel has set himself the most worthy task of rehabilitating the
> instrument which he plays with such wonderful skill, the poor flute
> so singularly compromised and abused by the *fantasias* and airs with
> variations of our frivolous age; we are indebted to him for revealing un-
> known artistic treasures, forgotten works in which the flute plays such
> a noble and interesting role, and which never cease to surprise us.[22]

So popular was the Gluck solo at the Société des concerts that it became
almost an annual event, and each time it must have given audiences and critics pause for thought. In December 1874, for example, Taffanel received a
standing ovation and another detailed analysis of the remarkable qualities of
his playing:

> It would indeed be difficult to play with more taste and style than this
> excellent artist, and the famous flutists whose incomparable prowess
> some of the regulars in the audience (*laudatores temporis acti*) persist
> in vaunting certainly could not have brought more feeling or delicacy
> to their playing; besides which, the imperfections of their instru-
> ments would not have allowed them to produce the smoothness of
> tone and evenness of sound and intonation possible today.[23]

Two other pieces would become just as popular and successful for Taffanel
at the Société des concerts: the Scherzo from Mendelssohn's incidental music
to *A Midsummer Night's Dream* and Bach's B minor Suite. In all, Taffanel gave

ten performances of the Gluck, ten of selected movements from the Bach, and seventeen of the Mendelssohn between 1872 and 1892, when he ceased to play in the orchestra. On five further occasions the second flute, Lafleurance, also shared some of the limelight, with performances of movements from Berlioz's *L'Enfance du Christ*, including the Trio for two flutes and harp.[24]

Return to the Conservatoire

Although Taffanel was to be denied the flute professorship at the Paris Conservatoire for another twenty years, in 1873 he began to exert some influence there by becoming a member of the jury for the annual *concours* for wind instruments. The composer Ambroise Thomas had been appointed the new Conservatoire director on 1 July 1871, following the death of Auber, and he was to prove a valuable friend and ally to Taffanel, eventually supporting his nomination as chief conductor at the Opéra. In 1873 Thomas appointed Taffanel to the Examining Board for Instrumental Studies, which meant that he was also involved in the twice-yearly preliminary examinations that preceded the *concours*. Then in 1888 Taffanel joined the jury for the ensemble class—recognition of the key role he was by then playing in the revival of wind chamber music— and in 1892 he became part of a special commission set up to review all aspects of the Conservatoire's teaching and administration. Finally, in 1896 Taffanel was invited to become a member of the Conservatoire's governing body, the *Conseil supérieur*, on which he continued to serve for the rest of his life.[25]

The wind jury of nine internal and external musicians (Taffanel was the only flute player) was chaired by the director, and in 1873 the flute *concours* took place on 31 July. Unusually, there were only three entrants and no first prize was awarded. In fact there were fewer first prizes generally at the Conservatoire that year, and comments were made about the rigorous approach of the new director.[26] Taffanel subsequently served on the wind instruments examining board and *concours* jury every year until 1893, and he kept his copies of the official mark papers.[27] These gave printed details of each candidate's name, age (in years and months), year of study, and awards already obtained, with a blank column for the examiner to write brief notes and comments on the performances as a guide to voting for the various awards.

Taffanel ruled columns on the 1874 *concours* paper and established a four-point criterion for judging the students: *son* (tone quality and intonation), *mécanisme* (finger technique), *style* (musical interpretation), and *vue* (posture and general impression). He then allotted marks in each category. Two students, Edmond Bertram and Charles Molé, both scored straight fours, but Molé's mark for *vue* was underlined and he was awarded the first prize while Bertram gained a second prize. Taffanel kept the same system for 1875, but from 1876 onward he began instead to write brief comments, sometimes combining these with a more general marking system for overall impression in the set piece (*morceau de concours*) and the sight-reading piece (*morceau de lecture à vue*).

The *concours* of 1879 was the only other year Taffanel used the full four-section marking system on his papers, but his comments and preoccupations clearly followed the same method throughout his time as an examiner. Tone quality came first on Taffanel's list, and it was obviously uppermost in his mind when listening to the students. The majority of his comments begin with observations on sound and intonation: "woolly sound (1876) . . . the tone does not carry (1877) . . . the sound lacks breadth but the quality is pure, good phrasing, must get rid of the throaty wobble (1878) . . . the sound is unclear and lacking in projection, tonguing unclear (1880) . . . a small sound but good in quality, good fingerwork, plays in tune (1882) . . . tone quite good, stylish, colorful (1883) . . . constantly out of tune (1884) . . . colorless playing, out of tune, very correct but cold, good tonguing (1885) . . . *good sound*, a little brassy and out of tune in the low register, tonguing *very good*, musical, stylish (1886) . . . *beautiful sound*, colorless interpretation (1887) . . . good sound, wobbly, uncertain intonation, sharp when ff, flat when pp (1888) . . . beautiful but weak sound, clear and neat passagework, interpretation a little cold, qualities of accuracy and lightness (1889) . . . good sound, exaggerated nuances, out of tune, adequate fingerwork (1890) . . . very big sound, warmth in the playing, shows good taste" (1892).

Taffanel's general comment on the examination paper for June 1877 is also revealing: "All those who have a pure sound have focused it without covering the embouchure too much." The implications of this are that while a good flute sound should be pure and focused, it should also be flexible and free, therefore the embouchure hole should not be covered too much by the lower lip. Most unusually, this comment was also entered on the official copy of the mark papers kept by the Conservatoire.[28] A hint to the professor Henri Altès, perhaps? Certainly it was the only year that anything like that appeared on these papers, and although there was a comment for three of the other seven wind and brass classes, there was nothing as technically precise. The oboe class was judged: "A good class. In general more care should be taken over the tuning of the instruments"; the clarinet class: "A rather poor class. Little sense of style"; and the cornet class: "Good technique. Bad style."

Taffanel's examination and *concours* comments on Adolphe Hennebains, who would eventually succeed him in the orchestras of the Société des concerts and the Opéra, also reflect the priorities of his own flute playing: "Good sound, very good finger technique, should succeed . . . the playing is less exaggerated than Feillou, but a little stilted (1879) . . . good sound—limpid, good all-round technique—good, clear tonguing . . . good resonant sound (sometimes plays flat), has musical taste, rapid tonguing (errors not his fault), very good, unanimous first prize" (1880).

Georges Barrère was maybe not alone in feeling disillusioned with Altès, declaring that "his very systematic teaching gave me no chance to develop [on] my own" (see chapter 11).[29] This was reflected in Taffanel's reports on four examinations just before he finally took over the flute class and Barrère became his student: "Out of tune, reasonable sound, exaggerated accents, quite good finger technique . . . better in tune, lacks color, playing is too cold (1892) . . . little progress, mediocre sound . . . wrong notes, clumsy breathing, aimless playing, good sound" (1893). "Aimless playing"—*chant sans intentions*—takes the concept of performance on the flute a stage further, particularly with the use of the emotive word *chant* in the original French. Even a beautiful sound will not be enough unless it is used as an agent of musical expression, to *sing* the meaning of the music.

Taffanel used the same marking system and musical criteria for assessing the other wind classes. There were eight in all: flute, oboe, clarinet, bassoon, horn, cornet, trumpet, and trombone. The terms *son, mécanisme, exécution, style*, and *justesse* formed the basis for many of his comments. During the 1880s, when Taffanel was directing his Société des instruments à vent, he frequently used the word *timbré*—resonant—along with a wide range of other adjectives to describe the quality and color of sound. He gave praise with words like "velvety," "supple," and "vibrant," and criticism with words like "cloudy," "meager," and "edgy." But among all this high seriousness there were also occasional moments of levity. Taffanel's mark sheet for the bassoon *concours* in 1886 has a sketch of the back view of an old man with boils all over his head! An absent-minded doodle during a dull afternoon, depicting a fellow jury member, perhaps?

A general remark on musical interpretation, or lack of it, in the 1889 oboe class indicates Taffanel's sensitivity to the concept of performance practice—the differing stylistic demands of the early repertoire he was rediscovering and playing: "Tempi often too fast. Interpretation not straightforward enough for music of the Masters—harmful influence of modern music—no *understanding* of the accompaniment." That same year Taffanel commented on the bassoonist Gaillet: "Has good taste, plays with style, good sound, the best bassoonist I've heard for a long time (quite a musician), is he at last the bassoonist of one's dreams?!" Unfortunately something must have gone wrong for Gaillet, and by the time of the 1890 *concours* he was judged to have a "bad sound" and "bad technique." But, behind Taffanel's first heartfelt comment lies some indication of the problems he must have faced with the Société des instruments à vent in finding players of like mind and like ability to achieve homogeneity of sound and style.

Not surprisingly, Taffanel's approach to judging voices at the Conservatoire also concentrated largely on their qualites of tone. Comments on the opera *concours* for 1895 include such adjectives as "weak," "tight," "uneven," "bright," and "resonant." Most revealing is the comment "salon voice, no substance." A few words that speak volumes—salon flute players beware!

Marriage to Geneviève Deslignières

Around the time that Taffanel first joined the Conservatoire flute jury, he received a visiting card with a quaintly worded message:

> Charles Lebouc called to ask his colleague Taffanel if in the early days of the month of August between 3 and 4 o'clock he could come to a school where he teaches and accompany 2 short pieces. He can only offer 30 francs, but it should take 2 hours at most, one for the rehearsal and one for the performance. He would be very pleased to have the opportunity to join forces with Taffanel again.[30]

That chance engagement to play with the cellist Lebouc at an end-of-year concert in a fashionable girls' private school resulted directly in Taffanel's marriage. The Pension Beaujon at 14 rue de Chateaubriand, in the smart eighth arrondissement close to the Arc de Triomphe, had been run since 1848 with prerevolutionary regality by the formidable Madame Marie Emilie Deslignières, née Rovérolis de Rigaud de Saint-Aubin. Her husband, Alexandre, was an architect, and they had three children: Marcel, Louise, and the youngest, Geneviève, born in 1852 (see fig. 6).[31] Marcel Deslignières adopted his late father's profession (Alexandre died in 1865), and he designed and constructed the house at 8 avenue Gourgaud where Paul and Geneviève Taffanel eventually settled. Louise married the painter Jules Lefèbvre, who was elected to the Académie des beaux-arts in 1890, and who later painted a portrait in profile of his brother-in-law Paul Taffanel (see fig. 23).[32]

Both Geneviève and Louise were capable pianists. They were taught at their mother's school by César Franck, who dedicated to them in 1873 an arrangement for piano and harmonium of his *Prélude, fugue et variation*, op. 18 for organ.[33] An ex-pupil of the Pension Beaujon, the Comtesse de Quigini Puliga, writing under the pseudonym Brada, painted a sympathetic portrait of "Poor Monsieur Franck!" as she called him: he seemed to have "such a solemn and serious face," but the girls held him in awe as "the organist of Saint-Clothilde who is very talented, they say." As for the strict Mme. Deslignières, she regularly castigated pupils as "hussy" or "silly goose," depending on the scale and nature of their misdemeanors, but "she seemed to have a treasure store of indulgence" for the artists and musicians who came to teach at the school.[34] So Charles Lebouc's young flute-playing friend could have counted on a warm welcome, and when he arrived to play at that concert in 1873 it was Geneviève Deslignières who accompanied him on the piano.

A year later when they married, Taffanel was enough of a celebrity for an announcement to appear in the pages of *Le Ménestrel*, where Madame Deslignières was no doubt gratified to have her school described as "one of the principal educational establishments in Paris, where good music is highly regarded."[35] The civil wedding took place on Saturday 1 August 1874 at the town hall of the eighth arrondissement, with a religious ceremony two days later at the society church of Saint-Philippe du Roule on the rue du faubourg Saint-Honoré. Again, *Le Ménestrel* reported it—and it was a quite a concert!

> The musical part of the ceremony was noteworthy, most of the soloists from the Opéra having wished to show their support for their excellent colleague. Messieurs Mohr, Cras, Roze, Garcin and Prunier performed various religious works. The organists were Messieurs Saint-Saëns and Fauré; Monsieur Bosquin sang Cherubini's *Ave Maria.* Two unpublished works were performed: an *Offertoire* by Monsieur Lebouc . . . and a *Panis Angelicus* by Monsieur Franck.[36]

The couple moved into a fourth-floor furnished apartment at 3 rue Saint-Arnaud (now rue Volnay) in the second arrondissement, conveniently situated for the Salle Ventadour in the rue Méhul, where the Opéra had been temporarily housed since the fire in October 1873 that had destroyed the Salle Le Peletier. But looking to the future, maybe they chose the rue Saint-Arnaud because it was in even easier walking distance of Garnier's long-awaited new opera house, where Taffanel would soon play in the gala opening the following January.

Meanwhile, there were other new things in the air in the mid-1870s. Shortly before Taffanel's marriage, he had made his first visit abroad as a soloist, appearing in London at St. James's Hall in June 1874, at the invitation of the conductor Sir Julius Benedict, and at a private soirée given by Lady Fitzgerald.[37]

Taffanel also took on extra responsibilities at the Société des concerts, beginning a first term of office as secretary in 1875. At the annual general meeting on 18 May he was elected by ninety-six votes. He served initially for two years and was later reelected to this important position for three more terms of office: 1879–81, 1883–85, and 1889–91. Later on he would also succeed Charles Lebouc as secretary of the *Caisse de prévoyance*—a contingency fund or provident society. Taffanel was elected initially to that in June 1884 and reelected in 1886, and he continued to serve until his eventual retirement as conductor of the Society in 1901.[38]

By 1875 there was also a new orchestra to play in, and an old friend to encourage—though not quite in the way he expected. On 18 March Jules Massenet's *Eve*, a "mystery in three parts," was receiving its premiere at the Cirque des Champs-Elysées. The concert was being given by Concerts de l'harmonie sacrée, an organization founded and conducted by Charles Lamoureux to present the sacred choral works of Bach, Handel, and modern French composers. Massenet, however, had a horror of attending performances of his own music, so he decided to wait in a café nearby and get Taffanel to come and tell him how it was going. "After each part, Taffanel ran across the road to bring me the comforting news. After Part Three, still very encouraging, he hastened to tell me that everything was over, the audience had gone and he urged me to come quickly and thank Lamoureux. I believed him, but what trickery!" In fact the performance had only just finished, and Massenet was hoisted onto the shoulders of his musician friends and carried into the hall to acknowledge the applause and cheers of the audience. "I fled, furious!"[39]

Jacques Taffanel

The most important event of 1875 for Taffanel was undoubtedly the birth of his son, Jules-Lucien-Jacques on 20 May. Taffanel was tremendously proud of Jacques, who grew up to become a brilliant mining engineer. He studied at the Ecole normale supérieure and the Ecole polytechnique, and quickly advanced his career until he was appointed controller of the mines at Clermont-Ferrand and then at Saint-Etienne. In the aftermath of a mining disaster at Courrières in 1906, he was put in charge of a research center at Liévin to work on the volatile nature of coal gas and dust underground, the prevention of explosions, and the development of breathing equipment. He later traveled all over the world giving advice to foreign governments—by chance he was in Russia in 1917 and witnessed the events of the Revolution at first hand. The latter part of his career was spent in managing the vast ironworks of the Compagnie des forges de Châtillon, Commentry et Neuves-Maisons, and he was decorated by the French government with the high honor of commander of the Légion d'honneur.

Though not a musician, Jacques was an ardent Wagnerian from the time of his first visit to Bayreuth with his father in 1892 (see chapter 9), and he returned on his own for the complete Ring Cycle in 1896. He married Marie Chancel, the daughter of family friends, in 1919, but she died tragically young in her early forties only a few years later in 1924. Jacques survived her for over twenty years, until 5 March 1946, raising a son and daughter, Claude and Jacqueline. An obituary paid tribute to "his good-humor and his lively and incisive mind."[40] He was his father's son.

CHAPTER 5

Composing for the Flute

A grande fantaisie for flute on Mignon by Taffanel, a bag of tricks
with repeated notes, huge arpeggios, flashy passagework for the
flute, then scales in octaves from one end of the keyboard to
the other for me, unison trills in both hands, chromatic
scales etc, all of that brings the house down!
—VINCENT D'INDY, LETTER TO MARIE D'INDY (2 JUNE 1874)

An excursion to the provincial town of Béthune, near Calais, with several
musician colleagues to play for the local Philharmonic Society in May
1874 brought the young Vincent d'Indy (he was twenty-three) once again into
contact with Taffanel. This time, instead of just hearing him play, d'Indy accompanied Taffanel on the piano. He wrote a long and lively letter about the
whole experience to his half sister, Marie, amused by the *Mignon fantaisie* and
scandalized to discover that the audience went wild after it, whereas they had
received the serious items on the program by Mozart and Weber with only polite enthusiasm: "Oh audience!" The letter also provides a rare description of
Taffanel at his most relaxed and playful. After the concert there was a cham-
pagne supper until 2 o'clock in the morning, and "Taffanel was the toast of the
evening, he knows all sorts of parlour games," wrote d'Indy, "he is brilliant at
saying the most absurd things so seriously that everyone *believes they must be
true.*" And he recounted a little game that Taffanel had played earlier in the
evening, when a local amateur musician who had never seen a flute with so many
keys asked him to explain what all the "little gadgets" on his instrument did:

> Taffanel looked as serious as could be: "Monsieur, they do absolutely
> nothing, it's just that in the past, instruments were made all of a
> piece, but they did not sell very well, so the dealers thought up the
> idea of adding lots of little accessories of every kind, for the sake of
> embellishing the instrument, since then they sell really well, which is
> understandable . . . Take you, for example, Monsieur, if you wanted

to have a house built, you wouldn't be happy if the architect quite simply piled stone upon stone without carving and ornamenting them . . . " (at this point there followed a lengthy screed on architecture) the poor man was completely lost, he could not understand what a disquisition on Herculean monuments had to do with a flute, and this interlude greatly amused us all.[1]

Five Fantaisies

The flute piece that Taffanel played at Béthune was published that same year by Heugel with the title *Grande fantaisie sur "Mignon," opéra d'Ambroise Thomas*, and a dedication "to my mentor and friend Louis Dorus." It had first been noticed the previous December when the *Revue et gazette musicale* reported that "the flutist Taffanel played with his customary skill a transcription of *Mignon*."[2] Whether Taffanel had ever played in the orchestra for the opera *Mignon*, with its delicate flute counterpoint to "Connais-tu le pays?" is not known. It was only premiered at the Opéra-comique in November 1866, after he had left to join the Opéra, but it may well have been given on one of the occasional nights when he returned as a deputy—by the end of 1867 there had been 148 performances.

Taffanel's *Mignon fantaisie* established the general format and style for the four others that followed, on Weber's *Der Freischütz* (published 1876), Rameau's *Les Indes galantes* (1877), Delibes's *Jean de Nivelle* (1881), and Thomas's *Françoise de Rimini* (1884).[3] An introduction sets the musical scene and provides the flute with a brief cadenza. Then follows a series of themes from the opera, embellished with variations: Mignon's aria "Connais-tu le pays?" Philine's aria "Je suis Titania"; the orchestral entr'acte that opens Act 2; and the "Forlane" that appears in the Overture and was originally included in an early draft of the conclusion of Act 3 but later omitted by Thomas.

Flutist-composers were, of course, a commonplace in the nineteenth century. Before Taffanel, the flute had become so marginalized as a serious solo instrument that players must have felt that if they did not write music for it, no one else would. There is nothing so very special therefore about the fact that Taffanel tried his hand at writing fantasias, and, as previously noted, he may well have done this from quite early on in his career. What set Taffanel apart was the fact that he had trained as a composer and therefore brought quite different skills to the task. Where the average flutist was intent only on producing a vehicle to display his virtuosity, casually overlaying someone else's original themes with acrobatic variations, Taffanel delved deep into the music of the original. He composed from the inside out.

Taffanel's next *fantaisie*, on *Der Freischütz*, demonstrates this perfectly. It is arguably the finest example in this genre by any player-composer, and primarily concerned with exploring the emotional world of Weber's opera. He carefully selects extracts from the Overture and each of the opera's three acts, notably key arias for Agathe, Max, and Aennchen. And although the variations are very taxing for the player, they seem to grow naturally from within the given melodies, rather than being superimposed from without. The treatment of Agathe's aria from Act 2 is particularly atmospheric, while later—a truly imaginative touch—Taffanel gives the original Act 3 flute solo to the piano and surrounds it with a gentle counterpoint on the flute.

On 12 August 1876 Taffanel and Saint-Saëns were in Dijon for the unveiling of a statue to Rameau (born in Dijon in 1683), and in the evening they took part in a concert at the theater. Taffanel played the obbligato part in the air "Rossignols amoureux" from the opera *Hippolyte et Aricie*, then he played what was simply described as an "Air de flûte" by Rameau. As there is no original solo flute music by Rameau, maybe Taffanel played a theme from what was to become his own *Fantaisie-transcription sur "Les Indes galantes,"* published the following year. This is the least "composed" of his five fantasias, and the least embellished. First comes a Maestoso that is actually the Overture to Rameau's *Hippolyte et Aricie*, then an Allegretto that uses the Minuets from Scene 2 of the Prologue of *Les Indes galantes*, and finally a Rigaudon based on the March, and two Tambourins from Scene 6 of the Première Entrée. The plan is straightforward throughout, with a simple cadenza after the opening Maestoso and clearly defined sections of variations after the Allegretto and Rigaudon that could easily have been added later.

Incidentally, the festival concert in Dijon ended with Taffanel, Saint-Saëns, and the cellist Johann Reuchsel playing four pieces from the *Pièces de clavecin en concert*: "La Livri," "Le Vésinet," "La Timide," and "L'Indiscrète."[4] The Rameau *Pièces* had also been played earlier that year at a concert at the Salle Pleyel given by the pianist Caroline Montigny-Rémaury with Taffanel, Lebouc, and Saint-Saëns, and they became favorites in Taffanel's recital programs from then on.

Some insight into Taffanel's musical preoccupations at this point in the sequence of composing his five fantasias comes from a draft of a letter to Louis Dorus in 1879. Taffanel signs himself "Ever your devoted student and friend" and asks Dorus for advice:

I have been captivated for some time by a very appealing melody of unstudied simplicity which I really think would work marvelously on the flute. This melody was played superbly by Sivori and followed by some extremely difficult variations. I ventured to try and make a transcription, or rather a transformation of it. And just as I was about to give it to the publisher I began to have qualms about it, concerned that the final variation would not have the desired effect, or indeed that it would exceed the bounds of virtuosity. Although I have often been able to play it, sometimes I have not managed to reach the end.[5]

Taffanel encloses the music (it is now lost and the actual melody was never identified) and asks Dorus to judge. No reply exists, but as Taffanel published no variations around this time, and there is nothing later that answers to the description in the letter, he and Dorus must have concluded that there was indeed a limit to the kind of virtuosity to be encouraged on the flute. The melody might have been borrowed from Camille Sivori—an Italian violinist popular in Paris at the time, whose playing was characterized by "passion and feverish excitement"—but that was all.[6]

In April 1880 Taffanel played the obbligato flute part in Arlette's "Rossignol" aria, from Delibes's opera *Jean de Nivelle*, in a concert partnering the soprano who had created the role at the premiere at the Opéra-comique the previous month. "Taffanel's flute literally ravished the audience," commented *Le Ménestrel*.[7] *Jean de Nivelle*, though now forgotten, was a great success at the time, and at the end of the year, at a concert at the Lycée Louis-le-Grand, Taffanel gave the first performance of his new *fantaisie* on themes from it.[8] It was published with a dedication to Taffanel's colleague in the Opéra orchestra, Johannes Donjon.

Avoiding the obvious, Taffanel did not include any of the nightingale music in *Jean de Nivelle*. Instead he chose another of the opera's most popular arias, the "Ballade de la mandragore" from Act 1. This celebrates the magic powers of the mandragora plant, around which the complicated action of the plot revolves. Taffanel juxtaposes it with the "Marche des archers" and the "Trio bouffe," and he opens and concludes the fantasia with the picturesque imagery of the watermill, the "Fabliau du moulin," from Act 2. It is all attractive but inconsequential. Taffanel seems to be continuing the process begun with the Rameau transcription of *Les Indes galantes*, attempting to transform a virtuoso genre into something more immediately lyrical—although a considerable technical challenge remains. But the result is a sort of hybrid with a limited amount to say musically.

The last of Taffanel's five flute *fantaisies* was based on Ambroise Thomas's *Françoise de Rimini*. Thomas's opera was inspired by the story recounted in Dante's *Inferno*. It was premiered at the Opéra in April 1882 but never equaled the success of his earlier *Mignon*, and was quietly forgotten after forty-one performances. Likewise, Taffanel's *Fantaisie sur "Françoise de Rimini"* in no way rivals the compositional skill of his earlier one on *Mignon*. Although a sense of atmosphere is created and well sustained in the first half of the piece, the ending appears to be just a straightforward potpourri of tunes.

Taffanel chose to base the *fantaisie* on instrumental sections of the score only: the Prologue and three dances from the Act 3 ballet music—"Adagio," "Saltarelle," and "Sevillana"—probably recognizing that these displayed Thomas's lightweight lyrical talent at its best. And it is the lyricism and pathos that Taffanel underlines in the first half of the piece, with the Prologue of Virgil and Dante arriving at the entrance to Hell, and the "Entrée de Virgile." The "Adagio" continues the mood, and the variation embellishes the melody in a shimmer of sixty-fourth-notes. But after this there only remains a straightforward presentation of the "Saltarelle" and "Sevillana." The overall effect is confusing, as in the *Fantaisie sur "Jean de Nivelle"*—a curious mixture of the musically introvert and extrovert, with neither gaining a convincing upper hand. There is a feeling that, for Taffanel at least, the *fantaisie* genre was nearly played out. This one carried no dedication, there were no press reports of Taffanel ever having performed it, and he never wrote any more such pieces. He needed to look elsewhere for a synthesis of lyricism and virtuosity in his music, and he soon discovered it in a quite extraordinary piece: the *Sicilienne-Etude* of 1885 (see chapter 7).

On one level these *fantaisies* appear to contradict the idea that Taffanel was trying to guide the flute away from superficiality. But such works were still hugely popular with audiences, as the concert at Béthune proved, and by now Taffanel was appearing at some of the most important political and aristocratic soirées in Paris—at the Elysée Palace, for example, and the salons of the minister of justice and the Comtesse de Chabrun.[9] What Taffanel demonstrated, particularly in his first two fantasias, was that with a good formal structure, with a true partnership between the two instruments rather than just chord vamping on the piano, and with the musical application of virtuosity, something valid could still be said.

Louis Fleury later wrote of Taffanel's "several brilliant *fantaisies* on themes from operas dating from his youth and regarded by him as unimportant," and liked to imagine a clean break with the old school.[10] But the truth seems to have been more complicated. Taffanel was almost thirty when he composed *Mignon*, and he would be forty when *Françoise de Rimini* appeared. His way was one of evolution rather than revolution. He would hardly have valued, for example, the vacuous variations presented in 1873 as the culmination of the flute *Méthode* by Joseph Duvergès, former solo flutist with the Régiment des guides de la Garde impériale. Nor would he have endorsed the exhaustive coverage in the author's method of fingering and articulation at the expense of breathing and embouchure. Nevertheless, Taffanel was a virtuoso player of his time, just as Patti was a virtuoso singer. The real difference between them and the others was the use to which they put their virtuosity: the quality and depth of their *musical* intentions. Something of this is caught in a review from 1876 when Taffanel paired his *Mignon* and *Der Freischütz* fantasias with the Saint-Saëns *Romance*:

> Monsieur Taffanel is absolute perfection; nobody could play the flute better. His technique is so marvellous that he seems, in the faster passages, not to move his fingers; the quality of sound that he draws from his instrument is so fresh, so delicate, so amazingly supple, that if the human voice could produce such trills you would think that Patti was hidden in the wings.[11]

New Transcriptions

As he was putting the finishing touches to his *Mignon fantaisie* in 1873, Taffanel embarked on a new series of transcriptions for flute and piano: *Répertoire de la Société des concerts du Conservatoire et des Concerts populaires*. Felix Mackar was the publisher and the first volume contained ten pieces, with further issues of ten separate pieces building up to a second volume between 1875 and 1886.[12] These "classical transcriptions" were originally made for violin and piano by the violinist Amédée Berthemet, and Taffanel's involvement in the first volume was limited to arranging alternative flute parts—a task similar to the one he had previously undertaken for the *Souvenirs du Théâtre-Italien* (1868). This time the pieces were favorite tunes from orchestral and chamber works by Mozart, Beethoven, Haydn, Boccherini, Viotti, and Mendelssohn. And Taffanel soon made his influence felt when Gluck's *Scène d'Orphée* appeared in 1875 as no. 11 of the series. Flutists, amateur and professional alike, must have welcomed the chance to play for themselves this glorious piece popularized by Taffanel.

The Wind Quintet

In May the following year Taffanel gathered together some colleagues to perform Hummel's Septet for piano, flute, oboe, horn, viola, cello, and double bass at a Conservatoire concert in aid of the Association des artistes musiciens. It prompted an unusual review:

> This performance would have been perfect if the delicacy of its nuances, pushed to extremes, had not sometimes almost completely extinguished the sound itself. You might have thought that the seven players had agreed among themselves to play constantly at *piano* and reduce the music to a murmur.[13]

That critic may have been unimpressed, but the subtleties of chamber music were much in Taffanel's mind in 1876, the year that he composed his

Wind Quintet. It was written in response to a competition run by the Société des compositeurs de musique. This was an annual event with two or three different categories of work chosen each year. In June 1876 they were announced as a piano quartet, a wind quintet, and a lyric *scena* for voice and piano.[14] Only French composers were eligible to enter the competition, and the works submitted had to be unpublished and unperformed. Each manuscript had to be clearly readable and submitted anonymously with a sealed envelope attached to it, bearing on the outside an epigraph of some sort, to identify the work to the jury, and on the inside the name and address of the composer.

Taffanel was particularly busy that summer, as he finally succeeded Henri Altès as first flute at the Opéra, on the personal recommendation of the conductor Ernest Deldevez.[15] Altès retired on 31 August (he actually played for the last time on the 18th), Johannes Donjon moved up to second flute, and Edouard Lafleurance was appointed third flute. Taffanel recorded the month leading up to Altès's retirement and the first two months of the new regime in his *Notes biographiques*, with details of the operas given and the roster of players involved, as he assumed responsibilty for the flute section. He also arranged a farewell lunch for Altès on 5 September, with Donjon, Lafleurance, and three other colleagues from the orchestra, Turban, Mayeur, and Triébert. Then, after the performance of Meyerbeer's *Les Huguenots* on 16 September (his thirty-second birthday), Taffanel took four weeks' leave, a late summer holiday during which he would have been able to concentrate in earnest on his Wind Quintet.

Fourteen quintets were submitted for the competition and judged by a jury chaired by François Bazin and including Ambroise Thomas, Léo Delibes, and Théodore Dubois. The result was announced by the Society on 20 May 1877: "a single prize of a gold medal and 300 francs awarded to Monsieur Paul Taffanel."[16] Soon after, Taffanel received a visiting card from Théodore Dubois: "With many congratulations on the Quintet. I had no idea it was by you when I read it, but I am not surprised."[17] And at the annual general meeting of the Société des compositeurs on 29 March 1878 Taffanel was admitted to full membership.

When the Quintet was published by Leduc the same year, it carried a dedication to Taffanel's former composition teacher, Henri Reber, who had himself studied composition with Antoine Reicha, the composer credited with inventing the form of the wind quintet. Taffanel, however, was unhappy with the Leduc edition, which "printed with unprecedented panic is embellished with mistakes on virtually every page. I cannot begin to correct them . . . but I must just rectify a piece of wrong phrasing and some inaccurate tempo indications."[18] Unfortunately, apart from the photograph of a single page (see fig. 7), the manuscript has since been lost, so there is no way of pinpointing the inaccuracies of the printed edition—but they evidently exist.[19]

The first documented performance of the Quintet took place on 3 May 1878 at the Salle Pleyel, in a program that included Beethoven's *Spring* Sonata and a D major Trio by Haydn for flute, cello, and piano. The Quintet was judged to be "an outstanding composition . . . very difficult to play," but "brilliantly rendered" by Taffanel, Lalliet, Turban, Alard, and Verroust.[20] The official premiere was at a prizewinner's concert organized by the Société des compositeurs at the same venue on 23 May. This time the performers were Donjon, Triébert, Turban, Dupont, and Verroust. *Le Ménestrel* declared it to be "delightful . . . a most distinguished work, made even more interesting by an excellent performance."[21] The critic of the *Revue et gazette musicale* particularly admired the second and third movements:

> The first movement is excellently crafted, with delightful harmonic effects and use of instruments, but I prefer the other two, the graceful and distiguished Andante—like Mozart brought up-to-date—and the Finale, a novel and elegant saltarello, a piece of high musical quality, quite apart from the skill with which it is written for the five instruments.[22]

Taffanel played the Quintet again on 5 July, at the fifth chamber music concert of the Paris Exhibition. This time he was joined by Gillet, Turban, Dupont, and Espaignet, and together they were soon to become the core quintet of his wind instrument society. The *Revue et gazette musicale* reminded its readers that it had already praised this "extremely distinguished work," but now expressed some doubts—not about the music itself, but about the instrumentation: "The Quintet . . . was written for a competition; we cannot therefore blame the composer for the unfavorable choice of the means used to realize his ideas."[23] The implication was clear: Taffanel should write some *real* chamber music, for strings rather than winds! That particular critic would have been by no means alone in dismissing wind instruments, and it must have been deeply frustrating for Taffanel. No doubt it spurred him on in his plans to create the Société de musique de chambre pour instruments à vent.

Théodore Dubois's elegant compliment on the Quintet was quite literally true, for no one was better placed than Taffanel to understand the demands of writing for wind instruments. His Quintet is an excellent example of the genre. Moreover, it points the way for the future. Taffanel weaves a musical fabric of rich, dark colors, in a basically contrapuntal style that constantly balances and rebalances the five instruments. All are soloists, all are accompanists, and nothing is ever predictable. In form and musical language the work displays the French classical–romantic ideals of Taffanel's teacher Reber, and even more of his mentor Saint-Saëns. The outer movements are both in sonata form, while the central Andante is an accompanied *romance*. The craftsmanship throughout is unfailingly impressive: the dovetailing into the recapitulation at bar 219 in the first movement; the atmospheric aural perspectives of the Andante; and the Mendelssohnian deftness of rhythm and texture in the last movement are immediately striking examples of Taffanel's keen ear and fastidious sensibility. He brought to fruition the early work of Reicha and freed the form of the wind quintet for future generations. Indeed, many decades later when the composer Arthur Honegger came across Taffanel's Quintet, he was amazed: "The Quintet . . . was a revelation to us all. This was no old-fashioned work, but a score full of delightful music, somewhat similar to Lalo, and masterfully written. Like me, many musicians were surprised never to have heard it before."[24]

8 avenue Gourgaud

The year 1876 had opened on a personal note with Paul and Geneviève Taffanel finalizing their plans to buy a plot of land and build a house, designed by Geneviève's brother Marcel, in the developing seventeenth arrondissement. It took them out of the immediate center of Paris to a residential area that still seemed like a separate village, where they could have more space and calm to bring up a family. The land and construction costs of over 10,000 francs were paid for from Geneviève Taffanel's dowry in a series of regular installments up to the beginning of 1877, by which time the couple had moved into the new house at 8 avenue Gourgaud, which they would occupy for the rest of Taffanel's life (see fig. 8).[25]

Avenue Gourgaud was one of several roads radiating out from the place Péreire—named after the bankers who had profited from the massive land and property speculations associated with Haussmann's rebuilding of Paris—and the back garden of the house connected with the property owned by Geneviève's mother at 116 boulevard Péreire. That was, however, a mixed blessing, as Madame Deslignières continued to be an autocratic and demanding presence until her death at the age of ninety in 1901. Taffanel's house remained in the family until the 1930s, when it was demolished to make way for a six-story block of flats. Various members of the family, including Taffanel's daughter, Marie Camille, and her husband, Charles Samaran, took apartments there, and the address still had direct family associations until quite recently.

Louis Diémer

A musical dedication to Taffanel in 1877 set the seal on an important new musical partnership with the pianist Louis Diémer, who was reputedly a difficult man and a rather "dry" player, but who became the stalwart resident accompanist to Taffanel's wind instrument society. When Diémer appeared in Vienna, the critic Eduard Hanslick chose his words carefully to commend a "most elegant, correct and finished style."[26] On that occasion Diémer played not only the usual pianist's fare of Beethoven, Liszt, and Chopin, but also pieces by Couperin and Rameau—like Taffanel, he was keen to rediscover an earlier, forgotten repertoire, and he was later a pioneer in the revival of the harpsichord. He and Taffanel were almost direct contemporaries: Diémer, born in 1843, had studied at the Conservatoire with Marmontel, Bazin, and Thomas, receiving his *premier prix* when still very young in 1856. He became a Conservatoire professor in 1887.

The flowery sentiments of Gabriel Marc's poetry in Diémer's *Sérénade* for voice, flute, and piano, combined with its picturesque ballad style, place it in the heady world of the salons: "If I, oh my love, / Were a perfumed breeze, / I would timidly steal to charm / And brush your laughing lips." The flamboyantly designed cover of the printed edition lists a selection of similar miniatures by Diémer, although this was the only one to include a flute. The singer Léonce Valdec shared the dedication of the *Sérénade* with Taffanel, and they performed it many times with Diémer. At a Société nationale concert it was described as "a delightful and ingenious piece which gave great pleasure," and at one of Diémer's own private concerts a critic reported that "the colourful accompaniment could not have been bettered."[27] The young Jacques Durand, son of the music publisher, particularly remembered attending Diémer's "very popular musical soirées . . . all the famous artists were happy to perform there . . . among the regulars at Diémer's salon was Taffanel, the king of the flute (it was a real treat when he took part in the program)."[28] And even when Taffanel no longer played the flute in public he would often still be there as a member of the audience. Some years later, in the 1890s, the violinist Jules Boucherit described the procession of smart guests and well-known musicians at Diémer's: "then without any fuss, somewhat hampered by the cord of his pince-nez, the unassuming conductor of the Société des concerts, Taffanel, slipped in."[29] It is a revealing snapshot of the kind of man Taffanel was.

Morceaux de lecture à vue

Taffanel's own activities as a composer took a new turn in 1877 when he wrote the first of a series of accompanied sight-reading tests for the Paris Conservatoire end-of-year examinations. It was customary to commission a new piece each year for each instrument, often from the composition professors (there are flute and piano examples by Massenet, Delibes, and Fauré), so it may have been Taffanel's recent success in the Société des compositieurs competition, as well as his standing as a regular examiner, that led the Conservatoire authorities to approach him. Taffanel went on to provide twelve sight-reading tests between 1877 and 1902: eight for flute and one each for oboe, clarinet, bassoon, and cello. The cello Andantino was the only one to be published during Taffanel's lifetime.[30]

The sight-reading piece for 1877, marked Allegretto scherzando, is typical of the series: a thirty-bar exercise in rhythm, control of register changes, dynamics, and especially subtle varieties of articulation. In effect it is a miniature song without words. Even the faster pieces like the Allegretto scherzando of 1892 are conceived so that the control of legato line is a priority. Incidentally, in four of the eight years that Taffanel composed the sight-reading tests (including 1877), there was no *premier prix* awarded—a relatively unusual occurrence.[31]

In His Own Words

The year 1877 is also significant in providing the earliest drafts of any letters that have survived from Taffanel. After the cryptic abbreviations of the *Notes biographiques* and the *Journal professionnel,* a more sustained and distinctive voice now emerges in a collection of notes and draft letters he kept.[32] The personality revealed is clear-headed, open, and aimiable, a musician with a busy and complicated professional life, constantly juggling the demands of the Opéra, private students, and solo appearances. "So often I seem to begin letters by apologizing," he writes, "life in Paris, and particularly the kind that I lead, leaves little time for reflection." And he goes on to refer to "numerous and very tiring duties which have brought on a severe chest infection." This same letter (to an unnamed friend) also discusses the choice of music for a projected concert at Valenciennes:

> You ordered from Paris the Weber Trio (bravo) but what edition have they sent you? I know at least six that are faulty. However, the one by Peters is the least inaccurate among them. Let me know which one you have and I will tell you what alterations, additions, or deletions to make. Here are the metronome marks for the trio. First movement = 112. Scherzo = 80. Shepherd's Lament = 92. Finale = 116 except for the few bars of piano at the beginning which are a little slower. I mentioned a Haydn Trio which is delightful and which would be excellent to finish the concert with. You can get it from Heugel; here is the title (29th Trio Sonata for piano, flute, cello in D major. Haydn). With these two main works we can easily complete our programme with a few classical transciptions for solo piano, or piano and flute, or piano and cello, and I think we should have the wherewithal to satisfy the good people of Valenciennes.

I hope that our Exhibition will tempt you and that while you are in Paris you will remember avenue Gourgaud. Let me know what day you are coming so that I can be "at home" and present my little family to you. When that day comes I won't have the sort of succulent tongue of beef to offer that only your country knows how to prepare, nor its fantastic vintage wines, but a warm welcome nonetheless and a real pleasure to see you, spiced with high spirits.

The classical transcriptions referred to may well have included a selection of Mendelssohn's *Songs Without Words* that Taffanel published in 1878. His choice of that particular composer and genre underlines once again an insistence on the lyrical and vocal associations of the flute.[33]

Meanwhile, away from the flute for a moment, in November 1877 Taffanel sketched a reply (again to an unnamed friend) to a request for guidance on buying a piano. He offered to go and try out an instrument and continued: "you pose a delicate question about the choice between a Pleyel and an Erard. Really it's entirely a matter of taste . . . As a guide for your decision I would say that it is generally agreed that Pleyels have much greater mechanical freedom and more immediacy of attack and repetition of notes. Erards have more fullness and *density* of tone."

1878 Paris Exhibition

The year 1878 began for Taffanel with the usual round of the Opéra and orchestral and chamber music concerts. On 6 January Edouard Lalo had his Overture to *Le Roi d'Ys* played at the Société des concerts, and he noted that Taffanel was one of the few members of the orchestra to applaud the work at its first rehearsal.[34] Meanwhile a new pattern was emerging in the concert halls, as music for the flute became more fashionable. Taffanel would first discover works and popularize them, then they would be taken up by other flutists. There is a review, for example, of Edmond Bertram, a recent Conservatoire *premier prix* of 1875, performing extracts from Bach's B minor Suite and joining with Eugène Damaré, a bandmaster-flutist, in the Trio from Berlioz's *L'Enfance du Christ*.[35]

Taffanel's own latest discovery was the flute music of Mozart: first the Flute Quartet in A major, K. 289, which he played at one of Lebouc's concerts. It was a discovery for the critics as well: "This charming little work was unknown in Paris . . . it was performed by our eminent flutist Taffanel . . . with great finesse."[36] Another performance of the Quartet was noted by the press on 8 February 1879, followed in March by the Concerto for Flute and Harp,

K. 299, composed exactly one hundred years previously in Paris in 1778 and now also welcomed as "a rarity."[37]

Taffanel's continuing interest in the history of the flute was fueled that year by the appearance of a new book, Lavoix's *Histoire de l'instrumentation*. His copy is annotated with queries, corrections, underlinings, and notes reminding himself to "look up" a number of points throughout the flute chapter. Clearly he had a greater knowledge of the subject than Lavoix, and he was actively involved in research of his own at this time, having acquired a reader's card for the Bibliothèque nationale.[38] But any thoughts of writing his own history of the flute, or a flute method, were subordinated for the moment to the pressing and practical issue of raising the status and broadening the repertoire of all the wind instruments. Maybe it was the spirit of innovation and adventure in the air during that year of the *Exposition universelle* that finally crystalized Taffanel's ideas for a wind instrument society, because he laid the plans that autumn, and the first rehearsal took place before the end of the year.

The 1878 Paris Exhibition was a triumphant symbol of successful national recovery after the War and Commune, proof to the world that France had confidently regained her wealth, power, and political stability. "Paris herself again—comelier, richer, gayer, more fascinating than ever" was the verdict of the English journalist George Augustus Sala, and *Paris Herself Again* became the title of the book he wrote with delight about his experiences in Exhibition year.[39]

Taffanel's involvement in the musical side of the Exhibition was considerable and earned him a commemorative medal as "flutist-composer."[40] There were various gala orchestral concerts in the newly built Trocadéro Palace, notably a soirée on 11 June at which he played the solo from Gluck's *Orphée* and the Scherzo from Mendelssohn's *A Midsummer Night's Dream*, and another on 11 July with the Société des concerts, in the presence of the king of Portugal, when the Mendelssohn Scherzo was again played and encored.[41] In addition there were sixteen official chamber music concerts, running from 5 June to 20 September in the Petite Salle of the Trocadéro at 2 P.M. in the afternoon. After the first concert, the *Revue et gazette musicale* praised the excellence of the performances, but complained about the noise of the trams in the place du Trocadéro and the hammering of workmen on a nearby site. Nevertheless, "everything went off splendidly."[42]

The programs were predominantly given over to chamber music for strings. When wind instruments were required for occasional works, Taffanel was invariably the flute player. He appeared in six of the chamber concerts, gathering around him a small group of wind-playing colleagues from the Opéra and Société des concerts (see list below). The lineup of performers and works directly prefigured the Société des instruments à vent, and even as he played these concerts, Taffanel must have been eagerly anticipating this momentous next step in his career.[43]

Concert	Date	Composer	Work and Performers
I	05.06.78	Onslow	Wind Quintet
		Lalo	*Allegretto et andantino* for 10 winds and strings
		Massenet	*Thème et variations* for 10 winds and strings: Armingaud, Turban, Mas, Jacquard, de Bailly (strings); Taffanel, Lalliet, Grisez, Espaignet, Dupont (winds)
3	21.06.78	Grandval	Suite for flute and piano: Taffanel, Fissot
5	05.07.78	Taffanel	Wind Quintet
		Barthe	*Aubade* for wind quintet: Taffanel, Gillet, Turban, Dupont, Espaignet
12	23.08.78	Reicha	Wind Quintet no. 3 in G: Taffanel, Lalliet, Turban, Garrigue, Espaignet
13	30.08.78	Farrenc	Trio for piano, flute, and cello: Miclos (piano), Taffanel, Rabaud (cello)
15	13.09.78	Reicha	Wind Quintet, Andante and Finale *La Chasse*: Taffanel, Gillet, Grisez, Garigue, Espaignet

CHAPTER 6

The Wind Society

I don't know if you have been following the wonderful little
concerts given by the Wind Instrument Chamber
Music Society at the Salle Pleyel . . .
— GUY DE CHARNACÉ, *LA GRANDE DAME* (APRIL 1893)

The story of Taffanel's Société de musique de chambre pour instruments à vent begins and ends with two eye-catching press reviews. In 1893, fifteen years after its founding, the Society had become such a fixture in the Parisian musical calendar that the critic Guy de Charnacé decided the time had come to recommend it to the refined female readership of the "fashionable, cosmopolitan" magazine *La Grande dame*. And so, after the latest news on the arts and spring hats, and in between advice on choosing the best perfumes and behaving with *le dernier chic*, an article appeared praising the Society's excellent performances and noting how it had grown from modest beginnings to become a force that had raised the whole level of awareness of chamber music. "It is a curious thing, but as this century draws to a close, the appreciation of musical instruments is beginning to seize hold of us in the same way as the appreciation of colour."[1] In other words, just as the exoticism of Art Nouveau was opening everyone's eyes, so the novelties of chamber music for winds were opening their ears.

Ironically, de Charnacé turned out to be writing shortly before the Society gave what proved to be its final concert. Taffanel had achieved his original aims in founding it—raising performance standards and public awareness and increasing the repertoire—but in so doing he had also experienced what Hugues Imbert called "an apprenticeship to the craft of conducting . . . while still playing his own part, he in fact led this little ensemble and took the keenest interest in studying scores."[2] All that had led him in a new direction. By the beginning of the 1893 season Taffanel was principal conductor of the Société des concerts du Conservatoire, and soon after it ended he was appointed principal conductor at the Opéra. His career as a flute player was thus effectively over, and the other members of the Wind Society voted to disband rather than continue without him.[3]

But back in February 1879 the story was only just beginning, and the advent of the Society was heralded in an unusually long and witty article in *Le Ménestrel*:

> The wind instruments of the Société des concerts have just hoisted the flag of mutiny against the strings, to whom they always have been subservient. The flute is weary of arguing with them; the clarinet is worn out launching its sad complaint into a vacuum; the oboe will groan no more; and the bassoon declares that it has grumbled for quite long enough without getting its rightful satisfaction. So, to avenge themselves once and for all on these squeaky fiddlers, Messieurs Taffanel, Gillet, Turban, Dupont, Espaignet and Villaufret of the Société des concerts have banded together with the aim of offering us, this winter, six chamber music concerts devoted to works for *wind instruments alone*, or with piano, because they will make that one concession and have granted Monsieur Diémer the honour of playing opposite them.[4]

The article goes on to note that Taffanel has wisely gathered around him mainly young players for this innovative enterprise, apart from the bassoons, who are rather more mature in years, "as befits the gravity of their occupation"!

The quality and distinctiveness of French orchestral wind playing had at one time been much admired. According to Henry Chorley, an English critic visiting Paris in the year of Taffanel's birth, the wind section in the Conservatoire Orchestra had "a unity and coherence—a like family resemblance among its separate members—a like sensitive delicacy which is beyond all praise. No unfortunate flute there chirps half a note before its time."[5] (That last comment was presumably aimed at English orchestras!) But for Taffanel, things were evidently not what they had been. As he wrote to an amateur who had contacted him to express support:

> It is precisely because the study of those instruments that make up the wind section is no longer what it was in the past, because the appearance in a serious concert of a virtuoso wind player has become extremely rare, that we wish to react against such a totally unjustifiable neglect. There are two reasons for this neglect, one the shortage of worthwhile works at a time when musical education is making astonishing progress, the other, it must be said, the apathy of musicians themselves.[6]

Those views were amplified later in Imbert's biography, in words that he can only have had from Taffanel himself:

At the Conservatoire, the wind players have no musical repertoire; beyond the actual technique of the instruments, they ignore most of the time the musical heritage of the old masters. Another oversight: they don't organize themselves in ensembles, they have never learned to play clearly on the beat without the help of the strings and they cannot play notes for their correct lengths.[7]

Taffanel was therefore determined to continue the work he had started with the Société classique some years before, but this time without the strings. He would draw on a neglected wind repertoire from the past—notably by Mozart and Beethoven—and stimulate the composition of new works. Only then could wind instruments become truly independent.

The First Season

Preparations for the first concert were unusually intensive for the period—a measure of the seriousness of the whole enterprise. Taffanel kept a careful register of eight rehearsals from 3 December 1878 to 5 February 1879, listing the names in an order that reflected their importance in the group: a hierarchy of first and second players of each instrument.[8] He had assembled a wind octet, with pairs of oboes, clarinets, horns, and bassoons—the classical *Harmoniemusik* formation of Mozart's time—plus flute and piano. Alongside Taffanel himself and his now regular pianist Louis Diémer (who just came in for the final two rehearsals), the nucleus of players for the first season comprised the oboists Georges Gillet and Auguste Sautet, clarinetists Charles Turban and Arthur Grisez, horn players Henri Dupont and Jean Garigue, and bassoonists Jean Espaignet and François Villaufret.

Apart from Sautet, they were all Conservatoire *premier prix*, and Gillet and Turban would also later become Conservatoire professors. Grisez and Garigue played in Pasdeloup's orchestra, and Sautet played for Colonne, while the others belonged to the Société des concerts, and all of them were members of either the Opéra or Opéra-comique orchestras. As for their ages, the bassoonists Espaignet and Villaufret were indeed the oldest at fifty-five and forty-five, respectively, while the others ranged from nineteen to thirty-seven. Taffanel himself was thirty-four.

The first concert took place in the small recital room of the Salons Pleyel et Wolff (the piano makers) at 22 rue de Rochechouart, a few streets away from the Conservatoire, on Thursday 6 February 1879 at 4 P.M. "precisely." Tickets for the 170 seats had been on sale in advance at the offices of *Le Ménestrel* and various of the Paris music publishers. They cost five francs for one concert, or twenty francs for a subscription to the whole series of six—a clever ploy to encourage audience loyalty.

The *Revue et gazette musicale* praised the first concert's "outstanding performances" and noted that the second concert had to be moved to the larger hall of the Salle Pleyel because of the demand for tickets.[9] This hall, with seating for 550, was the most prestigious chamber music venue in Paris (Chopin and Liszt had played there), and it became the Society's home for the duration of its activities. The acoustic must have been ideal, with oak paneling and a semicircular raised stage, not unlike the present-day Wigmore Hall in London.[10]

The rest of the season continued in a pattern of fortnightly Thursdays at 4 P.M., apart from the last concert, which had to be moved to a Friday. The dates were 20 February, 6 March, 20 March, 3 April, and 18 April. Each concert had four or five works in it and lasted between eighty and ninety minutes, with no intermission. Taffanel noted four rehearsals before the second concert, and after that he stopped keeping a register, but no doubt the principle of frequent rehearsals once in place was continued throughout the whole season.

The program of the first concert established the pattern and intention of things to come:

1. A classical ensemble work (Beethoven: Octet, op. 103)
2. A serious solo piece (Bach: B minor Flute Sonata, BWV 1030)
3. A contemporary foreign ensemble work (Anton Rubinstein: Quintet for piano and winds, op. 55)
4. A new French ensemble work (Adrien Barthe: *Aubade*)

Significantly, Rubinstein had also made an arrangement of his Quintet for piano and strings because wind ensembles were "neither numerous nor much appreciated in Russia."[11] Much the same could be said of the rest of Europe in 1879, so Taffanel's Society was quietly making history on that first Thursday afternoon.

Three of the four works played had previously been included in Société classique concerts, but Adrien Barthe's *Aubade* was completely new. It went all but unnoticed by the critics but was well received by the audience. "At the actual dawn of our chamber music concerts your delightful work earned us our first success," wrote Taffanel when the *Aubade* was eventually published with a dedication to him.[12]

Grouped according to the preceding categories, the complete first season of works comprised (in chronological order of performance):

1. Beethoven: Octet, op. 103
   Mozart: Serenade in E flat, K. 375
   Mozart: Quintet, K. 452

Beethoven: Quintet, op. 16
Beethoven: Trio, op. 87
Mozart: Serenade in C minor, K. 388
Beethoven: Sextet, op. 71
Mozart: Serenade in B flat, K. 361

2. Bach: Flute Sonata in B minor, BWV 1030
   Beethoven: Horn Sonata, op. 17
   Schumann: *Romances* for oboe, op. 94
   J. S. Bach: Flute Sonata in E flat, BWV 1031
   Saint-Saëns: *Romance* for horn, op. 36
   Berlioz: Trio from *L'Enfance du Christ*
   Weber: Clarinet Sonata, op. 47
   Clémence de Grandval: Flute Sonata
   Mendelssohn: *Concertstück* for clarinets, op. 114

3. Anton Rubinstein: Quintet, op. 55
   Spohr: Quintet, op. 52
   Röntgen: Serenade, op. 14
   Liszt arr. Lassen: *Trois pièces*

4. Adrien Barthe: *Aubade*
   Emile Pessard: *Prélude et menuet*
   Saint-Saëns: *Tarentelle*, op. 6
   Léon Kreutzer: Sextet
   Adolphe Deslandres: Scherzo
   Georges Pfeiffer: Musette

As the first season continued, it was monitored with interest and occasional reservations by the musical press. *Le Ménestrel* particularly noted Emile Pessard's Prélude et Menuet— "a charming little work . . . played very gracefully"—and Spohr's "significant" Quintet, "played with first class virtuosity." The *Revue et gazette musicale* commented that wind music was "a rather limited field, but so much the more interesting for being so little explored," and pointed out some balance problems in the ensemble, several times imploring Louis Diémer to play less harshly, "to moderate his tone a little when the instruments of limited force, like the flute and clarinet, have to struggle against the piano." The Serenade by Julius Röntgen, a young Dutch composer and pianist, was judged to be "hard to play" and "very well brought off," but Edouard Lassen's arrangement of pieces from Liszt's *Années de pèlerinage* "did not always encourage a good sound from the ensemble." Moreover, in that concert on 20 March it was the only work to include the flute, and "really we rather felt the lack of it." But overall the conclusion in the press was that the first season had been very successful and had prepared the ground for wider and greater appreciation of the Society's efforts.[13]

In the end the most impressive thing about the first season was the extent to which Taffanel had meticulously planned and thought out the whole concept. Successive seasons would follow in an immediately recognizable pattern of venue, dates, time, publicity, subscriptions, personnel, and programming, and from this stable base he would have the best possible chance of achieving his aims for wind chamber music. Only the name of the Society took some time to evolve. At the beginning, the programs were just headed *Six Séances de Musique de Chambre*. Then in 1882, the fourth season, the names of the nine main players were added. This format continued for two further seasons until 1885, when the definitive name of the society emerged as La Société de musique de chambre pour instruments à vent.

Meanwhile, that first season the Salle Pleyel concerts were not the Society's only appearances. Part of the first program was repeated at Henri Lemoine's music society called La Trompette on 15 February, and at a "Soirée Gilbert" on 18 February.[14] Then, after the second concert, an invitation arrived to perform at one of Jules Pasdeloup's popular Sunday concerts in the Cirque d'Hiver on 9 March. This, however, presented a potential clash of interests with the Société des concerts du Conservatoire (in principle no Conservatoire player was allowed to perform for a rival organization), so Taffanel had to seek permission from the Orchestra's committee.[15] Fortunately this was forthcoming, and the *Revue et gazette musicale* reported that the works played were the Spohr Quintet and a Beethoven Rondino for wind octet (later programmed by the Society in its second season). Both were interpreted "with technical perfection and a delicate sense of style; and the tonal effect did not sound at all thin in the vast rotunda of the circus arena."[16] But it appears that the performance scored only a modest success with the audience (probably it was too small-scale for what they were used to), and there were problems because Pasdeloup's first horn, Mohr, felt he should have been asked to play instead of Garigue, who was the second horn. Consequently, Mohr resigned from the orchestra, and Garigue was promoted in his place.

Personnel and Repertoire

From early on the Society began to call on extra players as it explored more varied repertoire than could be performed by the original lineup of nine, and from time to time the core personnel also changed. It is significant that as the years went on the extra players were drawn more and more from the ranks of recent Conservatoire graduates. Taffanel was in close contact with this source of emerging talent through his position on the juries for the annual examinations and *concours*, and the benefits were twofold: the young players gained valuable experience of chamber music (still an otherwise unusual activity for wind players), and the Society constantly renewed and rejuvenated itself. Details of all the players associated with the Society during its fifteen years are given in appendix 5, along with a complete repertoire list compiled from the printed programs. Each program was a single sheet printed on one side only with details of works and performers (there were no explanatory notes about the music), and Taffanel kept a complete set that he annotated when last-minute changes were necessary.

During the fifteen years of its life the Society performed 150 different works, including about fifty premieres. These only began to be indicated on the printed programs from the 1881 season onwards, although it is likely that some of the French ensemble works (e.g., by Barthe, Deslandres, Pfeiffer, and Gouvy) of the 1879 and 1880 seasons were first performances. From then on the composers listed with premieres were as follows:

1881   Gouvy

1882   Lefèbvre

1883   Handel, Mozart, Reinecke, Richard Strauss

1884   Bernard, Boisdeffre, Diémer, Grandval, Lalo, Lefèbvre, Mozart, Spohr, Widor

1885   Boisdeffre, Gounod, Herzogenberg, Klughardt

1886   Bériot, Diémer, Gouvy

1887   Diémer, Lefèbvre, Rheinberger

1888   Durand, Gouvy, Mozart, Saint-Saëns, Saint-Saëns arr. Taffanel, Schubert

1889   Nováček

1890   Herzogenberg, Lefèbvre, Thuille

1891   Alary, Hartmann, Périlhou

1892   Beethoven, Ehrhart, Lefèbvre, Pfeiffer

1893   Brahms, Lazzari, Reinecke

If the presence on this list of the names of Handel, Mozart, Beethoven, and Schubert is surprising, it only goes to show how conscious the Society was of introducing Parisian audiences to "new" wind music of all periods. The complete catalogue of wind works by Mozart and Beethoven had never been played in Paris before, and those two composers formed the classical nucleus of all the programs. No less surprising on the preceding list are the names of a number of contemporary foreign composers. Clearly Taffanel was aware of the wider European musical scene and aimed to reflect it in the Society's programs, even with composers such as Brahms and Richard Strauss who otherwise found little favor in France at that time. Strauss's Serenade, op. 7 was introduced in the 1883 season, the year following its composition, and Brahms's Serenade, op. 16 (played in 1881 and 1885) was a particularly unusual choice, not strictly either a wind or a chamber work, but Taffanel was obviously keen for it to be heard, even with reduced strings. This was in marked contrast to the Société nationale, for example, which made a point of excluding all non-French contemporary music from its programs until 1886.[17]

The list of ensemble works with the most performances over the fifteen seasons is a mixture of old and new:

Composer and Work	Performances
Mozart: Quintet for piano and winds, K. 452	11 from 1879
Beethoven: Octet, op. 103	11 "
Mozart: Serenade, K. 388	9 "
Rubinstein: Quintet, op. 55	9 "
Spohr: Quintet, op. 52	9 "
Mozart: Serenade, K. 361	8 "
Beethoven: Trio, op. 87	8 "
Hummel: Septet, op. 74	8 from 1880
Raff: Sinfonietta, op. 188	8 "
Gouvy: Octet, op. 71	8 from 1881
Mozart: Serenade, K. 375	7 from 1879
Beethoven: Piano and Wind Quintet, op. 16	7 "
Beethoven: Rondino, WoO25	7 from 1880
Lachner: Octet, op. 156	7 "
Onslow: Sextet, op. 30	7 "
Bernard: *Divertissement*, op. 36	6 from 1884
Gounod: *Petite symphonie*	6 from 1885

Two instrumental groupings proved the most popular for new music: the traditional wind quintet (flute, oboe, clarinet, horn, and bassoon) and a modified wind octet (flute, oboe, two clarinets, two horns, and two bassoons), which was in effect the *Harmoniemusik* lineup, but with the first oboe replaced by a flute. There were quintets by eight composers—Barthe, Deslandres, Gouvy, Lefèbvre, Liszt arranged by Lassen, Pessard, Pfeiffer, and Taffanel, and octets by seven composers—Gouvy (two), Lachner, Lazzari (including a cor anglais), Lefèbvre, Nováček, Reinecke, and Saint-Saëns (arranged by Taffanel). The sextet combination of piano plus wind quintet also proved popular, with works by

Diémer, Kreutzer, Pfeiffer, Rietz, and Thuille. But only two works—Colomer's Nonet, op. 51 and Gounod's *Petite symphonie*—actually employed all the original nine wind players, and only two double quintets were ever performed: Bernard's *Divertissement*, and Raff's Sinfonietta.

Taffanel did not exclude works that mixed wind and strings, but they were not allowed to dominate the programs as they had in the days of the Société classique. He also included occasional works that excluded the winds, usually because of visiting soloists like the violinists Joachim and Sarasate, or the pianist Saint-Saëns (this accounts for various non-wind pieces by Beethoven, Boccherini, Brahms, Chovan, Diémer, Fischof, Handel, and Mendelssohn). What Taffanel rigidly excluded was anything associated with the vapid musical world of the salons, in particular, virtuoso solo pieces and vocal items. The concerts were made up entirely of serious instrumental music in a judicious blend of small and large ensembles, and of old and new compositions. Even his own solo and small flute ensemble items were chosen to reflect the best of the old and a small selection of new works recently discovered or dedicated to him: for example, J. S. Bach's Sonatas, Schubert's Introduction and Variations, Reinecke's *Undine* Sonata, and Widor's Suite.

Second, Third, and Fourth Seasons, 1880–82

No documents have survived concerning the general administration of the Society (financial arrangements, lists of subscribers, and so forth), but from the very beginning Taffanel was anxious to ensure its continuation and he had the idea of applying for official government recognition and financial support through the minister for the arts. As there were no official channels for making such an application, he enlisted the help of one of the influential society hostesses, Marie Trélat, at whose salon he had played, and she delivered a letter by hand. Changes in the government then necessitated another letter, but by the second season Taffanel had still not received any reply. So he asked his colleague, the organist and composer Charles-Marie Widor, to make discreet enquiries via Mme. Trélat. "I am not used to the role of fund-raiser, even when I am acting on the behalf of others rather than myself," he told Widor. "Our little society, which you heard yesterday, is developing, as you could judge, in a way which entirely pleases me; but I have long thought that an incentive from the Minister would give my colleagues a boost and a confidence in themselves which would raise the standard of our performances onto another level."[18] Did he ever get a reply? Nothing has come to light.

The success of the Society was secure, however. Toward the end of the second season the *Revue et gazette musicale* reported an increasingly enthusiastic audience for the concerts, and, incidentally, anticipated the full name of the Society, which did not yet appear on the programs. The works singled out for particular praise included two foreign ones: Raff's Sinfonietta and Rietz's Concertstück.[19]

After the first concert of the third season, Le Ménestrel also lent its support: "We cannot encourage enough the efforts of this young society which has already won over the music-loving Paris audience."[20] But the reception for foreign works was more mixed. At the second concert the critic praised Lachner's Octet, especially the Scherzo, for its "happy combination of varied textures," but professed little enthusiasm for Brahms's Serenade, "more bizarre than ingenious."[21] Likewise, in the third concert, although he noted a full house (including a number of fellow critics) and praised the actual performance of Röntgen's Serenade, the work itself was judged "noteworthy more for the qualities of its workmanship than for the merits of its ideas."[22]

A cloud was cast over the fourth and fifth concerts by the death of Taffanel's second child, Juliette, aged only twenty-two months. She had been born on 25 May 1879, shortly after the end of the Society's first season, and she died on 29 March 1881. There were last-minute program changes, and Taffanel did not reappear until the final concert on 28 April. The new work in this concert was an Octet by Théodore Gouvy, who was to have a close association with the Society. This Franco-Belgian composer, by then in his early sixties, had studied partly in Germany and developed close ties there with Mendelssohn and other musicians. He was strongly drawn to orchestral and chamber music, and uninterested in opera, so he was somewhat out of the mainstream of French music of the time. However, he was very much a part of the foremost musical circles gathered around figures like the singer Pauline Viardot and frequented by composers such as Saint-Saëns, Lalo, and Widor—and therefore by Taffanel, who would also have known Gouvy as one of the founding members of the Société nationale back in 1871.[23]

Gouvy's Sérénade for wind quintet had already been performed by the Society the previous year, and the new Octet, op. 71, for Taffanel's preferred combination of flute, oboe, two clarinets, two horns, and two bassoons, quickly became a favorite. "What more can one say about Monsieur Gouvy's Octet, which we hear every year, and which Monsieur Taffanel and his colleagues play perfectly?" asked one critic some years later.[24] What certainly can be said is that this was a model work for its time and for the instrumental forces it uses. The ingeniously contrapuntal first movement is almost symphonic in scope, yet always mellifluous on the ear. A rippling Danse suédoise follows, and then the mood changes for a serious and deeply felt Romance. Finally, a spirited Rondo caps everything with chattering optimism, mirroring the confidence everyone could feel once again, a decade on from the dark shadow of war. No wonder the Parisian audiences lapped it up!

Taffanel also programmed the Octet for foreign tours, and Gouvy appears to have been a regular member of the audience at the Society's concerts. However, when his second Octet (composed in 1886, but never published) was premiered there, it did not attract the audience in the same way and there were no repeat performances. So Gouvy tried again, offering Taffanel a Septet for the anniversary season that was approaching in 1888. "Our tenth year of life could have no better start than a new work by our favourite composer," wrote Taffanel in reply, but his high hopes were only partially realized.[25] The Septet turned out to be just as carefully crafted but less musically imaginative than the first Octet, notwithstanding a playful Scherzo and echoes of Bizet's *Carmen* in the finale. Its instrumental combination of flute, oboes, clarinets, and bassoons, but no horns, also strikes the ear as less colorful. Taffanel programmed it for only two seasons, and by 1890 the Society was back to playing the evergreen first Octet.

Taffanel made plans for the Society to reach a wider audience from early on. The first excursion was to Amiens on 1 May 1881, immediately after the end of the Paris season. The local press waxed lyrical:

> Have you ever felt while looking at the splendid marvels revealed by the telescope that you could hear celestial music, a sweet illusion of the senses where the prismatic colours of the luminous waves of a thousand suns seem transformed into sound waves, into an exquisite melody . . . this heavenly concert, this discourse of angels, is what we heard.[26]

Back in Paris the following season, *Le Ménestrel* reported that even the large hall of the Salle Pleyel was now scarcely big enough to contain the audiences that flocked to the Society's concerts.[27] The new work in March that year was for wind quintet, two movements by Charles Lefèbvre, a direct contemporary of Taffanel, son of the painter Charles Lefèbvre (no relation to Taffanel's brother-in-law Jules), and another member of the Viardot and Saint-Saëns circle. Lefèbvre's music was in some ways like his father's paintings: well wrought in the French academic tradition—what the critics called *très bien écrit*. But whereas the father treated religious and historical subjects in oils on a large scale, the son was more of a musical miniaturist. Hugues Imbert likened his work to "the grace revealed in Rosalba's delightful pastels" and described him as an admirer of Mendelssohn.[28]

Lefèbvre's *Deux pièces* for wind quintet (expanded to three in 1884) are pleasantly diverting, as are the octet *Méditation* and the quartet *Intermezzo-Scherzando*, which followed in 1887 and 1892, but they were never more than light relief to the serious repertoire of the Society's concerts. Taffanel's own Wind Quintet, which he allowed to be played just once (on 13 April 1882), and even then only the second and third movements, is certainly of greater musical substance.

Fifth, Sixth, and Seventh Seasons, 1883–85

"Good luck and a following wind to these gallant players" was how *Le Ménestrel* hailed the opening of the 1883 season, adding that the Society in its fifth year could now be regarded as "solid and lasting." César Franck was noted among the audience for the last concert, warmly congratulating the players for their "great precision allied to excellent style and coloured with the utmost subtlety of nuance."[29] Among the new works that season was a Nonet by a Spanish composer resident in Paris, Blas-Maria Colomer, who was also having some success with new works at the Société nationale. Taffanel thought well enough of Colomer's Nonet to recommend it for publication, adding that he took "scrupulous care in choosing the works to be performed."[30]

Taffanel also felt it was time to spread the word farther afield about the Society, and a draft letter from around this time reveals that he was hoping to visit London: "the novelty of the works to be heard, the care taken over the most difficult technical challenges, seem to me to have a chance of success with music lovers."[31] Taffanel continued at some length to enquire which hall might be suitable, how much it would cost, where he could find an agent to deal with publicity, and even which hotels would be suitable to stay at. Unfortunately, nothing came of the project, and it would be another ten years before the Society crossed the English Channel.

There was plenty to keep Taffanel busy in Paris, however, as the sixth season was particularly rich in first performances, nine in all, including the *Divertissement* by Emile Bernard—a delightful work to rival Gounod's *Petite symphonie*—Lalo's *Aubade* (a revision of the two pieces originally written for the Société classique), and Widor's superbly idiomatic Suite for flute and piano. This became one of Taffanel's most often played recital pieces during the 1880s, along with the Reinecke Sonata. The season opened with a varied program of music by Dvořák, Beethoven, Diémer, and Mozart:

> The concert was crowded, and rightly so, it's good that people are keen to attend such unusual events. Thanks to this ensemble of virtuosi a whole repertoire is beginning to emerge from the shadows, and it can only increase. What composer would not be delighted to have as interpreters artists such as Taffanel, Gillet, Turban, Espaignet, Grisez etc.[32]

Le Ménestrel now dubbed the Society the *Société Taffanel* and reported its success at a brief appearance in Brussels between the fourth and fifth Paris concerts: "All the Brussels newspapers speak admiringly of our Parisian virtuosi and recount the endless ovations lavished on them."[33]

In retrospect, the seventh season in 1885 emerges as the most musically significant, with the premiere of Gounod's *Petite symphonie*, a work expressly crafted for Taffanel's original lineup of flute plus wind octet. It is the one new work that has found a lasting place in the repertoire, and to some extent it has also served as a benchmark for French wind ensemble music ever since. Curiously enough, although it was announced in *Le Ménestrel* as "an unpublished symphony by Monsieur Gounod written especially for this Society," there was no follow-up review after the first performance on 30 April. Incidentally, the program for that concert had to be reorganized at the last minute when Saint-Saëns stepped in for an indisposed Diémer (see fig. 9). The *Petite symphonie* was not mentioned until the second concert of the 1888 season (the fourth of a total of seven performances), when its "delightful" Andante and "charmingly original" Scherzo were praised.[34] But by the 1890 season it had become a firm favorite. The pianist Isidor Philipp, in his role as music critic, recognized "the distinctive charm of the composer of *Faust* . . . it contains in equal measures the qualities of harmonic purity, instrumental elegance and bewitching style."[35] Another reviewer thought it "overflowing with charm and humor and delightful instrumental color."[36]

Gounod himself, however, seems to have set little store by the work. At the time, he was preoccupied with more serious matters, the impending premiere of his massive oratorio *Mors et vita*. The *Petite symphonie* was just a trifle—a favor for his friend Taffanel—and in it Gounod returned to the rhythmic lightness and transparent textures of his two youthful symphonies written thirty years earlier. The gesture to Taffanel is most evident in the extended flute solo of the Andante. This lingering, "vocal" line with its ornamental flourishes must surely have reminded contemporary audiences of the solo from Gluck's *Orphée*, so often performed by Taffanel at the Société des concerts. Gounod is also masterly in his treatment of the other instruments, and their interplay as both soloists and accompanists, in a way that more than once recalls Taffanel's Wind Quintet. If that work had been written after the *Petite symphonie*, the influence of Gounod on Taffanel would be easy to point out, and parallels could be drawn of mood, style, and technique. But as the Quintet predates the *Petite symphonie*, could Taffanel the composer, as well as Taffanel the player, have had some influence on Gounod in writing for winds?

The 1885 season also saw a significant change in the Society's personnel. The clarinetist Arthur Grisez decided to retire, much to Taffanel's dismay, but there was a young Conservatoire graduate that he had his eye on, "a player of real quality, almost a carbon copy of Grisez. He may not yet be absolutely first class, with that innate sense of poetry which made Grisez unrivaled, but nevertheless he has a subtle tone, a fine technique, and he is a very good musician."[37]

This was Prosper Mimart, who much later would be the dedicatee of Debussy's *Rapsodie* for clarinet. The qualities highlighted by Taffanel, particularly the "sense of poetry" and "subtle tone," indicate the ensemble style he was always aiming at. Clearly he must have thought long and hard about the musical matching of his players. He thought equally hard about instrumental balance in the wind ensemble repertoire. In a draft letter, probably to François Gevaert, director of the Brussels Conservatoire, Taffanel advised on the choice of works for a student prize-giving concert:

> The most congenial works to show off wind instruments are those written for 2 oboes (or equally 1 flute and 1 oboe), 2 clarinets, 2 horns, and 2 bassoons. This combination allows the underpinning of a smoothly consistent harmonic bass line, and excellent tone color, and it is much preferable to the combination so favored by Reicha (1 flute, 1 oboe, 1 clarinet, 1 horn and 1 bassoon). If you have enough young players I advise you therefore to choose an octet to present.

Taffanel goes on to recommend octets by Beethoven, Mozart, Gouvy, and Lachner, and then turns his attention to wind quintets:

> If you can only muster a quintet, however, which would be regrettable, there is very little choice because I would rule out everything by Reicha as being dated and only useful for study purposes. And those pieces that do exist are only very short miniatures.

At this point the draft letter breaks off, leaving a space and four pen strokes, presumably for Taffanel to list four suitable works later, once he had had time to think what they might be. However, he has one final idea:

> But if you want to feature three good students playing oboe, clarinet, and bassoon, there is a very attractive short Musette which is always effective.[38]

That would have been the Musette by Georges Pfeiffer, which the Society had premiered earlier in the season on 19 February. Always on the lookout for good music, Taffanel was also keen that young students should benefit from playing something new.

First Foreign Tour

In the early days of the New Year 1886, the Society undertook its first extended tour away from Paris. They traveled via Nancy and Mulhouse to Lausanne and finally Geneva, appearing there for two concerts in the Salle de la Réformation. Raoul Pugno was the pianist in Nancy and Mulhouse, thrilling the audiences with his own compositions for solo piano. Louis Diémer completed the tour in Lausanne and Geneva and, not to be outdone, also played his own music, including a new "diabolically virtuosic" *Grande valse de concert*.[39] The wind players involved were Taffanel, Gillet, Turban, Grisez (making a brief reappearance), Espaignet, Bourdeau, Brémond, and Garigue. The first program in Geneva, on 9 January, included many of the Society's old favorites:

Beethoven	Quintet, op. 16 for piano and winds
Diémer	*Deux pièces* for oboe and piano
Gouvy	Octet, op. 71
Schubert	Introduction and Variations, op. 160 for flute and piano
Mendelssohn	*Concertstück*, op. 114 for clarinet, basset horn, and piano
Diémer	*Pièce romantique* for piano
Rameau	*Rappel des oiseaux* for piano
Liszt	*Hungarian Rhapsody* for piano
Saint-Saëns	*Tarentelle*, op. 6 for flute, clarinet, and piano

That first concert was remarkable not only for its considerable length, but also for being the only time that Taffanel was ever reported as playing the piano in public: he accompanied the Mendelssohn *Concertstück* (maybe to give Diémer a rest before his big solo pieces). Originally that was to have been the only concert in Geneva, but it was such a success—for example, the *Danse suédois* from Gouvy's Octet had to be encored—that a second concert was quickly arranged for 12 January with the added incentive of reduced prices in the stalls and first gallery. It was another lengthy program:

Mozart	Quintet, K.452 for piano and winds
Weber	*Grand Duo*, op. 47 for clarinet and piano
Lachner	Octet, op. 156 for winds
Saint-Saëns	Romance, op. 37 for flute and piano
Pfeiffer	Musette for oboe, clarinet, and bassoon
Diémer	*Grande valse* for piano
Handel	"Air varié" for piano
Gounod	*Petite symphonie*

The Gounod *Petite symphonie* in particular was singled out for praise, but a slight mystery remains: where did the extra player (the second oboe) come from to make up the numbers required for it?

The only discordant note in any of the reviews—as previously in Paris—concerned the loudness and harshness of some of Diémer's playing, comparing it unfavorably with "such soft, such mellow and melting sounds" from the winds. This was presumably the price that Taffanel had to pay for having the foremost French pianist of the day as a member of his Society. But the general critical opinion was ecstatic, noting uninhibited applause and demands for encores, and praising the choice of programs—"nothing at all monotonous, as had been feared"—as well as the performances:

> If I say that Taffanel's legendary flute is at the head of this wonderful band, you can well believe me when I claim that they are outstanding artists . . . How rarely we hear such a perfect performance, one with such polish in every detail, such precision of attack, such delicacy of sound and color.[40]

Eighth, Ninth, and Tenth Seasons, 1886–88

Back in Paris the first concert of the 1886 season, on 18 February, involved so many different combinations of players that Taffanel annotated the back of his program with the various seating plans for the five works: Rubinstein's Quintet, Beethoven's Rondino, a Handel Oboe Sonata, Schumann's *Romance* for four horns, and Mozart's Divertimento, K. 131 (see fig. 10). The only other time he did this was for a performance of the Serenade, op. 7 by Richard Strauss at the third concert of the 1888 season. Both plans look strange to modern eyes, with straight lines of players extending from the front of the stage to the back and sitting facing each other (the chorus at the Société des concerts du Conservatoire sat in a similar formation). The result, therefore, in a work like Beethoven's Rondino, was clear eye contact between the eight players in two lines of four, and this must have been the priority, rather than trying to ensure that all the players could also be seen clearly by the audience, as they are now in the modern semicircular octet formation, which seeks a sort of compromise for performer and spectator. The seating plan for Strauss's Serenade is even more unusual: a line of two flutes and two bassoons on one side of the stage faces a line of two oboes and two horns on the other, and together they flank three lines of two clarinets, two horns, and one double bass facing the audience.

Also in the 1886 season admission prices were reviewed, and the original season ticket concession of six concerts for the price of four (twenty francs instead of thirty) was discontinued. While a ticket for a single concert remained at five francs, and would do so right through to 1893, the cost of a season ticket rose to thirty. By now the Society was so popular that incentives for the audience were no longer necessary, and even a relatively small amount of extra income must have been useful to help cover expenses.

The ninth season saw the first performances of ensemble works by Josef Rheinberger, Charles Lefèbvre, and Louis Diémer, who must have been stimulated by all these years of partnering wind players to produce a work for quintet and piano. "Good ideas enhanced by delicate instrumentation" was the verdict of the critics.[41] Diémer's *Deux pièces* for oboe and piano were also played that season—a last-minute substitution on 17 March for J. S. Bach's B minor Flute Sonata because Taffanel had to have a tooth removed (he made a penciled note on his copy of the program). A printed note on the program for the next concert announced that the violinist Joseph Joachim would be passing through Paris the following week and wished to appear at the Society. The fifth concert was therefore brought forward a week, and Joachim played a solo with Diémer, the Brahms Sonata, op. 78, and joined the ensemble for Beethoven's Septet, op. 20 for strings and wind.

The final concert of this 1887 season also took place after a gap of only one week, and it was the only other time that Taffanel did not appear. He, Gillet, and Turban had left Paris for a tour of Russia with Saint-Saëns (see chapter 8), so it was a somewhat depleted Society that played Mozart's Clarinet Quintet, Mendelssohn's Cello Sonata, op. 58, Saint-Saëns's *Romance* for horn, and Beethoven's Quintet for piano and winds. Taffanel's wife, Geneviève, made sure everything ran smoothly and provided a rare glimpse behind the scenes in a letter to him:

> My own Paul, the performance went off very well, the hall was full, Laforge, still very pale, played as well as possible. Mimart had a great success with the Mozart, shaping all the phrases. Loëb, ill on Wednesday but completely recovered yesterday, was much applauded. Diémer was, I think, much more circumspect than usual, and the audience demonstrated its approval with constant murmurs of approval. This very lovely sonata was listened to attentively and with appreciation. Garigue must have been pleased; he was listened to with reverence and there were bravos at the end of each section; he just had a problem with the penultimate note, which was really unfortunate. The Beethoven went well for everyone except Boullard; I hope the audience was not as critical as me, but really he was quite inadequate; he counted the bars on his fingers and came in too early, and in a trill which he had with the piano and the other instruments in the first movement I think, he finished quite a bit before the others; still everything turned out well and I think it made a good and pleasing impression. Many of the subscription holders had given away their tickets, but there were few empty seats. I stayed in the foyer as you asked. Franck came to the concert, as did Messieurs Lyon and Bernard Wolff, each of them asking me for news of you with interest and affection.

Two days later, on 17 April, Geneviève continued:

> This morning's post brought a charming letter from Gouvy . . . he says that "Joachim is all-powerful in Berlin and could be a support to

you for your triumphant tour of Germany which will certainly happen this coming autumn."[42]

In fact the tour did not take place until 1891, and then not to Berlin. However, later in 1887 the Society received further encouragement and publicity from a lengthy notice in the first volume of a new annual survey of Parisian musical life by the critic Camille Bellaigue: "You won't hear, in Paris or elsewhere, more beautiful music, more beautifully played. *Spiritus flat ubi vult* [the wind bloweth where it listeth]." Two years later Bellaigue mentioned the Society again, contrasting it favorably with the Société nationale: "What a lot of concerts, from those of the *Société des instruments à vent*, which are always delightful, to those of the *Société nationale*, which are often interesting, but can also be the opposite."[43]

The Society's tenth anniversary season in 1888 was celebrated with various new works, including the Gouvy Septet (noted earlier); a *Romance* for flute and piano by Jacques Durand; the Paris premiere of the *Caprice*, op. 79 that Saint-Saëns had written for Taffanel, Gillet, Turban, and himself for their Russian tour the previous year; and an arrangement for wind octet (flute, oboe, two clarinets, two horns, and two bassoons) by Taffanel of Saint-Saëns's piano duet *Feuillet d'album*, op. 81. As a piano piece it is slight, lasting about three minutes, marked "Andantino quasi allegretto" and moving in a gently syncopated 4/4 with a recurring triplet figure. Taffanel's arrangement, however, subtly colors in a new dimension of tonal perspective, in much the same way that black-and-white prints of the period were hand-colored for postcards and greetings cards. This skillful miniature is in effect Taffanel's practical demonstration of the principles of harmonic stability, homogeneity, and sonority that he described in the letter quoted earlier concerning the wind octet as an ideal combination. When the *Feuillet d'album* appeared again on a program the following year, *Le Ménestrel* noted that this "adorable trifle" had to be encored.[44]

Tchaikovsky was in the audience at the second concert on 1 March. The program included Gounod's *Petite symphonie* and Bach's Fifth Brandenburg Concerto. "At the *chamber music* matinée at Taffanel's. Gounod. Acquaintance with him. He is very nice. Bach's Flute Concerto," wrote Tchaikovsky in his diary.[45] He had visited Paris two years previously to see the publisher Felix Mackar and resolve a family problem concerning an illegitimate child of his niece, Tatyana. Mackar, having acquired the rights to distribute Tchaikovsky's works in France, set out to introduce him to all the right people. "The old Mme Viardot enchanted me . . . Lemoine (eccentric personality) . . . the charming Fauré . . . Ambroise Thomas is very friendly." By the time Tchaikovsky returned in February 1888 he was a celebrity. Paris had succumbed to a sort of Tchaikovsky mania.[46] In his diary he records an endless round of meetings, soirées, receptions, and performances of his music. There are several references to Taffanel: first at Mackar's office, then at a rehearsal at the home of a wealthy Russian, Nicolas de Benardaky, who gave a brilliant musical reception on 27 February. The performers included Madame de Benardaky, who was a singer, Lassalle and the de Reszke brothers from the Opéra, Colonne and his orchestra, Diémer, and Taffanel.[47] Taffanel played his own arrangement for flute and piano of the *Arioso* from act 3 of Tchaikovsky's opera *Eugene Onegin* (1879), and he took the opportunity of playing it again as a last-minute substitution at the Society on 15 March (Gillet, who should have played a solo, was ill). Mackar published it the following year. Tchaikovsky and Taffanel met again at two lunch parties, and Taffanel played at the special reception organized by *Le Figaro* on 14 March, a few days before Tchaikovsky left Paris for London.[48]

Toward the end of the tenth-anniversary year there were plans afoot again to realize the projected tour to Germany. Taffanel corresponded with Hermann Wolff, of the piano firm Pleyel et Wolff in Berlin, referring to previous failed attempts and suggesting a ten- or twelve-day tour in the second half of November. But it was not to be. The Opéra-comique suddenly called extra rehearsals for a new work by Litolff and would not allow the players leave of absence.[49] Nevertheless, the Society's name and reputation were traveling far afield. A Mr. George Treherne from London was one of many who wrote to Taffanel, requesting copies of the Society's programs. In reply, Taffanel gave him an update on his aims:

> When I conceived the plan of giving wind instrument concerts . . . I thought that there would be enough interesting works by the great composers to lay the foundations of our programs, and that hearing our concerts, always prepared with great care, modern composers would be moved to write for us.

> The results have matched our efforts since, next month, we are about to embark on our 11th year of existence. To be exact I must say that quite often we are assisted by extras from the "strings," but we have never had to resort to including singers.[50]

Taffanel's ongoing search for new works can be tracked in the copybook he kept of his letters at this time. He regularly requested music from foreign dealers, particularly C. F. Schmidt in Heilbron and Hug frères in Basel, and obviously made a point of keeping up with all the latest publications of chamber music, new and old. When he had to return music sent in error, a Mozart quintet for example, he was at pains to cite the precise source of reference to what he wanted: "Mozart's *Sinfonia Concertante* for oboe, clarinet, horn, and bassoon, score and parts . . . recently published by Breitkopf."[51] When it finally arrived, it was played with a piano reduction of the orchestral accompaniment at the first concert of the 1889 season, and a note in the program read: "never before performed in Paris."

The audience was no doubt delighted to discover a "new" work by Mozart, but was maybe not always so welcoming of contemporary new works. When Jules Bordier, conductor of the concerts of the Association artistique in Angers, offered a piece of his called *Aubade*, with a dedication, Taffanel replied tactfully:

> At the "Wind" Society, as it's often called here, there is an abundance of new works this year, and considering the demands of our audience (unfortunately we must take them into account) which constrains us not to put a new work in every concert, it follows that we find it difficult to include everything that we would like to play; but as soon as there is a little gap free I shall know to slip your work in.[52]

The "little gap" never materialized and Bordier's *Aubade* remained unplayed at the Society, but the outcome was more successful for the Czech composer Rudolf Nováček. In March 1889 Taffanel acknowledged receipt of Nováček's Sinfonietta for his favorite octet combination and confirmed that he would perform it: "I find it charming in every way . . . with so much skill and colour."[53]

Eleventh, Twelfth, and Thirteenth Seasons, 1889–91

In January 1889 *Le Ménestrel* announced the formation of a new ensemble in Marseille based on Taffanel's Society and made up of a wind quintet plus piano. The flutist was Edmond Alexis Bertram, who had been a student of Altès and gained his Conservatoire *premier prix*, with Taffanel on the jury, in 1875. The names of the other players were given as Dorel (oboe), Bourdin (clarinet), Triotier (horn), Autran (bassoon), and Amici (piano), and "the piquant novelty of their program" was noted.[54] Meanwhile, Taffanel's Society entered the reference books, with a short article in the latest published volume of the first edition of *Grove's Dictionary*. It confidently claimed that "the works performed are classical" and then went on to list the composers as "Bach, Handel, Beethoven, Mozart, Weber, Schubert, Mendelssohn, Schumann, Liszt, Rubinstein, Saint-Saëns, Dvorák and Gouvy"![55]

Although the only advertised new work in the 1889 season was Nováček's Sinfonietta, which was well received, the Society also performed Vincent d'Indy's Trio for clarinet, cello, and piano, premiered the previous year by the Société nationale. This time the critics were harsher: "It took all the talent of

Messieurs Diémer, Turban, and Delsart to make us listen with any interest to a complex Trio by Monsieur d'Indy." Mozart's Adagio for wind octet later in the season was considered a much more pleasing novelty.[56]

The 1889 season ended on a high note for the Society, with a supplementary half-season at the Paris *Exposition universelle.* The Salle des congrès et des conférences at the Trocadéro Palace was the venue for three concerts in late June and early July. The programs for the second and third concerts have not been found, but the first shows the Society fielding the nucleus of its repertoire, with Beethoven's Quintet, op. 16, Gounod's *Petite symphonie*, J. S. Bach's B minor Flute Sonata, and Mozart's *Gran Partita*, K. 361. Then in November that year, as a footnote to the Exhibition, both Taffanel and Diémer were created Chevaliers of the Légion d'honneur.[57] The Wind Society was honored.

The 1890 season opened with an accolade from *Le Ménestrel* after performances of works by Rubinstein, Mozart, Barthe, and Bernard: "Perfection is said to be not of this world, but when you come away from there, you are very satisfied."[58] Later there were two more successful premieres by foreign composers: the Austrian Heinrich Herzogenberg and the German Ludwig Thuille. Of Thuille's Sextet, *Le Ménestrel* remarked wryly: "a pleasant work; the third movement was encored, certainly the least good of the four." Meanwhile the press was still catching up in its appreciation of earlier French ensemble works. Gounod's *Petite symphonie* and Emile Bernard's *Divertissement* were particularly praised, but a discordant note was sounded by the following verdict: "Octet by Lachner, a colorless work and quite dated."[59]

Before the opening of the 1891 season the Society was invited to appear at the second concert of the Cercle philharmonique in Taffanel's home town of Bordeaux. The concert took place at 2:30 P.M. on 11 January in the Salle Franklin, and there were ten items, so it was a long afternoon! According to the *Bordeaux-Journal* it was also a rather more "serious" concert than usual at the Cercle philharmonique. Nevertheless, it made a profound impression on both the regular members and "true connoisseurs and those lucky enough to be invited." The press reviews adopted the by now predictable tone of surprise and delight whenever the society appeared somewhere for the first time: "What wonderful ensemble, what absolute faithfulness to the nuances, what striking contrasts, though never exaggerated, in the Beethoven Quintet and the Gounod Symphony." Taffanel himself was lionized — "such pure and velvety sounds on the flute" — and even some ten years later a letter from the son of one of his childhood friends recalled this "lovely concert."[60]

Back in Paris there were three premieres that thirteenth season: a *Divertissement* by Albert Périlhou, a former student of Saint-Saëns, which was well reviewed; a Serenade by the Danish composer Emile Hartmann, which was pronounced "well written, but dull and insipid — the Scherzo was the only exception"; and a *Cavatine et intermezzo* by Georges Alary, faintly praised as "two interesting pieces, although a bit long and nebulous."[61] Unfortunately not all the composers attracted to writing for wind instruments had the talent of a Gounod or a Gouvy!

Second Foreign Tour

The most notable event in 1891 was the second extended tour made by the Society. It took place from the end of October into early November, and the itinerary comprised Basel, Mulhouse, Berne, Neuchâtel, Lausanne, Strasbourg, and Frankfurt. On a train somewhere between Neuchâtel and Lausanne, Taffanel found a quiet corner and a few brief minutes of rest to write to his nine-year-old daughter, Marie-Camille:

> My little one. You would not believe how busy I have been during this tour when we have had to give a concert each day, worry about hotels, halls, sorting out music stands, all of which I know about because I have to arrange everything. Also I have not had a moment to write to you. So while the carriage shakes me around, I have fled from the one with my colleagues in it, where you cannot see a thing because of the tobacco smoke, and come to say a brief hello to you. I think of you twenty times a day and more, and you will believe that when you know that your lovely notebook never leaves me, and I am writing everything in it about my travels. I have it almost always to hand: so you can see how useful it is.
>
> At the moment the weather is marvellous, but very cold: it is winter, I am wearing all the clothes I have, so I am very well protected. The North Wind has been blowing its strongest since yesterday and the lake seems like a little sea. Beyond it you can see the superb panorama of the Alps and the beautiful outline of the Jungfrau. In a few moments I shall be admiring the Lake of Geneva, we will arrive in Lausanne and I will prepare my concert, which I hope will go as well as the one yesterday. I was very pleased, so was the audience—all of my ensemble did very well.[62]

The notebook has not survived (Taffanel no doubt gave it to Marie-Camille when he returned to Paris), so the local press in the various towns and reports in the Paris press are again the main sources of information, apart from a copy of the program for the Strasbourg concert on 31 October.[63] It includes many of the old favorite works and confirms that the party consisted of

Taffanel, Gillet, Turban, Grisez (once again back with the Society although he had been replaced by Mimart for the Paris concerts), Garigue, Brémond, Espaignet, and Bourdeau. Diémer was the pianist for this concert and the one in Frankfurt, while Raoul Pugno played for the Swiss leg of the tour.[64]

There were ovations wherever the Society played. "Sensitive," "refined," and "delicate" were the adjectives used time and time again. In Lausanne:

> The hall was full to bursting. I do not think that we often hear a lineup of such virtuosi and players of this calibre, presented in such a natural, straightforward and unassuming way, so absolutely right, so accommodating and with no pretensions whatsoever . . . In the ensemble works, each played his part marvelously, none dominated, none was lost . . . Monsieur Taffanel's flute is truly the "magic flute" . . .

> The Octet by Gouvy, with its inventive use of instruments and graceful rhythms, perhaps showed off the ensemble talents of these Parisian musicians at their best. Notable also was the great success of Monsieur Taffanel (flute) in Bach's B minor sonata.[65]

Fourteenth and Fifteenth Seasons

The 1892 season opened with three new works, all in the first concert: the Sextet by Georges Pfeiffer, an *Intermezzo–Scherzando* by Charles Lefèbvre, and *Valses* by the Alsatian composer Jacques Ehrhart. Isidor Philipp had particular praise for Pfeiffer's "light and meticulous craftsmanship" and the "elegance" of Ehrhart's pieces.[66] And even this many years on in the Society's history, there were still "new" works to be discovered from the past. At the second concert a critic noted a "graceful, youthful work . . . being heard for the first time."[67] It was Beethoven's Trio for piano, flute, and bassoon, advertised in the program as "composed at the age of 16." At the fifth concert the Society played host to Sarasate, making a special appearance to play Schubert's Rondo, op. 70 with Diémer and (like Joachim before him) to take part in the Beethoven Septet. Then the final concert was rearranged at the last moment. The pianist Caroline de Serres was indisposed, so duo pieces by Gounod and Widor were abandoned in favor of two works by Saint-Saëns: his Scherzo for two pianos, played by Diémer and his student Edouard Risler, and the "witty fantasy," *Carnaval des animaux*.[68] Taffanel must have used all his influence with Saint-Saëns to secure permission for this rare public performance of *Carnaval*.

Meanwhile, it was not just the critics or the audience who were unimpressed by some of the modern music Taffanel programmed; sometimes a player would rebel. Silvio Lazzari, a young Austro-Italian composer, told the story of being commissioned by Taffanel to write a wind Octet:

> After the first rehearsal, Gillet the oboist got up and said: "Excuse me, Monsieur Taffanel, but I will not play this rubbish." And nothing could be done to change the mind of this admirable player. A year was wasted. I had to wait a year until another oboist agreed to play his part in the ensemble.[69]

However, the printed program for the first concert of the 1893 season, when the Lazzari Octet was given for the first time, still discreetly printed Gillet's name as the oboist!

There are no indications that the 1893 season was intended to be the last. It seems most likely that the Society was just overtaken by events later that year when on 1 July Taffanel was appointed principal conductor at the Opéra. It is ironic, therefore, that 1893 was the year when appreciations of the Society appeared in two books, and in the magazine *La Grande dame* (quoted at the beginning of this chapter). "How delightful the Société des instruments à vent concerts are, led by that incomparable virtuoso of the flute, Taffanel," wrote Oscar Comettant at the beginning of a lengthy essay.[70] Louis de Fourcaud's history of the Salle Pleyel also celebrated the important role played by the Society:

> The idea has been to make the public aware of an art that was virtually unknown, while at the same time familiarizing them with a very rich repertoire containing real masterpieces . . . The excellent society has dipped its hands deep into the foreign repertoire, bringing, or bringing back, into the light of day numerous compositions . . . But it has not stopped there, and it has offered generous opportunities to our French musicians, who, profiting from the means at their disposal, have been well disposed to write for it.[71]

Alongside Lazzari's Octet, which exacted no particular comment from the press, the fifteenth season included two other first performances in Paris: Brahms's Clarinet Quintet and Reinecke's Octet, op. 216, composed the previous year. This was once again for the particular form of wind octet (including the flute) favored by Taffanel, so maybe he had had some influence on its composition after meeting Reinecke in Leipzig in 1890.[72] *Le Ménestrel* pronounced it "well written, but a little lacklustre . . . only the finale escapes this criticism: it is brilliant and allowed Monsieur Taffanel once again to demonstrate that wonderful virtuosity of which he holds the secret."[73]

The premiere of the Reinecke Octet should have taken place on 2 March, but that second concert of the season had to be canceled. The stark realities of the outside world suddenly intervened when Taffanel was called on to serve as a replacement juror in the court case attempting to unravel the infamous Panama Affair, the biggest financial scandal of the Third Republic.[74] Literally dozens of ministers and leading political figures were implicated in accusations of bribery and corruption relating to a company that had secured large loans to dig a canal through the Isthmus of Panama—a project that simply did not materialize. Consequently, the Society's program was held over until 16 March, and there was an unintentional irony in the inclusion of the three *Fantasiestücke* by Schumann! A supplementary concert was then organized for 4 May 1893 to make up for the earlier cancellation, and the season ended in style with a performance of Mozart's *Gran Partita*. None of the players who left the stage of the Salle Pleyel that afternoon would have known it, but that was the Society's last appearance in Paris.

Final Appearance in London

Although Taffanel was no longer willing or able to continue the Society's former range of activities after the end of the 1893 season, he did accept an invitation with five of its members (Diémer, Turban, Reine, Letellier, and Van Waefelghem) the following year to appear in London at one of the Wolff Musical Union concerts. The program at St. James's Hall on 11 July 1894 included Rubinstein's Quintet, op. 55; Mozart's *Kegelstatt* Trio, K. 498; Beethoven's Serenade, op. 25; and Widor's Suite. It was reported in the daily press and musical journals.[75] *The Musical Times* called the players "artists of exceptional merit" and Taffanel "a flautist of superlative excellence." *The Times* agreed, noting that the Scherzo of the Widor Suite had to be encored, but expressing a general reservation:

> Perhaps no combination of instruments is so difficult to write for with anything like complete success as a wind quartet, since it is so easy to lapse into the trivial and commonplace. This was brought home to the listener somewhat forcibly in the *finale* of Rubinstein's unequal quintet . . .

The Musical Opinion paid Taffanel a rather backhanded compliment, observing that he had "almost succeeded by remarkable beauty of tone and phrasing in making the flute an enjoyable solo instrument!" As for the ensemble itself:

> It is to be regretted that the excellent violinist and organiser of these high class concerts, Mr Johannes Wolff, did not see his way to introduce the complete group of performers composing the famous Parisian Wind Instruments Society, in order to show to London au-

diences what individual *maestria* in conjunction with assiduous co-operation can achieve in this fertile but woefully neglected branch of musical art. The last named qualification must be understood to refer to the incorrigible apathy of the British amateurs (so-called), who, season after season, for some years past, persistently withheld their support from two metropolitan wind and string instrument societies of conspicuous merit.

Those two groups were the Wind Instrument Society and Clinton's Wind Quintet, and the flutist involved in both of them was Frederic Griffith, who had studied for a while with Taffanel in Paris in 1888.[76] The rival activities of the two societies were trenchantly described by Bernard Shaw during his stint as a music critic, and he concluded:

> It is important that both enterprises should receive sufficient support to keep them going, for the sake of opportunities they afford for turning mere bandsmen into artists. At present the dearth of first-rate wind players is such that important concerts and rehearsals may be made impractical by the pre-engagement of two or three players—a ridiculous state of things in a city like London.[77]

Successors to Taffanel's Society

By 1894 there was certainly no dearth of wind players in Paris, but even thirty years later in London, Louis Fleury, writing for English readers, observed that the idea of wind chamber music "still appears to our contemporaries as a new idea . . . 'in the margin' of genuine chamber music."[78] In the same article, Fleury briefly recounts the story of Taffanel's Society and how it was only some years later that an entirely new group was formed. This reconstituted society was described in an article in *Le Monde musical* in 1901 which explained that Gillet and Turban were the first to try to revive Taffanel's Society, but that it was the clarinetist Mimart who eventually succeeded in 1898, joined the following year by Philippe Gaubert, who as Taffanel's favorite student easily gained his support.[79] The Society gave concerts up to the beginning of the First World War and then there was another, much longer gap until the sudden death of Philippe Gaubert in 1941 prompted a group of wind players, led by Louis Bleuzet and Fernand Oubradous, "to raise the Phoenix from the ashes once again."[80] In October 1941 the Society, now claiming in the program to be in its sixty-second year (!), gave a concert in the Hall of the Paris Conservatoire in homage to Gaubert. It opened with Mozart's C minor Serenade and included Gaubert's *Sonatine* for flute and piano, Taffanel's Wind Quintet, and Gounod's *Petite symphonie*. The tradition lived on.

However, the society that was most successful, not only in continuing but also in developing Taffanel's work, was the Société moderne des instruments à vent founded by another Taffanel student, Georges Barrère, with the express purpose of playing and encouraging contemporary wind music. The Society began with three concerts during the 1895–96 musical season, and Barrère later wrote that "Taffanel helped me greatly in the formation as well as the maintenance and perpetuation of such a venture."[81] By the time Barrère compiled a tenth-anniversary publicity booklet he could claim state funding and sixty-one new works by forty composers played by the Society. He was, however, somewhat rewriting history to maintain that in 1895 "chamber music for wind instruments seemed to be . . . completely neglected."[82] Nevertheless, Taffanel contributed a letter of congratulation, printed with a series of others from a wide range of composers as an appendix to the booklet:

> I salute your first jubilee with heartiest congratulations and great satisfaction.
>
> As a sort of "grandfather," or, if you wish, uncle of wind instrument societies, I am happy when I see one such as yours persevere on the straight and narrow, with no other aim than that of seeking perfection in performance; and dreaming only of cultivating the blossoming of new works to enrich a limited repertoire.
>
> In both these respects, you have, during these last ten years, worked wonders, and I am very delighted to confirm it.

Interestingly, some of the composers who wrote in support of the Société moderne in 1905, like Lazarri, Lefèbvre, and Pfeiffer, had previously written works for Taffanel. Reynaldo Hahn was too young to have done that, but he did have vivid memories of going to the concerts:

> During my early years of musical study I attended, filled with wonder, the concerts of the Société des instruments à vent, and can confirm that yours are comparable in every way, and that one finds the same well-matched ensemble, the same effortless and skillful technique, the same impeccable taste in every detail. The artistry of Taffanel, Turban, Gillet, Brémond, Espaignet, and Teste, that refined artistry that they brought supremely to perfection, lives on, thanks to you and your colleagues, in all its brilliance and rare nobility. The French school of wind playing is unequaled throughout the world.

When Barrère emigrated to New York that same year to join the New York Symphony Orchestra, Fleury took over, and by 1924 he could claim that the Society had "brought out no less than *one hundred and twenty-five works* for the first time, and revived all the classical or modern works of any importance."[83] In France, at least, the battle was won, and every significant French composer in succeeding generations would contribute something to the rapidly growing repertoire of wind chamber works.

Not surprisingly, Taffanel's society was copied throughout Europe and beyond. François Gevaert was the first to found a similar ensemble in Belgium, in the mid-1880s, followed a few years later by Frederic Griffith in England. Just a few months before he died, Taffanel received a letter, signed Mariano San Miguel from the Madrid Society of Wind Instruments, "honored to report its first success achieved chiefly with your magnificent *Quintet*."[84] In the United States, Barrère immediately continued the activities he had pursued in Paris, founding first the New York Symphony Quintet (with the encouragement of Saint-Saëns), then the Barrère Ensemble in 1910, and later the Barrère Little Symphony.[85]

One of the most interesting societies influenced by Taffanel was the Longy Club of Boston, founded in 1900 (before Barrère arrived in America) by the oboist Georges Longy, who had migrated from Paris the previous year to join the Boston Symphony Orchestra. Longy, a former student of Gillet, had appeared as an extra player with Taffanel's Society on several occasions (the first in March 1889), and had later helped to restart it with Mimart. He was assisted in Boston by relatives of two original players, Grisez and Sautet, and the Longy Club was closely modeled on Taffanel's Society. The concerts, which continued to 1917, comprised a similar mix of solo and ensemble items, and much of Taffanel's repertoire was duplicated, including many of the works originally premiered by him. Added to this was an increasing number of new works from various countries written since Taffanel's retirement.[86]

Achievements of Taffanel's Society

Taffanel's legacy through his Société des instruments à vent was aptly summed up after his death in a tribute presented in the 1909 Report of the Association des artistes musiciens. The Secretary, Francis Waël-Munk, claimed four particular achievements "thanks to this Society and its founder:"

> that the study of wind instruments in this country has increased so greatly . . . that wind instrument makers have worked ceaselessly, over the last thirty years, to make numerous improvements to the construction of their instruments . . . that many composers have enriched the repertoire with so many beautiful works for wind instruments . . . that our school of wind players, already the foremost in the world, has achieved a perfection which is recognized by all the European countries.[87]

It was victory on every front: the appreciation, making, composing, and playing of wind instruments. Perhaps it could only have happened in France. Unlike the Germanic countries, France had never been totally committed to instrumental music—the operatic tradition was paramount. So, when interest in chamber music began to develop from around 1850 onward, the string quartet and other traditional ensembles were important, but not exclusively so. It left open the possibility for wind instruments to be accepted, and Taffanel turned that possibility into a far-reaching reality.

CHAPTER 7

The Magic Flute

Monsieur Taffanel, a flute player, but what a flute player! . . .
he is—if you will forgive an unfortunate play
on words—a magic flute.
—*JOURNAL DE LIÈGE*, (8 FEBRUARY 1887)

The success of the first season of the Société des instruments à vent seems to have provoked in Taffanel's mind thoughts about the direction his career should be taking. Should he continue as an orchestral player when he had long ago achieved all that he could? What about his activities as a soloist, his new Society, composition, even conducting? He had a realistic and pragmatic view of the world, however, as he showed in a letter to one of his relations in Bordeaux, Joseph Celly:

> You must understand, Joseph, we live in a fundamentally confident, materialistic age. If the arts find a place in it, it is a more and more limited one, and it is becoming increasingly difficult to make a career. The public does not like to "share" its favors: it rushes to embrace this or that performer whose every fault it forgives and whose slightest thoughts and deeds it dotes on, and that's that . . . More than one Planté or Ritter has given up the fight in the face of this unjust public indifference and resigned himself to a tiresome and thankless teaching job. If you are setting your sights on the career of a composer many other setbacks await you.
>
> Success and fame nowadays come only to those composers who write for the theater. Symphonies, oratorios, and quartets lead nowhere. Paris is the only place there is for music, the provinces don't exist, and in Paris there are openings in only one or two theaters. These theaters

are controlled by a few individuals, with nothing to choose between any of them. I could name a sad number of young composers returned from Rome, previously filled with hope and enthusiasm, who have never managed to have even a poor little one-acter played at the Opéra-comique, and who, in despair, now give singing or violin lessons in schools. Don't think I am exaggerating, it's the absolute truth.[1]

Wise advice, particularly as Taffanel struggled with the frustrations of his own position in the early months of 1880. On 3 February, in the first of a sequence of three letters to the director of the Opéra, Emmanuel Vaucorbeil, he tendered his resignation from the orchestra, a post that although prestigious was also a day-to-day drudgery.[2] Vaucorbeil was understandably reluctant to let Taffanel go and looked for some alternative solution. The conductor, Ernest Altès, acted as a go-between in the negotiations that dragged on until early June. Taffanel suggested a compromise to safeguard his pension, whereby he would take eight months unpaid leave each year and then work for four months at whatever salary they liked to suggest. Vaucorbeil could not agree to this, however, fearing the reactions of other members of the orchestra to such preferential treatment. The government minister in charge of the Opéra's affairs also raised objections. Taffanel promptly resigned again.[3]

Then a few days later he sent another letter: "I am writing to ask you to agree to grant me six months' leave of absence from the coming 1st July. The state of my health, much affected by the rigors of the exceptionally hard winter just past, constrains me to beg your indulgence in this matter."[4] Did Vaucorbeil perhaps suggest this six-month leave of absence for Taffanel again to reconsider his resignation? The answer is not known, but for whatever reason, Taffanel remained in the Opéra orchestra until he was appointed its conductor, and he does not appear to have taken any more extended periods of leave.

While all this was going on, Taffanel was also facing another grim reality of life. On 17 June he purchased a plot of land for a family grave in Père Lachaise Cemetery, and his baby daughter Juliette was the first to be buried there, less than a year later in March 1881.[5] Jules Lefèbvre sketched a small oil portrait of her—a chubby-faced little girl in a pink-and-white bonnet—and inscribed it to Geneviève. It was a sad memento.[6] On a happier note, in October 1880 Taffanel bought another plot of land, this time down in the south of France in Hyères, where he had a holiday home built.[7] Hyères was a favorite haunt of a number of musicians, including the composer Ambroise Thomas, and Taffanel's "Villa des Oiseaux" was perched on the side of a hill, between the town and the sea in the area called Costabelle.

The Altès Method

During 1880 Taffanel would have noted the publication of Henri Altès's *Méthode pour flûte système Boehm*. This exhaustive, rigorous, and in many ways admirable tutor, in three volumes and 429 pages, encapsulated what Georges Barrère later called Altès's "systematic teaching . . . strictness and severe training."[8] Altès leads the student painstakingly through every aspect of technique, and the emphasis throughout is on the development of a secure finger technique: "play precisely" is the motto. To this end, numerous exercises and studies in duet form accompany each section. Altès's directions on embouchure and breathing, however, are much less detailed than those on fingering—indeed, there is no separate section on breathing, merely footnotes on pages 20 and 286. Much of the advice on embouchure is also general rather than specific: "the character of the flute requires a tone which is by turns gentle, soft, full and resonant . . . mellowness is the dominant character of the flute." As for posture, "maintain an absolutely fixed position."

Although Altès asserts that technique must always be allied to "sensibility," and refers much to "good taste," the sections of the *Méthode* where he attempts to discuss the aesthetics of playing are generally the most vague. On interpretation, for example: "a true artist, worthy of the name, will understand this innately and study will develop it." But the music recommended for that study reflects the virtuoso tradition to which Altès belonged, *fantaisies* and airs with variations by Berbiguier, Tulou, Lindpaintner, Demersseman, and others. Although the section headed "Bibliothèque du flûtiste" includes the names of Bach, Beethoven, Haydn, and Mozart, the longest list of works is by Altès's teacher, Tulou, and when Altès includes a duet arrangement of one of Handel's op. 1 Sonatas, he presents it as something unusual, "interesting, I think."[9]

There is something old-fashioned about Altès's *Méthode*, even for 1880, and it must have been anathema to Taffanel, whose repertoire was built on quite different musical foundations and whose attitude to playing was much more flexible. "My predecessor, very narrow in his views and completely of the old school, knew and taught only a very limited number of old-fashioned works which had no musical value whatsoever," wrote Taffanel to the Danish flutist Joachim Andersen after he had succeeded Altès as professor of flute at the Conservatoire.[10] The conclusion is clear: for Altès, flute playing was a skill, for Taffanel it was an art. Adolphe Hennebains, who graduated from Altès's class that year (Taffanel was on the jury), would have been the first to agree. In 1890 he joined the Opéra orchestra, and a year later succeeded Taffanel as principal flute: "I was therefore Monsieur Taffanel's colleague for a year and his example and the influence of his immense artistic talent contributed greatly to my development. *Monsieur Taffanel is my true teacher.*" Taffanel responded when he became conductor of the Société des concerts and Hennebains also succeeded him there as first flute, with the gift of a photograph of himself—a significant token at that time—inscribed "to my dear friend Hennebains, Nov '92."[11]

Marie-Camille Taffanel

The birth of Taffanel's second daughter, on 17 June 1882, was a source of great joy and completed his family (see fig. 11). It also strengthened his relationship with Camille Saint-Saëns, whom he invited to become godfather. However, in the light of Saint-Saëns's own broken marriage and the deaths of his two sons, the invitation had to be presented very carefully. Taffanel first confided in Saint-Saëns's mother, and then a few weeks before the birth again broached the subject: "Have you spoken to Camille about my audacious idea?"[12] Saint-Saëns's response was immediate:

> My dear friend. I had vowed that I would never again be a godfather. I have two reasons for that. The first you can guess, and then there is my loathing of religious ceremonies. However it seems to me that there should be a way of resolving everything by having some friend or other stand in for me at the ceremony. On that condition I will accept and with great pleasure.[13]

From that point on, there was regular social as well as professional contact between Taffanel and Saint-Saëns, reflected in their correspondence. After Louis Dorus, Saint-Saëns was the most important influence on Taffanel's career. They were kindred musical spirits. Saint-Saëns's "classical" stance, as both a composer and a performer, answered to similar sympathies in Taffanel, first as a flutist and later as a conductor. It is not hard to find, for example, in Isidor Philipp's evaluation of Saint-Saëns as a pianist, resonances of descriptions of Taffanel's flute playing: "Above all he valued sincerity of expression and clarity. He detested mannerisms and affectation . . . You could not have had piano playing with more wit, rhythm, naturalness, and life. His personality, more balanced than exuberant, was equally suited to interpreting the classics as it was to modern works."[14]

As for Marie-Camille Taffanel, she grew up devoted to her fascinating and diligent godfather. To her delight, Saint-Saëns regularly sent her letters and postcards from glamorous foreign places—Alexandria, Cairo, Venice, Naples—followed by presents of trinkets and sweets, flowers and exotic fruits. She responded with lively thank-you letters telling him all about her life.[15] The exchange of correspondence in January 1892, while Saint-Saëns was in Algiers, sets the tone. Marie-Camille was nine:

> Godfather. Thank you so much for the lovely brooch you sent me, it is very beautiful and I like it more than all my other New Year's pres-

ents. Mama has allowed me to write whatever I want to you, I hope you will get my letter and see how pleased I am. I go to school now and work as hard as I can, I came first in French, in reading and in recitation, arithmetic is the only thing that I don't like and don't do well. I practise the piano a lot and hope you will be pleased with me when you return. My dolls are lovely, I had three for Christmas. I am very busy sewing for them; I also have a canary that I have tamed called Riquet who eats sugar from my hand. Mama says I am writing for too long, but I want you to understand everything that I care about because you are my godfather and I love you with all my heart.

My dear child. I was so pleased to receive your kind letter, which would have pleased me even more if you had let me have news of your father and mother. If you want me to be proud of you on the piano, try to play in time and do not let your right hand trail behind your left, when they should be sounding together, and also give rests their exact duration; otherwise your godfather will roll his big eyes, which would be dreadful. I hesitate to be too forward, but maybe you could present my humble respects to Monsieur Riquet. I also had a tame canary who lived to be twenty and whom I loved passionately. I used to peel the pips of apples and pears and give him the kernels; and as soon as he saw anyone with apples or pears he would get excited. Try this and see if Monsieur Riquet likes it.

Saint-Saëns decorated the bottom of this letter with a sketch of the musical staff and two octaves of the whole-tone scale—like a row of musical pips. Marie-Camille, however, soon reported that Riquet did not like eating kernels. "Then there's nothing to be done," replied Saint-Saëns, "you will have to find something else to give him for treats." And they went on to discuss donkeys . . . Marie-Camille had had a donkey and cart at the seaside that summer, which reminded Saint-Saëns that all last winter he had also had one: "My donkey was called Pegasus and he went like the wind; no one could stop him. He sang delightfully and had such poetic ears."

"Mind the crabs!" warned Saint-Saëns the following summer, 1893, when Marie-Camille was at the seaside. "Their pincers are fiercely sharp and will cut through your fingers like butter." And turning for once to musical matters he went on: "Your father is covering himself with glory at the Opéra, which pleases me greatly, although unfortunately I can't benefit from it at the moment. Someone will explain to you what that means."

Marie-Camille was fast growing up. In her teenage years she would submit her poetry to Saint-Saëns, and he, gently but nonetheless firmly, would advise her on style and sentiment. She would also report on the failing health of her father. But childlike high spirits remained the keynote of their correspondence, and never more so than when Saint-Saëns sent her a picture postcard of himself in 1901, standing on a broad boulevard outside a hotel in Cairo, walking cane in hand: "The two balcony windows above my silly old head are where I am staying. It seems to me that I look for all the world like one of those particularly majestic animals that you see in menageries." *Carnaval des animaux* was never very far away!

Taffanel's own letters to his daughter reveal him to be the most loving of fathers. The seventeen letters from him that Marie-Camille carefully kept span the period 1887–98, when she was aged between four and sixteen.[16] Taffanel sent them either while he was away on concert tours, or while Marie-Camille was away on various family holidays, often with her aunt and cousins, the Lefèbvres.

"I think about you all the time, my little one, and really wish you could be here with me," he writes in February 1887. The letter is carefully copied in a clear, printed script, so presumably Marie-Camille was beginning to read by then. Two months later, on tour to St. Petersburg with Saint-Saëns, he tells her: "When I go down to lunch or dinner I always look out for a pretty little girl who will climb onto my back and pat me gently on the head to make me move along, but I never find one."

For her name day on 15 August, when she is seven, Taffanel sends Marie-Camille a blotter and the most fashionable sort of writing paper, so she can write her own letters. Later he will compliment her on how well her handwriting is developing, and gently chide her for not always abiding by the rules of grammar. Meanwhile, he has news of Jacques, who is on holiday with a friend and his badly behaved dog, Louis, and he also describes visiting the Eiffel Tower and meeting Thomas Edison (see chapter 8).

In April 1890, on a trip to play a concert at Bayeux, Taffanel visits the church and the famous tapestry: "Imagine seventy meters (not less) of canvas, about eighty centimeters high, on which countless figures are embroidered in wool, the whole design just in outline and more naïve than anything you could imagine! Much of it is absolutely comical." A visit to Hamburg in November the same year provokes a detailed account of the journey, including the inconvenience of having to change trains unexpectedly at Liège and travel in a smoking compartment. It is cold and wet on arrival in Hamburg, and Taffanel describes the rickety houses and even sketches one for her. The hotel is very grand, with a lift, but the ships' horns plague him, and he notates their dissonant pitches (see fig. 12).

Marie-Camille's pet canary — Taffanel calls him "Master Riquet" — is the subject of a charming letter in August 1891.

> He makes the most delightful music for us; as if he wants to console us for your absence and take the place of your chatter. His place, during the day, is always on the windowsill of the stairs; each time that I

go up or down I lean my head near to his cage and straight away Master Riquet, leaving his usual place, invariably comes and settles on a particular perch, always the same one, which is his perch for receiving visitors, and there he listens attentively to everything you say, nodding his head to left and right and looking as though he understands perfectly. Believe me, he is a very delightful friend. However, he is no real substitute for you, and we long to see you again.

Later that year Taffanel writes another travelog for Marie-Camille while he is on tour with the Société des instruments à vent (see chapter 6). The next summer, 1892, when Marie-Camille is ten, Taffanel describes how he has impersonated her by using one of her nicknames: "Even though you are far away we talk about you often and don't forget you. Only the other day, when I was in my study, I came out and I called Petite Maman who ran quickly up the stairs asking what was the matter; and I replied quite simply . . . 'Vavatikou!' Petite Maman was furious."

The Taffanel family was fond of nicknames and changed or modified them over time. Marie-Camille and her brother were sometimes Totote and Jajacques, sometimes Toutou and Jacquiche. Geneviève and Taffanel himself could be Petite Maman and Papatin, or Mouche (fly) and Petit Papa. Indeed, the subject of nicknames fills most of a letter Taffanel wrote while he was in Bayreuth with Jacques that same summer of 1892: "My sweet Totote, or Boubout, or Marie, or Camille, or Britz, or Boulet de Canon [cannonball], or Toutou [doggie], or Bouchon de carafe [bottle stopper], or Chienloup [wolfhound], or Vavaticou, or Trouloulou, or Mitzie. Is that all? Have I exhausted the list?"

The following summer he describes life in Paris with all the family away: "Would you believe that since Petite Maman left I have been conducting every night! And that's quite something: *Lohengrin, Salammbô, The Valkyrie!*" Taffanel found these enforced absences from the family very tedious, before he could join them on holiday later in the summer. "At the moment I am endlessly conjugating the verb to be bored until it is time to go to bed," he writes in 1895. And so the childhood years passed, with the threads of everyday details that weave the fabric of family life, and suddenly it was June 1898: "It is frightening to have to wish happy birthday to a grown-up girl of 16!! How that ages the poor parents! Ah well, one must give in . . . Papa is happy and sends his grown-up daughter all his love and kisses."

Marie-Camille later studied at the Sorbonne and in 1912 married Charles Samaran, an eminent historian who was to become director of the Archives de France and an active member of the Institut de France until shortly before his death at the age of 101 in 1982.[17] The couple had three daughters, two of whom became professional musicians: Annette was a violinist and Charlotte a pianist. The youngest, Jeanne, trained at the Conservatoire as a cellist and sub-sequently became a music librarian there.

Proust, Lalo, and Schubert

The Paris daily newspapers and weekly magazines in the 1880s offered a lively run-ning commentary on the musical scene—part serious reporting, part gossip—and Taffanel's name figured frequently in reports of concerts. While Altès was musing over the unusualness of Handel Sonatas, Taffanel was playing them regularly in recitals, notably on one occasion at a soirée at the home of the Comte Greffulhe, whose young wife Elisabeth was one of the most influential patrons of the arts. A dazzling beauty, she was the inspiration for Proust's Duchesse de Guermantes in his *A la recherche du temps perdu*.[18] Is there also a fleeting glimpse of Taffanel in the pages of Proust's epic novel, playing a piece so closely identified with him at the salon of another society lady, Madame de Saint-Euverte? "Swann had gone forward at Madame de Saint-Euverte's insis-tence, and in order to listen to an air from *Orphée* which was being played by a flutist, had positioned himself in a corner from which, unfortunately, his view was blocked by two ladies of mature years seated side by side."[19]

Highlights of this period include the premiere of Edouard Lalo's ballet *Namouna* at the Opéra in March 1882. Preparations and negotiations for this were complicated and acrimonious, with the leading dancer, Rita Sangalli, being particularly difficult to please. Lalo in desperation complained to the di-rector, Vaucorbeil:

> Yet another objection has been raised by Mademoiselle Sangalli: she wishes to replace the flute solo by another instrument. But no other instrument is agile enough, supple enough, to take the place of the flute in this very difficult solo entrusted to Taffanel. Even Sarasate's marvellous violin itself would be ineffectual and ridiculous. Made-moiselle Sangalli maintains that she cannot dance to a flute.[20]

Lalo stood his ground, Mademoiselle Sangalli eventually relented, Taffanel played, and all were rewarded with ecstatic reviews for the sensuous *Danse de Namouna*. Sangalli was even gracious enough to come down to the footlights and acknowledge Taffanel during the applause after her solo with the flute. Lalo later published the piece as *Introduction et allegretto* in an arrangement for flute and piano, dedicated to Taffanel.[21]

Meanwhile the press continued to chart the development and expansion of the solo flute repertoire played by Taffanel. In February 1882 he had made another visit back to his hometown of Bordeaux to appear at a Cercle phil-harmonique concert at the Salle Franklin. Alongside his own *Fantaisie sur Freischütz* and another favorite virtuoso piece of his at this time, the *Fantaisie pastorale hongroise* by Franz Doppler, he played the Schubert Variations: "his truly magic flute produced an ideal purity and incredible richness of sound; with what ease he made light of any difficulties, and with what expressiveness he let the andantes and romances gently murmur!"[22] Back in Paris, a further performance of the Schubert Variations drew another admiring review: "no other flute player today has such an elegant and refined style, such flexibility and exquisite perfection . . . he alone has that mellow sound, soft and velvety." But there were reservations about the actual music: "Just one thing rather spoils, I think, this lovely work by Schubert . . . it is the final variation in the style of a march which seems a bit ordinary."[23]

This is a revealing point, for if the Schubert Variations are treated by the flutist in the old bravura manner, the weaknesses of the marchlike finale are not really noticeable. Only when the player relates the variations to the tragic emotional world of the original lied from *Die Schöne Müllerin*—as Taffanel obviously did—does it become difficult to sustain Schubert's intentions right to the end, and the March can indeed seem ordinary, even flippant. Writers on Schubert have usually dismissed these Variations. The perceptive Hans Gál, however, was in no doubt as to their seriousness: "It is partly Schubert's fault that the deep personal significance of this rarely played piece almost invariably remains misunderstood . . . In so many other cases, a rugged exterior impedes access to a work of art; with Schubert it is often a gentle, pleasing surface that conceals its profundity."[24] It must have been precisely this "profundity" that kept Taffanel playing these Variations long after he had abandoned those by lesser player-composers.

Taffanel was also offering Paris audiences at this time "an unknown sonata by Christophe Bach," and an arrangement of "Hungarian suites by Brahms."[25] Then there was a Serenade by the contemporary German composer Heinrich Hofmann for flute, string quartet, and double bass, which created "an absolute sensation."[26] Taffanel amusingly recorded the preparations for a further per-formance of this work, with the Lefort Quartet and the bass player Emile de Bailly: "Rehearsal at Lefort's house for his two chamber music recitals. Hof-mann septet. A good session, despite de Bailly who, never one to miss his meals, left us before the end."[27]

By now almost any concert including Taffanel was guaranteed to be a suc-cess, so he was in demand by instrumentalists and singers making their debuts. At the end of 1882 he had promoted his own cousin Joseph Jemain, recently graduated from the Conservatoire as a pianist.[28] In March 1883 he appeared at a soirée with the young American soprano Emma Nevada, newly arrived in Paris. Years later in 1900, when Taffanel became an Officier of the Légion d'honneur, she wrote congratulating him and declared: "It is such a long time since I have seen, or heard, that angelic flute which I shall never forget."[29]

The Romance Style

The defining characteristics of that "angelic flute" inspired another dedication to Taffanel: the *Romance* by Alfred Bruneau, published in 1884. The mood is *lent et soutenu*, the low and middle registers are particularly featured, the phrases are long, and the *dolce espressivo* demands a richly vocal quality from the instrument. As Taffanel later wrote in the draft text for his *Méthode*: "Quality of tone is the most important thing to cultivate on the flute."[30] The manuscript of Bruneau's *Romance* (dated 1 October 1884) is particularly revealing. It has various differences in tessitura and phrasing between the solo part, marked "violin," and the score with a solo line, which has evidence of scratchings-out and rewritings. This score and a flute part extracted from it became the published version, and the separate violin part was suppressed, even though the work was still described as "for flute or violin." It is likely, therefore, that Bruneau consulted Taffanel, who suggested the various changes that make the phrasing more varied and subtle and keep the tessitura mainly low, with the highest note, a^3, reserved for special effect at the very end.[31] Two years later, Taffanel played at Bruneau's wedding: "Taffanel and his magic flute," noted Bruneau in his diary.[32]

In April 1884, at a Société des instruments à vent concert, Taffanel gave the premiere of another important work (although it was not published until 1898), the Suite by Widor. At various later performances this work was described as "very well received" and "quite outstanding." Taffanel was praised for extracting "all the essence of this music," it was "most elegant . . . delightful . . . the two inner movements are gems of refinement and grace," and "the performance was wonderful, the eminent flutist is truly extraordinary and despite the very serious style of the work he made a great impression on the audience."[33]

That last comment about the seriousness of the work is telling, for this was the first large-scale piece of any musical stature to be written for and dedicated to Taffanel. It succeeds in being both lyrical and dramatic. There are echoes of Schumann (the clarinet *Fantasiestücke* and oboe *Romanzen*) in the melodic line, the textures are richly contrapuntal, and the harmony is wide-ranging, with some of the chromatic elements that characterize Widor's organ music. The form throughout is carefully crafted and controlled, and the Finale is a dramatic orchestral canvas of sound that stretches the voice of the flute to its limits and far transcends the salon.

The most intimate of the four movements is the *Romance*, listed only as Andante at the first performance but given its final title by March 1885, when

Taffanel played the Suite again at the Société des instruments à vent. And in September that year this movement appeared in the incidental music that Widor wrote for Auguste Dorchain's verse comedy *Le Conte d'avril*, adapted from Shakespeare's *Twelfth Night*, at the Théâtre de l'Odéon.[34] In the score of *Le Conte d'avril*, published by Heugel in 1892, the *Romance* is no. 14bis (pages 103–7), following the text, "Night made for love, oh gentle April night." The scoring is for solo flute, harp, and strings, with occasional wind chords, and the heading reads: "In the theater this *Romance*, which comes after the Wedding March no. 17, is not performed with full orchestra. It is played in the wings. It is orchestrated here for concert performances." The flutist Raymond Meylan comments:

> This is a poem in which the flute replaces the text; it supplies the imagery, it expresses the characters, it is at one and the same time the April night and the lovers who are there united. This poetic imperative in instrumental performance seems to me to announce the launch of the modern French School. When, even today, I listen to my teacher Marcel Moyse (born in 1889), I seem to detect this imaginative thread, this pursuit of Orpheus's potency, which he himself felt, at the beginning of the century, with Taffanel.[35]

Not surprisingly, Taffanel continued to perform the whole Suite regularly, and from 1885 onward a steady stream of pieces in *Romance* style began to appear, dedicated to him:[36]

Emile Bernard	*Romance*, op. 33 (1885)
René de Boisdeffre	*Trois pièces*, op. 31 (1885?)
François Borne	*Ballade et danse des lutins* (1886)
Alphonse Catherine	Nocturne (1900?)
Johannes Donjon	*Rêverie*, op. 16 (1887)
Jacques Durand	*Romance*, op. 7 (1888?)
Léon Fontbonne	*Chasse aux papillons* (*Sérénade*), op. 30 (1890)
Benjamin Godard	*Suite de trois morceaux*, op. 116 (1890)
Charles Lefèbvre	*Deux pièces*, op. 72 (1889)
Emile Pessard	*Deuxième pièce*, op. 28 (1886)
Gabriel Pierné	*Sérénade*, op. 7 (1887)
Louis Reynaud	Nocturne (1896)

The beginning of 1886 saw Taffanel playing another new work written for him, described by *Le Ménestrel* as "a delightful sonata" for flute and piano by Charles-Wilfrid de Bériot.[37] Taffanel gave the first performances, accompanied by the composer, in a concert devoted to de Bériot's works at the Salle Erard on 18 January and at a charity concert on 2 February. Further performances followed at the Société des instruments à vent in April, and at the Société nationale in March the following year.[38] De Bériot was the son of the violinist Charles-Auguste de Bériot and the famous singer Maria Malibran. He was trained as a pianist by Sigismond Thalberg and later became a professor at the Paris Conservatoire, where his students included Ravel. Unfortunately, to modern ears, his three-movement Flute Sonata, op. 64 is chiefly distinguished by its long-windedness, apart from a disconcertingly short twenty-six-bar Adagio that prefaces the Vivace second movement. From the point of view of expanding the flute repertoire, it has admirable intentions, treating the flute with the scale and depth usually reserved for the violin, but its invention overtakes its ideas. There is, however, no other comparable French flute sonata from this period. It was obviously a tribute to Taffanel's seriousness of approach, but he was right to have preferred another contemporary work, Carl Reinecke's *Undine* Sonata, op. 67 published in 1883. Significantly, Taffanel played this piece three times at the Société des instruments à vent (in 1883, '89, and '93), but the de Bériot Sonata only once.

A Mozart Revival

On 1 May 1882, with the Société des symphonistes conducted by Léopold Deledicque, Taffanel gave what was described as "the first performance in Paris" of a flute concerto by Mozart: "Suffice it to say that the interpretation was the equal of the work."[39] The next reference to this concerto is in Taffanel's *Notes biographiques* for 1884: "21 December Brussels (Mozart Concerto first performance)." In neither case was the actual concerto identified, but it was undoubtedly No. 1 in G major, K. 313. In 1888 Taffanel requested the newly published orchestral parts for this work from the dealer Hug in Basel, stating that he already had the score. At the same time he wrote to the conductor Paul Martin, confirming that he had handwritten copies of the orchestral parts.[40] These must have been prepared for the Paris and Brussels performances.

The Brussels premiere of Mozart's G major Concerto came about by invitation of François Gevaert, director of the Brussels Conservatoire. Gevaert had been music director at the Paris Opéra for three years from 1867, so Taffanel already knew him and was grateful not only for the invitation, but for a set of cadenzas by Gevaert:

> The cadenzas are perfect, very effective, and I do not want to change anything about them. Consequently I have got rid of mine. I am only embarrassed at the efforts you have gone to for me and I cannot thank

you enough. For the cadenza in the Finale, I put it, as you do, on page 26 (98). But I link it to the final reappearance of the motif, page 29 (101), therefore making a cut. I am afraid that the length of the Finale will detract from the effect of such a musical work, and this little trimming of a work that already lasts a good 20 minutes would seem to be the right thing to do. However, if you do not approve, we will play it all. The pitch used at the Conservatoire is 870, is it not?[41]

Although at that point Taffanel may have discarded his own cadenzas, he seems to have taken them up again at some later date (he played the G major Concerto many times up to 1891) for both the G major and the D major Mozart Concertos. These cadenzas were eventually included in the Taffanel and Gaubert *Méthode*. However, there is some uncertainty here, because Marcel Moyse once claimed that these cadenzas were by Gevaert.[42] If so, it is strange that Gaubert did not credit them as such, but it may be that Taffanel developed them from elements of Gevaert's original ideas. The only other reference to them was in 1907 in a letter to Taffanel from an Italian flutist, Gilbert Gravina (he gave his address as "Villa Wahnfried, Bayreuth"), who had heard from several German players that Taffanel had written cadenzas for the Mozart G major Concerto and was anxious to obtain them as he could not find them in any published edition.[43]

After the Brussels performance, a reply from Taffanel to an enquiry about editions of the Concerto also yielded a rare comment about Bach's music:

The Mozart Concerto that I have just played at the Brussels Conservatoire is unfortunately not available in piano reduction. It is scored for the accompaniment of strings plus 2 oboes and 2 horns. I would very much like to know the Bach Sonata you told me about. I assume it is an extract from the "Musical Offering" which Bach wrote for King Frederick of Prussia who, as you know, was a fanatical flute player. If this is indeed the work I am describing, it is a very remarkable piece, long-breathed, it is true, but it is excellent Bach! I once played two movements of it, the Adagio and Finale, with Sarasate and it made a great impression.[44]

Incidentally, Taffanel helped celebrate the bicentenary of the birth of J. S. Bach in 1885 with a performance of the B minor Sonata, accompanied by Diémer, at a special concert on 21 April.[45]

Taffanel returned to the subject of the Mozart G major Concerto in November 1888, in a letter to Paul Martin, conductor of the Société des concerts populaires in Lille:

I regret not being able to come sooner to work with you. I say work, because this concerto is indeed written as a continuous dialog with the orchestra and demands to be studied with the care that one would give a symphony . . . Here are a few pointers for the performance. So as not to cover the flute, it would be a good idea to divide the desks of strings: one half playing all the time, the others only joining in for the tuttis. Depending on your resources and distribution you can decide the division yourself . . . There are, as always in Mozart, numerous appoggiaturas: they are written as small notes, but *with their real value*; they must therefore be played according to the context as quavers or semi-quavers and with the leaning style of appoggiaturas, never as modern, short grace notes . . . Finally, one last recommendation, please use *mutes* for the Andante.[46]

The concert in Lille on 18 November was a great success, and the local press reported that "Monsieur Taffanel filled his listeners with wonder."[47] Exactly what it was that Taffanel brought to Mozart was observed at a performance in Liège the previous year: "a delicacy, a scrupulous observation of the nuances, an understanding of how to illuminate the smallest details, an unrivalled refinement of style."[48]

Whatever might now be thought about a cut in the Finale, Taffanel's suggestions make clear his sensitivity to the historical perspective of Mozart's Concerto. For him, this was not just music to be remade for the 1880s with a large orchestra, a big flute sound, and modern ornamentation. He obviously recognized that there would originally have been fewer and lighter strings, and therefore no balance problems with the flute, and that orchestral compromises should be made to recapture the spirit of the original—particularly enlightened thinking for the period.

Joachim Andersen

Early in 1883 Taffanel made contact with the Danish flutist Joachim Andersen, who had recently become a founding member of the Berlin Philharmonic Orchestra. There followed the only sustained correspondence with a fellow flute player that has come to light, and it includes many valuable insights. Andersen, born in 1847, had studied in Copenhagen and played there at the Tivoli Concerts and in the Royal Orchestra from 1869 to 1877. He had then moved to St. Petersburg to play in the Italian Opera Orchestra, and finally on to Berlin, where he remained in the Philharmonic for ten years, until 1892, when a paralysis of the tongue forced him to give up flute playing. He then made a new career as conductor of the Tivoli Concerts back in Copenhagen, and he taught at the Royal Danish Academy of Music. Toward the end of his life he was honored by the government in recognition of his services to Danish music.

During his entire active career he always played an old-system flute, only afterwards conceding the advantages of the Boehm system.[49]

Most importantly for Taffanel, Andersen was also a composer. In the first letter to him Taffanel explains that he is to give two performances at the Société des concerts on 28 January and 4 February of the *Concertstück*, op. 3, which he much admires: "With its skillful craftsmanship and its high musical ideals it must rank above everything which has previously been written for our instrument."[50] Taffanel goes on to say that having received the parts from Hamburg, he has constructed a full score and eradicated all the printing errors. The conductor of the Société des concerts, Deldevez, is also enthusiastic about the *Concertstück* and has promised to devote three rehearsals to it. Taffanel's next letter reports the success of the performance:

> I account the greatest part of this success, and the best, to your composition that I studied, rehearsed and performed with ever increasing pleasure. In the fourteen years that I have had the honor to occupy the post of first flute at the Conservatoire concerts, I have always refused to appear as a soloist, not finding a piece worthy of figuring on the programs of the Société des concerts. Thanks to you, Monsieur, I have now had that satisfaction.[51]

Taffanel claims that the *Concertstück* has even confounded the gloomy predictions of Parisian "lovers of the flute" and their prejudice against foreign music. However, he confesses that he did make a few changes in the orchestration (particularly to the clarinets and bassoons) to lighten the texture and avoid the flute having to struggle to be heard. He regrets that he cannot send any press cuttings, as these are semiprivate concerts and not usually reported on, but again he thanks Andersen for the offer of new works and suggests that they should exchange photographs.

In fact there was a review in *Le Ménestrel*, which Taffanel maybe tactfully witheld because it misspelled Andersen's name and mistook his nationality!

> Our famous flutist Taffanel performed a concert piece by the Swedish composer Anderson; it is a well-written work, lavishly orchestrated. The recitative for flute that opens the work is most effective, as is the difficult cadenza which Taffanel dispatched with delightful virtuosity and charm.

> The audience showed its appreciation to this congenial performer with unanimous and prolonged applause, not only for all the pleasure just received but also in recognition of the care and attention he constantly takes over his playing in the orchestra.[52]

The Secretary of the Société des concerts, Alfred Viguiez, also paid tribute to Taffanel's performance in his report at the end of the 1883 season.[53]

In his next letter, Taffanel thanks Andersen for his photograph and for the "flattering offer" of the dedication of two flute pieces. These were the Impromptu, op. 7 and the *Moto perpetuo*, op. 8. Taffanel promises to do all in his power to publicize them. He also offers to speak to the publisher Brandus about the *Ballade et danse des sylphes* and to act in any other way as a go-between for Andersen. He commiserates with him over some recent problems (no details are given), congratulates him on escaping "the slavery of the Opéra," and hopes that his new-found freedom will allow him to go on enriching the flute repertoire with "ravishing works."[54]

Taffanel wrote again on 11 November with thanks for copies of Andersen's new compositions:

> Your works are skillful from the threefold point of view of expressiveness, craftsmanship, and suitability for the instrument . . . The pieces that you have honored me by dedicating to me are delightful. The "Impromptu," so full of poetry, is a gem. The "Moto perpetuo" with its inexorable semi-quaver rhythm in the accompaniment will have a tremendous effect. Mind you, the three-thousand or so notes in it will demand first class lungs! But I am not at all daunted by it.[55]

Taffanel goes on to praise the *Ballade et danse des sylphes,* which Andersen had copied out by hand for him, but regrets the difficulty of the piano part. In Paris he has a good accompanist, but on tour in the provinces that cannot be guaranteed. Taffanel also feels that there may be another problem: "Could not the tutti in the middle of the "Danse des sylphes" be shortened a little? I am worried that this interlude will cast rather a chill when it is not accompanied by the orchestra." Finally he thanks Andersen for some "poetic salon pieces" (no other details are given) that he intends to make the most of before yielding them up to other flute players.

After an undated New Year greeting card (probably 1884), the surviving correspondence breaks off until 1888, but there is enough from this first period to underline Taffanel's admiration for Andersen. Taffanel clearly recognized in him someone with shared aims, a flutist-composer who understood the capabilities of the instrument without exploiting its facility, and who believed the flute could have something meaningful to say, could engage in dialogue with the orchestra. Later, he also came to value greatly Andersen's many books of flute studies and to use them with his students at the Conservatoire. These are technically inventive and, above all, musical. They have remained mainstays of flute instruction, unlike Andersen's concert pieces for flute, which have not so far found a lasting place in the repertoire.

Marcel Moyse remembered Taffanel calling Andersen the "Chopin of the flute," and the Impromptu, op. 7 does share something of the same sound world, but neither it nor the *Moto perpetuo*, op. 8, a sort of Mendelssohn scherzo, really set their sights beyond the salon. The *Concertstück*, op. 3, however, is quite another matter. This work launches the flute into the world of late romanticism, leaving Chopin for Tchaikovsky, Brahms, and Wagner. In 1883 the *Concertstück* was the only work of its kind, and if Taffanel had been waiting for a significant contemporary work, as he maintained, this was undoubtedly it. However, its strong vein of Germanic profundity was hardly likely to have pleased Parisian audiences—hence the observation quoted above that the Conservatoire patrons were applauding Taffanel as much for his regular orchestral playing as for this performance. Not surprisingly, the *Concertstück* was not played again at the Société des concerts. Taffanel was ahead of his time.

Sicilienne-Etude

Taffanel's own *Sicilienne-Etude*, published in 1885 at the height of his career, confirmed this challenging new trend in flute music. It is a quite extraordinary work, extremely difficult to play, both technically and musically, and confounds expectations. The key and the meter are favorite choices for Taffanel—G minor and compound time (6/8 in this instance)—but the lyrical flute theme of the first section is embellished throughout with chordal grace notes, and the gently rocking piano part becomes progressively more chromatic. Then in the middle section the piano presents a new melodic line in chorale style, pitched within vocal range but with darkly chromatic Wagnerian harmonies, around which the flute weaves a whirlwind of scales marked *p molto legato*. The first section then returns, but with the piano part rhythmically fragmented, and there is a final brief *sempre pp* shimmer of notes from the flute as it climbs to a final high G.

From a musical point of view the *Sicilienne-Etude* is something of a manifesto. Taffanel appears to be saying that flute players must find a balance between two extremes—call them the *circus* and the *salon*. Having delivered the instrument from mere virtuosity (*circus* acrobatics), he is equally determined that it should not fall into the comfortable trap of just playing pretty tunes (*salon* trifles). The flute is a lyrical and virtuoso instrument, but it belongs in the real world of late-nineteenth-century harmony, and it has more to say than can be expressed in just a simple melody or in showers of notes over a vamped piano accompaniment. So he turns both the salon and the circus upside down. He makes the flute embellish its own melodic line harmonically, and he reduces its scale passages to the status of an accompaniment to the melodic and harmonic piano part.

The secret of the *Sicilienne-Etude* lies in this balance of lyricism without sentimentality, and virtuosity without exhibitionism. It is also an eloquent witness to Taffanel's own capabilities and style. A successful performance of the piece is impossible without the utmost stamina and flexibility of breathing, suppleness of embouchure, sureness of fingering, and delicacy of articulation. This is precisely the order of priority for technical training, with control of the breath paramount — "the breath is the soul of the flute" — that Taffanel and Gaubert later expounded in the *Méthode*.[56]

The *Sicilienne-Etude* was published by Félix Mackar as Taffanel's op. 7, with an imposingly engraved cover. Taffanel himself seems to have particularly valued the work. In 1900 when he was asked to contribute to a collection entitled *Autographes de musiciens contemporains* for display at the Paris Exhibition, he copied out the first six bars of the *Sicilienne-Etude* in purple ink, signed and dated "Paul Taffanel, July 1900."[57] He also inscribed a fragment from it on a visiting card: "To Madame Dornès. With much respect and affection. Paul Taffanel" (see fig. 13). And he included the piece in a suggested recital program around 1885, combining it with the Gluck *Danse*, as well as arrangements of a Minuet by Boccherini and two of Mendelssohn's *Songs Without Words*.[58]

Taffanel dedicated the *Sicilienne-Etude* to Walter Stewart Broadwood (his middle name was misspelled "Stuart" on the printed edition). The precise details of Taffanel's contact with Broadwood are unclear, but it may be that Taffanel was introduced to him when visiting London and it seems likely that Broadwood already knew Dorus (see chapter 1). Broadwood, born in 1819, was a grandson of the original John Broadwood who founded the firm of piano makers, but in Walter Stewart's generation, his elder brother, Henry Fowler Broadwood, was the active partner in the firm. It was Henry who had first contacted Boehm in 1843 for general technical and mechanical advice, and Walter had continued the correspondence on his own behalf. Walter remained a major shareholder in the firm until sometime around 1888, when he resigned his partnership and demanded to be bought out, which the company had to do, but at a very difficult time financially. It caused a total breach in the family.[59]

Shortly before the appearance of Taffanel's *Sicilienne-Etude*, Walter Broadwood's name appeared in Paris in connection with a performance at a Lebouc matinée of a flute quintet by Molique. *Le Ménestrel* described it as written for Broadwood, "a most distinguished amateur flute player," and published by him after Molique's death.[60] Broadwood was possibly the recipient of a letter in December 1882 that gives some insight into the network of contacts Taffanel undoubtedly had with others interested in the flute. That year Broadwood had edited a newly discovered document by Boehm, adding an explanatory preface and a collection of Boehm's letters, and he was obviously in the forefront of any developments regarding the instrument.[61] Taffanel's letter exists only in draft, and the sole clue as to its intended recipient is the mention of a work explaining the fingering of the Boehm flute:

> I have pondered much and constantly researched the subject of the fingering of the Boehm flute; therefore I was delighted to learn that you are also very keen to make a study of it, convinced that you could throw some light on this question, hitherto so inexplicable to us all. A perusal, necessarily rapid, of your book has confirmed my theory, and the principles of fingering, barely outlined in Boehm's brochure, are now, thanks to you, completely established. I have promised myself to study your work with all the care that it deserves, and if you will kindly allow me I shall send you my own very humble thoughts on the subject.[62]

Alternatively, the letter could have been addressed to another Englishman, Christopher Welch. His *History of the Boehm Flute* was published a few months later, in 1883, and he might have submitted a draft copy to Taffanel for comment.[63] Taffanel's papers include a translation in an unknown hand of part of Welch's book, annotated by Taffanel, so he may have been planning a French edition.[64]

Etudes and Encores

The extent of Taffanel's flute technique was further demonstrated in 1886 by three solo studies that he composed for inclusion in a reprint of the Etudes, op. 126 by Louis Drouet. Either Taffanel or the publisher, Brandus, must have realized that these would be a neat selling point: "The studies composed by L. Drouet stop at no. 97. The following three which complete this edition have been written by Monsieur Taffanel." In fact this was Taffanel's only contribution to the edition. Although the title page credits him with "revising" and "correcting" the other studies, the text, engraving, and plate numbers for the four volumes are exactly the same as for the original.[65]

Taffanel's three studies are a ne plus ultra: fingering exercises of exceptional difficulty, ranging systematically through all the keys, and requiring once again considerable stamina and flexibility of breathing and embouchure. Here are the technical bare bones, the necessary foundations (albeit later concealed) on which his art was built. The only other set of studies, or study-solos, revised by Taffanel were the *Six Divertissements*, op. 68 by Friedrich Kuhlau, a contemporary of Beethoven. These were issued in two formats, one for solo flute and one for flute and piano. While there is no record of Taffanel using the Drouet studies for his own teaching, several of the Kuhlau *Divertissements* were studied by his Conservatoire students and played at the periodic examinations.[66]

Taffanel also began a new association with another publisher, Auguste Durand, in 1886 and produced a major new series of arrangements for flute and piano that continued to be issued until 1909. This was his last series, and part of the attraction must have been that Durand was Saint-Saëns's publisher. Not surprisingly, more than a third of the pieces in the collection are by him. The others are a balance of interesting and by no means obvious choices from the eighteenth and nineteenth centuries. Taffanel used some of them as encores, and generally this is a much more personal anthology than had been possible with the previous collections published by Mackar.

Marchesi and Melba

It was said that you could always pick out a Marchesi-trained singer in any operatic cast throughout Europe, and from March 1885 Taffanel became involved in concerts she organized in Paris.[67] Mathilde Marchesi (née Graumann) was born in Frankfurt in 1821 and trained as a singer (she was a mezzo-soprano) first in Vienna and then in Paris with Manuel Garcia, brother of Maria Malibran and Pauline Viardot. Significantly, Garcia was the chief exponent of the art of Italian bel canto, and the first person to make a scientific study of singing—he invented the laryngoscope.[68] Marchesi inherited Garcia's students when he retired and also had a brief performing career before concentrating on teaching, first in Vienna, then Paris, Cologne, and Vienna again. Finally in 1881 she moved back to Paris.[69] Marchesi's tuition was rooted in Italian bel canto—the style that Taffanel had admired in Patti from the 1860s—and was summed up in the method she published in 1886. She was always critical of the French Conservatoire approach:

> *Le chant soutenu* is forced into the background by the florid school so much cultivated in France, and this is, no doubt, the reason that there is such a dearth of dramatic singers. But all dainty little Frenchwomen are admirable *sujets d'opéra comique,* and their talent for acting covers many of the defects of their singing.[70]

According to *Le Ménestrel,* Marchesi's rigorous training produced "supple . . . well-placed voices with smooth tone production in all the registers and throughout the whole dynamic range."[71] In other words she worked for a beautiful legato sound—*le chant soutenu*—an ideal complement to Taffanel's flute playing.

Marchesi promoted an annual concert in aid of the Association des artistes musiciens and held regular, fashionable soirées as a showcase for her students at her spacious new home in the rue Joffroy. She enlisted the assistance of some of the most eminent musicians of the day. In May 1886, for example, the performers included Saint-Saëns, Taffanel, and Emma Calvé, with Franz Liszt and Anton Rubinstein among the members of the audience.[72] Marchesi was much given to teaching arias with flute obbligato—"La Fauvette" from Grétry's *Zémir et Azor*, Mysoli's aria from Félicien David's *La Perle de Brésil*, Catherine's aria from Meyerbeer's *L'Etoile du nord*, and the "Air de rossignol" from Victor Massé's *Les Noces de Jeannette*—and so Taffanel was a regular performer at her concerts. It was also a creative relationship, as Nellie Melba well remembered. When one of her admirers wrote out from memory the voice and flute cadenza from the Mad Scene in Donizetti's *Lucia di Lammermoor*, Melba commented: "this *cadenza*, which has now been printed, was composed by Madame Marchesi and Taffanel during my student days in Paris. Many were the hours we spent in perfecting it."[73]

Melba studied with Marchesi for a few months from December 1886, and three years later she sang *Lucia* at the Opéra in an old production that was universally ridiculed, apart from the interpretation of the Mad Scene:

> The other performers in *Lucia* were mediocre, apart from Monsieur Taffanel's magic flute, which did not stray for a second, or rather a third (oh! pardon!) from Madame Melba's agile voice. It was to Monsieur Taffanel, and not to Monsieur Vianesi [the conductor], that the singer should have made her bows.[74]

There was at least one other performance of the *Lucia* cadenza with Melba and Taffanel, at a charity concert at the Trocadéro in 1891.[75] They also appeared together at the Société des concerts in January 1890 in Handel's *Ode to Saint Cecilia*, and on Good Friday the following year in Handel's *L'Allegro, il pensieroso ed il moderato*: "Madame Melba . . . Monsieur Taffanel . . . called and replied one to the other, nightingale to nightingale, and the audience swooned! . . . Good old audience!"[76]

All this had such an impression on Melba that when she made her first London recordings in March 1904 she insisted that Taffanel's student, Philippe Gaubert (Taffanel had long since retired from playing), be brought specially from Paris for the flute obbligati in *Lucia* and *L'Allegro*.[77] Only the best would do! Incidentally, Melba also remembered hearing Patti at the Paris Opéra revival of Gounod's *Roméo et Juliette* in 1888, and in a rare moment of generosity to another singer declared that "hers was perhaps the most golden voice to which I have ever listened. The *timbre* of it was exquisite, the diction crystalline. I took my lesson from her, for she had much to teach."[78]

Le Carnaval des animaux

On 3 March 1886 Taffanel took part in the golden wedding celebrations of
Louis Dorus at the church of Notre-Dame-des-Victoires. With the cellist
Hippolyte Rabaud (Dorus's son-in-law) and the harpist Alphonse Hasselmans
he played a Trio from Beethoven's *Prometheus*.[79] Taffanel and Hasselmans had
already given another performance that year of the "delicious" Andante from
Mozart's Flute and Harp Concerto, at one of Charles Lebouc's matinées.[80]
Now Lebouc was to be host to a particularly famous premiere:

> Monsieur Lebouc managed to assemble a definitive line-up of emi-
> nent performers: Messieurs Saint-Saëns, Diémer, Taffanel, Turban,
> Maurin, Prioré, de Bailly and Tourcy who, after a very interesting
> program, took part in the first performance of a very witty fantasy
> burlesque, composed for this concert by Saint-Saëns and entitled the
> *Carnival of the Animals*. This zoological fantasy was received with
> great enthusiasm.[81]

The elderly Lebouc was therefore the first cellist to play *Le Cygne,* and it
was soon dubbed his "swan song."[82] This was the only number from the work
that Saint-Saëns allowed to be published during his lifetime. The brilliantly
swooping and diving *Volière*, written specially for Taffanel, is conspicuously
absent from the list of his arrangements of Saint-Saëns's works mentioned earlier. A few days after the premiere, *Carnaval* was repeated at Lemoine's society,
La Trompette, and then at Pauline Viardot's home, at the request of Liszt, who
was passing through Paris. But fearing for his reputation as a serious composer,
Saint-Saëns strictly controlled the number of other performances he allowed.
They were all semiprivate — apart from the one at the Société des instruments
à vent in April 1892 (see chapter 6) — and often took place with the musicians
wearing masks of the heads of the various animals they represented.

A Reputation Made

Two documents from this period sum up perfectly the spread of Taffanel's
reputation and the sheer amazement that his playing provoked. The first is the
fragment of a letter to the elder statesman, former prime minister, and philoso-
pher Jules Simon, who was an ardent republican. Simon must have penned an
appreciation of Taffanel's playing, and on 14 July 1886 (Bastille Day) Taffanel
drafted a note of thanks, with maybe an indication of his own political sympathies: "I cannot, to Monsieur Jules Simon, send a card, as if to a kindly
critic . . . but it is impossible for me not to say to such an eminent man whom

I respect and admire, how honored I am by the compliments he makes about my poor talent."[83]

Then there is this review of a concert given by Taffanel in Brussels. Witty and perceptive, it says it all:

Taffanel is the magic flute, *il flauto magico*: set apart from all gratuitous virtuosity, he has the sound which charms and a nobility of style; you don't hear him breathe and he never runs short of breath. This flute is a revelation. The audience could not get over it. Imagine: an intelligent flute, a distinguished, musical flute. That has never been seen before.[84]

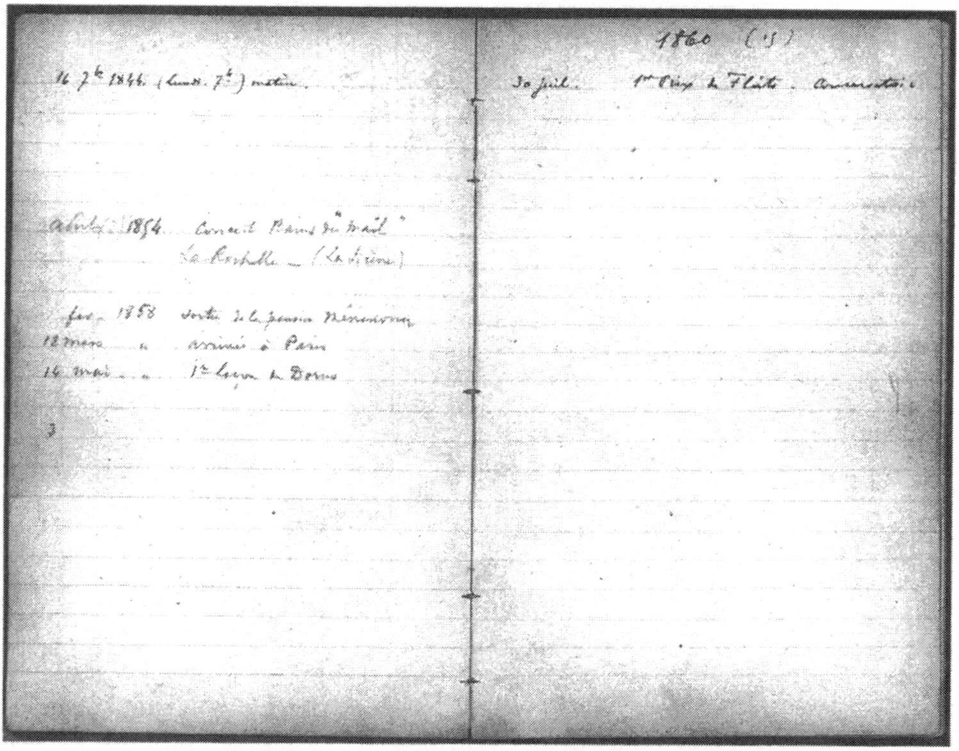

FIGURE I. Opening page of Taffanel's *Notes biographiques* with details of his birth and early life.

(All photos are graciously provided from a private collection.)

FIGURE 2. Taffanel and his father, c. 1854.

FIGURE 3. Louis Dorus, c. 1865.

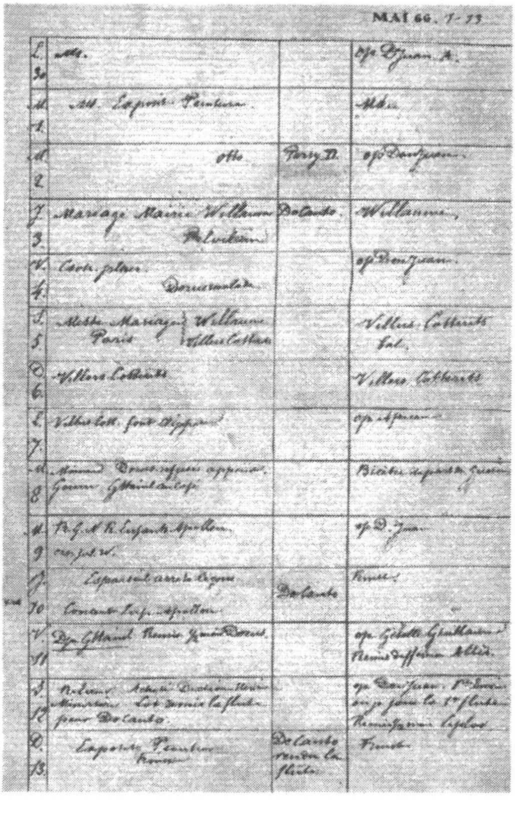

FIGURE 4. Page from Taffanel's
Journal professionnel with a reference
to playing Mozart's *Don Giovanni*
on 12 May 1866.

FIGURE 5. Taffanel in his
mid-twenties, c. 1871.

FIGURE 6. Taffanel's future wife,
Geneviève Deslignières (left), with her
mother and sister, c. 1871.

FIGURE 7. Manuscript page from Taffanel's
Wind Quintet (1876), showing the opening
of the second movement.

FIGURE 8. Taffanel's house and garden
at 8 avenue Gourgaud in Paris.

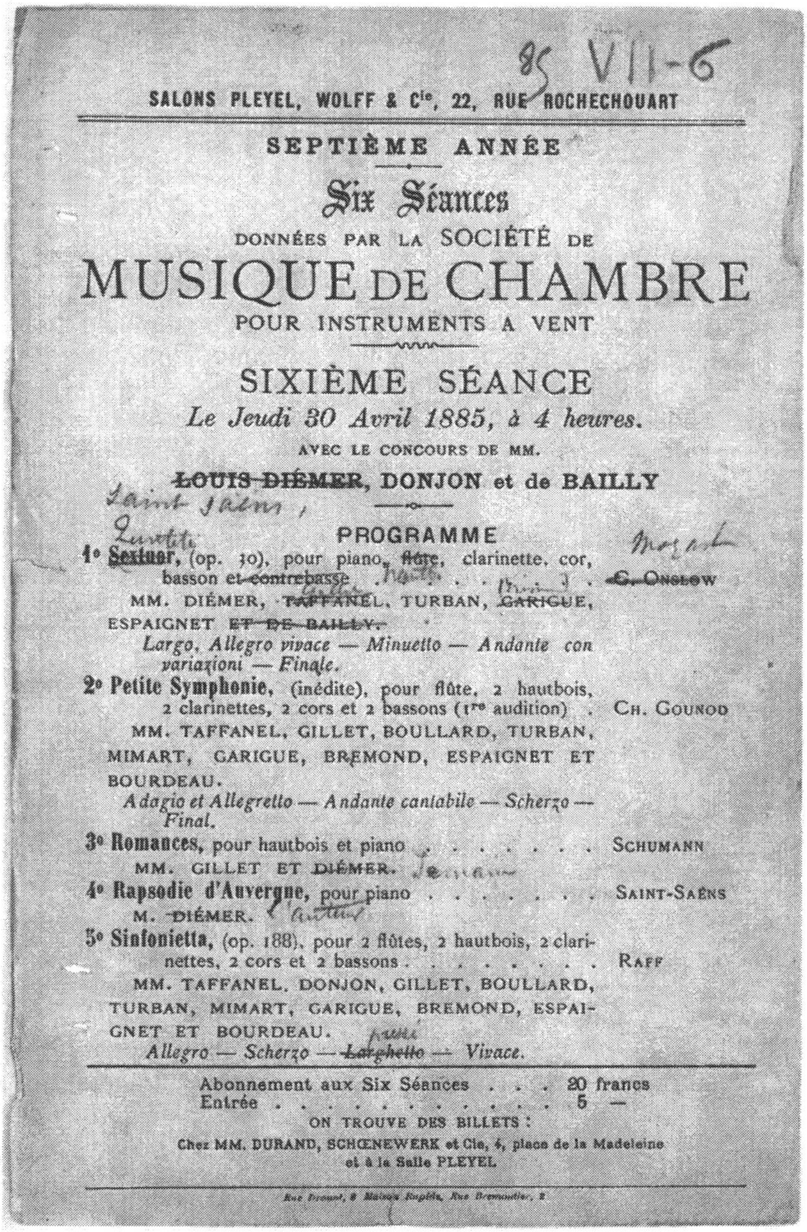

SALONS PLEYEL, WOLFF & Cⁱᵉ, 22, RUE ROCHECHOUART

SEPTIÈME ANNÉE

Six Séances

DONNÉES PAR LA SOCIÉTÉ DE

MUSIQUE DE CHAMBRE

POUR INSTRUMENTS A VENT

SIXIÈME SÉANCE

Le Jeudi 30 Avril 1885, à 4 heures.

AVEC LE CONCOURS DE MM.

~~LOUIS DIÉMER,~~ DONJON et de BAILLY

Saint Saëns,

PROGRAMME

1° **Sextuor,** (op. 30), pour piano, ~~flûte,~~ clarinette, cor,
basson et ~~contrebasse~~ . . . . ~~C. ONSLOW~~ *Mozart*
MM. DIÉMER, ~~TAFFANEL,~~ TURBAN, ~~GARIGUE,~~
ESPAIGNET ~~ET DE BAILLY.~~
*Largo, Allegro vivace — Minuetto — Andante con
variazioni — Finale.*

2° **Petite Symphonie,** (inédite), pour flûte, 2 hautbois,
2 clarinettes, 2 cors et 2 bassons (1ʳᵉ audition) . CH. GOUNOD
MM. TAFFANEL, GILLET, BOULLARD, TURBAN,
MIMART, GARIGUE, BRÉMOND, ESPAIGNET ET
BOURDEAU.
*Adagio et Allegretto — Andante cantabile — Scherzo —
Final.*

3° **Romances,** pour hautbois et piano . . . . . . SCHUMANN
MM. GILLET ET ~~DIÉMER.~~

4° **Rapsodie d'Auvergne,** pour piano . . . . SAINT-SAËNS
M. ~~DIÉMER.~~

5° **Sinfonietta,** (op. 188), pour 2 flûtes, 2 hautbois, 2 clari-
nettes, 2 cors et 2 bassons . . . . RAFF
MM. TAFFANEL, DONJON, GILLET, BOULLARD,
TURBAN, MIMART, GARIGUE, BRÉMOND, ESPAI-
GNET ET BOURDEAU.
Allegro — Scherzo — ~~Larghetto~~ — Vivace.

Abonnement aux Six Séances . . . . **20** francs
Entrée . . . . **5** —

ON TROUVE DES BILLETS :

Chez MM. DURAND, SCHŒNEWERK et Cⁱᵉ, 4, place de la Madeleine
et à la Salle PLEYEL

Rue Drouot, 8 Maison Euglès, Rue Bergère, 8

FIGURE 9. Program for the premiere of Gounod's
Petite symphonie at the Wind Society on 30 April 1885,
annotated by Taffanel.

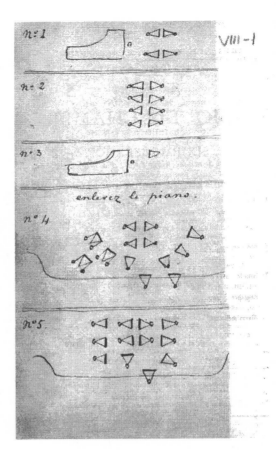

FIGURE 10. Taffanel's diagram of
the seating plans for works
by Rubinstein, Beethoven, Handel,
Schumann, and Mozart
on the Wind Society program
of 18 February 1886.

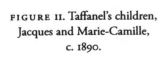

FIGURE 11. Taffanel's children,
Jacques and Marie-Camille,
c. 1890.

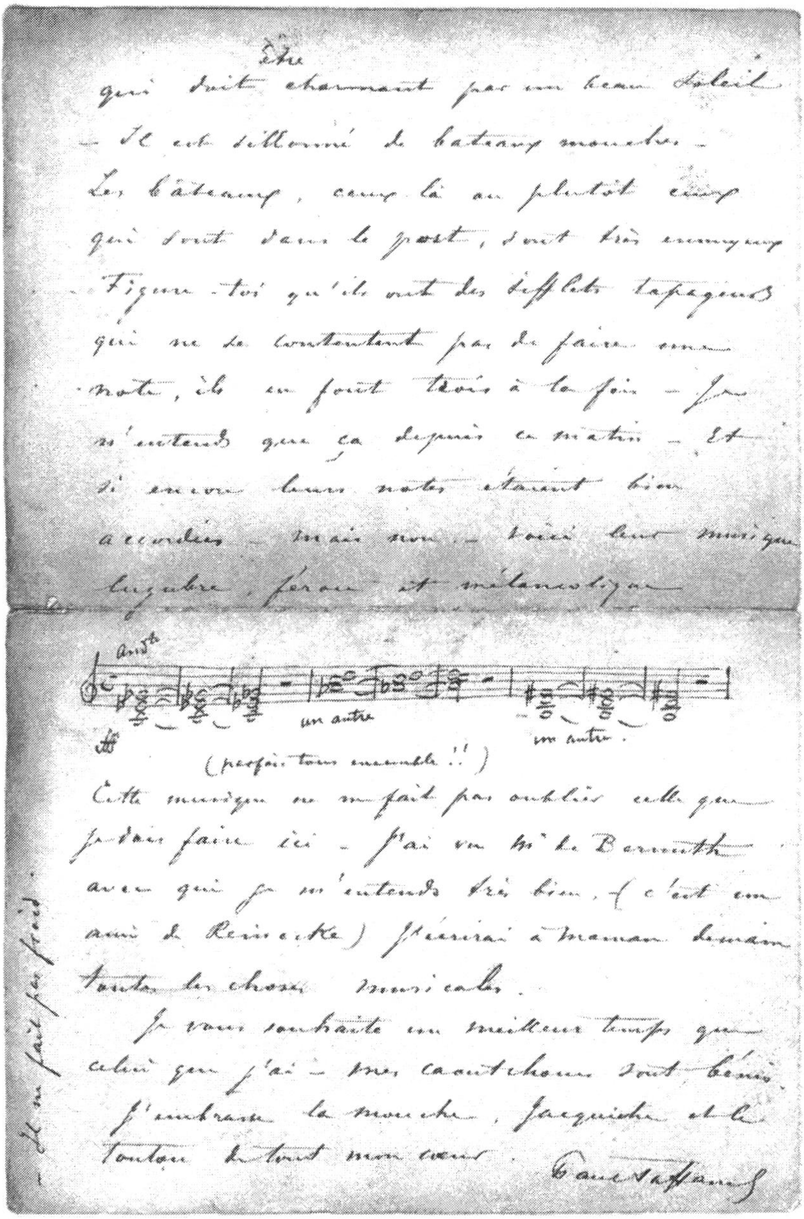

FIGURE 12. Page of a letter from Taffanel
to his daughter, 5 November 1890,
with musical notation of noisy boats' whistles.

FIGURE 13. Visiting card from Taffanel inscribed with the opening bars of his *Sicilienne-Etude* (1885).

FIGURE 14. Description of Taffanel on his passport for travel to Russia in 1887.

FIGURE 15. Photograph of Taffanel inscribed
to Philippe Gaubert, January 1895.

FIGURE 16. Photograph
of Philippe Gaubert inscribed
to Taffanel, October 1898.

FIGURE 17. Cartoon in
Le Charivari, 11 February 1896,
of Taffanel conducting
at the Paris Opéra.

FIGURE 18. Taffanel preparing the score of Verdi's *Otello* while on holiday in August 1894.

FIGURE 19. Taffanel and his flute class
at the Paris Conservatoire, 1895.

M.TAFFANEL

FIGURE 20. Cartoon of Taffanel
as both conductor and flute player
(Charles Giraud, 1894).

FIGURE 21. Sketch of a flutist
in a letter from Saint-Saëns
to Taffanel, 17 April 1899.

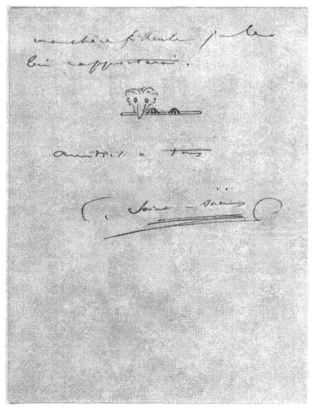

FIGURE 22. Lithograph of the Saint-Saëns
fiftieth-anniversary concert on 2 June 1896 (J. Grigny).

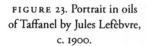

FIGURE 23. Portrait in oils
of Taffanel by Jules Lefèbvre,
c. 1900.

FIGURE 24. One of a series of photographs of Taffanel
demonstrating flute embouchure, c. 1906.

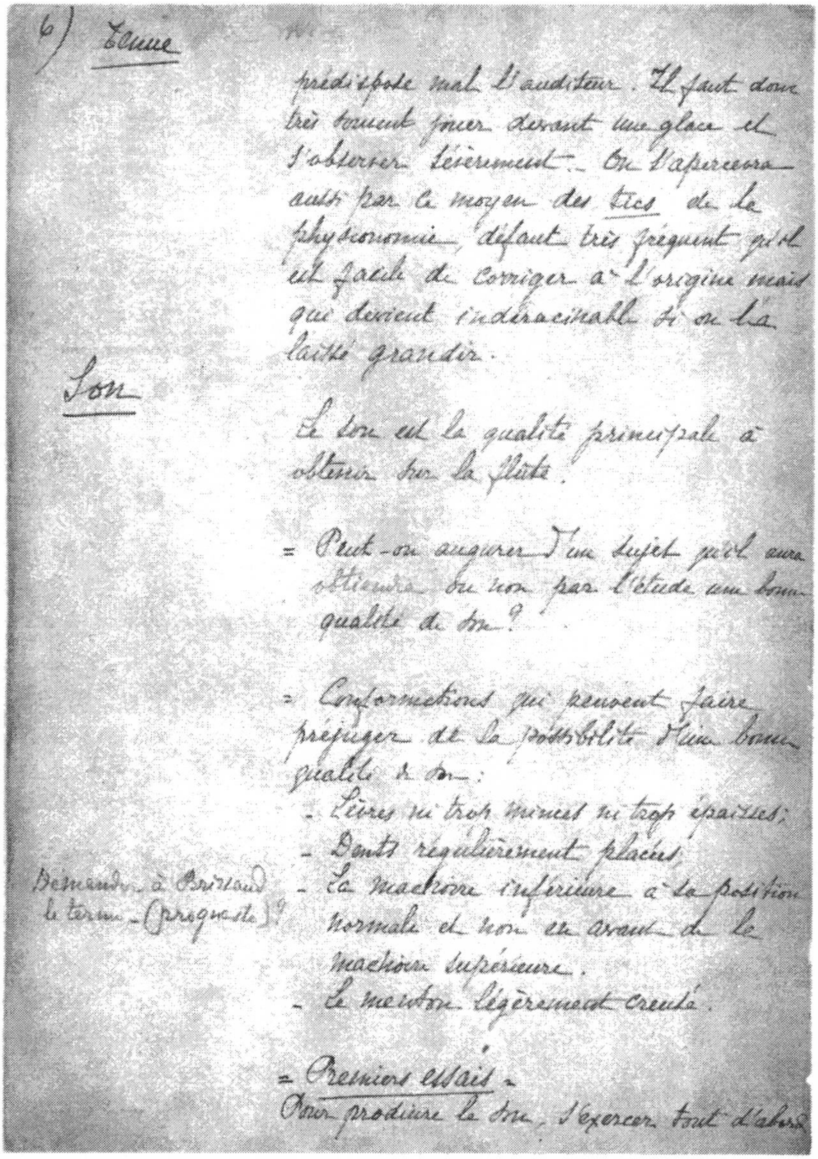

prédispose mal l'auditeur. Il faut donc très souvent jouer devant une glace et s'observer sévèrement. On s'apercevra aussi par ce moyen des tics de la physionomie, défaut très fréquent qu'il est facile de corriger à l'origine mais qui devient indéracinable si on la laisse grandir.

Son

Le son est la qualité principale à obtenir sur la flûte.

= Peut-on augurer d'un sujet qu'il aura obtenue ou non par l'étude une bonne qualité de son?

= Conformations qui peuvent faire préjuger de la possibilité d'une bonne qualité de son:
- Lèvres ni trop minces ni trop épaisses;
- Dents régulièrement placées
- La mâchoire inférieure à sa position normale et non en avant de la mâchoire supérieure.
- Le menton légèrement creusé.

Demander à Barrère le terme (proposé)?

= Premiers essais.
Pour produire le son, s'exercer tout d'abord

FIGURE 25. Page of manuscript notes for the *Méthode de flûte*, c. 1906, with a reference to the vital importance of tone quality.

⤗ CHAPTER 8 ⤛

From Russia to the Paris Exhibition

April Visit *St. Petersburg Moscow* with Saint-Saëns, Gillet, Turban.
4 June *London* Concert with Saint-Saëns, Gillet,
Turban. St. James's Hall.
—PAUL TAFFANEL, *NOTES BIOGRAPHIQUES* (1887)

After several years when Taffanel wrote virtually nothing in his *Notes bio-graphiques*, these two entries for 1887 suddenly stand out. The three wind players, Taffanel with oboist Georges Gillet and clarinetist Charles Turban, were invited to Russia by Saint-Saëns under the auspices of the French Red Cross, which had engaged him for seven concerts during Easter Week with the Imperial Opera Orchestra. In the days before passport photographs, Taffanel's visa for this trip carried a concise description of him (see fig. 14):

Age 42 / height one meter 63 centimeters / chestnut-brown and grey hair / high forehead / chestnut-brown eyebrows / brown eyes / medium nose / medium mouth / chestnut-brown and grey beard / round chin / oval face / clear complexion / short-sighted[1]

Saint-Saëns went on ahead to begin rehearsals and was greeted rapturously—particularly when he demonstrated that he could count in Russian during rehearsals.[2] Taffanel, Gillet, and Turban left Paris by train on 12 April and traveled via Berlin, where Taffanel had hoped to meet Joachim Andersen, but a letter was waiting to say that he had had to stand in for a colleague and conduct a concert. Their meeting eventually took place during Taffanel's return journey, although it was only a limited success, as Andersen spoke little French and Taffanel little German.

Taffanel, Gillet, and Turban arrived at the Grand Hotel in St. Petersburg on 15 April (or 3 April according to the Russian calendar, which was twelve days behind the European). The first concert was in the hall of the Imperial Riding School three days later:

119

On the first day there was a gala evening, attended by grand dukes, grand duchesses and princes of the court. On the third day the theaters re-opened and claimed the best of the performers. Then the snow, which had held off until then, began to fall. In that enormous hall the audience caught cold and did not come again. Nevertheless the concerts had become very fashionable; for the first time the audience had applauded solos on the flute, clarinet and oboe, instruments that it was unusual to hear played on their own.[3]

The highlight of the programs was the *Caprice sur des airs danois et russes* for piano, flute, oboe, and clarinet, which Saint-Saëns had specially written just before leaving Paris. This piece was dedicated to the empress Marie Feodorovna, who was a Danish princess by birth. She had married the heir apparent in 1866, and he had acceded to the throne as Czar Alexander III in 1881.

The *Caprice* finds Saint-Saëns at his most relaxed and entertaining. The form is simple: an introduction followed by three sections of melody-plus-variations, the last a semi-fugue. The melodies (whether authentic folk tunes or not) are gently plaintive and also lend themselves to more vigorous treatment. The mood, texture, and choice of register are constantly changing as Saint-Saëns shifts the focus around the wind instruments and the piano. The low-register statement of the first d minor theme by the flute, for example, after the opening tutti flourishes, must have been particularly atmospheric and perfectly tailored to Taffanel's playing. This is salon music of the finest quality, with all the old Second Empire sparkle of the Piano Concerto no. 2, which Saint-Saëns also played on this tour. It catches precisely the luxurious spirit of the Russian court that was so sympathetic to French culture— an "enchanted world" of "snow and gilt" so brilliantly evoked by Sacheverell Sitwell.[4]

The other works on the programs also reflected popular court taste. There was ballet music from Saint-Saëns's operas; various other piano solos and transcriptions by him; oboe solos by Handel, Gillet, and Diémer; and clarinet works by Weber, Mozart, and Saint-Saëns. Taffanel played Saint-Saëns's *Tarentelle*, the *Romance* and *Prélude du Déluge* (both with orchestra), and pieces by Doppler and Chopin:

The greatest success fell to Monsieur Taffanel who sings on his metal flute with an incomparable expressiveness and sweetness of tone. He worked wonders, especially with Doppler's *Pastorale hongroise* and a transcription of Chopin's *Nocturne* in F sharp. As for the latter's *Waltz* in D flat, it whipped up an absolute storm; the flutist interpreted it in the most exquisite manner, and while adopting the fastest possible tempo he preserved the limpidity of the best pianists who play this piece.[5]

Anton Rubinstein, director of the St. Petersburg Conservatoire, was so impressed that he made all the wind students attend the final concert on 26 April (14 April, Russian calendar) so they could get some idea of exactly what could be achieved on these instruments.

After the last St. Petersburg concert, the four musicians traveled on to Moscow for two concerts, and then back home via St. Petersburg, Berlin, Warsaw, Vienna, and Strasbourg, arriving in Paris on 8 May. During the tour Taffanel kept all sorts of scraps of paper with numerous financial calculations and notes, and he seems to have acted as a sort of banker for the three wind players, with reminders that "Taffanel owes Gillet / Turban owes Taffanel / Turban payed / Gillet owes Turban." Each of the wind players had been promised 1000 francs for the tour, but only two of them were paid at the time, so after their return Taffanel had a lengthy wrangle with the agent, Adolphe Mauriès (who pleaded poverty), for payment of the final 1000 francs.

Taffanel's collection of hastily scribbled notes also details a sequence of rehearsals, concerts, and receptions—the minutiae of life on tour: "a day of snow and gale-force winds . . . supper of broth, bread and beer . . . left visiting cards with the ambassador and princess . . . met Auer . . . dinner with Saint-Saëns, omelette, cutlet, and coffee . . . Rubinstein soirée . . . tea with Köhler . . . Olsoufieff . . . *Grand Duchess*." Although this gives only a fragmented picture of the tour, it does show that Taffanel had contact with the Russian court (Comte Alexandre Olsoufieff was aide-de-camp to the emperor, and the reference to the Grand Duchess is explained below) and with leading Russian musicians, including Anton Rubinstein, as well as Leopold Auer, who was head of the violin department at the Conservatoire.

The other significant figure mentioned is Ernesto Köhler, first flute of the Imperial Opera Orchestra. He also taught the flute at the Prinz Oldenburg Institute and directed the student orchestra of the Imperial Institute of Engineering. Köhler began his career in his native Italy, where he was born in 1849. He was a pupil of his father, then moved to Vienna, and finally in 1871 to St. Petersburg at the invitation of the flutist Cesare Ciardi, whom he eventually succeeded in the Opera Orchestra. Köhler was a renowned soloist in his own right, and a prolific composer of over a hundred works for the flute— studies, duets, and virtuoso concert solos—as well as an opera, *Ben Achmed,* and several ballets. When Taffanel was later asked to suggest a flutist for the 1889 summer season at St. Malo, he recommended Köhler and wrote encouraging him to apply for the job, as he knew Köhler was keen to come to France.[6]

For his part, Köhler dedicated the third volume of his op. 33 flute studies, *Der Fortschritt im Flötenspiel,* to Taffanel in 1888. These studies were specially composed to complement the course of instruction in Köhler's flute method, the *Praktische leicht verständliche Schule,* and the third volume contains just eight technically advanced studies, culminating in an expressively decorated Adagio that must have particularly pleased Taffanel.

Rather more is known about the day-to-day details of what went on back home in Paris during the Russian tour. Geneviève Taffanel wrote nearly every day, occasionally enclosing little notes from the children, a catalog of family life and concerns. Chief among them were Jacques' new bicycle; his piano lessons (from his mother); reading lessons (from his grandmother Deslignières) and his return to school; Marie-Camille's fever and nosebleed; and Taffanel's father's mild heart attack, from which he recovered by the end of the month, except that he could not bear drinking the milk the doctor prescribed, and he missed his wine. Geneviève urged Paul to keep warm, speculated about a possible war with Germany, and feared for his safety while traveling.

Taffanel's regular letters back to Geneviève have not survived, but Geneviève sometimes commented on them:

> It really is most annoying that the Emperor did not hear you play, but better a large public audience than he himself all alone, and I much enjoyed hearing about the Grand Duchess's reception. It is truly a blessing to know that you are in such high-spirits and such good health.

Following the success of the Russian tour, Saint-Saëns immediately invited the three wind players to accompany him to London for a further concert on 4 June at St. James's Hall. Taffanel played the Saint-Saëns *Romance*, a Bach Sonata, and his transcriptions of Chopin.[7] London was in a party mood, celebrating Queen Victoria's Golden Jubilee, and *Le Ménestrel* quoted at length a report from *The Times* observing how much of a novelty solo wind instruments were for English audiences. However, while there was praise for the original flute works by Saint-Saëns and Bach, along with a Handel Oboe Sonata and a Weber Clarinet Duo, the various arrangements were judged less idiomatic for the instruments: "Thus, a waltz by Chopin played on the flute had a curious effect, although the beauty of Monsieur Taffanel's tone and phrasing earned him genuine success."[8] *The Musical Times* was less qualified in its enthusiasm, declaring: "Each player is a perfect master of his instrument, and their united performances gave the liveliest satisfaction to those who were present. The programme was far too long, but it was highly interesting, and every item was received with much enthusiasm."[9]

As a postscript to the whole tour, there was a final, unofficial concert when the *Caprice* was published. The work had almost been lost when the manuscript was burned in the devastating fire at the Opéra-comique in May 1887, and it had had to be reconstructed for the printers by Saint-Saëns and Taffanel. So it was with some feeling of achievement and celebration that Taffanel wrote to Saint-Saëns: "Here it is then, our dear 'Caprice' engraved! Would you give me the very great pleasure of letting Madame Saint-Saëns hear it?"[10] And

Saint-Saëns responded by arranging a private performance just for his mother and a close friend, Pauline Viardot.

A Life in Letters

Fascinating glimpses, illuminating the pattern and preoccupations of Taffanel's life over the next fifteen months, emerge in a copybook of letters that he kept from June 1888 to September 1889.[11] There are letters to some eighty different people, and while many of them are of limited interest—much of the first part of the copybook is taken up with official letters concerning the liquidation of the Opéra contingency fund, the *Caisse de prévoyance*, of which Taffanel was the secretary[12]—they provide the most sustained account of Taffanel the man and musician in his own words. Alongside important letters quoted elsewhere in this book, there are ones to foreign music publishers, for example, which demonstrate the extent to which Taffanel was always on the lookout for new solo and ensemble flute music to play. The copybook also reveals that while the members of the flute section at the Opéra (Taffanel, Donjon, Lafleurance) got on very well together, they were prey to various health problems and other frustrations of the job. "What a section of invalids!!!" Taffanel exclaims at one point. And with the summer holidays fast approaching, fraught with complications about the roster of available players, he sighs: "There was a performance at the Opéra yesterday, and let's hope that that will be the last Saturday!"

There is also a first mention of the Léopold Lafleurance, Edouard's nephew born in 1865, who was a private student of Taffanel's at this time. Léopold had avoided joining Altès's class at the Conservatoire, although he studied solfège, piano, and harmony there, gaining prizes between 1878 and 1884. The final letter in Taffanel's copybook, written on 6 September 1889, is a progress report to Léopold's father, declaring Taffanel's faith in him: "I firmly believe that if Léopold does not neglect his studies he will make a good career for himself in Paris; because, as well as the remarkable aptitude which he has as an artist, he already possesses qualities of character which will certainly help him to achieve success." Léopold Lafleurance went on to be appointed fourth flute in the Opéra Orchestra not long after, in January 1891, and his career did indeed develop successfully from there, both at the Opéra and the Société des concerts, and as a soloist. He was appointed temporary professor of flute at the Conservatoire during the First World War, assuring the Taffanel succession after the death of Hennebains and before the arrival of Gaubert.[13]

Another significant private student of Taffanel's came all the way from Wales to study with him. His name was Frederic Griffith and he was the protégé of a Mr. John Rutson. Taffanel agreed to accept Griffith as a student from

October 1888 and sent Rutson a progress report, and a note declining to charge his usual fee, the following month:

> I am very pleased with him. He is very attentive, punctual, he understands and makes every effort to succeed. I believe he has it in him to be a good performer. The "expressive" side of his playing is not yet very evident; but I don't doubt that it will appear one day, because it is there.
>
> The quality of tone is good. The pursuit of loudness has somewhat distorted it in the low register, we have just about managed now to make the sound even in all registers. When studying our instrument we must beware that in aiming for *quantity* of sound rather than excellence of *timbre* we do not make the flute into an instrument which is no longer true to itself.
>
> To sum up, I have great hopes for his progress, but one cannot learn everything in a few days, and I would like to keep him here as long as possible.

By implication, this report neatly sums up how Taffanel viewed the essential differences between the French and English styles of flute playing. English and German players preferred the wooden flute, and their style was generally robust and reedy, with the lips stretched back across the teeth and the airstream devoid of vibrato. To the ears of Taffanel, who favored a metal flute, such playing lacked flexibility and expression, substituting quantity for quality. It distorted the essential nature of the instrument.

Griffith had come to Paris after already pursuing a course of study at the Royal Academy of Music in London, and he learned his new lesson well. "He excelled as a soloist," wrote one of his contemporaries, "belonging in style to the French School. He invariably played high class music . . . and by practising always *pianissimo* attained exquisite delicacy of tone."[14]

Griffith returned to London to join the orchestra of Covent Garden Opera, and he also toured with Nellie Melba (continuing the Taffanel connection). He was the dedicatee of two flute works by Edward German—a Suite and *Saltarello*—and in 1900 he wrote to Taffanel recommending the music of his friend: "the most gifted composer and beautiful orchestrator that we have over here. In fact he is quite different to any other English composer, whose works generally I confess I do not care for." Griffith enclosed a score of German's *The Tempter*: "if you would be so kind as to perform it on your orchestra it would be honouring him and very greatly obliging me . . . your grateful student."[15]

In turn-of-the-century England, Griffith would have been something of a lone voice, not only in his exaggerated opinion of Edward German, but also in his adoption of Taffanel's style of flute playing. And whatever Griffith's personal influence may have been during his brief tenure as professor at the Royal Academy of Music, the tide of English flute playing did not really begin to turn until some decades later, in the 1930s, when Geoffrey Gilbert rethought the English Style after hearing Marcel Moyse and taking lessons from René Le Roy.[16]

The Summer of 1888

The most personal letters in Taffanel's copybook are those to his wife, Geneviève. At the beginning of the summer holiday period, as in other years, the family dispersed for a few weeks. Taffanel was left in Paris for most of August — the Opéra was still playing—while the others visited friends and relatives. Then toward the end of the month they all traveled together to their villa in Hyères, where they stayed until the beginning of October. This particular year Geneviève and Jacques were staying at a boardinghouse, the Etablissement d'Alise Sainte-Reine, near Les Laumes in the Côte d'Or. Marie-Camille, accompanied by her German nanny, Betty Prümm, was at Tourgéville on the Normandy coast with her Aunt Louise and Lefèbvre cousins.

In a sequence of thirteen letters to Geneviève beginning on 5 August, Taffanel recounts the day-to-day happenings (mainly nonmusical) during their separation and reveals how closely knit the family was. Just as Geneviève had written when Taffanel departed the previous year for Russia: "Yesterday after leaving you we felt quite alone . . . I was very listless," so now Taffanel echoes her: "This evening I feel much more alone than in other years—this separation from you all is sad." But as well as his various professional commitments, Taffanel busied himself with all the minutiae of domestic life. There are frequent references to a whole network of relatives, including his father (*grandpère*) and Geneviève's mother (*bonne maman*), who was also away on holiday, so Taffanel also kept her abreast of the news.

On that first rainy evening without the family, and after a day at the Conservatoire attending the annual *concours* (where he encountered César Franck, who sent warm wishes to Geneviève), Taffanel consoled himself at home by playing Wagner on the piano: "I took up arms against the Valkyre, it was enough to subdue all the stray dogs in the neighborhood!" A friend who dropped by was treated to four pages of this still controversial composer and had to admit that "it wasn't too awful!"

"My Geneviève, I would give anything to be with you," Taffanel wrote a couple of days later, and began to outline a neat plan to make a fleeting visit to Les Laumes the following weekend:

> I have received a telegram from Elkan asking if I would like to come
> to Aix on Saturday for a concert in the evening. I telegraphed back

yes, without saying that I have the Opéra on Friday and that I could only arrive in Aix at 8:30 in the evening. I didn't want to worry him, and it doesn't bother me as I've done it before. I haven't yet consulted the timetable for the return journey, but I'm quite sure that I can arrive at Laumes very early on Monday morning, leave again at 1 o'clock and arrive in Paris at 6 o'clock, ready for the Opéra. It's a bit like playing truant, and a bit tiring perhaps . . . but *zut!* as Papa would say.

This idea continued to develop over the next few days, and on Thursday he continued:

This morning a brief note [from Elkan] just thanking me for accepting, asking what time my train arrives and if I need a room booked. So I have no idea what sort of concert it will be . . . I have just sent him a telegram saying: "Colleague at the Opéra ill. Cannot leave until Saturday morning arriving at 8 in the evening." I am sending the music on ahead . . . I hope they have good pianists in Aix.

So, I shall leave on Saturday by the 8:50 fast train. We will pass by Les Laumes around 1 o'clock or 1:30 (I don't know exactly) but at top speed! If one of you happens to be there, you will see me waving my handkerchief, I will sit to the left of the engine.

On Sunday I will take the 9 o'clock evening train that will get me to Laumes at 4:30 in the morning. Don't worry about me—if it is pouring with rain I will doze in the waiting room until 7 o'clock. If it's fine, I shall come knocking on your door, having walked the short distance. If it's bad weather, someone can come and get me at 7.

All went according to plan—thanks to the efficiency of the French railway system—and Taffanel was soon back in Paris:

I was so happy to embrace you all yesterday and find you in such good health; carry on taking life as it comes, not worrying about anything, sleeping well, eating well, after all, that's the ideal human existence. If the holiday runs its course to the end I defy the Parisians to recognize you on your return.

My journey went well—I had the memory of your two happy faces and that easily made me forget my tiredness. However, I must admit that in the evening, during *L'Africaine*, I let myself drift into a gentle sleepiness (that's a polite way of putting it) and that this morning the alarm didn't go off until 8:30!

Then it was back to more mundane pursuits, like trying (unsuccessfully) to buy Geneviève a particular pair of shoes at her favorite department store,

Le Louvre; arranging for Marie-Camille's and Betty's return to Paris and the onward journey to Hyères; and wondering if it would be better to call the chimney sweep now or wait until their return from holiday.

The weather in Paris continued hot and thundery: "I am prudently staying at home, working and writing. I'm so pleased to know that only a week now separates us and I'm already preparing for our departure." Meanwhile, has Geneviève packed some music for Marie-Camille and Jacques for Hyères? The cost quoted for a cook during their stay seems exorbitant—how much does Madame Lebouc pay?—they really don't need cordon bleu! And what about arrangements for the delivery of beer and wine at Hyères, and for hiring a donkey and cart?

Then the weather suddenly turned cold: "I've sneezed six times while writing this letter!" Would they be warm enough at Hyères? Should he buy a rug at Bon Marché? With only a few days to go, a letter suddenly arrives from Edouard Lafleurance asking to extend his holiday and delay his return to Paris and the Opéra orchestra by a couple of days. But it's too late to change their arrangements, and besides, writes Taffanel, "I've had enough of the 'pit'!" So he looks for something diverting to do: "I am bored, oh! but enough of that! To throw off my dark mood I went to the circus yesterday evening to see the 'famous cats' [trained to perform a dressage act]. They are truly very curious, I will tell you all about their antics, and also those of a mischievous little donkey."

"You are prudence personified!" he tells Geneviève on 22 August as she ties up the final loose ends in their holiday arrangements. "Until tomorrow, then. Much love, your Paul."

Advice on Flute Making

One of the most intriguing letters in the copybook was written on 15 August 1888 while Taffanel was waiting for that summer holiday. It was addressed to Alfred Quesnay, professor of flute at the Lille Conservatoire and a former student of Louis Dorus, and it uncovers an otherwise undocumented aspect of Taffanel's involvement with the firm of Louis Lot. Quesnay had written to Taffanel expecting him to know all about a new design of Lot flute embouchure. The answer must have astonished him, for Taffanel revealed that this design had originally been his own idea, but that he had abandoned it the previous year after the maker Debonneetbeau at Lot's had failed to make it work:

> Imagine my surprise when I received, like you, a brochure announcing
> a new embouchure with a chin support, signed by Debonneetbeau-
> Lefèbvre! It is exactly, in principle, my modification.

If my proposed aim has been achieved, bravo! But I doubt it, because there were some difficulties to overcome which it does not seem that anyone has addressed.

The amusing thing about the whole affair is that I was at the makers and we talked about all sorts of things, but not a word was breathed about the aforesaid invention.

What a silly carry-on, isn't it?

H. D. Villette had taken over the Lot firm after Louis Lot's retirement in 1876, and been succeeded in 1882 by Debonneetbeau, who was himself soon to retire in May 1889.[17] In the light of this incident it is not surprising that Taffanel had been open to an approach from an independent flute maker, Djalma Julliot:

> I examined with great interest the modified Boehm system flute that you submitted to me and was pleased to discover the ingenuity of the alterations you have devised. While conserving the usual fingering layout, your new system of keywork is easy to adjust and gives perfect precision to the various *interconnections*. This matter of adjustment, which is often so annoying for players who do not have an expert technician to hand, has become a very simple thing thanks to your new system. I congratulate you.[18]

Taffanel went on to make various suggestions to Julliot regarding possible improvements to his designs, and Julliot also worked in collaboration with François Borne, a flutist-composer and professor at the Toulouse Conservatoire who wrote a popular *Fantaisie sur Carmen* and dedicated a flute piece to Taffanel, the *Ballade et danse des lutins*. In 1905 Borne and Julliot published an explanatory *Notice* about their flutes, also dedicated to Taffanel, and carrying a *Foreword* by him: "Monsieur Djalma Julliot, with his inventive mind and his great skill, seems to me to have brought the Theobald Boehm flute to the highest peak of perfection that any player could hope for."

The book credited Taffanel with a particularly significant development. In 1889 he had alerted Julliot to defects of the Boehm flute caused mainly by the closed G-sharp key adopted by French players (Boehm's original design was with an open G-sharp). There was a particular problem with the note E in the third register, so Taffanel suggested that Julliot should look for some way to duplicate the benefits of open G-sharp fingerings on a closed G-sharp flute. "Helped by the invaluable advice of the king of the flute," wrote Borne and Julliot, "we at last managed to solve the problem."[19] The result was the "split-E" mechanism, which, by dividing the action of two otherwise connected keys, duplicated the open G-sharp effect for this note. It is the one modification designed by Julliot that has been commonly adopted by subsequent makers and is widely used today.[20]

Taffanel also pointed out problems with the flute's faulty intonation, which Julliot set himself to solve. In all there were ten models of Julliot flutes, and the final one was unique in also having embouchure modifications: "An embouchure of correctly adjusted proportions giving great security of attack, aiding the production and sonority of the low register, and assuring the sweetness of the high notes."[21] Those must have been exactly the qualities Taffanel himself had been searching for.

By the time Julliot's first flutes were produced, after his patent of 1895, Taffanel had given up playing regularly in public, so there was no question of his abandoning Louis Lot instruments. He also seems to have still considered that Lot flutes were the best instruments for his students, whatever may have happened to the firm since Louis Lot's own day. Maybe the easy availability of these instruments (the firm still had a contract with the Conservatoire) played a part in that. But Julliot obviously benefited hugely from Taffanel's advice, and the blueprint of one of Julliot's later patented flutes was inscribed: "Improvements to the Boehm system flute / Offered to the king of flute players / By one of his most modest admirers / La Couture-Boussey, 25 December 1901."[22]

Exercices journaliers

When François Gevaert was preparing the second volume of his treatise on orchestration (*Cours méthodique d'orchestration*, 1890), he turned to Taffanel for advice on the flute section. Taffanel corrected him on which trills were easy, difficult, and even impossible, and where Gevaert had named the keys of C, G, D, and A major as "the brightest and easiest" for the flute, he observed: "You could add F and B flat which, on the Boehm flute are perhaps more congenial than D and A."[23] Part of that congeniality was the ease of fingering in those keys, and it was to develop facility across the whole flute that Taffanel developed a unique system of practice.

A letter in the copybook dated 13 October 1888 to a Monsieur Richaud in Paris requesting the return of some borrowed "exercises" is the first recorded mention of an important composition by Taffanel: the set of daily exercises that he would use as a technical foundation throughout his Conservatoire professorship, and that were eventually incorporated into the *Méthode* by Philippe Gaubert after his death. Despite the forbidding title they were given in the method—*17 Grands exercices journaliers de mécanisme*—these are creative exercises, built on two principles: that every scale and arpeggio should cover the complete range of the flute (not just two octaves, and not always beginning in the low register or on the tonic note), and that repetitive fingering patterns, constantly expanding in range and key, would lead most effectively to mastery of the instrument. A good exercise, therefore, is not isolated to a couple of octaves in a particular key up and down the flute, it is an extended exploration of the instrument, working progressively through all the keys and in all the registers. In that way it becomes a more relevant preparation for the random technical demands that real music makes.

It is worth remembering that Taffanel would have come into close contact with dancers as well as singers at the Opéra, because there is a clear analogy here with a dancer's training, where daily repetition of progressive exercises both warms up the body's present state of technical capability and develops it further: "Regular and careful practice of these exercises is essential for every flute player. They include all the instrument's difficulties."[24]

Taffanel's *Exercices journaliers* have proved the most influential section of the *Méthode*. They have long been available published separately and continue to be widely studied. They quite likely evolved over a number of years, initially for Taffanel's own practice, and were even the subject of a court case after his death, when one of his former Conservatoire students, Henri Bouillard (*premier prix* 1904), published an adapted version of them under his own name.[25] A student of Philippe Gaubert's brought a copy to one of his lessons in 1913, and Gaubert alerted Geneviève Taffanel and provided her with a letter of attestation as evidence of the real authorship of the *Exercices*.

> I declare that from 1890 with my teacher Paul Taffanel I worked on the exercises that have lately been published by Bouillard. From the time when he was appointed professor at the Paris Conservatoire, in 1893, my teacher made all the students in his class work on *his* exercises. Each student could copy these studies, but they remained, although not published, the property of my teacher. Moreover the idea would have been unthinkable for any student of my generation to claim these studies for himself.[26]

Théodore Dubois, director of the Conservatoire from 1896 to 1905, made a similar declaration, and the case was won. Bouillard's studies were withdrawn by the publisher and the remaining copies destroyed.

Flute and Orchestra

From time to time in the copybook Taffanel answers requests from other flute players on what music to play and what books to read. For the latter he particularly cites works by and about Theobald Boehm. But while literature on the flute was expanding, Taffanel was obviously still finding its solo repertoire with orchestra limited. As he explained in a letter to a young flutist (and future student of his), Alfred Lorentz, in Strasbourg: "The repertoire of works for flute and orchestra is not rich, by which I mean those works which can appear honorably on modern programs."[27] Taffanel lists only the two Mozart solo concertos, "for which Andersen has written cadenzas;" a *Concertstück* by Heinrich Hofmann; the *Concertstück, Ungarische Fantasie,* and *Fantaisie caractéristique* by Andersen; Saint-Saëns's *Romance*; and a concerto by Ferdinand Langer. He had also been trying out a Divertimento for flute and string quintet by the contemporary German composer Friedrich Gernsheim, who wrote suggesting a performance with orchestra. Taffanel replied:

> I confess that until now I have thought it the height of folly to pitch a feeble flute against sixty strings! . . . Your letter makes me think again and query whether my terrors are not exaggerated. At least the experience is sufficiently interesting to merit a try. That is why I spoke about it yesterday to Monsieur Garcin, conductor of the Société des concerts, who received my suggestion eagerly.[28]

But no performance ever took place. Instead Taffanel appeared at the Société des concerts on 13 January 1889, along with the violinist Henri Berthelier and pianist Louis Diémer, playing J. S. Bach's Fifth Brandenburg Concerto: "The ferocious audience at the Conservatoire seemed to appreciate this rather bold venture and gave us a warm welcome," reported Taffanel to a friend.[29] Incidentally, that same letter contains an early reference to Taffanel's interest in Wagner. This was to become an important aspect of his subsequent conducting career in the 1890s when he championed Wagner's works at the Opéra:

> Allow me, Madame, to present you with the little book on Wagner about which we spoke; I think you will have pleasure reading it: it is so unusual to see Wagner judged with neither infatuation nor hostility, whether it comes from proselytizing or ignorance.

Meanwhile, later that week on 19 January, Taffanel played part of the Ferdinand Langer Concerto he had recommended to Lorentz. It was at a concert with the Colonne Orchestra organized by the pianist Marie Jaëll, and Taffanel had pragmatically suggested the Andante (second movement) because it would be possible to prepare with only little rehearsal.[30] "I have a horror of makeshift performances," he declared on another occasion.[31]

Langer was a cellist as well as a composer, and when he was appointed to the Mannheim Court Orchestra in 1865 the resident flutist, Franz Neuhofer, immediately requested a concerto from him. Langer, at first reluctant to write for an instrument he did not really know, agreed if he could check on matters of technique and capability of the instrument. Neuhofer replied that nothing was impossible on the Boehm flute. The Concerto was duly written, in very quick time in 1867, and the conductor Franz Lachner was so impressed that he programmed it for one of the Mannheim Academy Concerts.[32]

The work is virtually unique for its period: a romantic flute concerto by a non-player-composer. It is likely that Taffanel had known it for some time, although this is the first recorded occasion on which he played it, and he regarded it highly enough to set extracts from it as the *concours* piece in 1894, at the end of his first year of teaching at the Conservatoire. He also appears to have composed a cadenza for the first movement, maybe for his Conservatoire students.[33]

The Concerto's three movements play without a break, but the central, lyrical Andante is extractable. For much of the time the flute is in the middle and upper registers, but there is a passage beginning seventeen bars from the end, in long notes in the bottom register, that caught the ear of the critic of *Le Ménestrel* when Taffanel performed it: "you could not play the flute better and you could not make more of the lower notes of the instrument."[34] "Thank you my dear Taffanel. You are a marvelous flutist and friend," was the response from the conductor Edouard Colonne.[35]

The low register had always been the weakest area of the flute. English and German players tended to overcome this on wooden flutes by tensing the lips and forcing the airstream (as described earlier). The result was loud and reedy. Taffanel brought a flexibility of embouchure, and particularly of airstream, to the Louis Lot flute that allowed the thin silver tube to resonate with the column of air, giving an expansiveness to the low notes without forcing. The resonating tube is something the player can clearly feel through the fingers in all the registers on the Lot flutes, with their open holes and minimum of light keywork, but only when the instrument is being played relatively gently. If driven too hard, Lot flutes lose their resonance. Loudness is better achieved by intensity of focus in the sound than by sheer volume of the airstream, which perhaps explains some of Taffanel's comments already noted regarding the solo flute pitched against the orchestra. The point is underlined by Taffanel's student Louis Fleury in the article for Lavignac's *Encyclopédie*: "It should be noted that the flute is an instrument of limited resources, that the range of its tone is constrained, and that certain effects or the expression of certain emotions are denied it."[36] Nevertheless, the text of the Taffanel and Gaubert method insists that the flute can "express the profoundest feelings."[37] In other words, there is the potential for great power of expression within clearly defined limits—a good working definition of Taffanel's French flute school.

This sense of balance and proportion certainly answered to Taffanel's own character. He was far from being a wild, impulsive virtuoso, and his blend of imagination and common sense in life, for example, is reflected in two letters in the copybook to his young cousin Joseph Jemain, as it had also been some years previously in letters to another relative, Joseph Celly (see chapter 7).

Jemain had not long before taken up an appointment in Aberdeen, Scotland, teaching the piano, and he was deeply unhappy. He had ambitions to be a composer. Taffanel observes that "the joy of composing is one of the greatest joys we can experience," and that "the harvest of the mind requires silence, solitude, and not the tedious and demanding clamour of 'teaching'!" but also offers him sound advice about the realities of life, the need for patience, and the value of time "and a period of testing" for revealing true artistic ability.[38] It was not just advice that was on offer, however; later letters in the copybook reveal that Taffanel used his influence to help Jemain gain a better post at the Lille Conservatoire and discreetly settled his debts in Aberdeen.

Toward the Baroque Flute

After his return to Paris from his summer holiday in Hyères in 1888, Taffanel turned his mind to planning a special series of concerts of contemporary music for flute and string ensemble, the first series devoted exclusively to the flute that he had promoted since 1875.[39] He wrote to the Viennese composer Robert Fuchs requesting a copy of his Serenade for flute and string quintet, and also collected similar works by Heinrich Hoffmann, Arnold Klug, and Friedrich Gernsheim. Alongside these contemporary pieces he decided to place some early instrumental music, and he also consulted François Gevaert in Brussels about including early vocal works.

The series, when it eventually took place, however, seems to have been limited to two concerts of "old and new music" at the end of January 1889. They were announced as: "Part one: modern works; part two: works by seventeenth- and eighteenth-century masters played on period instruments."[40] Only the first concert was reviewed in detail, so the complete programs are not known, but *Le Ménestrel* pronounced Gernsheim's Divertimento "quite long, quite colorless and quite tiring"—not even Taffanel could always carry the critics with him when he strayed off the path of the well known! The early works were much better received, with music by Marais, Leclair, Handel, Legrenzi, Milandre, and Rameau—his *Pièces de clavecin en concert* for keyboard, flute, and continuo. For the Rameau, and for a Loeillet Gigue that was encored, Louis Diémer played a harpsichord and Jules Delsart a bass viol, thus introducing the contemporary audience to "instruments, unknown today, of which we can have only a very approximate idea."

There is no mention in *Le Ménestrel* of what sort of flute Taffanel played, but it is unlikely to have been an original eighteenth-century one. When the two concerts were repeated in June 1889 at the Paris Exhibition, the critic Julien Tiersot wrote of the Rameau *Pièces*: "Monsieur Taffanel, on the same flute which he can make into a true bravura instrument, applied himself to softening the tone to evoke the gentle flutes of yesteryear."[41] The implication that Taffanel adapted his sound on his modern flute is confirmed by a review of the same players on original instruments two years later. It clearly states: "Monsieur Taffanel with his modern flute . . . "[42]

There seems no aesthetic reason why Taffanel would not have wanted to use an eighteenth-century flute, but presumably there were irresolvable problems of pitch and tuning. Diémer's harpsichord, built at current French pitch (a^1 = 435), would have been considerably higher than any of the early flutes that Taffanel might have borrowed from the Conservatoire museum or have himself owned. But the fact that he "softened" his tone argues knowledge of early flutes and performance practice many decades before such notions began to be explored systematically.

Patti Returns to Paris

The musical sensation of autumn 1888 was undoubtedly the first production at the Opéra on 28 November of Gounod's Roméo et Juliette (first given at the Théâtre-Lyrique in 1867), conducted by the composer and starring Adelina Patti. The complicated, and in itself operatic, saga of Patti's reappearance (complete with a ticket scandal) was charted by the press from the beginning of the month.[43] When the few scheduled performances finally took place, the reviews were considered (Patti was by now forty-five) but generally admiring. Le Ménestrel thought that her voice still had "the penetrating tone and freshness which make up its charm," and that meanwhile the virtuosity of her performance had become "more human and flexible, creating today a complete and often moving artist."[44] Another critic, Camille Bellaigue, listed various charges made against her of vocal insecurity, diminished virtuosity, and advancing age, but concluded: "Some high notes are no doubt less pure, less easy, but what freshness the others have retained! As for virtuosity, no one else can get anywhere near her."[45]

Patti's return to the Paris stage after so many years prompted one of the most revealing letters in Taffanel's copybook (quoted in part in chapter 2). In the wake of the Roméo et Juliette performances, he acknowledges his debt to specific aspects of Patti's art, and muses on the transitory nature of performance:

> Not having been able to find you, I assume that, like so many others who were called, you had to give up the idea of being one of the few chosen. But since you have been an admirer of that incomparable voice don't be too regretful and disappointed. Like you, in times past I often went to the Théâtre des Italiens; and I must say that for me she was an invaluable model of sound production and limpid tone.

Nowadays our ears are assailed so constantly that it is pleasant to have the echo of a great artist . . . but where is our Patti who sang Linda and Rigoletto and La Traviata? . . . What an astonishing career . . . and how fruitful! But also, could there ever be anything more barren? One seethes with frustration to see such wonderful gifts disappear without leaving the slightest trace behind them.[46]

This last point is particularly telling, for Taffanel himself would leave nothing behind him that captured the actual sound and artistry of his playing. Patti did make some commercial recordings, in 1905 and 1906, but by then she was in her sixties and almost a caricature of how she must have sounded in her prime when her voice first captivated Taffanel.[47]

Russia and Tchaikovsky

A letter in the copybook from Taffanel to his father, Jules, for his name day in October 1888 gives the first inklings of a return visit to Russia. Louis Diémer had originally been invited, but he was fearful of the bitter Russian winter, and therefore the invitation was likely to be extended to Taffanel, who relished the idea of revisiting Moscow: "It must be wonderful in the snow and I very much hope that Diémer gets cold feet!"[48]

Diémer did indeed back out, and so Tchaikovsky, who was one of the directors of the Moscow division of the Russian Imperial Music Society, wrote to Taffanel confirming the invitation for the following February:

We are absolutely delighted at the chance to hear you and have you among us for a while. Unfortunately for me, I cannot personally do you the honors in Moscow, because from the end of *January* I am undertaking an extensive *tour* of Germany and it is very likely that I will be in Paris at the same time that you are in Moscow . . . but be assured that we will do everything possible to make your visit to Moscow enjoyable and memorable.

The conductor of our Society, Mr *Max Erdmannsdoerfer* begs you to let him know what piece, or pieces, you will play and to tell him where and how he may obtain the scores and parts of the works you are performing for the Muscovites. I am sure that the St. Petersburg branch of our Society will take the opportunity of your visit to Moscow to invite you to play in Petersburg. I will talk to them about it this evening and give them your address. My very warmest wishes, my good and dear friend. I am very disappointed to think that I shall not be there when you come.[49]

Taffanel suggested the Mozart G major Concerto and, if other works were required, in order of preference, the Saint-Saëns *Romance*, his own *Sicilienne-Etude*, and a Chopin Waltz. The reply came that two works would be acceptable, so Taffanel sent off the scores and parts for the Mozart and Saint-Saëns.

Tchaikovsky left Moscow on 1 February (21 January, Russian calendar), having sent a note to P. Jurgenson, director of the Imperial Music Society: "Do all you can to make Taffanel happy while he is here." Jurgenson replied: "Taffanel arrives tomorrow. Simon will go and meet him, the committee will give him dinner, Simon—supper."[50] Antoine Simon was a French pianist and composer who had settled in Moscow in 1871 and become conductor of the Théâtre-bouffe. "You received me in that far country like one welcomes a brother," Taffanel wrote to him after returning to Paris, and he reeled off a whole list of names of other people to whom he was grateful for hospitality. One couple, Monsieur and Madame Boesch, sent him back to Paris with a present for Marie-Camille of a beautiful doll that she named Tatiana and "literally adored."[51]

As for the concert (incidentally, there is no record of any offer to appear also in St. Petersburg), it took place on 9 February (29 January, Russian calendar), and its success was reported back in Paris: "Our excellent flute player Monsieur Paul Taffanel . . . played a Mozart concerto to enthusiastic applause from a most supportive audience numbering at least three thousand."[52]

Tchaikovsky actually arrived in Paris later than he had expected, on 20 March, for a stay of three weeks. He recorded in his diary meeting Taffanel at his hotel shortly before he left again for London.[53] At some point he promised to write a flute concerto for Taffanel, and he referred to this the following year in a letter to the singer Désirée Artôt.[54] The concerto was mentioned again in the autumn of 1893 in conversation with the young cellist Yulian Poplavski: "Piotr Ilitch was waiting then for the libretto of a new opera he wished to compose (he did not say what); in October he was intending to write a flute concerto for which he had had an idea (and which would be for Taffanel, the famous Parisian virtuoso)."[55] But Tchaikovsky died only a few weeks later, on 6 November, and no evidence has yet come to light that he had begun work on the concerto.

Exposition universelle, 1889

French society and culture reached another milestone in 1889 with the Paris Exhibition, which opened on 7 May. The mood of the time was upbeat. The Third Republic was proud of its continuing progress, and it symbolically celebrated the centenary of the French Revolution and the fall of the Bastille with the raising of a brand-new tower, a triumphant feat of engineering by Gustave

Eiffel. As the emblem of the Exhibition, and its greatest scientific achievement, the Eiffel Tower was linked to two other of the newest inventions on display: elecricity and the phonograph.[56] This was also the exhibition that created a vogue for things Oriental. In the visual arts it was the inspiration for art nouveau, and in music, with the Javanese gamelan, it prefaced the new sound world of the young Debussy.[57]

Taffanel involved himself in both the forward- and the backward-looking aspects of the Exhibition. The early music concerts he had given earlier in the year were repeated as a sort of living demonstration of the large exhibition of musical instruments made in France, a panorama stretching back several centuries. It included a display case of rare and particularly fine examples, among them two flutes donated by Taffanel. His official receipt from the Exhibition authorities described them as: "1. Flute in A, signed Boehm and Grève, Munich, made of wood. / 2. Alto flute, known as a flûte d'amour, in G, metal, Munich 1867."[58] In the official catalog the former instrument was credited as the first example of a Boehm flute that had been brought to France, while the latter had been presented at the 1867 Exhibition.[59] It is likely that both these instruments would have been originally owned and played by Louis Dorus. They represent what was no doubt a much larger number of flutes collected by Taffanel and dispersed piecemeal after his death.

Julien Tiersot waxed lyrical over the musical instrument exhibition, regretting only that they had to be "played by the eyes," and applauding the efforts of Taffanel's two concerts to revive the works of earlier composers "on their own instruments." Incidentally, he deplored the specially constructed small concert hall on the fourth floor of the Trocadéro, with its glass room and open staircase that meant you either boiled or froze nearly to death.[60]

The three concerts given by Taffanel's Société des instruments à vent at the Exhibition have already been noted (see chapter 6), and he would also have played in various other official orchestral concerts that involved members of the Opéra and Société des concerts. The great enigma of the Exhibition, however, concerns a possible recording of Taffanel's playing. On 13 August he wrote to Marie-Camille, who was away on holiday: "Today I lunched at the Eiffel Tower and I went right to the top, into Monsieur Eiffel's little room. There was a gentleman with us called Monsieur Edison, who invented the little electric lights which you saw when you visited the Exhibition at night."[61]

At that point there was no mention of a recording, but elsewhere at the Exhibition Edison was already demonstrating his other invention, the phonograph. Tiersot described hearing "reproduced right in front of me a flute solo played by Monsieur de Vroye."[62] Then in November *Le Ménestrel* reported:

> More news of the Exhibition: Monsieur Eiffel has just presented Madame Adiny, Messieurs Vianesi, Taffanel, Turban, Berthelier, and

Melchissédec, of the Opéra, with magnificent silver gilt medals as souvenirs of the concert which these performers took part in, at the summit of the tower, for the unveiling of the phonograph which Monsieur Edison gave to the distinguished engineer.[63]

So it seems that Taffanel's playing would have been recorded at least once, but no other information has come to light. He was not included a few years later in *Appréciations sur le gramophone*, a volume of facsimile letters from many French musicians to the inventor of the gramophone supporting it as a great improvement on the phonograph, and there are no references to him ever having played for the gramophone.[64] So did that one recording ever make it down from the Eiffel Tower (albeit not in any lasting form on the still primitive phonograph), and did anyone else ever hear it apart from the members of that concert party? The answers may never be known.

What is known, however, is that Taffanel was decorated with the order of Chevalier of the Légion d'honneur, crowning that Exhibition year at a ceremony on 30 November 1889. He was in good company among musical colleagues similarly honored, including the composers Godard and Delibes (who was promoted to Officier), the conductors Garcin and Vianesi, and his friends Delsart and Diémer. *L'Art musical* listed him simply as "Paul Taffanel, artiste-compositeur."[65] *Le Ménestrel* was more informal and more poetic: "Taffanel, known as 'the magic flute,' son of Pan and Apollo, his lips are god-like."[66]

CHAPTER 9

Toward a New Career

The most distinguished virtuoso of our time
is also a first-rate musician.
—JULES BORDIER, BIOGRAPHICAL NOTE ON TAFFANEL (1890)

The award of the Légion d'honneur at the end of 1889 put an official seal of approval on Taffanel's career as a flute player, but also heralded its end. Taffanel himself must have felt he had arrived at a watershed. He was at the peak of his abilities as a flutist; he had established a whole new profile for the instrument; he had led a great revival in chamber music for wind instruments; and he was only forty-five.

As already noted (see chapter 6), Taffanel's role in organizing and directing the Société des instruments à vent had also pointed him in another direction:

> Therefore, when, on 25 January [1890], at the Opéra, he mounted the podium as third conductor to direct *Faust*, it was, it is true, the first time that he had found himself in charge of an orchestra; but he had been gradually familiarizing himself with the skills required and, helped by his innate ability, he was ready to be an excellent conductor.[1]

In an age before the cult of the conductor as personality had taken over, Taffanel no doubt felt conducting to be a natural development onward from his career as an instrumentalist, albeit an unusual one for a non-string player. Certainly his musical horizons had never been circumscribed by just the flute. It is interesting to speculate, however, on what might have happened if Henri Altès had not held on to the flute professorship at the Conservatoire for quite so long. If, like many of his colleagues, Taffanel had already become a professor by 1890, perhaps he might never have become a conductor. His decision to accept the professorship when it was finally offered in 1893, even though by then he was principal conductor of both the Société des concerts and the Opéra, argues a strong desire to complete what he had started on the flute and pass on the tradition to the next generations. Certainly the Conservatoire flute class was the last of his appointments to be relinquished—and then only at his death.

"Monsieur Taffanel is appointed third conductor from 1 January 1890," runs the entry in his personal file at the Opéra.[2] He succeeded Zéphirin-Joseph Lancien, a former leader of the second violins, who was retiring after less than three years as third conductor.[3] Le Ménestrel registered surprise at the appointment: "It is the first time that anything like this has happened at one of our big theaters, and that a conductor has been chosen elsewhere than from the ranks of the strings."[4] But when Taffanel came to conduct Faust later that month he was well prepared, having noted the precise metronome markings of the various tempi at its five hundredth performance in November 1887, conducted by Gounod himself. He would eventually pass these on to his successors.[5]

Taffanel's conducting colleagues were Augusto Vianesi and Madier de Montjau, and at first, as third conductor, he was also expected to continue playing in the orchestra. During this final period that he was still principal flute, Johannes Donjon retired and two new appointments were made on 1 January 1891: Adolphe Hennebains and Léopold Lafleurance became, respectively, second and fourth flutes, with Léopold's uncle, Edouard, remaining as third flute.[6]

Philippe Gaubert

With retrospective neatness, 1890 was also the year that Taffanel's direct successor as a flute player appeared on the scene: Philippe Gaubert, aged eleven. Gaubert was born in Cahors in the southern Lot region of France on 5 July 1879. His father was a cobbler and an amateur clarinetist. When Gaubert was seven the family moved to Paris and set up business at 34 rue Poncelet in the seventeenth arrondissement, not far from avenue Gourgaud, where Taffanel lived. Gaubert's aptitude for music was noticed first by Taffanel's father, who taught him the rudiments of theory and began to teach him the flute, "on the same old-fashioned instrument which had formerly been used by his own son. Giving in to insistent entreaties, Monsieur Paul Taffanel then agreed to take care of the little chap's musical education; the teacher was severe, but the pupil was studious, so progress was rapid."[7]

Gaubert was soon provided with a Boehm-system flute, and he remained a private pupil of Taffanel's until the latter was appointed to the Conservatoire professorship in 1893, at which point Gaubert also joined the flute class (an earlier application to Altès's class on 20 October 1892 had been withdrawn).[8]

Once in the Conservatoire, Gaubert gained a *premier prix* at the end of his first
year, aged fifteen, playing the Concerto by Ferdinand Langer.

Already there were parallels with Taffanel's own early life and relationship
with his teacher, Dorus, and from then on they became even more marked. In
1897 Gaubert found playing positions in the orchestras of the Société des concerts and the Opéra. He also built a reputation as a chamber music player and
often performed as a soloist in some of the most exclusive Parisian salons. By
day he continued to study harmony and composition at the Conservatoire,
and he also took up the violin and piano for a while. His teachers were Raoul
Pugno, Xavier Leroux, and Charles Lenepveu, and in 1905 Gaubert won second prize in the Prix de Rome. This was the notorious year that Ravel once
again failed to win the prize (his fifth attempt). There was outcry and scandal,
the director, Théodore Dubois, resigned, and Gabriel Fauré was appointed in
his place. Meanwhile, the previous year Gaubert had been appointed assistant
conductor of the Société des concerts after a competitive audition for which
Taffanel had given him conducting lessons. This was the subject of the only
letter that has survived from Taffanel to Gaubert:

> My dear Philippe, here is the sticking point in your letter: "As for ac-
> tually conducting an orchestra, although until now I have rarely had
> the chance to take up the baton, I have no fear of any test the Soci-
> ety may well wish to impose." What are you thinking of? And why
> haven't I seen you again? Have you changed your mind? Your old
> teacher, Paul Taffanel.[9]

The story was amplified many years later in an article Gaubert wrote
when he was retiring as chief conductor of the Société des concerts:

> I joined at the age of eighteen, when my dear teacher Paul Taffanel, a
> great artist, was the conductor. A few years later (at the time when I
> was competing for the Prix de Rome) the post of second conductor
> became vacant and it was decided to have a competition for it. Taffanel
> said to me: "Put yourself forward!" "But I have never conducted!"
> "Come and see me." He gave me two lessons . . . and there I was
> conducting the finale of the Ninth and the Scherzo of Schumann's
> First Symphony, totally foolhardy. What cheek! I was elected; I was
> twenty-five . . . my conducting career was marked out.[10]

Gaubert sent a copy of this article to Marie-Camille Taffanel with a covering letter: "every time that I have a chance to declare publicly my admiration
and my gratitude to my dear, great Maître, I do not miss it! Artists such as he
are very rare and it is important that younger generations should know it!"
That year, 1938, Gaubert was elevated to the rank of commander of the Légion
d'honneur, and he wrote in response to congratulations from Jacques Taffanel:

The other evening, at the Opéra, the orchestra invited me to the foyer to celebrate my decoration. . . . My reply was simple: I invoked the name of my venerated Maître, Paul Taffanel, to whom *I owe everything*, I talked of my arrival at the Opéra, in 1894, following my flute prize, as 4th additional flute in Die Walküre, which was actually what I was conducting this evening! Many of the older players had performed under my Maître's baton; his memory still lives in this house as in the Conservatoire and I can assure you that his name was acclaimed not without a certain emotion.

Heavens! what a long time ago it was in the garden at avenue Gourgaud. . . . when I used to play on the swing before having my lesson! I worked hard . . . but with such a mentor and such a guide, such a spiritual father, my life was made, and what I am today I owe, solely, to him.[11]

In January 1895 Taffanel inscribed a photograph of himself "to my dear student, Ph. Gaubert," and in October 1898 Gaubert returned the compliment with a photograph inscribed "to my dear Maître M. Paul Taffanel. Grateful and affectionate wishes. Your most devoted student, Philippe Gaubert" (see figs. 15 and 16).[12] Gaubert's first published composition in 1903, a *Tarentelle* for flute, oboe, and piano, was dedicated to Taffanel, as were two later works for flute and piano, *Nocturne et allegro scherzando* (1906) and the First Sonata (1918). In 1931 Gaubert presented a copy of this Sonata to Léopold Lafleurance, "In memory of our great and revered teacher Paul Taffanel, whose noble style has never been equalled, neither as a flute player, nor as a teacher on the conductor's podium."[13] Taffanel's role was indeed that of mentor and musical father to Gaubert, just as Dorus had been for him. Gaubert's direct contemporary and friend, the composer and conductor Désiré-Emile Inghelbrecht, stressed the similarity of Gaubert to Taffanel:

While still a child, he had been noticed by Taffanel who, struck by the configuration of his lips, had foreseen in him his successor as a flute player. Those who had heard Taffanel declared that indeed with Gaubert you rediscovered that extraordinary sound which the best flute players have never equalled since . . . From childhood, Taffanel mapped out the path which would lead his spiritual son most naturally to the positions he himself had occupied at the Opéra and the Société des concerts.[14]

In 1919, when musical life in Paris was returning to normal after the First World War, Gaubert was appointed principal conductor of the Société des concerts and professor of flute at the Conservatoire. The following year he also became chief conductor at the Opéra, and eventually, in 1931, artistic director. From 1923 onward he played the flute only rarely in public, although, like Taffanel before him, he continued to teach. Throughout his career he played on Louis Lot flutes, always retaining the same headjoint acquired when he first began to study with Taffanel. On 8 July 1941, several days after the premiere of his own ballet *Le chevalier et la demoiselle* at the Opéra, he died suddenly of a cerebral hemorrhage.[15]

The artistry of Gaubert's playing survives on two recordings he made with Nellie Melba in 1904 (see chapter 7) and on a few solo recordings he made for the French Gramophone Company in 1919.[16] His flute sound is mellow, yet rich and penetrating, with a wide tonal range and discreet use of vibrato. His supple control of legato and impeccable virtuosity of fingering and articulation inform an essentially musical approach and seriousness of interpretation clearly inherited from Taffanel. It is very much as described by Gaubert's contemporary, Gustave Samazeuilh: "a sustained sound, incisive in its power, particularly penetrating in its sweetness, extremely fluent, and knowing never to be hard or garish."[17] It seems that Gaubert was a totally natural player. One of his former students, Robert Hériché, told the story that when someone in the Conservatoire class admired Gaubert's tone on one occasion and asked how he developed it, he just shrugged and said that when he first went for lessons, Taffanel said: "Philippe, you have a lovely sound; look after it well!"[18]

Any difference between Taffanel and Gaubert lay in their basic personalities. Unlike Taffanel, Gaubert was very much the extrovert, the *bon viveur*. But they shared a basically pragmatic and certainly optimistic outlook on life, reflected in two Gaubert letters from the 1930s to the conductor and composer Henri Busser. After describing his recently completed symphony, Gaubert ranges over subjects as diverse as the political maneuverings at the Conservatoire, the precarious state of the French franc, and the relative merits of the Opéra and Opéra-comique. "Enough—just let them all wallow in it [*laisse pisser le mouton*] as my dear, great Taffanel used to say—you will be at the Conservatoire until you are 70, and from now to then you can be sure that there will be many changes." He concludes: "Ah! Paris! Ah! intrigues! But I don't give a damn . . . I just love music! So aren't I the happiest of men?"[19]

Leipzig and Ascanio

Ironically, just as Taffanel was beginning to change careers in 1890, he experienced two of his greatest successes as a flutist. In February he appeared as soloist in Mozart's G major Concerto in Leipzig with the Gewandhaus Orchestra, conducted by Carl Reinecke, and no doubt at his invitation—Taffanel had long championed Reinecke's Flute Sonata. He also played Benjamin Godard's newly composed *Prélude, idylle, et valse* in a program that included Wagner's Overture to *Die Meistersinger*, Beethoven's Second Symphony, and vocal items by Saint-Saëns, Brahms, Wagner, and Schubert, with the soprano Clara Polscher.[20]

The date, 13 February, was the anniversary of the death of Wagner, and the concert was a unique occasion: the only time that the Gewandhaus Orchestra would perform a complete Mozart flute concerto until 1968.[21] It also marked the meeting of two very different cultures in terms of flute playing, as had been the case when Taffanel played in England. The Gewandhaus's flutist, Maximilian Schwedler, played a typically heavy German flute, non-Boehm system, with a wooden body and metal headjoint, and in 1899 he patented his own "Reform Flute."[22] The German style was correspondingly forceful, just like the English (see chapter 8). The Gewandhaus audience, noted *Le Ménestrel*, was also "severe, and nearly always rather cold and unbending," but in this instance "the audience was electrified."[23] As so often, the musical eloquence of Taffanel's playing was persuasive. One Leipzig critic praised his "technical mastery" and "tasteful interpretation."[24] Another declared that his playing possessed "every possible virtue," and was well placed to reverse prevailing prejudices against the flute as a solo instrument:

> Monsieur Taffanel entices from his silver instrument bewitching, silvery sounds, pure and bright; his whole technique is as brilliant as it is flawless, and with what sheer musicality his performance binds everything together . . . We have special reason to be grateful that he acquainted us listeners with the Mozart G major Concerto . . . The Prelude was the most pleasing of the Godard pieces on offer; the other two have too much "haut goût" or are at the very least too perfumed.[25]

The three pieces by Godard were published later that year (for flute and orchestra or piano) with the title *Suite de trois morceaux* and a dedication to Taffanel. Urbane and scintillating, there is something Chopinesque about them, as if Taffanel had asked Godard to provide him with modern alternatives to the Nocturne, op. 15, no. 2 and the Waltz, op. 64, no. 1, which he had previously used as encores to the Mozart Concerto. He played Godard's pieces again, soon after, in March at the Société des instruments à vent.

News of the Leipzig concert traveled fast, and Taffanel was invited to Hamburg for a similarly successful concert in November that year. Meanwhile, back home he had scored another playing success—a particularly unexpected one. Saint-Saëns's *Ascanio*, on the story of Benvenuto Cellini, was premiered at the Opéra on 21 March 1890, and all the critics picked up on a moment in the act 3 ballet music: "The flute variation which Monsieur Taffanel glided through with such speed and limpidity would have made the great god Pan himself jealous."[26] The audience applauded so wildly after it that Taffanel had to rise and take a bow—"something, I believe, unprecedented, at least in Paris"—and the variation had to be encored![27] "My dear Taffanel," wrote the critic René de Récy in *La Revue bleue*, "if you carry on playing like that, they will never let you onto the podium, but goodness knows we need a conductor at the Opéra."[28]

The *Adagio et variation* comes in the mythological ballet-divertissement at the point when, according to the score, "Amour makes Psyché appear." The Adagio is pure song, in the low and middle registers of the flute, and the Variation is all brilliant double-tongued arpeggios and swirling legato scales. It is a classic piece of writing tailored by Saint-Saëns to Taffanel's skills. The two pieces were quickly published in a version for flute and piano, with "played by P. Taffanel" printed in bold letters on the cover.

Victorin Joncières, writing in *La Liberté*, also noted another flute melody in *Ascanio*: "a ravishing accompaniment by the flute to an archaic-sounding melody when François I presents Benvenuto to the Duchess!"[29] Another critic, Charles Malherbe, explained that it was "a *recurring motif* which depicts the character's elegant, admirable and sensitive nature."[30] Significantly, Saint-Saëns quoted a few bars of this melody at the end of a letter two years later when Taffanel was appointed chief conductor of the Société des concerts. He headed the letter with a quotation from Virgil's *Aeneid*, which in translation reads: "When the first is rent away, a second, no less golden, succeeds."

Uno avulso non deficit alter Aureus . . .

I went to the Opéra hoping to congratulate you, you were not there! And I leave for Switzerland tomorrow without seeing you, nor my charming goddaughter, nor her charming mother. But I will be back, at least I hope so, and we will see each other again!

What is so very sad, is that you will no longer play the flute, and nobody will ever again play it like you.[31]

Final Solo Tour

In February 1891 Taffanel undertook a last major tour abroad as a flute player. In his *Notes biographiques* he recorded the itinerary as Strasbourg, Mulhouse, Basel, Zurich, Berne, Lausanne, and Geneva, with concerts on the way back through France in Lyon and St. Gall. Part of the same route through Switzerland was duplicated later in the year on the tour previously noted with the Société des instruments à vent (see chapter 6). *Le Ménestrel* was quick to report Taffanel's success in Strasbourg playing the Mozart G major Concerto, Godard's Suite, and the Chopin Waltz as an encore.[32] The same story was taken up by the local papers throughout the tour: in Lausanne the Mozart Concerto was "played with such impeccable technical assurance, perfect nobility of style, and subtle variety of nuances." "His flute is silver, but the notes which come from it are the most liquid crystal, nothing could be more mellow and smooth." "Lausanne quite frequently hears true artists of the violin, but we never would have believed that anyone could draw such wonderful sounds from the flute, with so little apparent effort."[33]

After that there was very little the Geneva press could add, except that one review does significantly mention the clarity of Taffanel's low notes, his control of breathing, and the sheer naturalness of his playing, with no obvious physical effort: "however much and however attentively one watches him, it is impossible to catch the moments when he breathes . . . such perfection and ease that you might believe these were simple things which anyone could do."[34]

Other notable concerts that year included the first performances in Paris of J. S. Bach's B minor Mass, given by the Société des concerts on 22 February— Taffanel was back from tour just in time. The work caused a great stir, and Taffanel's obbligato in the *Domine Deus* was much noted in the reviews.[35] The music scholar Camille Benoît later sent a copy of his analytical study of the work to Taffanel, inscribed "Hommage et souvenir," and in it referred to him as not just *a* flute, but *the* flute.[36]

Meanwhile, the critic Willy (Henry Gauthier-Villars) had his ironic pen poised. On 4 April he was at a Société nationale concert when Taffanel played Clémence de Grandval's *Valse mélancolique* for flute and harp, Fauré's Berceuse (originally for violin), and an "Allegro" by Paul Fournier:

> Diémer hurled himself at the piano. Such ferocity! . . . Taffanel, armed with a merciless flute, launched the offensive, aided by Hasselmans, on a *Valse mélancolique* by Madame de Grandval. Georges Hüe contorted himself with extravagant gesticulations, the audience began to get worried, evidently he had fallen prey to some illness, while that annoying flute kept trotting out its banal and dull tune to an insipid harp accompaniment.[37]

And just to ram the point home, Willy filed a second review of the same concert a few days later. It has the dubious distinction of being the only uncomplimentary account of Taffanel's playing to have come to light:

> The tipsy *Allegro* by Paul Fournier isn't bad. But the tipsy *Valse* by Madame de Grandval is very bad. Oh yes! As for Fauré's *Berceuse*, the

Society's Pan babbled it out wildly. Play in a more seemly manner, don't get so worked up, it's pointless to get *all hot under the collar.*[38]

Willy's final phrase is an untranslatable pun on Taffanel's name—"intuile de mouiller *ta fanelle*"—referring to the flannel undershirts worn by gentlemen at that time (the nonexistent word *fanelle* is a play on the word *flanelle*). Incidentally, this turned out to be Taffanel's last appearance at the Société nationale—though not, presumably, because of Willy's review!

Changes at the Opéra

The entry for 8 April 1891 in Taffanel's *Notes biographiques* reads: "Letter Gounod Thomas supporting my application 1st conductor Opéra." This letter seems subsequently to have been lost in the Opéra files, but Taffanel's own covering letter has survived, applying for the post owing to the imminent retirement of Vianesi and reopening the subject of retirement from the position of principal flute: "the years I have spent at the Opéra qualify me for a retirement pension, and I have resolved, for some time and absolutely, to give up my career as a player and claim my pension: I could therefore devote myself, as I wish, entirely to conducting."[39]

But despite the support of two eminent operatic composers, Charles Gounod and Ambroise Thomas, the latter also director of the Conservatoire, the time was not yet right for Taffanel. The director of the Opéra, Pedro Gailhard, and his partner Eugene Ritt (soon to be succeeded by Eugène Bertrand) were looking to capitalize on the vogue for Wagner's music that had been gathering momentum during the previous decade, once the memory of Prussian humiliations in 1870 had begun to recede. They decided it was high time to begin staging Wagner regularly at the Opéra and looked first to Charles Lamoureux, who duly conducted the Opéra premiere of *Lohengrin* in September 1891, and then to Edouard Colonne, who did the same for *Die Walküre* in May 1893.

Like Taffanel, both conductors were natives of Bordeaux, but somewhat older than him—Lamoureux was born in 1834 and Colonne in 1838. They had also proved themselves already as ardent Wagnerians with their respective orchestras in their popular Sunday concerts. However, neither of them lasted long amidst all the intrigues of the Opéra. Lamoureux had already had one unhappy period as conductor there between 1877 and 1879, and the Opéra audience took firmly against Colonne after the first few performances of *Die Walküre*. Then it would be Taffanel's turn, but for the moment, in 1891, he continued as third conductor, assisting Lamoureux with the run of eighteen rehearsals for *Lohengrin.*[40] He also finally got his wish to relinquish the position of principal flute and was succeeded in November by Hennebains.

Conducting Is the Future

Taffanel's first recorded appearance conducting in the concert hall was at the Salle Erard on 6 March 1891. It was at a charity concert, organized by the pianist Caroline de Serres (née Montigny-Rémaury) in aid of the Association des dames françaises. The program included a Beethoven piano concerto and extracts from Delibes's ballet *Coppélia.*[41] There was also a work by Gabriel Pierné, who reminded Taffanel of the occasion some years later: "I rediscovered among my collection of papers a most amusing letter from you! Your beginnings as a conductor: with my Scherzo caprice played by Madame Montigny-Rémaury. Do you remember?"[42] Maybe the specially assembled orchestra for the occasion left something to be desired and was the source of the amusement, but the charity still benefited, and Caroline de Serres was satisfied. She marked the occasion with a gift to Taffanel of a black ivory and silver engraved baton.[43]

Then another opportunity suddenly opened up. At the end of the 1891–92 season of the Société des concerts, the conductor, Jules Garcin, resigned for reasons of ill health. The second conductor, Jules Danbé, who was also conductor of the Opéra-comique, had already deputized for him several times that season.[44] The appointment of a new conductor was by election, arranged for 3 June, with each member of the Society eligible to vote. At the end of May Taffanel submitted a brief letter of application: "If the Society finds me worthy to direct its activities it can be assured that I will give it all the diligence and dedication of which I am capable."[45]

There were four candidates: Danbé, Taffanel, Benjamin Godard, and the violinist Gabriel Marie. After five rounds of voting, Godard and Gabriel Marie were eliminated, and a result was reached in favor of Taffanel by forty-eight votes to Danbé's thirty-seven, with two abstentions. Danbé immediately resigned, resisting all attempts to persuade him to stay (he was later made an honorary member), and the violinist Désiré Thibault was elected as second conductor. Hennebains was subsequently brought in from the Lamoureux Orchestra to become first flute.[46] Among the letters of congratulation on Taffanel's appointment was a joking one from the pianist Edouard Risler and a group of close friends including composer Florent Schmitt, addressing him as "Dear old Hen" and sending "joyful cluckings."[47]

There followed a period of waiting. The new season of the Société des concerts would not start until November, so there was time to think and plan. Meanwhile, Wagner continued to top the Opéra agenda, and in August 1892 Taffanel visited the Bayreuth Festival to report back on its productions. He took his son Jacques (then aged seventeen) with him, and the whole trip developed into a sort of grand tour of Switzerland, Germany, and Italy.

They saw four Wagner operas at Bayreuth— *Tannhäuser, Die Meistersinger, Tristan und Isolde,* and *Parsifal*—and Taffanel must have been delighted that Jacques was immediately bitten by the Wagner bug. They also attended a performance of Verdi's *Otello* at the Teatro Carlo Felice in Genoa, and everywhere they went Taffanel kept mementos of their travels: tickets and programs, maps and menus.[48] He also made sketches of the orchestra layout at Bayreuth, and these were later reproduced in Albert Lavignac's popular guidebook for French Wagnerians, *Le Voyage artistique à Bayreuth.* Taffanel went on to collect the complete scores of Wagner's operas, along with books on the composer and on German philosophy.

Geneviève Taffanel kept in touch via regular letters full of family news, including the progress of renovations at 8 avenue Gourgaud and also at their villa in Hyères. Various members of the family, especially Geneviève's mother, were being troublesome, and to add to the problems there was a heat wave and a cholera epidemic that summer. Nevertheless, Geneviève had bought a bicycle— all the rage in Paris—and Marie-Camille's canary, Riquet, was learning to sing! Geneviève also recounted an anecdote from the critic Stany Oppenheim, who had met Taffanel in Bayreuth and had come to call on her:

> He told us that for a long time he had had a grudge against Monsieur Taffanel, because when he was young he got together a little orchestra that he used to conduct, but his flutist smoked cigarettes all the time, blowing the smoke out through his flute, and replying to anyone who said anything: "I am a student of Taffanel, and I do this at my lessons!"[49]

Taffanel's letters back to Geneviève have not survived—no doubt he would have made some crisp rejoinder to this story—but there is a charming note to Marie-Camille, describing daily life in Bayreuth:

> Papa and your Jacques are well and think about you a lot. We are delighted to know that you are learning to swim with Aunt Louise. How marvelous it must be to live in the water during this dreadful heat. As for us, we are living in dust instead, and we are literally baking. Yesterday it was 36 degrees in the shade. And to reach the theater we have to travel 2 kilometres, without much shade. Mind you, once we get there, we are rewarded with beautiful music, which Jacques enjoys very much, even though it is very complex. As all the lights are put out in the theater, it is not too hot. Once the act is finished, everyone goes out to eat and have ice creams in the restaurants nearby. It is still daylight, because it begins at 4 o'clock so that it will be over at

10 o'clock. And that is how we are spending every day, right up to Sunday.[50]

After traveling on to Italy, they ended their tour with a few days in Hyères, but as there was still construction going on at their own villa they stayed in the home of Taffanel's old friends, the cellist Charles Lebouc and his wife. The Leboucs were away, and Taffanel drafted them a letter, the most personal and revealing to have survived among his papers:

> Here we are under your hospitable roof resting from the wear and tear of our extensive journey and building up our strength for the approaching year's work. For me this year will be tough, with such a great assignment allotted to me. At a point of such profound change in my artistic career how can I not remember, my dear friends, those true tokens of affection you have both given me during the course of my life, and the support you have always provided for me. You are certainly in large part the authors of my fortune, you, dear Lebouc, setting my foot on the ladder of the Conservatoire, baptising my young Society; both of you giving me my much-loved companion, she, who has given me courage each day and helped me so well to reach my goal. What will my destiny now be? . . . Faced with the unknown, so marvelous and so threatening, I tremble sometimes, and yet I also have the most wonderful dreams . . . The coming year will determine everything. Nowhere, better than here, dear friends, could I gather my thoughts for the supreme night before battle, and it is once again under your protection that I make the most significant move of my artistic life.[51]

That moment of introspection, however, yielded immediately to one of action. On the same piece of paper, Taffanel followed his draft letter to the Leboucs with a report to Pedro Gailhard on his visit to Bayreuth, suggesting *Die Meistersinger* for staging at the Opéra: "I think the Opéra could stage it as well, if not better, as regards the principal singers and the orchestra. For the chorus, there would certainly be problems, but not impossible ones."

Principal Conductor at the Conservatoire

Back in Paris, Taffanel's first concert conducting the Société des concerts took place on Sunday 27 November 1892. The program was wide-ranging: Beethoven's *Leonora* no. 3 Overture and his *Eroica* Symphony; Saint-Saëns's tone poem *Le Rouet d'Omphale*; a work for chorus and orchestra by Gounod, *Près du fleuve étranger*; and two unaccompanied choral pieces, *O felix anima* by Carissimi and *Fuyons tous d'amour le jeu* by Lassus.[52]

Hugues Imbert, who was in the audience, asked the question uppermost in everyone's mind: "One wondered how the faultless player would conduct this wonderful orchestra . . . even though he had already proved himself as third conductor at the Opéra." He was relieved to find Taffanel "completely successful," although "a little feverish at the beginning," and concluded that things augured well for the future.[53]Arthur Pougin, in a lengthy review in *Le Ménestrel*, agreed, observing only that "perhaps a little more precision would not come amiss in the way of prompting the initial attack of a work."[54] The general tone of the reviews was summed up succinctly by Willy: "My word, Taffanel conducts well!"[55]

Taffanel had consulted Saint-Saëns over a point in the bowing of *Le Rouet d'Omphale* and made sure he had a ticket for the concert. The next day's post brought a "delightful" letter from him in response to the performance and a considerably less delightful one from Julien Tiersot, the Conservatoire librarian and music scholar who wrote the Society's program notes.[56] But Taffanel welcomed Tiersot's comments:

> For a long time now, as a darling of the audiences, words of praise have had only a feeble effect on me . . . but I attach quite a different value to reasoned criticism like yours. At the start of my new career I feel so greatly the *necessity* for these criticisms, that I often accuse myself of imaginary musical crimes in order to elicit from those I am talking to something other than insipid compliments.

Tiersot accused him of conducting too fast and of failing to respect the traditions of the music and of the Conservatoire Orchestra, and Taffanel delivered a spirited and comprehensive defense to these charges, answering them one by one in relation to each piece. He pointed out, for example, that a particular accelerando in *Le Rouet d'Omphale* had actually been requested by Saint-Saëns, and that another accelerando in the finale of the *Eroica* Symphony was very much a Conservatoire tradition. "I have never thought to change the noble character of our masterpieces," he insisted, but he took the point that not everything may have turned out exactly as planned, and pleaded the "extenuating circumstances" of his inexperience as a conductor, "of which you can have no idea, you, who have only been a spectator and never a performer." A neat point, intended to hit home—but for Taffanel there was something fundamental at stake here:

> In taking command I felt I needed to react against a torpor, a real laziness which paralysed the attack of notes; the attitude to performance seemed to me to be lacking in any life; it was devoid of spontaneity, of drive. My conducting arm no doubt unfortunately speeded things up, and I must watch that when it leads me away from the true

tempo. The fault that I wished to correct has not, I think, completely disappeared, but I would not want to replace it with a worse one. So your observation will bear fruit.

Alongside the politeness and the apology, Taffanel was clearly throwing down the gauntlet. He was not going to allow the Société des concerts to rest on its laurels, and one of the first things he did was to fling its doors wide open to the music of Wagner. In February 1893 he performed the complete third act of *Tannhäuser* (cause of the famous scandal surrounding Wagner at the Opéra back in 1861). This time it was acclaimed by audience and critics alike.[57] For Taffanel, it was also a useful move in establishing himself as a Wagner conductor, and the message was presumably not lost on the directors of the Opéra. Taffanel sent out a similar message about championing all modern music when he conducted an orchestra at the Salle Erard the following month in a concert organized by the pianist Isidor Philipp, featuring works by Widor, Rubinstein, Saint-Saëns, Lefèbvre, and Bernard.[58]

Principal Conductor at the Opéra

The long-awaited premiere of *Die Walküre* took place at the Opéra on 12 May 1893, conducted by Colonne. The reviews were mixed, some very hostile, others hinting at problems between Colonne and the orchestra and speculating that he might resign and be succeeded by Taffanel. Colonne immediately wrote to *Le Temps* denying all these rumors, and for the moment the performances continued.[59]

Meanwhile, in early June, Taffanel agreed to meet Hugues Imbert to give him information for a projected biographical article, "although I am absolutely unworthy to appear in a gallery of 'Contemporary Masters!'"[60] Between their conversation and publication of the article in *Le Guide musical*, there was just time for Imbert to insert a few words on the latest development in Taffanel's career: "when E. Colonne declared his intention of resigning from his post of conductor at the Opéra, Paul Taffanel was quite naturally nominated to replace him."[61] The news broke in *Le Figaro* on the morning of 30 June 1893: "Monsieur Colonne will conduct for the last time this evening the performance at the Opéra." The article went on to explain that in future the three conductors at the Opéra would have equal status. Nevertheless, it listed them in a particular order, and the descriptions spoke for themselves:

Monsieur Taffanel is a distinguished artist. The Opéra Orchestra has lost in him an incomparable player, it will rediscover a conductor who is skilled, intrepid, liked by all: Monsieur Taffanel proved himself last winter, at the head of the Société des concerts, which had the good idea of entrusting him with Habeneck's baton.

Monsieur Madier de Montjau is a conscientious artist who has been allotted for some years now the direction of most of the repertoire works and is appreciated in that role for his sound qualities.

Monsieur Paul Viardot [son of the singer Pauline Viardot], who has not yet "had a career," is a young violinist whose debut revealed a most talented player, an artist of more than ordinary interest. He bears a famous name, one that we would once again wish to acclaim.[62]

L'Univers illustré capped this by publishing photographs of the three conductors, with Taffanel's reproduced larger than the other two.[63]

Taffanel was officially appointed from 1 July 1893, and he conducted *Die Walküre* for the first time two days later. "His precision, command and fervor left nothing to be desired," declared the critic Arthur Pougin.[64] Saint-Saëns, writing to Marie-Camille Taffanel, observed: "Your father is covering himself with glory at the Opéra, which pleases me greatly."[65] It was reported soon after that the Opéra had decided to adopt for all future productions the new orchestral seating plan devised for *Die Walküre*, with the conductor placed in the middle of the players rather than right up in front of the stage. This new layout had been the idea of Pedro Gailhard, against the wishes of Colonne, and was no doubt yet another cause of the discontent that led to Colonne's resignation.[66]

Taffanel's appointment made him something of a celebrity—after all, the Opéra was as much a social institution as a musical one. The first of what were to be many newspaper and magazine features on him had already appeared in 1890, giving details of his career and concluding with a brief character sketch: "He is a modest and charming artist, a kind and witty conversationalist."[67] Now more articles and photographs began to appear, including one in *La Gironde* from his hometown of Bordeaux, as the press did their best to make a "personality" of him. Most notably, in 1902, a photograph of Taffanel conducting at the Opéra was used for the front cover of the first issue of *Musica*, a new monthly magazine.[68]

Gailhard was keen to push forward with his plans for more Wagner at the Opéra, so in 1893 he publicly promised to stage one per year up to the 1900 Exhibition.[69] He therefore dispatched Taffanel to follow up the visit he had made to Bayreuth with one to the Munich Opera (archrival to Bayreuth) to evaluate their methods and styles of production. Taffanel drew up a plan of Munich performances and decided to go there in the second half of September when there would be a chance to see seven different Wagner operas. He took Jacques with him once again, and they left Paris on 16 September, Taffanel's forty-ninth birthday. He kept a small dossier of notes, tickets, and programs, as he had done from Bayreuth, and it shows among other things that he met the flute player Rudolph Tillmetz, professor at the Munich Academy and a former student of Boehm, and went searching for books at Philipp Reclam's Universel-Bibliothek.[70]

Taffanel drafted reports back to Gailhard on three of the operas in Munich: *Tristan und Isolde, Tannhäuser,* and *Die Meistersinger.* He followed everything in the minutest detail, score in hand, and his comments indicate that he knew the music intimately. He had scant praise for the performance of *Tannhäuser*—quite well sung, but poorly played under the conductor Franz Fischer, "in short, a mediocre provincial orchestra." For *Die Meistersinger,* on the other hand, conducted by Felix Mottl: "What a beautiful performance! Nothing but praise to give, or at least, only the mildest of criticisms, so as not get out of the habit!" Taffanel did, however, have a problem with the style of singing:

> If I express reservations it is from my French vantage point. I do find it difficult to get used to these German voices which, even if they don't have that abominable French affliction, wobbly vibrato, have on the other hand, from the men, a constantly guttural sound, and from both men and woman a total absence of expression, an absolute uniformity of diction and of vocal timbre, whatever the situation, and a way of articulating which is so harsh that the melodic texture is distorted at every turn.

Translate all that into flute-playing terms, and it speaks volumes about the particular aesthetic of sound and style pursued by Taffanel.

Finally, there was *Tristan.* It, too, was conducted by Mottl, and the music, if not all aspects of the performance, won Taffanel over completely: "Tristan made a deep impression on me . . . I had, several times, to close the score and give myself up to the stage, so compelling is this work." At that point he concluded that *Tristan* should be the next opera for Paris, even though it would be "a tall order for French ears, and for French eyes, given the simplicity and length of the scenes," and he made sure he included the Prelude at the opening concert of the next season of the Société des concerts in December 1893.

Taffanel's plans to stay on in Munich until *Götterdämmerung* at the end of the month were thwarted by a scandal back at the Paris Opéra. Paul Viardot, possibly drunk, broke down while conducting *Die Walküre* on 20 September and had to be replaced by the chorus master, Edouard Mangin. Viardot later claimed he was ill and produced two doctor's certificates confirming a disease of his right ear.[71] Nevertheless, he resigned as third conductor and Mangin was appointed in his place, but Taffanel was recalled early from Munich, arriving on the day of the next performance of *Die Walküre,* 27 September, so that he could conduct it.[72] From then on, he would be the Opéra's undisputed chief conductor.

CHAPTER 10

Wielding the Baton

Taffanel-House, 2 rue du Conservatoire
—WILLY, *NOTES SANS PORTÉES* (1896)

While Taffanel's career as a flute player received ever increasing acclaim, his career as a conductor proved more controversial. It rapidly became apparent that since he had emerged into a wider public arena he was subject to much closer scrutiny than before, by people with all sorts of vested interests and partisan affiliations. The veteran violinist Charles Dancla, for example, took the opportunity in his memoirs of 1893 to fire a broadside against any conductor who had not previously been a violinist. "As the strings are the heart of the orchestra," he argued, this was only logical. He carefully did not name Taffanel, but in giving a list of all the French conductors who had been violinists, including Taffanel's second conductors at both the Société des concerts and the Opéra, he made his implication clear: "In my opinion, a musician who is a stranger to that instrument will not usefully be able to indicate in a symphonic work, and even in an opera, the bowings and logical fingerings which vary the timbre of the strings and give a performance the right ensemble, smoothness, and polish."[1]

That was a common prejudice, so Taffanel started in the eyes of many with a severe handicap. Consequently, when he faltered he was immediately damned by some, and even when he triumphed others could not forgive him. The absence of flamboyant histrionics on the platform also left many unconvinced — solid musicianship and calm expertise are not visual virtues. Nevertheless, there are abundant examples of praise for Taffanel's conducting in reviews in the weekly musical press and daily newspapers.

There is, however, something ironic about the fact that he took a "provincial" instrument, the flute, and established it internationally, while his wielding of the conductor's baton remained "provincial" in the sense that he never left Paris. Willy's glib reference to the Société des concerts quoted at the beginning of the chapter has something of a bourgeois ring to it.

The critic and composer Gustave Samazeuilh perhaps evaluated Taffanel's tenure at the Société des concerts most dispassionately:

> He proved to be the guardian of tradition, with energy, conviction, a certain absolutism as well, but with technical qualities and style which were admired even by those who reproached him for a certain lack of expression and expansiveness. After the great masters of the past, Saint-Saëns was his favorite composer.[2]

It is also revealing to see Taffanel through non-French eyes. The Irish novelist and travel writer Hannah Lynch was a shrewd chronicler of French cultural life in 1900. She visited a solemn session of the Académie française, for example, called it "only a club," and sighed over "the utter vanity of the whole affair." She also confidently dismissed Notre Dame as a "second-rate edifice" compared to Sacré Cœur. In short, she was critical of received opinion and scornful of snobbery. So when she went to the Société des concerts she ignored the stuffed shirts in the audience and fixed her attention on the unassuming figure on the rostrum:

> Monsieur Taffanel, the able conductor of the Conservatoire orchestra, cannot compare with the great German conductors; he has not the genius of Mottl, nor the magical temperament of Weingartner, nor the individuality of the French conductor, the late Lamoureux. But in his quiet, measured way he is an incomparable artist, to judge by the results of his lead . . . Monsieur Taffanel has not a suspicion of affectation or histrionism. He is simplicity itself, the very model of impersonality. He so effaces himself that you are only conscious of his presence by the perfection of his orchestra. He is so easy and subdued that he hardly seems necessary in this admirable triumph of art.[3]

Taffanel was a conscientious *kapellmeister* in an age that was witnessing the rapid rise of the conductor as virtuoso. He was a respected colleague of the Wagner conductors Felix Mottl at Bayreuth and Hermann Levi at Munich, but none of them had the international reputation of Hans von Bülow, Hans Richter, or Arthur Nikisch. And by the following generations the "star" quality was paramount, with Felix Weingartner, Arturo Toscanini, and Wilhelm Furtwängler.[4]

Taffanel certainly had age on his side. At forty-eight in 1892 he was considerably younger than his predecessors at both the Société des concerts and the Opéra. His approach was correspondingly alert: "He had the superior advantage of personal authority, by virtue of which he transformed the methods of

working and improved their effectiveness. Swifter than any other of his colleagues, and with the minimum of preparation, he obtained the desired results."
Pasdeloup, for example, had been famous for long, dull orchestral rehearsals—
his musicians used to bring bread, sausages, and chocolate to eat during the
bars of rest when it got past lunchtime! "Taffanel succeeded, on the other hand,
in reducing to the bare minimum the effort required of his troops: a measure
of the status, knowledge and skill of a general."[5]

The conductor Désiré Inghelbrecht, noting that the triumvirate of conductors at the Opéra meant in reality that Taffanel was first and the others "assisted" him, pushed the idea of "personal authority" one stage further: "Paul
Taffanel dared to impose his absolute will on his musicians, as on his directors.
Having come from the same orchestras which he now directed, this stooped
little man, with short and precise gestures, radiated merciless authority."[6] But
this impression of "merciless authority" is tempered by an incident, recounted
by Marcel Moyse to his son, Louis, in which Taffanel seemed uncomfortable
in his professional dealings with the people. He reportedly used his influence
to have a player sacked from the orchestra, then later assured the musician in
question that he had had nothing to do with it: "My father was most unhappy
about this story. Maybe sometimes it is necessary to bring our gods down to
human level."[7]

There was one critic for whom Taffanel could do no right: Pierre Lalo, son
of the composer Edouard Lalo, and a passionate Wagnerian. Lalo wrote in *Le
Journal des débats* and *Le Temps,* where he pursued a merciless vendetta:

> . . . a makeshift conductor, whose lack of innate talent and acquired
> experience do not cut him out for the formidable task of interpreting
> Wagner.

> . . . it just will not do, for a flute player, however skilled he may be at
> playing the flute, to take on the role of a Kapellmeister; that requires
> a true musician, and a great musician.

> . . . the regrettable metamorphosis of Monsieur Taffanel has produced,
> out of an unrivalled flute player, a very ordinary conductor.[8]

But Pierre Lalo should be compared with other critics writing about the
same productions—Catulle Mendès, for example, on Berlioz's *La Prise de Troie*
at the Opéra in November 1899:

> Fortunately, in the orchestra, ardently conducted by Monsieur Taffanel,
> the passionate, wild and thwarted spirit of Berlioz cried, wept, howled,
> yelped, and roared magnificently. [Mendès]

> The orchestra conducted by Monsieur Taffanel is adequate, but col-
> ourless and inexpressive: if this music does have a certain coolness in

places, neither this orchestra nor its conductor are capable of sorting it out. [Lalo]⁹

Lalo, however, also vented his critical spleen in other directions, not just at Taffanel. His anti-Ravel campaign, for example, lasted some forty years. Although he damned all of Taffanel's Wagner productions, he could elsewhere very occasionally find some faint praise: "his interpretation is, in *Armide*, very superior to what it was in *Tristan*; it lacked neither breadth, nor purity, nor style."¹⁰ Interestingly, Taffanel entered in his *Notes biographiques* that Gluck's *Armide*, his next-to-last new production, premiered in April 1905, was the first for which his name had appeared on the publicity posters. Usually it was only the singers, and sometimes the scenery and costume designers, who were considered worth advertising by the Opéra.

Among the reviews of other critics, the pronouncements of Willy (or rather the team of hacks he hired to do much of his reviewing for him) were usually supportive and often entertaining. For those who criticized Taffanel for staidness of interpretation, Willy had an anecdote of an incandescent performance of Beethoven's Second Symphony at the Société des concerts. Hermann Levi was in the audience, and he emerged from a box, "stunned by such speed . . . and meticulously beat the tempo in the vain hope of making Taffanel, who had got the bit between his teeth, slow down a bit. Now look here, Paul, just take it easy!"¹¹

In the pro-Taffanel camp, the composer and critic Paul Dukas admired his "artistic sensibility . . . and his skill."¹² Saint-Saëns, too, who was notoriously difficult to please regarding conductors and at times had his differences of opinion with Taffanel, was also ready to congratulate him. "The orchestra was perfect, and more than perfect," he wrote after the premiere of *Frédégonde* at the Opéra, "a phalanx of heros conducted by Caesar!" And when he missed a performance of his First Piano Concerto at the Société des concerts, he remarked: "it seems the concerto was well received . . . how I would have liked to hear it, with the myriad details of the 1st movement brought out by you as only you know how."¹³ Another colleague, the pianist Francis Planté, was impressed by the "poetry" of Taffanel's "magic baton" in a concert with the soloist Alfred Cortot.¹⁴

When the Berlin Philharmonic Orchestra and Nikisch visited Paris in May 1897, *Le Monde musical* bullishly declared that Paris orchestras had nothing to fear from any comparison, and that if Nikisch could have heard the recent performance of Beethoven's Fifth Symphony at the Société des concerts, "he would have had to salute Monsieur Paul Taffanel as a maestro and acknowledge the considerable superiority of the Société des concerts."¹⁵ In the same journal, Arthur Dandelot, historian of the Society, appended a plea for proper recognition of Taffanel's worth to his glowing review of Bach's B minor

Mass in 1899: "Finally a word for the master of ceremonies Monsieur Taffanel, who achieved the sort of results that should silence any biased critics, surely such a magisterial account of the B Minor Mass confirmed him as a first-class conductor?"[16]

Wagner at the Opéra

Whatever the reviews, Taffanel himself seems to have viewed the situation with equanimity—at least when he wrote to Joachim Andersen in May 1895:

> Since we met, my musical career has changed greatly; I have all but abandoned my flute for the conductor's baton.

> By a combination of circumstances, which I think has few parallels, I have in the course of five years taken on one of the most desirable conducting positions in Paris—I who had never picked up a baton in my life. Today I am successor to the legacy of the great Habeneck at the Société des concerts du Conservatoire and at the Opéra, a heavy legacy to shoulder and one which I would not dare to hold on to if I did not feel myself supported favorably by the Parisian audience which I am proud to have been able to win over . . .

> I leave you now to go and conduct one of the final rehearsals for "Tannhäuser." We are staging the work at the moment and in 8 days time we will give the *4th* performance. 34 years have gone by since the first 3! It will be quite an event for Paris![17]

This time, *Tannhäuser* was acclaimed by audiences and critics alike, although the latter were divided on the merits of the actual performance.[18] Eugène d'Harcourt, the aristocratic composer and conductor who was a member of the same Jockey Club that had booed *Tannhäuser* off the stage in 1861, went as far as publishing a book detailing forty shortcomings of the performance. It was clearly directed at Taffanel but carefully did not name him, except to note that "courtesy of Taffanel's school of playing" the piccolo should have been more prominent at a certain point in act 1.[19] Incidentally, Taffanel had reorganized the seating of the orchestra for *Tannhäuser*, grouping the strings around him and raising the brass and wind for greater clarity.[20] Several reviews picked up on Taffanel's verve when conducting the Overture to *Tannhäuser*—he received an ovation after it on the first night—so when, a few months later, some masonry was dislodged from the roof of the Opéra, a cartoon appeared of Taffanel in the Opéra pit turning to the orchestra and saying: "Gentlemen, let's launch into the Overture . . . but not too loudly. It's probably the Wagner vibrations which made stones from the Opéra fall into the street" (see fig. 17).[21]

During his tenure at the Opéra, Taffanel assumed prime responsibility for Wagner and other new productions, while Madier de Montjau looked after general repertory operas and Edouard Mangin conducted the ballets. In 1896 de Montjau was succeeded by Paul Vidal, who went on eventually to succeed Taffanel. Mangin then moved up to second conductor, and Henri Busser became the new number three.[22] The precise chronology is uncertain, as no official documents of retirement for Taffanel have been found, and he never made an entry in his *Notes biographiques*, beyond details of the operas he conducted up to 1905. However, he is not mentioned in reviews of the Opéra after the end of that year, and Busser, who conducted for the first time in December 1905 (the premiere of his own ballet *La Ronde des saisons*), referred then to Taffanel's "imminent retirement." By that time, Taffanel had already been retired from the Société des concerts for four years, but his withdrawal from the Opéra was probably a more gradual process and Inghelbrecht maintained that he still had influence there right up to his death.[23]

The new production of *Tannhäuser* was followed by the Opéra premieres of Wagner's *Die Meistersinger* (1897), *Siegfried* (1901), and *Tristan und Isolde* (1904).[24] *Die Meistersinger* in particular seems to have been close to Taffanel's heart. Back in 1892, after seeing it at Bayreuth, he had recommended it to the director, Gailhard, and the following year in Munich he had been even more delighted by it, conducted by Felix Mottl (see chapter 9). There were reservations about the German cast, but:

> Listening to this masterpiece, I substituted good French singers, good musicians, and I could see, back home, a production of this finely etched, fantastic marvel. I am sure that the work would become popular, and increasingly so, even though it is reputedly so fundamentally German. But the music must be married to absolute refinement of language. It is indeed a musical comedy. And as not a word must be lost, it must not sound like gibberish. The overture sets the tone, in a manner more resolute than weighty, as the score indicates. I very much like that pace . . . I thought the scene about poetic style was delightful, whereas I used to find it childish. From start to finish I was much more won over by this work than I had been last year in Bayreuth.[25]

During his meticulous preparation of *Die Meistersinger*, Taffanel made copious notes and corresponded with, among others, Alfred Ernst, who was preparing the French translation, and the pianist Edouard Risler, who was then working as a *répétiteur* at Bayreuth. Taffanel had known Risler since inviting him to deputize for Diémer at the Société des instruments à vent in 1890, the year after Risler had graduated from Diémer's class at the Conservatoire. Their correspondence dissects Bayreuth traditions and performance practice, and Taffanel invited Risler to return to the Opéra as a *répétiteur* for the production.

With such care and attention it was no surprise that the whole enterprise was a great success.[26]

The memory of *Die Meistersinger* was still strong in the 1920s, at least for the composer and by then Opéra conductor Gabriel Grovlez:

> The good old snobs are always ready to tell us about brilliant performances abroad! Nothing is any good unless it happens in Bayreuth, Munich, or Dresden, and nowadays performances in Vienna are the ultimate . . . Let those who were there recall the musical splendour of the premiere of *Die Meistersinger* at the Paris Opéra, conducted by Taffanel![27]

Verdi at the Opéra

The other international highlight of Taffanel's reign at the Opéra was the long-awaited French premiere of Verdi's *Otello* on 12 October 1894.[28] Ever since the scandal that had surrounded the revival of *The Sicilian Vespers* at the Opéra in 1863, and resulted in the dismissal of the conductor Pierre Dietsch, Verdi's dealings with the "grande boutique," as he called it, had been intermittently stormy. His attitude is summed up in a letter to his friend Count Arrivabene in 1876: "At the Opéra, the productions are splendid, and their costumes, their good taste, are superior to all other theatres. But the musical side is awful, the singers are always the most mediocre . . . the orchestra and chorus are lazy and lacking in discipline."[29] Verdi therefore made little attempt to secure a French production of *Otello* after the premiere at La Scala in 1887.

But Pedro Gailhard was persistent, so negotiations dragged on for years until Verdi finally agreed. Taffanel assumed responsibility for the musical side of the production, and he took the score of *Otello* away with him on holiday to study it during the summer of 1894 (see fig. 18). Before beginning rehearsals in September, he decided to write to Verdi with various queries: "I have found quite a number of discrepancies between the score and the parts—playing directions omitted or positioned differently. In the main I have had to use my own judgement, but there are several places where I have not dared."

It was a difficult letter to write. After covering six sheets of paper with rough notes, Taffanel settled on the idea of sending Verdi a chart listing the alternative versions in the score and the orchestral parts and asking him to delete the wrong ones. Verdi did as requested and also expanded on several points in a covering letter on 6 September:

> For the rest, my dear Monsieur Taffanel, if there are any other points to note, a few minutes together should suffice for us to sort things

out. You are too intelligent, and too good a musician, for us to need more than a few minutes. Thank you for your charming letter.

On his arrival in Paris, accompanied by his librettist, Arrigo Boito, Verdi supervised the final rehearsals, and the gala premiere of *Otello* was a triumph. It was also a glittering social occasion. During the first intermission, Verdi was invited to President Casimir Périer's box and decorated with the Grand Cross of the Légion d'honneur, and he returned to Italy reasonably satisfied. True there had been the usual compromise over providing a ballet—an absolute requirement for Paris audiences—but the critics were unanimous in their praise of the rest of the score and the performance.[30]

The whole experience forged a particular link between Taffanel and Boito. In November 1897 Boito returned to Paris for the premiere of *Die Meistersinger* and afterwards spoke to Taffanel about some choral works he had been urging Verdi to complete: the *Pezzi sacri*. Taffanel suggested that they might be premiered at the Société des concerts during the coming season, but the project had to be shelved almost immediately when news came of the death of Verdi's wife, Giuseppina. Boito returned to Italy at once, and the subject was not reopened until he wrote to Taffanel on 4 January 1898, once again urging him to approach Verdi about the pieces:

I am sure such a distraction would be of inestimable benefit to him. As an opportunity above all for mental effort, it would tear him away from his sad thoughts . . . The four compositions are amongst the most beautiful of the Maestro's works. They are each enlivened by the flame of pure inspiration, and by a truly wonderful power of expression. Two especially (the most extensive) the Te Deum and the Stabat, for choir and orchestra cannot fail to make an exceptional impression, comparable to the success of the Requiem and more . . . The best time for the performance would be at the beginning of April during Holy Week . . . Drop Verdi a line then immediately and I'm sure the deal will be settled.

Taffanel explained to Verdi that the Société des concerts had been obliged to move for one season to the Opéra because the concert hall of the Conservatoire had been declared unsafe and was undergoing structural repair. The acoustics were not as good at the Opéra, but a much larger audience could be accommodated to appreciate Verdi's "latest masterpiece." Thinking that Taffanel meant he wanted to perform only one of the pieces, Verdi politely declined, but once that misunderstanding was cleared up, he agreed to the *Pezzi sacri* being premiered on Maundy Thursday and Good Friday, 7 and 8 April 1898, adding that he would hope to come to Paris himself toward the end of March.

Then suddenly Verdi had second thoughts. He decided that the *Ave Maria*, composed as an exercise on an "enigmatic scale," did not fit with the other pieces and spoiled the balance of the program. He decreed that it must be omitted. He further insisted, via Boito, that the *Laudi alla Vergine Maria* (the third of the four pieces) must be sung by four solo female voices. These changes tightened the dramatic impact of the work considerably, leaving the *Stabat Mater* and *Te Deum* as two colossal pillars of powerful choral and orchestral sound to support the central arch of the delicately reflective solo *Laudi*. The *Ave Maria* may be a beautiful solution to an academic problem, but arguably it detracts from the impact of the stark opening and raw power of the *Stabat Mater*.

The arrangements for the premiere began to take shape. The orchestra would number seventy and the chorus one hundred. Tito Ricordi visited Paris several times to meet with Taffanel, and on 8 March he reported back Verdi's latest demands: "He is absolutely convinced that the present layout of choir and orchestra is defective and won't help the performance of his works one bit." Verdi was concerned about the distinctive Conservatoire layout, which had the orchestra at the back of the stage with the choir seated in front in two blocks, turned inwards to face the conductor, who stood in the middle. The choir therefore sang across the stage toward each other rather than out to the audience.

Verdi's solution, which he sent as a sketch plan with Ricordi's letter, was still to divide the choir in two, on either side of the stage, but turn them toward the audience and arrange them standing in successive rows of sopranos, altos, tenors, and basses, right to the back of the stage. In between these two choir blocks, but now at the very front, stood the conductor, facing the four soloists, then the orchestra, with a careful layout of instruments extending from violins and high woodwinds at the front to low brass, double basses, and percussion at the back. Verdi therefore created three columns of sound—from left to right, choir, soloists with orchestra, and choir: a stereophonic effect. It would be fascinating to see and hear a modern performance that reproduced this layout to judge its impact on these pieces.

Taffanel telegrammed his agreement on 11 March, and next the names of the soloists were finalized: four stars of the Opéra—Marie Héglon, Aïno Akté, Louise Grandjean, and Marie Delna. Then on 27 March Boito wrote regretfully to Taffanel that Verdi had been advised by his doctors not to come to Paris, and that he himself would come instead for the final preparations. A letter from Verdi followed a day later, and via Boito he also sent a large signed portrait of himself on which he had meant to inscribe the words "to my old friend Paul Taffanel," but having confused two French adjectives (*ancien* and *vieux*) he actually wrote, "to my former friend Paul Taffanel"! Fortunately, that was not an omen of disaster, and the final rehearsals, with Verdi in constant

touch via letters to Boito, went smoothly, as did the two premiere performances. Boito was pleased, and Verdi in a final letter on 1 June was thankful: "I
know that if this music has had some little success I owe it to the masterly performance of the Société. My profound thanks to you, the gallant conductor of
all these excellent performers."

Paradoxically, the Parisian audience, so used to musical pomp and gran-
deur, most appreciated the *Laudi* for four unaccompanied voices, and it was
encored, although the critics bemoaned the cold vastness of the Opéra as a
venue for such delicate music.[31] But for Verdi it was a final reconciliation with
Paris: he had subdued the "grande boutique."

New Productions at the Opéra

Die Meistersinger and *Otello* may have been the most significant Paris Opéra
premieres during Taffanel's time, but there was a succession of other important
new productions and revivals for him to prepare and conduct every year from
1894 to 1905, apart from 1902:[32]

Date	Composer	Work	Description
16.03.94	Massenet	*Thaïs*	premiere
12.10.94	Verdi	*Otello*	premiere
05.02.95	Holmès	*La Montagne noir*	premiere
13.05.95	Wagner	*Tannhäuser*	new production
18.12.95	Guiraud/Saint-Saëns	*Frédégonde*	premiere
03.02.96	Donizetti	*La Favorite*	revival
24.04.96	Duvernoy	*Hellé*	premiere
19.02.97	Bruneau	*Messidor*	premiere
07.06.97	Meyerbeer	*Les Huguenots*	revival
05.11.97	Wagner	*Die Meistersinger*	premiere
09.05.98	Meyerbeer	*Le Prophète*	revival
08.06.98	Rousseau	*La Cloche du Rhin*	premiere
23.12.98	Vidal	*La Burgonde*	premiere
16.04.99	Chabrier	*Briséïs* (Act 1)	premiere
20.09.99	Reyer	*Salammbô*	revival
15.11.99	Berlioz	*La Prise de Troie*	premiere
15.02.01	Leroux	*Astarté*	premiere
23.10.01	Saint-Saëns	*Les Barbares*	premiere

31.12.01	Wagner	*Siegfried*	premiere
06.03.03	Reyer	*La Statue*	premiere
18.05.03	Saint-Saëns	*Henry VIII*	revival
17.04.04	Erlanger	*Le Fils de l'étoile*	premiere
31.05.04	Verdi	*Il Trovatore*	new production
11.12.04	Wagner	*Tristan und Isolde*	premiere
12.04.05	Gluck	*Armide*	new production
27.10.05	Weber	*Der Freischütz*	new production

Of the new French operas, only Massenet's *Thaïs* found a continuing place in the repertoire. After the premiere a grateful Massenet wrote to Taffanel: "What a joy it has been for me to follow your work, and see how your great talent and musical good sense so quickly brought things to life and clarity; once again I felt more than ever your strong and devoted friendship."[33]

New Music at the Conservatoire

Ten days before Taffanel's first concert conducting the Société des concerts, the composer Emmanuel Chabrier wrote thanking Hugues Imbert for having "sounded out" Taffanel. "He is someone to cultivate, for here he is, a great man, and if you meet him again, don't forget to tell him that I have plenty of talent, that will make a good impression."[34] Music by living French composers had been infrequent at the Société des concerts and Chabrier had only ever had a brief extract from his opera *Gwendoline* performed there, so he probably did not hold out much hope. He was rewarded that first season, however, at only the third concert in January 1893, with the first public performance of his choral ode *A la musique*.

The development of Taffanel's thinking about the Société des concerts and its repertoire is fascinating to follow in the reports for the annual general meetings he wrote during his years as secretary to the Society before he became its conductor. In 1881 he was content to say: "Our Society . . . has continued to interpret, as it should, the classical masterpieces which have established its reputation. In addition it has allowed into its repertoire, but prudently and carefully, some modern French and foreign works." By 1890 the Society's terms of reference had taken on an added dimension for him: "The Society's true role, in the current climate of musical struggle, is to reveal works to the public that it alone can tackle and perform, thanks to the exceptional means at its disposal. We have the possibility and it is in effect our duty." The following year, his final one as secretary, he was recommending "two watchwords that should be constantly in our minds: discipline and artistic integrity." The Society should "move on and grow."[35] It was inevitable, therefore (as noted in chapter 9), that he was going to direct the Society forward.

Taffanel's predecessor, Jules Garcin, had made a move against the deeply conservative audience of the Société des concerts when he programmed music by Saint-Saëns, Gounod, Lalo, Massenet, Franck, and a few of the younger generation of French composers, and it was a lead that Taffanel was happy to follow, particularly when it came to Saint-Saëns. During Taffanel's nine seasons, he conducted sixteen different works by Saint-Saëns, several of them more than once:[36]

Work	Date(s) of Performance			
Le Rouet d'Omphale	27.11.92	22.03.96	17.04.98	17.12.99
La Lyre et la harpe	12.02.93	08.12.95	30.01.98	
Ave Verum	19.03.93	28.01.94		
Violin Concerto no. 3	31.03.93	22.12.95	22.01.99	
Symphony no. 3	09.04.93	16.04.97	21.04.01	
Piano Concerto no. 3	23.03.94			
Danse macabre	22.04.94	27.11.98		
Piano Concerto no. 4	16.12.94			
Le Déluge	10.02.95			
Symphony no. 2	17.03.95			
Piano Concerto no. 5	29.11.96			
Nuit persane	03.01.97	17.03.01		
Requiem	31.03.99			
Marche héroïque	11.03.00			
Piano Concerto no. 1	23.12.00			
Violin Concerto no. 1	05.04.01			

Taffanel therefore played a key role in keeping Saint-Saëns's music regularly performed at a time when it might otherwise have been overshadowed. He also allied himself with the wider cause of contemporary music, both French and foreign: "he was quite clearly focused on the present, and took a certain pleasure in satisfying the least reactionary taste of his audience."[37] He championed the symphonies and Requiem of Brahms, for example, when French audiences still found his music difficult and severe and only a minority of French musicians thought it had any worth. Alongside the core repertoire of composers like Haydn, Mozart, Beethoven, Weber, Schumann, and Mendelssohn (and excluding the works of Saint-Saëns listed separately above), each season therefore had its modern novelties (see list below).[38]

Season	Composer	Work
1892–93	Chabrier	*A la musique*
	Wagner	*Tannhäuser,* Act 3
	Thomas	Chorus of Nymphs from *Psyché*
1893–94	Verdi	*Pater noster*
	Wagner	Prelude to *Tristan*
	Grieg	Piano Concerto
	Borodin	Extracts from *Prince Igor*
	Paladilhe	Extracts from *Les Saintes-Marie de la mer*
	Brahms	*Gesang der Parzen*
1894–95	Brahms	Symphony no. 3
	Wagner	Overture and Chorus from *Der fliegende Holländer*
	Dubois	*Non fecit taliter*
	Bernard	Violin Concerto
	Lenepveu	Extracts from *Requiem*
1895–96	Brahms	Symphony no. 2
	Joncières	*La Mer*
	Indy	*Symphonie cévenole*
	Bourgault-Ducoudray	Extracts from *Stabat Mater*
1896–97	Dubois	Extract from *Le Paradis perdu*
	Rousseau	*Libera me Domine*
1897–98	Dubois	Piano Concerto no. 2
	Massenet	*Scènes alsaciennes*
	Verdi	*Pezzi sacri*
1898–99	Holmès	*Hymne à Apollon*
	Fauré	*La Naissance de Vénus*
	Dubois	*Ave Maria*
	Brahms	Symphony no. 4
	Massenet	Extract from *La Vièrge*
1899–	Dubois	*Le Baptême de Clovis*
1900	Brahms	Symphony no. 1
	Ropartz	*Psaume 136*
	Lefèbvre	Extracts from *Judith*
	Brahms	*Requiem*
1900–01	Charpentier	*Impressions d'Italie*
	Pierné	*L'An mil*
	Dubois	Violin Concerto

Vidal	*Ecce sacerdos magnus*
Massenet	*Alleluia*
Fauré	*Requiem*

Taffanel also made time for other new works to be tried out in rehearsal, even if not all of them were eventually performed in concert. In 1894, for example, Imbert once again acted as a go-between, this time on behalf of the young composer Paul Lacombe. Taffanel replied: "Believe me, I have not forgotten Monsieur Paul Lacombe's Symphony. The coming season will, I hope, be less encumbered with new works than the last and I really think I will be able to keep an old promise . . . the Symphony is certainly very interesting and I would be very pleased to hear it played."[39]

Meanwhile, Taffanel kept the work of recent generations of French composers alive, notably Bizet, Lalo, Gounod, Franck, and Berlioz, who was still considered a home-grown, difficult composer. However, only a small minority of the subscription audience lived in the present, musically speaking, or even in the near past, and Taffanel's way (as it had been during his flute-playing career) was one of evolution rather than revolution, so a carefully chosen mixture of the new along with the old became a characteristic of his program building, to satisfy his patrons, his committee, and himself. But even when keeping the music of the old masters regularly on the programs, there could still be some revelations. J. S. Bach's B minor Mass had been performed just once before, in 1891 (postponed from 1890, when it proved too challenging to prepare in time). In his secretary's report that year he had praised its "emotional intensity and sublimity," and now when Taffanel conducted it himself in January 1895, Paul Dukas hailed the "intense life" that he brought to the work.[40]

Taffanel's detailed preparation of contemporary scores was also much appreciated by their composers. Vincent d'Indy wrote of the "perfect" performance of his *Symphonie cévenole* in 1896: "it was a real pleasure to hear all the effects which I have dreamed about, without ever having achieved them, rendered in such a way."[41] Another grateful friend was Raoul Pugno, one of a distinguished line of soloists, including Eugène Ysaye and Pablo de Sarasate, who played under Taffanel's baton. Pugno, previously an organist and teacher, made his debut as a pianist at the Société des concerts in December 1893 and became a celebrity overnight. "My dear Paul," he wrote in his New Year's greetings some years later, "my loyal gratitude to the *godfather* who brought me good fortune—for my success dates from that concert at the Conservatoire . . . and I shall never forget it."[42] Taffanel sketched a few words of reply on a scrap of paper he kept with the letter:

> Your little note really touched me! My only merit was *to believe in you* as the great artist that you were all the time that your modesty persisted in hiding it . . . If the world has its dark side, sometimes it has

glimmers of Truth, and it did a good thing on the day that it recognized and celebrated you.

Pugno kept in contact from various locations on his concert tours, and in his 1900 New Year's greetings reported from Russia that Taffanel was still remembered there: "At Petersburg—I talked at length about you."[43]

Competitions and the Classe d'orchestre

From time to time the Société des concerts and Opéra orchestras were called upon for official concerts, to greet a visiting head of state, or accompany some formal occasion or award at the Institut de France. From 1893 onward Taffanel conducted these concerts, including the ones for the *concours Rossini*, and the *envois de Rome*—the works-in-progress sent back by winners of the Prix de Rome composition prize during their stay in the Villa Medici. Henri Busser recalled that in 1893, before he set off for Rome, his prize-winning cantata *Antigone* was one of the works that "enjoyed a perfect performance."[44] Taffanel was also a member of various juries for new music prizes, for example, the Ville de Paris competition in 1892–93, one at Rennes in 1897, and one sponsored by the journal *Musica* in 1903. A photograph published in *Musica* shows the deliberations of the jury for the piano trio prize. Taffanel is standing next to Debussy, looking at the score on the piano during a performance of one of the trios. On his left, looking inscrutable, is Pierre Lalo.[45]

In January 1897 Taffanel took on a new conducting responsibility, one that became particularly dear to his heart. It was at the instigation of Théodore Dubois, who had succeeded Ambroise Thomas as director of the Conservatoire the previous year. Dubois wanted to revive the practice of holding *exercices d'élèves*—student concerts—open to the public as a showcase for the Conservatoire, and he created a professorship for Taffanel to direct an orchestra class. The aim was to give the instrumental students experience of playing in an orchestra and a chance to learn the repertoire. The concerts began in May that year and continued annually until Taffanel was forced by ill health to retire after the performance in May 1908.

Percussion players for the orchestra class were often recruited from among the composition students, and they included Edmond Maurat, later director of the Conservatoire at Saint-Etienne:

> Taffanel was a man liked by everyone: natural, sensitive, affable, and lit by the flame of a born musician. The student orchestra was enthusiastic and compliant; one morning we were working at the overture to *Manfred*, exulting in a Schumann-like fervor, with the music bursting forth. When we got to the great viola and cello passage, which,

like a stream of lava, plumbs the depths of the orchestral abyss before rising again and bursting forth in a sky of fire, the air literally trembled in the empty but overheated hall. With a sharp click of his baton Taffanel stopped the orchestra: "My friends, your youthfulness is magnificent, I am overwhelmed, but an artist must know how to master himself, or else, without self control, he cannot be true to himself . . . let us continue."

At the end, I accompanied him out to the boulevard Montmartre. He told me that he had just experienced one of the most wonderful moments of his career. When I mentioned the Opéra, the Société des concerts, he continued in a disenchanted tone of voice: "Yes . . . Yes! but that is something else . . . it is not overwhelming." I thought of that phrase of Schumann's: "In art nothing great is made without enthusiasm."[46]

1900 Paris Exhibition

Enthusiasm, combined with sheer hard work, was something Taffanel needed endless supplies of as the 1900 *Exposition universelle* approached. He was chosen by the minister for the arts to be responsible for a series of official concerts dedicated to French orchestral and choral music. The inaugural concert opened the Exhibition on Saturday 14 April and was followed by ten others, on Thursday afternoons at fortnightly intervals from the end of May to the beginning of October. Massenet, Saint-Saëns, and Dubois shared the honors at the inaugural concert, and thereafter a wide variety of old and new French music was performed, sixty works in all:[47]

Composer	Work
Auber	Overture *Lestocq*
Berlioz	*Roméo et Juliette*
Bizet	*L'Arlésienne* Suite no. 1
Boieldieu	Overture *La Fête du village voisin*
Bourgault-Ducoudray	Extract from *Thamara*
Bruneau	Extract from *Messidor*
Chabrier	*España*
Charpentier	*Impressions d'Italie*
Chausson	*Viviane*
Cherubini	*Sanctus* and *Agnus Dei* from *Requiem*

Coquard	Overture *Esther*
David	Extracts from *Herculanum*
Debussy	*La Damoiselle élue*
Delibes	Extracts from *Coppélia*
Dubois	*Le Baptême de Clovis*
Dukas	*L'Apprenti sorcier*
Duparc	*Invitation au voyage* and *Phidylé*
Duvernoy	*La Tempête*
Erlanger	*Kermaria*
Fauré	*Requiem*
Franck	Extract from *Les Béatitudes*
Gigout	*Méditation*
Gluck	Extract from *Alceste*
Godard	Extract from *Le Tasse*
Gounod	Extract from *Ulysse*
Grétry	Extract from *Silvain*
Guilmant	Symphony with organ
Guiraud	*Carnaval*
Hérold	Overture *Le Pré aux clercs*
Hillemacher	Suite from *Claudie*
Holmès	*Irlande*
Hüe	*La Belle au bois dormant*
Indy	Extract from *Le Chant de la cloche*
Jannequin	*Le Chant des oiseaux*
Joncières	Overture *Dimitri*
Lalo	*Symphonie espagnole*
Lambert	*Tanger, le soir*
Lefèbvre	*La Messe du fantôme*
Lenepveu	Extracts from *Jeanne d'Arc*
Leroux	*Vénus et Adonis*
Lully	Extracts from *Alceste*
Maréchal	*Antar*
Marty	Extract from *Merlin enchanté*
Massenet	*Marche solennelle*

Méhul	Extract from *Stratonice*
Messager	Suite from *Les Deux pigeons*
Paladilhe	Extract from *Les Saintes-Maries de la mer*
Pierné	*L'An mil*
Puget	Prelude to *Beaucoup de bruit pour rien*
Pugno	*Concertstück*
Rameau	Extracts from *Quam dilecta*
Reyer	Extracts from *Erostrate*
Ropartz	Finale of *Symphonie sur un choral breton*
Rousseau	Extracts from *Mérowig*
Saint-Saëns	*Le Feu céleste*
Spontini	Extract from *La Vestale*
Thomas	Prologue to *Françoise de Rimini*
Vidal	Ballet extracts from *La Burgonde*
Widor	Symphony no. 3
Wormser	*Les Misérables*

An orchestra and chorus of 250 musicians were assembled for each concert in the vast Salle des fêtes of the Palais de l'électricité at the Trocadéro. The nucleus was drawn from the Société des concerts, augmented by players and singers from the Opéra and elsewhere, and no doubt it was with these forces in mind that the flute maker Djalma Julliot presented Taffanel with an extra-large, patented baton! The arts minister convened a music committee to assist in deciding policy and voting on repertoire, but Taffanel was in overall charge of every aspect of these concerts, artistic and administrative. The whole enterprise, "this exhibition of French music from its origins to modern times," was later summed up by Alfred Bruneau in a published report to the minister praising Taffanel and his chorus master Samuel Rousseau, who had "dedicated themselves heart and soul," and noting the "huge audiences extremely supportive of our musicians" who had guaranteed the success of the whole venture.[48]

For Taffanel, there were various official rewards for all this hard work. He was already a Chevalier of the Order of the Crown of Italy (awarded in 1894 when he conducted *Otello*), and he held the Order of St. Anne of Russia, third class (awarded in 1897). Now he became an Officier of the Persian Order of the Lion and the Sun (he was decorated by the Shah of Persia during a performance of Gounod's *Faust* at the Opéra), and he received the Swedish Order of the Polar Star and membership in the Swedish Royal Academy following the Swedish Concert at the Exhibition. Finally, on 14 December 1900, after the

Exhibition was over, he was promoted to the rank of Officier of the Légion d'honneur, and the following day the Société des concerts presented him with a bronze medal inscribed simply *La Musique*.[49]

But the reward that meant most to Taffanel was personal: the dedication of Saint-Saëns's cantata *Le Feu céleste*—celestial fire—composed in praise of the new "enchantress electricity" and in honor of the Palais de l'électricité, which was one of the great attractions of the Exhibition. In fact this work for narrator, soprano solo, chorus, and orchestra was little more than a routine *pièce d'occasion*, but it fulfilled a particular dream for Taffanel: "so often I have envied those whose names you placed beside your own—and this time you thought of me."[50]

Among the many letters of congratulation for the Exhibition concerts and for his elevation to Officier of the Légion d'honneur, one from the composer and Conservatoire history professor Louis Bourgault-Ducoudray was particularly apposite. It praised Taffanel's "dedication to the French School, which you proved heroically this summer."[51] Taffanel remained receptive to new directions in French music to the end of his life (unlike the reactionary Saint-Saëns), and having conducted Debussy's *La Damoiselle élue* at the seventh official concert of the Exhibition, he was a keen member of the audience in 1902 at one of the early performancess of *Pelléas et Mélisande*. Henri Busser, who was conducting that night, found Taffanel "completely carried away" by the work, and Taffanel himself enthused about "that meticulous score . . . I found it delightful from beginning to end . . . Debussy is a most charming musician and he will make a name for himself!"[52]

The preparations for *La Damoiselle élue* at the seventh official concert on 23 August 1900 had been complicated by the vexed question of singers. Debussy had had no trouble in choosing Blanche Marot as the "blessed damozel" of Dante Gabriel Rossetti's poem—he had recently accompanied her in the premiere of his *Chansons de Bilitis* at the Société nationale—but he turned to Taffanel for help with the other solo part of the *récitante*:

> I was expecting to find both of the singers that are needed for the performance of the *Damoiselle élue* and here I am with only the damoiselle? . . . therefore you must please get me *a narrator*. That does not require an enormous voice, charm and goodwill are all I need! Thank you in advance for all you are doing for me.[53]

Various singers were considered by Taffanel and Debussy, and a solution, if not an ideal one, was found in Laure Beauvais from the Opéra. Debussy was pragmatic:

> It should undoubtedly be Mademoiselle Beauvais who will sing the narrator—she has a rather big voice, but that will impose itself with

authority, and she also has nothing "Pre-Raphaelite" about her. One cannot have everything . . . With grateful thanks . . .[54]

La Damoiselle élue was on the program sandwiched somewhat unpromisingly between what *Le Figaro* called music by "one of the most austere of our organists" (the *Méditation* for violin and orchestra by Eugène Gigout) and by "one of the most exuberant of our female composers" (*Irlande*, a symphonic poem by Augusta Holmès).[55] *Le Monde musical* also revealed that there had been lively debate by the program committee about whether the music of this "young prix de Rome" should be included at all.[56] In any event, the audience was completely won over by this seductive score. Debussy was delighted, and the critics were complimentary—even Pierre Lalo![57]

Whether Debussy's and Taffanel's paths crossed again after the *Musica* competition is not recorded, but Debussy's reviews during his time as a music critic include a mention of the conductor that same year, 1903. Maybe he was remembering Taffanel's efforts to make the best of things, and overcome the cavernous Trocadéro acoustic at the Exhibition, when he wryly commented at the premiere of Reyer's *La Statue* at the Opéra: "The orchestra, which Monsieur Taffanel's conducting tried hard to drag out of the doldrums, could have been wonderful."[58]

Retirement from the Société des concerts

All this work was taking its toll on Taffanel's health. In April 1898 he had recorded in his *Notes biographiques* a first attack of *gravelle*—gallstones—and he had been seriously ill with influenza for six weeks from the middle of January 1900, before his grueling schedule at the Paris Exhibition. In February 1901 he requested leave of absence for two concerts of the Société des concerts owing to continuing pressure of work at the Opéra.[59] Then, on 27 April, just as he was about to conduct at the Opéra, he was crippled by another bout of illness—this time a renal attack. He handed the baton to Paul Vidal, but the next day he somehow managed to conduct Beethoven's *Missa Solemnis* and Saint-Saëns's Third Symphony at the Société des concerts. "He had made a superhuman effort . . . and Taffanel who normally shied modestly away from applause, turned spontaneously toward the audience and waved. It was, alas, his goodbye that he was directing at his faithful regulars."[60]

Taffanel submitted an emotional letter of resignation to the Committee of the Société des concerts the following morning, 29 April:

> In writing you this letter, I am undertaking the hardest act of my artistic career! As my health now requires great care and attention, I am regretfully obliged to leave our dear Society! You understand the full extent of the sacrifice my loved ones are imposing upon me, you

who know what place our work has held in my life, work that has been my chief aim for 36 years. The Société des concerts has filled me with joy, and the support it has given me so many times has been the crowning point of my career: I will always feel profound gratitude and fraternal affection until my last breath.[61]

His resignation was considered at a meeting of the committee on 7 May, and a delegation immediately visited Taffanel to try and persuade him to reconsider. But he was adamant, and at a further meeting a week later the resignation had to be accepted. At the annual general meeting on 29 May, Théodore Dubois, president of the Société des concerts, gave a speech in appreciation of Taffanel, who was immediately elected Honorary Life President.[62] All that remained was for Taffanel to encourage Philippe Gaubert to follow in his footsteps when the time came (see chapter 9), and on 29 November 1904 Gaubert was elected second conductor. The succession was guaranteed, in conducting as in flute playing.

However, there was an unpleasant footnote to Taffanel's tenure at the Société des concerts. When Taffanel died in 1908, the secretary, Théodore Heymann, sent condolences and a wreath, but no representative of the Society to the funeral. Then at the annual general meeting the following May he made minimal reference to Taffanel in his report. When challenged on this the following year, 1910, Heymann launched an open attack on Taffanel, accusing him of embezzling public finds set aside for the Society's remuneration and expenses for providing music at the funeral of President Carnot in 1894. André Messager, the Society's new chief conductor, and Edouard Nadaud, who had been the secretary in 1894, were astounded and demanded proof. None was forthcoming. Finally, after endless discussions in committee and demands for Heymann to appear and explain himself, an extraordinary general meeting was called on 19 November. At it, the government department responsible confirmed that the available money had simply not been used, apart from 426 francs to pay for hire of instruments. Taffanel's name was completely cleared, and Heymann grudgingly had to accept his error. But Heymann refused all calls for his resignation and eventually had to be forcibly voted out of the Society, and his name struck off the register, the affair having developed into a full-blown scandal.[63]

The Art of Conducting

Taffanel's own apologia as a conductor is contained in his only completed piece of writing, *L'Art de diriger*. This extended article appeared in Albert Lavignac's *Encyclopédie de la musique et dictionnaire du Conservatoire*. But Taffanel never saw it published, as the encyclopedia only began to appear in 1913 and then, interrupted by the First World War, was not finished until 1931. Two other projects would have complemented the conducting article but remained incomplete at Taffanel's death. The first was a translation of Ebenezer Prout's book *Instrumentation* (1896).[64] Significantly, Taffanel adds a footnote to chapter 7, paragraph 194. When Prout claims that "the orchestra becomes subordinate" once the voices enter in an opera, Taffanel writes: "The author forgets the Wagnerian orchestra which illuminates the characters' very souls." The second project was an article on the new Decastieu system of metronome. Taffanel planned it during the last year of his life and gave his notes to Joseph Jemain when he became too ill to continue.[65]

Taffanel collected all his notes and drafts for his conducting article inside a folded wedding invitation for May 1906, so he was obviously working on it during the final years of his life, after he had retired from the Opéra.[66] *L'Art de diriger* is a very personal statement. Conscientious and rigorous, it recognizes both the responsibilities and the glories that the music brings, and rejects any hint of showmanship or of pandering to the audience. Taffanel's philosophy is summed up in one telling phrase that leaps from the page: "Conducting is a small thing, knowing how to rehearse is everything."

The article is in three sections: "General Observations," "The Conductor's Gestures," and "Some Practical Advice." The first section is the most extensive, an exposition of the essential qualities of a good conducter. For Taffanel, it all comes down to "*natural ability* and *practice*." "The musician who posesses this natural ability, a precious and rare gift, will feel an inexpressible joy to find himself at the head of his orchestra." Meanwhile, practice is equally vital, especially in the theater, where so many things can go wrong in performance.

The conductor's gestures should all be analyzed and linked to profound musical understanding. Therefore the conductor should be something of a composer; have knowledge of all the instruments; ideally be a pianist-accompanist, so he can make piano reductions of new scores for his own practice; have an enquiring musical mind and study all periods and styles; be familiar with Italian, English, and German (in addition to French); and also have administrative capabilities.

Profound analysis of the construction and orchestration of a work is the conductor's first and most important responsibility: "He must assimilate it to the point of thinking that he is himself the composer." Tempi need to be considered, following the metronome markings if supplied by the composer, but these should be taken only as a guide, for no absolute tempo exists for any work. Therefore there is no virtue in two identical performances by the same conductor, "because if the conductor is sensitive and dynamic, he will find it impossible to keep rigidly to time." The metronome is actually a mixed blessing, as Beethoven, Berlioz, and Wagner all found. (Taffanel refers several times to Berlioz in the article, including his *L'Art du chef d'orchestre*.)

The moment of truth arrives with the orchestral rehearsals. "If the conductor knows, by his character, by his personality, how to win undisputed authority, the respect of all, his task will be easy." But even then, the results of a first rehearsal of a new work can be near chaos, and this is where the real work begins, a patient disentangling and rebuilding, with the conductor feeling "the delight of a sculptor who makes life itself spring from a base lump of clay." Civility and courtesy are important, but the conductor "must be steadfastly firm and always make people respect his wishes." He must be realistic in his demands, having worked everything out carefully before the rehearsal, and there must be a clear reason for repeating any section, or the musicians will think he is just using them to learn the music himself! In short, "the conductor must possess the qualities of a *leader of men*, always a difficult task, and an even more delicate one where musicians are concerned."

The second section concerns the conductor's gestures, both technical (beating time) and expressive (shaping the musical ideas). Use of the baton is almost always necessary, except with small groups of musicians. With the arm lightly lifted, and economy of gesture from the wrist, the conductor will be able to make himself absolutely clear. The baton should move within the line of vision that links the conductor and his players, for having learned his score by heart, the conductor will be free to have eye contact with the players, to sustain a sort of magnetic field that will allow him to "play" the orchestra. The conductor's left hand is there to underline points of expression, and contain any indiscretion, but it is more effective the less it is used. On no account must it just copy the right hand in beating time. It is also important that the gestures should not provide a distraction, or contradict the spirit of the music. The conductor is the link between the players and the audience, and his gestures should be the interpretation made visible. "The need to establish this correlation is why conductors sometimes overstep the mark, and become lamentably exaggerated, especially nowadays, when conductors set great store by their own importance." All gestures should harmonize with the music, for the maximum effect is obtained with the minimum effort.

Finally Taffanel provides a section of practical advice to aspiring conductors, drawn from his own experience. In a sequence of succinct paragraphs he covers control of ensemble in pizzicato; beating pauses; beating cross rhythms; subdividing the beat; conducting recitatives, particularly in modern operatic music; knowing when *not* to beat time; uniformity versus non-uniformity of bowing (concluding that there are occasions for both); marking breathing in the wind and brass parts, and also in the strings so they will develop a sensitivity to phrase endings; training the winds and brass to breathe earlier before playing and to attack notes absolutely *on* the beat; and marking the parts (particularly in operas) with frequent cue points to obviate confusion and endless counting of bars in rehearsals.

If Taffanel did not always manage to practice what he preached, according to some critics, the evidence of both good sense and imagination in this article is still impressive. Whatever Pierre Lalo may have believed, Taffanel's faults were certainly not those of incompetence. More likely, any dull performances resulted from situations where the work was really still "in progress." Taffanel's was a systematic method of approach that required ample rehearsal time—then, as now, not always possible. His was also an approach that presupposed, and was inspired by, intelligence. No doubt there were times when the musicians just could not rise to the occasion. They might have been goaded into life by a display of histrionics, but this was foreign to Taffanel's temperament. The sheer range and achievement of his conducting career, however, can safely be left to speak for themselves.

CHAPTER II

Teaching the Flute

As for my classes at the Conservatoire,
I will keep those right to the end.
—PAUL TAFFANEL, CONVERSATION
WITH FERNAND BOURGEAT (1908)

While Taffanel was discussing the details of his biography with Hugues Imbert on 3 June 1893, his career was about to take yet another new turn. That same day Henri Altès tendered his formal resignation as professor of flute at the Conservatoire. He was sixty-seven and in rapidly failing health. "I have no strength even to come to the Conservatoire to carry out the examination of my students," he wrote in a personal letter soon after to the director, Ambroise Thomas, and he enclosed a written report and suggested that the *concours* piece for that summer should be Tulou's *Fourth Solo*.[1] No doubt as a compliment to Altès, the set piece was changed to his own *Eighth Solo*. Altès died just over two years later on 24 July 1895 in a Paris nursing home, leaving as next of kin only his younger brother, the conductor Ernest Altès.

October came, and with a new academic year approaching, a replacement flute professor had to be found at the Conservatoire. A sheet of paper preserved in the archives lists the candidates: "Cantié, Hennebains, de Vroye, Donjon, Bertram," with their dates of birth and the year when each one had gained a *premier prix*.[2] This seems to be the only record of its kind for appointments to the flute class. There is no trace of a short list for 1859, 1868, or 1908, maybe because there was usually an obvious successor, irrespective of how many others may have written letters of application to the director. Cantié, for example, had enlisted the support of the composers Gounod and Joncières. In 1893 the obvious successor would have been Taffanel, except that he was by now firmly committed to his two conducting positions. The absence of his name from this list suggests that either he had already been approached and had declined, or that he had not yet been approached but in case he did say no, alternative names were being prepared. But whatever negotiations may have taken place, the outcome was soon clear: the director nominated Taffanel to the arts minister, Raymond Poincaré, who replied on 10 November with a decree naming Taffanel as *professeur de flûte*, with a salary of 1500 francs per annum. This rose eventually to 2400 francs, by increments of 300 francs in 1897, 1900, and 1903.[3] Taffanel's appointment was announced in *Le Ménestrel* in the same issue that carried an obituary notice for Tchaikovsky.[4]

Taffanel's only recorded comment on his appointment was made obliquely two years later to Joachim Andersen, in the course of outlining other developments in his career: "what is more, two years ago I had to accept the position of flute professor at the Conservatoire."[5] But even if there had been some coercion involved, this appointment proved to be one of the great satisfactions of his life: Taffanel was a born teacher.

From Altès to Taffanel

In the final year of Altès's professorship at the Conservatoire there were fourteen flute students in the class: Danis, Leclercq, Deschamps, A. Macquarre, Barrère, Boyrie, Grenier, Pascal, Leducq, Million, Balleron, Hennion, Leduc, and Stenosse. The most significant of these was Georges Barrère, born in 1876, although his reports from Altès in the twice-yearly examinations were not exactly glowing. In 1892: "Has made progress, shows promise," then "Slow progess, intelligent student." In 1893 the comment for both examinations was "Has made some progress." (The first time this was actually written as "ditto" from the previous student and continued to the next!)[6] Barrère later filed his own report, a comparison of Altès with Taffanel:

> Henri Altès was a great teacher but I did not progress as well as I should under his tutorship. I still believe his very systematic teaching gave me no chance to develop [on] my own . . .

> In October 1893, all the flute students of the Conservatory were called to the Director's office and I still remember dear old Ambroise Thomas presenting to us our new master, Paul Taffanel. I always considered that day as the turning point of my life. While I have a reverent memory of Altès's strictness and severe training, I must avow if it were not for all Paul Taffanel did for me, I should not, today, be tooting upon what the wood flute players so irreverently call the "Gas-pipe."[7]

Similar sentiments were expressed by Louis Fleury, born in 1878, who joined the class in 1895:

It is no disrespect to the memory of his predecessor, Altès, a good musician perhaps, but a second-rate artiste, to assert Taffanel's immense superiority and note the change that his arrival brought. Incredible as it might seem, the Bach Sonatas, Mozart Concertos, and in general all that makes up the riches and adornment of the flute's repertoire had never figured in Altès's teaching. The good man had written a three-part method in which he encased his students, like wearing sandwich boards.[8]

The flamboyant Barrère and introspective Fleury both found what they needed in Taffanel's teaching and were two of the most successful graduates from his class. In 1905 Barrère was invited by the conductor Walter Damrosch to New York, where he became a vital influence in teaching the French style to several generations of American players and teachers. His most important student was William Kincaid, who played for many years in the Philadelphia Orchestra and taught at the Curtis Institute. In 1913 Barrère composed a Nocturne for flute and piano that he dedicated "to the memory of my dear teacher Taffanel." And Barrère himself, with his platinum flute, was the inspiration for Edgard Varèse's *Density 21.5* (1936), a seminal work that launched the flute into the world of the twentieth-century avant-garde.[9]

In contrast, Fleury became the scholar of the French School. By all accounts he was never very highly regarded as a player by his contemporaries, but he was a widely read and cultured musician. He made a career mainly as a chamber music player, inheriting the Société moderne des instruments à vent from Barrère in 1905. He also edited many new editions of eighteenth-century flute music, wrote a series of well-researched articles on the flute and its music, and completed the article on the flute that Taffanel had planned for Lavignac's *Encyclopédie*.[10]

Among Fleury's many articles, two particularly stand out: "The Flute and Flutists in the French Art of the 17th and 18th Centuries," which elegantly explores the baroque antecedents of Taffanel's style; and "The Flute and Its Powers of Expression," which is a closely argued statement of the new French flute aesthetic. The flute is "first and foremost an instrument of expression, and it achieves expression by remaining within its peculiar limits." Fleury cites examples of old and modern music (Bach, Blavet, Mozart, Beethoven, Debussy, Lalo, Saint-Saëns) to delineate the essential characteristics of the flute: "Melancholy sweetness . . . pathos . . . wit and gaiety." As he readily acknowledges, these were the qualities that Taffanel brought to the flute and the repertoire that he rediscovered and inspired, in contrast to his predecessors, "those dismal manufacturers of Airs with Variations."[11]

Between them, Barrère and Fleury were responsible for the premieres of two of the most influential works in the flute's orchestral and solo repertoire, both by Debussy. In December 1894 Barrère was the flutist at the Socété nationale for the first performance of *L'Après-midi d'un faune*, and in December 1913 Fleury was the first to play *La Flûte de Pan*, published later as *Syrinx*, at a performance of Gabriel Mourey's play *Psyché*.[12]

Debussy, as a young student in Paris in the 1880s, would very likely have heard Taffanel play. Certainly his approach to writing for the flute, both in these pieces and elsewhere, underlines the suppleness of the French style, and the characteristic use of the low register so often remarked in Taffanel's playing. It is also fascinating that the flute's first note in *L'Après-midi* is the second-octave C-sharp—its open note (no closed keys), with the palest, least clearly focused sound. Did Debussy know that, and consciously exploit it? The French flute is often talked of as an Impressionist instrument, but here in effect is the Symbolist flute, more subtle and mysterious. From this point the flute moved on through the other "isms" of the twentieth century, and none of them found it wanting in aesthetic resonance. It is unlikely, however, given the instrument's earlier nineteenth-century history, that any of this could have been achieved without Paul Taffanel. He provided the aural background of a distinctive style that Debussy and other French composers grew up with.

For Fleury, Debussy represented a link with the flute's distinguished past, a revival of a once broken tradition: "Who can say that the opening phrase of *L'Après-midi d'un faune* is not an echo of a performance of Bach or Gluck?"[13] Did he get that from Taffanel? There is only an oblique indication of what Taffanel may have thought of *L'Après-midi*. His presence at a performance in 1895 that included his friend in Dorus's class, Auguste Cantié, was described by the critic Willy: "To Taffanel's great joy, Cantie's flute poured its gentle melody over an audience 'bathed in harmony.'"[14] Taffanel's contact with Debussy in 1900 and his enthusiasm for *Pelléas* have already been noted (see chapter 10), and although he never lived to hear *Syrinx*, the *Sonate pour flûte, alto et harpe*, and the later works of Ravel or Roussel, they were the true musical realization of his ideals. Meanwhile, the continuing influence of his Conservatoire students would be a force in bringing the French flute school to maturity, until writing for the instrument became the norm rather than the exception, first for composers in France, then throughout Europe and America.

The Conservatoire Flute Class

Taffanel gave his first class on 15 November 1893. Like the other instrumental classes, it lasted two hours and took place three times per week. Twice a year, in January and June, there was an internal examination (until 1906 when it was reduced to once a year), and he chose a test piece for each of his students and reported on their progress. The best students were then allowed to go forward and compete in the annual public *concours* in July. Extracts from Taffanel's reports, and other detailed information on his tenure of the Conservatoire professorship from 1893 to 1908, can be found in appendix 6.

The numbers in the class fluctuated from time to time. In 1894 they declined from fourteen to ten, remained constant at that level until 1901, when they increased to eleven, dropped back to ten in 1904, and finally increased to twelve in 1906. Not all of the students were intending to become professional players, as the Conservatoire still functioned as a training school for military as well as civilian musicians, although the records for this period do not differentiate between the individual students. This explains, however, some of the less than complimentary reports written by Taffanel, as only the civil students had gained their places by competitive audition. It was always a class, therefore, of mixed abilities and ages, and there were intermittent absences for periods of military service—something not even the civilian students could always avoid.

There were two changes of Conservatoire director during Taffanel's time as professor. Théodore Dubois succeeded Ambroise Thomas in 1896, and was himself succeeded by Gabriel Fauré in 1905. There were also various administrative and educational reforms within the Conservatoire. Fauré's reforms placed greater emphasis on ensemble classes in orchestral and chamber music for the instrumental students, and provided more time for this by abolishing the January examinations. There were, however, still January reports from the professors on each student's progress.[15]

Alongside Barrère and Fleury, the most significant graduates of Taffanel's Conservatoire class were Philippe Gaubert, Daniel Maquarre, Gaston Blanquart, Georges Laurent, and Marcel Moyse. In addition, Jean Boulze (who joined the class right at the end of Taffanel's life, in November 1908) became first flute at the Opéra and in the Lamoureux Orchestra; Paul Krauss became professor at the Strasbourg Conservatoire; Gaston Bladet played in the Boston Symphony Orchestra; Urbain Bauduin and René Grisard played in the Concerts Colonne; Henri Bouillard (noted in chapter 8) was professor at the Lille Conservatoire; Georges Delangle played in the Opéra Orchestra; René Bergeon was professor at the Bordeaux Conservatoire; and Fernand Dusausoy was professor at the Roubaix Conservatoire. Four others might well have been destined for prominent careers, but they were killed during the First World War: Antoine Million, Gustave Cardon, Jules Pascal, and Léon Joffroy.[16]

Daniel Maquarre, born in 1881, emigrated to the United States like Barrère, along with his elder brother, André, born in 1875, who was the last graduate from Altès's class in July 1893. Both André and Daniel played in the Boston Symphony Orchestra. Daniel also taught at the New England Conservatory and became solo flute of the Philadelphia Orchestra from 1910 to 1918, but he returned to France toward the end of his career.[17]

Gaston Blanquart, born in 1877, remained in Paris, where he became solo flute of the Concerts Colonne. He was said to have had quite a small, rather breathy flute sound, but it was finely focused and carried well in a large hall. He was noted for his interpretation of *L'Après-midi d'un faune*.[18]

Georges Laurent, born in 1886, was yet another Taffanel student who settled in America. His influence on the style of American flute playing should have been greater, as his recordings reveal a purer French flute sound than that of Barrère, whose often wobbly vibrato was widely copied by his students. But Laurent did not arrive until after the First World War (before that he was first flute of the Société des concerts), when he became solo flute of the Boston Symphony Orchestra and taught at the New England Conservatory. By then the Barrère style was firmly established. Nevertheless, Laurent helped to complete the colonization of America for the French flute school.[19]

Taffanel's mantle of great teacher undoubtedly fell on the shoulders of Marcel Moyse, born in 1889. While Gaubert and other Taffanel students were remembered by their own students as remarkably inspiring, it seems to have been largely a case of "listen and copy"—learning by example rather than by systematic instruction. Moyse, following Taffanel most closely, managed to combine inspiration and method, although the technical lengths to which he went in his many books of studies and exercises might well have been viewed as excessive by Taffanel. After Gaubert, Moyse was the most celebrated player in Paris. In the 1920s he inherited Gaubert's playing positions when the latter turned to conducting, and in 1931 he succeeded him as professor at the Conservatoire. Dissatisfied with life back in Paris after the Second World War, Moyse resigned from the Conservatoire in 1948 and moved first to Argentina, then to North America, teaching and playing at Marlboro with Rudolph Serkin. From the 1960s until his death he became a guru figure for flutists, attracting students from all over the world until his death in 1984. During those years there were few major players who did not at some time or other have lessons from him.[20]

Daily Life in the Class

Louis Fleury never forgot his first audition for the Conservatoire class. He played a piece by Kuhlau—"quite badly, I think"—and gained a vivid first-hand impression of the professor:

> Short, slightly stooping, greying, keen-eyed behind his pince-nez, his
> mouth strong and kindly under the short, square-trimmed beard, his
> hands broad and his fingers short, fingers which were always curved
> in the shape they assumed over the keys of his flute, his voice a little

husky, with a hint of a Bordeaux accent, that was Paul Taffanel as I saw him for the first time in the autumn of 1894. He was the kindest man in the world, and the most welcoming.

He circled around me with the agility of a squirrel, standing on tiptoe to examine my embouchure, the formation of my hands, the position of my fingers. He tapped me on the shoulder with the most encouraging smile and wished me much success. He had laid siege. After a pitiful audition I was completely quashed and did not become his student until the following year.[21]

Moyse, who joined the class in 1905, also on his second attempt, remembered Taffanel's initial regime as several months of exercises, scales, and studies. Only after that was a student allowed to go on to pieces.[22] Fernand Caratgé, a Conservatoire student of Gaubert's in the 1920s (*premier prix* 1924), who later revised the Altès *Méthode*, maintained that "there was rivalry between Altès and Taffanel," and that Taffanel completely changed the Conservatoire style of teaching.[23] The Altès *Méthode* was abandoned and Taffanel's *Exercices journaliers* substituted as the main technical course of study. Moyse added that, in particular, Taffanel taught them all to play numbers 1 and 5 very slowly to concentrate on legato and homogeneity of tone, and they followed the routines for daily practice later set out at the beginning of the *Méthode*. Gaston Crunelle, also a Gaubert student (*premier prix* 1920, and later flute professor from 1940 to 1969), remembered that Gaubert inherited the *Exercices journaliers* and continued to make each new student copy them out, just as Taffanel had done.[24]

Taffanel also recommended Louis Lot flutes and if a student arrived with a different instrument would urge him to change. André Castel told Caratgé that when he joined the class in 1905 with a Bonneville flute, Taffanel said: "Yes, very good, but listen, a Lot flute will give you a better tone." Caratgé dated the French preoccupation with *sonorité*—tone quality—to the arrival of Taffanel at the Conservatoire: "What was astonishing was Taffanel's low register. When he played *Namouna*, it was like a trombone . . . it was the first time the flute had sung in the low register." For Taffanel, this sonority seems to have resided mainly in the headjoint of the instrument. Various of his students recounted to Caratgé how Taffanel kept his own flute headjoint in his inside jacket pocket, and would take it out and fit it onto one of his students' flutes to demonstrate during the class. Once each student found a headjoint that suited him, Taffanel advised him to keep it throughout his career, transferring it to successive new flutes.

Although Taffanel would have considered the earlier nineteenth-century virtuoso repertoire long since outmoded on the concert platform, he continued to find it useful as teaching material, with pieces encapsulating every imaginable technical difficulty. Once the *instrument* had been mastered, then the student could proceed to better *music*. Meanwhile, the best of the virtuoso repertoire included lyrical interludes that were as valuable for developing expression as the other sections were for pure technique. Taffanel chose carefully, and certain pieces recurred frequently. Not until a student had successfully performed some of this repertoire in the twice-yearly examinations would he be allowed to proceed to Bach, Handel, Mozart, or Saint-Saëns.

Taffanel's reports on his students followed the usual Conservatoire format of a few succinct phrases. Not surprisingly, he was particularly concerned with quality of sound, followed by fingering and tonguing technique. He also addressed the broader aspects of general musical aptitude. The development of his students as musicians and as people emerges clearly from these reports, and thoughts of the flute class must have been ever present in his mind. A rehearsal timetable for May 1900 (found among his papers for the Paris Exhibition) has notes on the reverse with a list of students matched to specific pieces he had chosen for the June examinations. Taffanel's favorite composers for these examination pieces were Demersseman and Tulou, closely followed by Lindpaintner and Kuhlau, then Briccialdi, Mozart, Andersen, and Pratten. He also set the most popular examination choice, Demersseman's *Sixth Solo*, op. 85, for the *concours* in 1896 and 1900. Demersseman subtitled the piece "Concert italien," and it has a lilting 6/8 *chanson napolitaine* and a *saltarello* that make it almost the prototype of the two-movement, slow–fast, lyrical–virtuosic pieces that the Conservatoire began to commission at this time.

Morceau de concours

The flute *concours* always took place toward the end of July, on an afternoon that included all the other wind instruments. The composition of the jury changed much more in these years than it had when Taffanel was first involved in the 1870s, but the voting procedure for the various prizes was essentially the same as when Taffanel himself had competed for his *premier prix* back in 1860 (see chapter 2). Because he was now the professor, Taffanel did not serve on the wind jury, but he was on various other ones, including those for strings, opera, and brass, from 1895 onwards, and he even composed the cello sight-reading test in 1902.

The pieces set as flute *morceaux de concours* are of mixed quality, although most of them have remained popular in the repertoire, in particular those by Fauré, Chaminade, Gaubert, and Taffanel himself. Taffanel's influence on the competition pieces is significant, and not just for the flute. For years Altès had alternated virtuoso solos by himself and by Tulou, but Taffanel immediately introduced a work in a more modern style, which he himself had recently been playing: the Langer Concerto (described in chapter 8). The logical next step was to ask a living composer to compose a new flute piece, and once that principle was successfully established, Taffanel persuaded the Conservatoire authorities to formalize the commissioning process for other instruments with limited solo repertoires. From 1897 onward all the wind and brass instruments benefited from new music. In time a whole Conservatoire repertoire was created, and the annual *concours* became something of a showcase for new music.[25]

The idea to commission Joachim Andersen for the 1895 competition brought Taffanel back in contact with him after a six-year gap in their correspondence. He wrote to Andersen in May that year, first bringing him up to date with details of his conducting career (quoted in chapter 10), then moving on to the flute. He describes how he has introduced his students to Andersen's studies and concert works — they have become "great favorites" — then asks him for a new piece and gives a succinct description, almost a blueprint, of the style required:

> The piece should be short: 5 or 6 minutes at the most. I will leave the form of it entirely up to you; whether an Andante followed by an Allegro, or a single movement, but it needs to contain the wherewithal to test the examinees on matters of phrasing, expression, tone control, and virtuosity. The accompaniment should be for piano.[26]

Andersen agreed, and Taffanel wrote again, requesting that the piece should be delivered by 10 June if possible. "I have introduced your 'School of Virtuosity' to my class," he adds, "and my youngsters are battling away with the very interesting difficulties you have filled it with."[27] The studies referred to are Andersen's op. 60, virtuosic indeed, but also of real musical value — exactly the sort of teaching pieces Taffanel was looking for.

Andersen managed to deliver the competition piece by 6 June via a friend who was visiting Paris, but there was a problem: the work lasted *ten* minutes. It was much too long, bearing in mind not only the number of flute students who had to perform it, but all the other wind instrument students who had to be heard in one afternoon: "around 80 or 100 pieces for the poor members of the jury . . . I gave myself that little treat for twenty years!!" Taffanel therefore suggested a substantial cut about halfway through, and the insertion of an extra cadenza-like section to show off the students' techniques — with apologies for requesting such "made-to-measure" music![28] But time was evidently too short, Andersen had conducting commitments in Lübeck that summer, and Taffanel had to substitute the *Concertstück*, op. 3 for the 1895 *concours*. Andersen's *Deuxième morceau de concert*, op. 61 was eventually set in 1897, presumably with a cut, or some sort of modification, as the published version still lasts about ten minutes. It was dedicated to Taffanel by the composer, as were the works commissioned from other composers for the flute *concours* over the next twelve years.

As a footnote to the Taffanel–Andersen relationship, Marcel Moyse often told the story of Andersen's visit to the Conservatoire class in the spring of 1906. Taffanel was teaching Moyse and the other students Andersen's G major Study, op. 15, no. 3, and he began by demonstrating how it was constructed on a legato theme:

> After he had wiped the mouthpiece and adjusted his moustache, he began to play soh, ray, tee, fah . . . At the beginning Andersen watched him, smiling, then he became more and more interested, his face took on a different look of satisfaction, eventually tears began to come to his eyes, he was very moved, then finally he said to Monsieur Taffanel, "This is an absolute revelation, I had no idea that I had written such beautiful studies."[29]

Moyse remembered that Taffanel often used this device of "skeleton practice," reducing a study or a piece to its most important notes, its basic architecture, then building it up again, "with appropriate tone colour changes at crucial points in the music."[30] It was a technique Moyse was to make much of in his own teaching.

Correspondence has survived from four of the other composers commissioned by Taffanel to write competition pieces: Gabriel Fauré (1898), Alphonse Duvernoy (1899), Louis Ganne (1901), and Cécile Chaminade (1902). Louis Ganne's letters say nothing about the music itself, but they do reveal the extent to which all these composers deferred to Taffanel for advice and modifications in matters of phrasing and articulation, and in the basic style and standard of the pieces. There was a general recognition that these were *pièces d'occasion* and should be tailored to requirements. Their subsequent identification with the French School, therefore, is somewhat artificial. None of these pieces is great music inspired by Taffanel's example, but each is a valuable indication of the technical and aesthetic ideals he brought to the Conservatoire.

Two letters from Fauré, who was at that point professor of composition at the Conservatoire, concern arrangements to discuss the competition piece — his *Fantaisie*—with Taffanel, and later to play it through with him to make a final check of all the details. June 1898 was a busy time for Fauré, with the premiere in London of his incidental music for Maeterlinck's play *Pelléas et Mélisande*. He wrote to the director of the Conservatoire, Théodore Dubois, just before he left for England: "I have given Taffanel the flute piece. It lasts four-and-a-half minutes and is in two movements. I have urged Taffanel to modify any passages that would be impractical and show it to you. On my return I shall write the little sight-reading piece."[31] The manuscript of this sight-reading piece (*pièce à déchiffrer* as Fauré called it) eventually bore the date "14 July 1898"—Bastille Day.[32]

Meanwhile, Taffanel had taken the opportunity of revising the *Fantaisie*, though not without a certain hesitation. Fauré wrote from London to reassure him: "Forgive me for not having thanked you immediately: I have been constantly busy here. Your revision is perfect and I beg you to make any changes you want, and not to worry at all. I will be extremely grateful."[33] There is a hint here that Fauré not only had confidence in Taffanel's artistic judgment, he was also positively relieved to have some help with a relatively unimportant task. It is unlikely that he set much store by the *Fantaisie*, although he did incorporate the opening lyrical Andante into his incidental music for *Pelléas et Mélisande*. This is the most effective part of the piece, and its legato scale line is like a slow-motion version of one of Taffanel's *Exercices journaliers*. Incidentally, Saint-Saëns's last flute piece, *Odelette* (1920), is also strongly reminiscent of the famous daily exercises—whether by accident or design, as with Fauré, it is impossible to say. The attractive, but rather routine, scales and arpeggios of Fauré's second movement, however, bear little relationship to anything else, and it is difficult not to feel that the *Fantaisie's* enduring success has had more to do with the reputation of its composer than with its intrinsic merit. Interestingly, Taffanel did not choose Fauré's *Fantaisie* in the only two years that he repeated a *concours* piece: 1900 (Demersseman's *Sixth Solo*) and 1905 (Ganne's *Andante et scherzo*).

When Alphonse Duvernoy was approached for the 1899 piece, he got right down to basics: "Do tell me what the tempo of the flute examination piece should be and also the key."[34] The manuscript of his Concertino then passed back and forth as both he and Taffanel made various alterations before publication. Duvernoy was concerned to get the phrasing absolutely right: "If my memory serves me correctly, you said that when the motif of the *Lento* comes back an octave higher it only needs slurs without dots and you have shown it with dots. Are you changing your first opinion or have you made a mistake? In short, please, dear friend, be kind enough look over the whole thing again."[35] The answer in the printed edition (no written reply has survived) is that Taffanel had revised his previous opinion: the motif from rehearsal figure 2 returns in the high register in the fifth bar of figure 3 with exactly the same tongued–legato combination of dots and slurs. As Duvernoy was a pianist, Théodore Dubois invited him to be the accompanist for his Concertino at the competition—not a particularly enticing offer! Duvernoy declined, choosing instead to sit on the jury for that year.

In 1902, Cécile Chaminade, or "C. Carbonel-Chaminade," as she signed her letters, took the whole process very seriously indeed. She was very agitated by the sequence of revisions and proofs. With time pressing, and her usual copyist unavailable, she laboriously copied out the whole work herself for the printers. Then there was the vexed question of the title:

> "Caprice" or "Fantaisie" has been suggested, but I think those titles have an unfortunate ring to them, given all the horrors committed in their names, especially in the wind instrument repertoire. For the time being I have put "Concertino;" it is unpretentious, although it does evoke a rather developed piece in several movements. If you do not disapprove of this title we will leave it, if it does not seem good to you then please baptize it yourself, I accept your title in advance.[36]

No problem there: Concertino it was. But Chaminade had got rather carried away with the length of the piece and it needed a cut for the *concours*. This was restored for the printed edition (page 8 of the Enoch piano score). Like others before her, Chaminade also deferred to Taffanel for the final details of nuances and phrasing in the flute part, and she requested an opportunity to try out the piece with him. After the competition she sent a congratulatory note: "I was delighted to hear that excellent class."[37]

Chaminade was not the only one to be impressed. The following year the young writer Colette was doing a brief stint as a music critic for the newspaper *Gil Blas*. Witty and irreverent (a *Claudine* to Willy's *Ouvreuse*), she sampled the Conservatoire competition that July:

> We drink in Périlhou's *Ballade* like a soothing love potion! Through the gentle languor that envelops me, cradled by waterfalls of flutes, their droplets of trills and rocketing scales, I can still single out the merits of these young people: Grisard, with his fluid, lovely sound; Delangle, who sounds like a horn in the low register; Puyans, absolutely delightful; Racnilalao [*sic*], a prince charming; finally, Cardon, the best; my word, these Taffanel fledglings are talented![38]

A single scrap of paper found with Taffanel's other notes on the flute gives the only idea of his thinking about possible composers for the *concours*. "1. Gaubert / 2. Catherine / 3. Hennebains / 4. Lagorsse / 5. Lamy, E. / 6. Goldberg."[39] The intriguing thing about this list is that it avoids the names of the well-known composers of the day, in favor of those with strong flute-playing connections. Gaubert and Hennebains are self-explanatory; Alphonse Catherine had already dedicated a Nocturne (1900) for flute and piano to Taffanel; Lagorsse was an amateur flute player and former private student of Taffanel's; Alfred Goldberg was the author of the recently published book of biographies and photographs of flute players; only Ernest Lamy was an unknown quantity as regards the flute. The year was 1906, when Philippe Gaubert wrote his *Nocturne et allegro scherzando*. Marcel Moyse remembered that instead of Taffanel playing through the piece for his students before they began to learn it, as he usually did, that year Gaubert himself came and played to the class, accompanied by Taffanel on the piano.[40]

Recognition and Reward

In 1895 the Conservatoire celebrated its centenary, and photographs were taken of each of the classes. Taffanel's group photograph—formally posed, with no hint of the bubbling creativity of the class itself—includes Gaubert, seated on Taffanel's right (see fig. 19).[41] But Gaubert had graduated in 1894, so he should by rights have left the class by then. He seems to have been the first, therefore, followed later by Barrère and Fleury, to attend the class beyond graduation for extra coaching from Taffanel. This was a new departure for the Conservatoire, the beginning of a modern concept of musical study extending beyond mere success in examinations.

In August of the centenary year 1895 Taffanel was presented with the Palmes académiques—an academic honor awarded by the government—followed in 1902 by promotion to the rank of Officier de l'instruction publique.[42] But even in 1895 an article on Taffanel referred to him as "the most noteworthy personality at the Conservatoire after its director, Ambroise Thomas."[43] The article bemoaned Taffanel's modesty, however, which made it difficult to conduct interviews with him!

Le Monde musical remarked on Taffanel's class in the 1896 *concours*, particularly the musical qualities of his students: "in the forefront are Messieurs Maquarre and Grenier. Since the last examination, the former has developed an exceptional tone; he played like a virtuoso. . . . On the other hand Monsieur Million phrased with exquisite taste and read at sight very well."[44] The critic went on to report the tribute paid by the arts minister to Louis Dorus, who had died on 9 June, just three months after his sister, the singer Julie Dorus-Gras.

Taffanel himself began to have serious health problems from 1898 onward (see chapter 10) and in the latter years of his life asked Hennebains to deputize for him from time to time at the flute class.[45] Presumably he felt that Gaubert was too young and inexperienced, but this created another curious parallel in their careers. Just as Taffanel had been too young to inherit the flute class when Dorus retired in 1868, and therefore the direct line of succession was diverted, so Gaubert would be passed over by the Conservatoire authorities in 1908 when Taffanel died. Like Taffanel before him, Gaubert had to wait his turn—in his case, until after the First World War.

Taffanel's reputation as a teacher spread far and wide. In 1898 the American writer Henry Clay Wysham cited a certain Lancelot Bayly from Boston "who has been studying for some years with great success with Taffanel in

Paris."[46] Bayly may have been joined by others, for example F. Sanchis from Alger-Mustapha, who wrote to Taffanel requesting lessons in 1899; or Auguste Giroud from Lausanne, who wrote the following year: "my aim has always been to study with you, and I make so bold as to say that I am not just an ordinary flute player and I am sure I am worthy of your famous teaching."[47] But probably Taffanel was too busy, and toward the end too ill, to expand his teaching much beyond his Conservatoire class. In 1902 when Eugène Crosti requested lessons, Taffanel recommended that he should contact Gaubert instead.[48]

The final accolade bestowed on Taffanel by the Conservatoire, albeit a minor one, was his election in 1907 as an honorary member of the league of former students—the Association des anciens élèves du Conservatoire.[49] By June 1908 he was too ill to come to the class to prepare his students for the competition piece, so they came to him:

> Taffanel loved his students profoundly; he was their friend, their companion, while always knowing, however, how to retain his status and authority. "I will never," he said, "leave my students, I will keep my class until my death" . . . On 14 May . . . he achieved his final triumph at the head of his orchestral class and, several weeks later, laid low by illness, stretched out on his deathbed, he prepared his students from the flute class for the end of year examinations. Obviously he could not be present at the examinations, but he had, at least, the satisfaction of knowing his final successes.[50]

Ironically, only a few days before Taffanel died, a letter arrived from the minister of public instruction renewing his term of office on the Conservatoire's governing council, the Conseil supérieur d'enseignement, for a further three years.[51]

The French Flute School Lives On

The tangible legacy of Taffanel's years of playing, studying, and teaching the flute should have been the publication of his two major projects, a *Méthode de flûte* and a treatise on the instrument's history and construction for Lavignac's *Encyclopédie*. But neither was realized before he died. What remained was at once more ephemeral and more vivid: the memories of Taffanel's Conservatoire students. And as well as passing on the tradition by word of mouth to their own students, several of them left written accounts. These are remarkably consistent in general tone and detail. Taken together, they build up the picture of Taffanel's nondidactic, inspirational teaching method.

Barrère maintained he began to take the flute seriously only under Taffanel's skillful and flexible guidance:

> He was careful to assign to his pupils such work as would enable them to progress surely and rapidly. Unlike Altès, he did not pay strict attention to school routine. Many times we would stay after class to listen to solos that he would play for us in his own inimitable style. While he was teaching one pupil the remainder of the class would listen attentively to every observation or suggestion made to improve our friend's work . . . Each pupil was a musical son.[52]

When the time came to leave the class, Barrère was reluctant, and he asked to be allowed to continue an extra year. Taffanel was pleased at this request, and they worked particularly on the solo repertoire and on chamber music: "I became very intimate with him, being then a young man to whom he could speak in a different way than to the lad he found me when I first entered his class."[53] The solo repertoire included the Mozart concertos, sonatas, and suites by Bach, Handel, Reinecke, Widor, and Godard, and the Schubert Variations. By then Taffanel was making only occasional public appearances as a flutist, but Barrère never missed a chance to hear him:

> Quality as well as quantity of tone and fine technique were only a small part of his splendid characteristics as a flute player.
>
> His musicianship, his style particularly, was hugely inspirational. He loathed cheap sentimentality, excessive expression, endless vibrato, or shaking of tone, in a word, all the cheap tricks that are as undignified as they are unmusical.[54]

Barrère also benefited from Taffanel's help in forming the Société moderne des instruments à vent (see chapter 6), and in persuading the directors of the Opéra to release him to accept Damrosch's first invitation to appear in America. "I know that Barrère," said Taffanel. "He will never come back; I am sure he will succeed there."[55]

The initially timid Fleury, whose playing developed only slowly, also had ample opportunity to watch and listen:

> Taffanel brought wide-ranging ideas to the Conservatoire and a teaching method that was infinitely skillful and flexible. He left much of the initiative to us, taking account of the individuality of each, and imposing no system . . . Let me add that this great artist was the most conscientious and the most patient of teachers . . . and that he helped us to make a living by every possible means in his power (life was difficult at that time).[56]

Fleury, like so many others, was amazed at Taffanel's playing, and grappled with the problem of how you could ever describe it to anyone who hadn't heard him:

> His virtuosity was phenomenal. He made his fingers do, quite literally, whatever he wanted. When I knew him, he had just given up the flute for the conductor's baton and he no longer practised; but his playing had solid foundations. I still remember the dazzle of his lightning scales, launched at full speed and slowing down or stopping at will, and I can still hear a certain Schubert Variation, played with an evenness and simplicity that were the height of artistry. Add to that, exquisite tone, warm and rich, and an allure that I just cannot describe.[57]

Fleury's *Souvenirs* were written in 1925, about the same time that he completed the *Encyclopédie* article, which included a final page of tribute to Taffanel:

> Taffanel's artistry was essentially refined, supple and sensitive, and his prodigious virtuosity was made as little apparent as possible. He hated ostentation, followed the printed text with absolute respect, and the fluid flexibility of his playing concealed an absolute rigor in the observance of tempo and rhythm. He had spent much time studying the problems of acoustics and sound production.[58]

Fernand Dusausoy, born in 1882, gained his *premier prix* in 1902, and went on to become professor at the Roubaix Conservatoire. Writing to Taffanel's granddaughter, Jeanne Samaran, in 1949, he recalled the moment each year when Taffanel would play through the competition piece for his students for the first time: "As soon as the piece was finished, we all looked at each other with the same thought, if only we could play it like him on the day of the examination!" Dusausoy may have been a diligent flute student and proud to be in Taffanel's class, but he neglected his other musical studies and partway through his course he was expelled from the Conservatoire. Taffanel appealed to Dubois, the director, and had him reinstated: "so you can see how much I owe him, and I have never forgotten it."[59]

Writing the same year, René Bergeon remembered Taffanel in both the flute and the orchestra classes:

> An exceptional teacher, he was not satisfied to concern himself with just the musical side of his students, he took the trouble to get to know their characters and personalities. The lessons he gave us were captivating and the two hours of study passed without us realizing it.
>
> I was also lucky to have him as my teacher for the orchestra class, where all the young players of the moment who made up the section

were lost in admiration for the explanations that he lavished on the works to be performed, about the ways they should be interpreted, and about the contribution and importance of each one of us so that the sum total might be perfect.[60]

Bergeon, born in 1887, was a contemporary of Marcel Moyse (both graduated in 1906), and he was subsequently offered the position of flute professor in Berlin. He declined to become a naturalized German, however, so he had spent the last thirty-three years in Bordeaux, teaching and playing at the Grand Théâtre and also at the Casino at Vichy. A native of Bordeaux, he felt that Taffanel had a special affection for him. En route for Biarritz one year, Taffanel had stopped off to give Bergeon's parents news of him, and he had several times welcomed the young man to his home in avenue Gourgaud: "my shyness disappeared completely," wrote Bergeon, "even though I was overawed by the sheer greatness of his talent." Equally overawed was the young Georges Cléton, who whispered in Moyse's ear one day during the flute class: "Don't you think Monsieur Taffanel is perfect? Like the Good Lord himself! "[61]

No doubt many of Taffanel's students felt some sort of special relationship to him, hence the memories they cherished for the rest of their lives. In a letter to Jeanne Samaran in 1970, Marcel Moyse declared: "He was a 'father' to each one of us, understanding all our problems . . . I dare to claim that few had a deeper understanding of his mind—and grasped what he really was—not only a great flute player of phenomenal talent, but a great musician with perceptive insight, no matter who the composer."[62] Moyse was "filled with wonder" every time Taffanel took up a phrase of Bach, or Mozart, or Saint-Saëns to demonstrate during the class: "His playing was like the rising of the sun: it did not astonish you, it transfigured you, as the sun gently but powerfully brings light everywhere . . . There were so many colors in his sound . . . I learned to sing from Taffanel."[63]

This poetical-musical use of analogy was characteristic of Moyse, and he never broke faith with what he had learned. He remained close to not only the spirit but also the letter of Taffanel's teaching, continuing to use the repertoire of nineteenth-century bravura pieces and *morceaux de concours*, although he devised many books of his own technical studies. In 1950, when the American flutist Charles DeLaney approached Moyse for lessons, he was sent a list of core repertoire that could have come from Taffanel himself—Kuhlau, Tulou, Andersen, Doppler—and an explanation of how Taffanel had structured his teaching to progress from the virtuoso pieces to the serious repertoire of old and new music for the flute.[64] But whether Taffanel would still have been teaching Kuhlau, Tulou, and Doppler if had he been alive in 1950 is an open question. All the evidence about him suggests that his ideas were always evolving, and that he was ever receptive to new music.

Moyse's veneration for Taffanel is all the more persuasive as he seems to have struggled to come to terms with some less than perfect aspects of his character. Moyse was unhappy about two stories in particular that he told about his teacher: one concerned the dismissal of a player from the Opéra orchestra (quoted in chapter 10), the other recounted what must have been a rare and therefore unnerving display of absolutism in the flute class:

> Taffanel always started his lessons with scales played melodically. On this particular Monday morning, a new student was having his first lesson. The boy played a scale badly. Taffanel asked, "Do you play all the scales?" "Yes, every day," the boy said. Taffanel replied, "O.K. let's hear the rest." The boy could not do it. "You will learn all the scales by next Monday or you have had your last lesson," said Taffanel.[65]

Robert Hériché, a Gaubert student at the Conservatoire (*premier prix* 1921), also recalled this tougher side to Taffanel. Blanquart told him he was once evicted by Taffanel after straying backstage at the Opéra. Taffanel was dressed formally in top hat and tails, and appeared very severe.[66]

Moyse's Epilogue on Taffanel

Moyse contributed one of the most illuminating attempts to analyze Taffanel's art in an unpublished page of notes (a sort of stream of consciousness) sketched in the final years of his life. He headed it "Vibrato"—a thorny subject about which he had tried to write at various times before, with mainly confusing results.[67] Here, he hardly gets going before his enquiring mind encounters the wider question of what it was that made Taffanel unique. The result is something of a philosophical meditation. It is worth quoting in full:[68]

> Vibrato—With Monsieur Taffanel vibrato was integral to the sound. Thanks to his effortless tone production, the lips completely relaxed, he obtained a discreet vibrato by a light trembling of the lips—as he used to say—on the low notes. His great mastery—mobility, flexibility of the embouchure. He maintained this ease of tone production in the middle and even the upper register, whatever the nuance. Everything was held in balance—the guiding principles remained the same.
>
> His sound was like the natural voice of a true tenor, rich and fully resonant.
>
> All the notes were rich in vitamins whatever the tessitura.
>
> Those who never heard him cannot have any idea.

Was it a natural gift? I tend to think so. But I have always thought that in any case his innate talent (above all an exceptional intelligence) had been developed by work over a long period.

His interpretations certainly got to the heart of things.

The gift of observation.

Nothing was left to chance.

He certainly did not say here I will use vibrato no. 3 or no. 5.

His inspiration was direct. He followed the unfolding of the phrase—the sound followed—the lips, the breath obeyed.

The sound was serene and lightly vibrant at its source because it was free, it was by turns bright, dark, expressive on the appoggiaturas. It became animated as the music developed and climaxed.

Each note, each point of expression justified itself—sensitivity; simplicity—sincerely.

He expressed himself on his flute with the same ease with which he would have talked, or sung.

His flute was second nature to him, belonging to him like excellent vocal chords belong to a singer.

CHAPTER 12

Last Words on the Flute

Taffanel, the conductor in whom the flute player lives on.
—WILLY, *GARÇON L'AUDITION* (1899)

P en-and-ink portrait—Giraud," wrote Taffanel in his *Notes biographiques*
for August 1894. This cartoon-like color sketch was one of a series that the
artist Charles Giraud made of personnel connected with the Paris Opéra. He
depicted Taffanel standing on a chair (an allusion to his short stature), slightly
stooped, with pince-nez and a rather serious expression, a baton in one hand,
and a flute (one-keyed!) supported on his chin and tucked under his other arm
(see fig. 20).[1] It neatly sums up how audiences in the 1890s would have seen
Taffanel, for however important his career as a conductor was, he remained
first and foremost *the* flute player of his generation to those who had heard
him. Even Saint-Saëns, commenting on a performance of his *Requiem* conducted by Taffanel at the Société des concerts in 1899, concluded his letter with
a cartoon drawing of a flute player (see fig. 21).[2]

Taffanel's actual appearances as a player, however, became rarer after 1893.
Apart from performances with the Société des instruments à vent, the musical
press reported only five other chamber concerts that year in which he took part
(playing music by Beethoven, de Bériot, Bernard, Weckerlin, and Widor), and
all between February and April.[3] Meanwhile, Adolphe Hennebains's name
began to appear increasingly in the reviews, as he began to assume Taffanel's
role—for example, he now played the solo in Gluck's *Orphée* at the Société des
concerts—though not with anything like the same critical adulation.[4] Soon,
however, Taffanel handed the torch to the young Philippe Gaubert, his chosen
successor. "How vexed I am not to be able to answer: yes!, but truly I am in no
fit state," Taffanel wrote in April 1896 to Hugues Imbert, who had asked him
to play in a concert:

My flute is totally neglected and only resonates now like a cracked reed; and alongside the virtuosi who have promised to take part I would only inspire pity. Saint-Saëns's fiftieth anniversary will force me to retune my pipes (the first time for 4 years!) but I still have six weeks ahead of me. For 9th May I would definitely be unable to make a sound; therefore, would you like me to ask my student, Gaubert, soloist at the Opéra Concerts, who plays the flute ten times better than me, if he is free on that date? This kid of 16 will amaze you.[5]

In fact Taffanel was still playing from time to time, usually to please old friends, or for some special occasion. He noted a soirée in Rouen in January 1894, for example, and he had appeared at one of Diémer's concerts the following month, along with Saint-Saëns, for a performance of *Le Carnaval des animaux* that "ended up in roars of laughter."[6] And he was still enough of a flute player when conducting the premiere of Massenet's *Thaïs* in March 1894 to decide that the violin *Méditation* would suit the instrument admirably. He quickly made a flute transcription of it, published later that year by Heugel. He was also tempted in July that year (as noted in chapter 6) to play a final time in London with five former members of his Société des instruments à vent. Incidentally, on that occasion he was keen to see the workings of the Covent Garden Opera House, and he took with him a letter of introduction from Massenet to the director, Sir Augustus Harris.[7]

Photographs from August 1894 (rather more flattering than Giraud's cartoon!) while Taffanel was on holiday in Thun show him looking still youthful at forty-nine (see fig. 18). But during the next decade illness and overwork aged him dramatically, and by the time the series of flute demonstration photographs was taken around 1906 he appears an old man, although only in his early sixties (see fig. 24). A puzzling reference to his health was also signaled in May 1895 in a letter to Joachim Andersen, who was having problems with paralysis of the tongue. Taffanel sympathized with Andersen over having to give up playing in public and confided: "I myself had, for a whole year, a weakness of my lips which prevented me from playing higher than e^3—I thought I would never regain the ability, but it returned one day, however, just as before. I very much hope it will be the same for you."[8]

When was this "whole year"? Everything seems to indicate that Taffanel's playing career was continuous, apart from a six-month leave of absence negotiated with the Opéra in 1880 (see chapter 7). Presumably he managed somehow to conceal the problem, although quite how remains a mystery, when so much of the solo and orchestral flute repertoire includes the third register above e^3. Dental problems, however, are mentioned from time to time, and they persisted. In 1899 Taffanel told Raoul Pugno he was making great efforts "to blow my pipes again," preparing for another concert in Rouen, and that it had meant a visit to the dentist "to pull out a molar which didn't like the flute!"[9] That concert in February 1899, like the earlier one in January 1894, was organized by a Canon Davranches of Rouen Cathedral, who was also a singer. Taffanel kept a copy of the program on which he appeared with Davranches and another singer, Jeanne Raunay, the pianist Raoul Pugno, and the cellist Jean Gérardy. Alphonse Catherine was the accompanist for part of the program, but Pugno partnered with Taffanel for the Weber Trio (with Gérardy), J. S. Bach's Sonata in B minor, and three movements from Rameau's *Pièces de clavecin en concerts*.[10] Taffanel entered the Rouen concert in his *Notes biographiques*, along with a concert identified simply as "Soirée de Fels" in May that year, and they were his last mentions of playing the flute.

Both of those concerts would have been semiprivate events, and by then Taffanel's last major public appearance had already taken place. Appropriately enough, he had bowed out with one of the defining pieces of his career: the *Romance* by Saint-Saëns. The concert was at the Salle Pleyel on 2 June 1896, and it attracted great attention because it celebrated Saint-Saëns's *cinquantenaire*— fifty years on the concert platform (referred to in Taffanel's letter quoted earlier). It was given in aid of the musician's union—the Association des artistes musiciens. Special presentation programs were printed on silk (Geneviève and Marie-Camille Taffanel carefully kept theirs), and after the concert a souvenir book was published. It comprised an essay by Louis de Fourcauld, a copy of the program, an account of the evening by "Th. Lindenlaub," and a lithograph by J. Grigny, reproduced from the magazine *La Grande dame*. The latter showed Taffanel conducting the orchestra at the concert, with Saint-Saëns at the piano and Pablo de Sarasate playing the violin—an idealized view, as there was no work that involved violin, piano, and orchestra at the same time (see fig. 22).[11] The program, which included two first performances, was as follows:

Mozart	Overture, *The Marriage of Figaro*
Saint-Saëns	Piano Concerto no. 5 (first performance)
Saint-Saëns	Introduction to Act 2 of *Phryné*
Saint-Saëns	*Romance*, op. 37 for flute and orchestra
Saint-Saëns	Sonata no. 2 for violin and piano, op. 102 (first performance)
Massenet arr. Saint-Saëns	*La Mort de Thaïs* for solo piano
Mozart	"Fourth" Piano Concerto in B flat [K. 450] (played at the concert in 1846)

A chamber orchestra of twenty-five strings, with wind, brass, and percussion, was made up of members of the Société des concerts (Hennebains, Léopold Lafleurance, and Gaubert were the flutists). Saint-Saëns played the piano, including accompanying Sarasate, and he also conducted the orchestra in the extract from *Phryné* and the *Romance*. Taffanel conducted the other orchestral items. The audience was full of fellow musicians, critics, and Parisian high society. Paul Dukas was impressed by "the beautiful and noble melancholy" that Taffanel brought to the *Romance*; *Le Monde musical* declared that Taffanel "still has that beautiful sound which is his hallmark and that captivating way of playing that one hears, alas, so rarely nowadays"; and Lindenlaub was struck by how Taffanel had made both the flute and this particular piece of music his own.[12] Saint-Saëns, in an elegant tribute, sent Taffanel a faïence plate from the fashionable art shop, Th. Deck, in the rue Halévy, accompanied by a card on which he had inscribed the first two bars of the *Romance*. Taffanel immediately gave it pride of place, mounted on the wall of his study.[13]

La Trompette

Alongside Saint-Saëns and Diémer, the eccentric Emile Lemoine was one of the very few who could tempt Taffanel out of retirement as a flute player. Taffanel's connection with Lemoine dated back to 1879, when he had first played at the Société La Trompette. This originally amateur society, founded at the Ecole polytechnique in 1860 by Lemoine and still directed by him, now held its concerts in the Salle Erard. Lemoine had managed to attract more professional musicians as the years went on, but he still restricted entry to the concerts to a semiprivate audience of "enlightened amateurs" largely chosen by himself. Nevertheless, the society had played an influential role in the rise of chamber music, and Taffanel had become part of Lemoine's inner circle of friends that also included Lalo and Saint-Saëns.[14] After the 1884 series of La Trompette concerts Lemoine had sent Taffanel a bronze medal inscribed "to Taffanel, the amiable charmer," and early in 1897 he turned his own persuasive powers on Taffanel in a series of witty, begging letters. Taffanel at first left these unanswered, then countered by suggesting Gaubert as a replacement. But Lemoine kept up the attack with fragments of doggerel verse:

> Respond quickly when I yell,
> My dear Monsieur Taffanel.
> For anguish will flee,
> When your pen runs free . . .

> May almighty Aeolus lend us his wind,
> And breathe upon Taffanel a breeze from the sea.
> To enliven his pipe, and make him rescind,
> That on 25th March he will play for me . . .

Hope brings relief, it is true,
And lulls for a while our despair,
But Taffanel, naught without you
Can succeed, so I beg you be there.[15]

Taffanel finally gave in and agreed to take part in a performance of Saint-Saëns's *Carnaval des animaux*, complete with animal-head masks. At the last minute Lemoine asked him to direct it as well as play, and after the performance he sent a quirky note of thanks: "Whoosh! . . . you still know how to fire up the rockets of those staccato scales!"[16] And he even managed to talk Taffanel into making two more annual appearances at La Trompette.

A Final Composition

New works continued to be dedicated to Taffanel during the last years of his life. Among them, in addition to the Conservatoire *concours* pieces, were Léopold Lafleurance's arrangement of Six Chopin Etudes (1895), Alphonse Catherine's Nocturne (1900), and Jules Mouquet's *Divertissement grec* (1908).[17] Then on 12 May 1907 Taffanel completed his own last work for flute and piano, the *Andante pastoral et scherzettino*.[18] In his first published work, the *Grande Fantaisie sur "Mignon"* (1874) dedicated to his teacher Louis Dorus, Taffanel had reflected the old tradition from which he had come. Now, although confined to some extent by the formal constraints of a competition piece, he handed on a new tradition and dedicated the piece to his student Philippe Gaubert. He thus articulated in musical terms the principles being laid out at the same time in his article on the history of the flute and in the *Méthode*. Since those two projects were destined to remain unfinished at his death, his last complete statement would be this music.

The title *Andante pastoral* and the use of lilting compound meters (12/8, 6/8, 9/8) recall eighteenth-century models, in particular the *Sicilienne* from Blavet's Sonata, op. 2, no. 4, also in G minor. The entry of the flute in bar 5 introduces a swirling figuration within falling phrases, dying away to the cadence in bar 7, and these arabesques recur throughout the movement as a restrained ornamentation of the melodic line. The *Andante pastoral* is paced in long legato phrases that have a natural, breathed quality about them, and the shape and range of the melodic line suggest clear parallels with vocal music. When Louis Fleury later wrote, "the highest compliment that one could pay to a flutist is that his instrument sings like a beautiful voice," he was no doubt aware that the compliment *had* many times been paid to Taffanel.[19] It was the ideal he had passed on to his students.

Taffanel's melodic line proceeds with much stepwise and restrained angular movement. Wide leaps are sparingly used for calculated effect—for example, in bars 20 and 42. There, the downward leap to d¹ is accompanied by a crescendo to *forte*, demanding a flexibility of embouchure and breathing that were always noted in Taffanel's own playing. Again, following his own preferences, Taffanel writes extensively in the low register, also recalling the eighteenth-century repertoire that he did so much to revive. The range for most of the *Andante pastoral* is d¹ to d♯³, with one low c¹ in bar 6 and a long, expressive top g³ in the final two bars, marked *piano*. Taffanel's detailed phrasing and dynamic markings require the utmost attention from the player, both technically and musically. His own approach in this gently nostalgic piece would no doubt have been similar to the directions given in the *Méthode* for interpreting Xavier Leroux's *Romance* (1897), also in a lilting compound meter: "aiming to imbue it with the pleasing and fanciful colors it requires, without however falling into sentimentality and affectation."[20]

The *Scherzettino* exhibits the same careful attention to detail and clarity of textural effect, even though the flute tessitura often lies within the range of the piano part. It also requires considerable control of breathing, particularly in the almost continuous passagework of the final twenty-two bars. When the flutist William Bennett was recording this piece and others by Taffanel, he observed that the most striking technical aspect of the flute writing was its "almost impossible, but just about manageable" demands on breathing.[21] Yet considering that this was a competition piece, its most significant feature is the absence of virtuosity of the kind exhibited in the former test pieces of player-composers like Tulou and Demersseman. The range of the flute part for much of the movement is e¹ to e³, with an occasional f♯³ (bar 88) and a³ (bars 12, 31, and 77); the passagework is restricted to running sixteenth-notes in scale and arpeggio figurations; and there is a central songlike *espressivo* section, marked *poco più mosso*.

This restrained virtuosity and poise are also reminiscent of much earlier models—for example, the juxtaposition of more and less technically demanding sections in the Chaconne of Michel de La Barre's Sonata *L'Inconnu*, or the interplay of moods in the solo sections of the Allegro movements of Michel Blavet's A minor Concerto. That Taffanel was not just concerned with finger virtuosity is also strikingly illustrated by the complexity of articulation patterns throughout the *Scherzettino*. The basic grouping of four separately tongued sixteenth-notes appears in five other combinations of tongued and slurred notes (see, for example, bars 10, 14, 17, 23, and 58), and often several of these different patterns are combined within only a few beats. Not for nothing does the *Méthode* open with the clear aim "to make the instrument *speak*."[22] So while the purely musical value of the *Andante pastoral et scherzettino* should not be exaggerated, it does represent in essence the style and sound world of the French flute school.

Toward the End

From 1891 onward Taffanel recorded more frequent references to his family life in his *Notes biographiques*. There is a regular catalog of Easter and summer holidays, and details of the progress of Jacques's education and the beginnings of his career. Marie-Camille's operation for appendicitis in 1901 is recorded, and the marriages and deaths of relatives and friends, notably the death of Geneviève's mother, Madame Deslignières, on 17 October 1901 at the age of ninety. The litany of entries from 1898 onward to the disease of the gallbladder and kidneys that led to his own death makes somber reading. From time to time Taffanel noted periods of convalescence in Biarritz or the spa towns of Contrexeville and Chantreauville to rest and take the waters, and there was a family trip to Italy in September 1907, when all four of them visited Milan, Florence, Siena, and Pisa. After that, nothing: it was his last diary entry.

Taffanel's final illness began in June 1908, when (as noted in chapter 11) he was unable to leave his bed to prepare his Conservatoire students for the *concours*. He died on Saturday 21 November at 8 o'clock in the evening, and his death was duly reported the following Monday morning by his son, Jacques, and by an artist friend, Bernard Wolff, who lived nearby.[23] Saint-Saëns had been one of the last people to visit Taffanel the previous Sunday before leaving for Barcelona, and he immediately wrote to Geneviève:

> Despite the encouraging things I said to you, I knew only too well that I had seen him for the last time; and I am so grateful to you for having arranged that last meeting. Because of it I will see to the end of my days his face and his smile, which were once again those of the past.

> Why do my friends who are ten years younger than me pass away before me? I blame myself for having lived so long when it is they who should have outlasted me.

> Be brave, you have your children, they have their mother; I myself have nobody except my works, and that is not the same thing.[24]

Geneviève replied:

> Dear dear friend; you had his last real smile, his last look of recognition, for a moment he remained radiant with joy at having seen you again and embraced you, then he slept heavily and the glimmers of consciousness were so wavering on Monday, Tuesday, and Wednesday

that I do not know if he was still with us; on Thursday evening he did not recognize our son.

Now all is emptiness, a dreadful emptiness, I no longer wish to live![25]

By then the funeral had taken place, on Tuesday 24 November at the local parish church of Saint-François de Sales and at Père Lachaise cemetery. Francis Waël-Munk, in his secretary's report to the annual general meeting of the Association des artistes musiciens, described the scene:

> His funeral had an imposing simplicity about it, he had lived simply and wished to depart simply, without pomp, without ceremony, accompanied by only the liturgical music of his religion. But what his modesty had not been able to prevent was the invasion of the church of Saint-François de Sales by the multitude of his friends and admirers who had come in droves from far and wide to pay him their final respects. At the cemetery, many speeches were given by Messieurs Bourgeat, on behalf of the Conservatoire; Théodore Dubois, on behalf of the Société des concerts; Gailhard, on behalf of the Opéra; Nadaud, on behalf of the Association des artistes musiciens; Combarieu, on behalf of the Société des professeurs du Conservatoire; Gustave Lyon on behalf of Taffanel's personal friends; Philippe Gaubert, on behalf of the students of their much missed teacher.

> His family and his art, those were Paul Taffanel's sole passions; he devoted his entire life to them, that life which can be summed up in these three words: talent, simplicity, kindness.[26]

Waël-Munk was wrong in one detail: Théodore Dubois actually represented the Institut de France, while the Société des concerts sent a wreath and condolences, but no representative (that was the beginning of the scandal described in chapter 10). Meanwhile, "talent, simplicity, kindness" were themes that echoed through the many obituary notices.[27] Then there were personal tributes in the many letters that Geneviève received, including one from Dorus's daughter, Juliette: "Oh! if my father had still been here, how grief-stricken he would have been, he loved him like a father."[28] There was also a letter from the young Nadia Boulanger, recently graduated from the Conservatoire as a composition student: "his kindness, his generosity, and his invaluable and sympathetic advice bound me very closely to him and it is with a heavy heart that I share your overwhelming distress."[29] Taffanel's influence had been far-reaching.

Taffanel left everything in his will to Geneviève, Jacques, and Marie-Camille. The legal process of settling his estate was begun the following January and revealed total assets of a little over 130,000 francs, most of it bound up in property, house contents, stocks, and bonds.[30] He had indeed lived both modestly and wisely.

Unfinished Business

"Translation, still continuing . . . flute method, ditto," Taffanel jotted on a scrap of paper along with a whole list of other jobs to be done. During his final years he had managed to complete an article on conducting (see chapter 10), but he was still working at a series of projects relating to the flute.[31] One of these was a translation of the monumental *Treatise* by Richard Shepherd Rockstro. It had been published in London in 1890 and included Taffanel's name among the list of subscribers to the first edition. Despite Rockstro's theory that Boehm plagiarized the ideas of a certain Captain Gordon when remodeling the flute (refuted soon after by another writer, Christopher Welch), this was the most comprehensive book on all aspects of the flute to have appeared since Quantz's *Versuch* (1752). Taffanel worked on various different sections of Rockstro's book simultaneously, but he managed to translate only about a quarter of its 647 pages. Shortly before his death he gave his copy of Rockstro's book to Louis Fleury, and it was eventually passed on to René Le Roy.[32] At one point in the fifth of the six notebooks Taffanel used for his translation, he recorded the place and date, "Nice, March 1906," and throughout he made margin and footnote annotations, querying various points, or indicating the need to consult a particular source in more detail. Incidentally, his reaction to Rockstro's attribution of the remodeling of the flute to Captain Gordon rather than to Boehm is summed up in the scribbled comment, "What cheek!" at the end of paragraph 631.

When the flute *Méthode* finally appeared in 1923, completed by Gaubert, the preface pointed out the scope of Taffanel's ambitions: "Throughout his long career, Paul Taffanel, pursuing his plan, ceaselessly amassed the materials for a vast treatise which would bring together in complete synthesis all the historical, theoretical, and practical knowledge relating to the flute."[33] Taffanel's aim had been to produce an *Art of the Flute* comparable to the great violin treatise *L'Art du violin*, published by Pierre Baillot in 1834. In addition, Albert Lavignac had requested a comprehensive article on the flute from Taffanel for his projected *Encyclopédie de la musique*. There is virtually nothing left of the material that Gaubert must have used for the *Méthode*. As a close friend of the family, Gaubert appears to have kept most of what was passed on to him by Taffanel, and the manuscript of the *Méthode* has never come to light. It is likely that it was among a collection of personal papers in Gaubert's office at the Paris Opéra that disappeared immediately after his death in 1941, during the German occupation of Paris.[34] It is not possible, therefore, to be completely sure of the precise demarcations of Taffanel's and Gaubert's individual contributions to the *Méthode*.

The situation regarding the *Encyclopédie* article is a little clearer. Fleury returned to Geneviève Taffanel a large amount of the material he had used for the published version. Geneviève, however, gave away all of Taffanel's music and many of his books after his death, so what remains represents only a small nucleus of Taffanel's once comprehensive collection. It is likely that Taffanel would have bought, or been sent, a copy of virtually everything published on the flute. Four letters from the Leipzig publisher Zimmermann, for example, refer to complimentary copies enclosed of flute studies by Köhler and Wehner, and of Emil Prill's book on flute repertoire, *Führer durch die Flöten-Literatur* (1899).[35] Taffanel also obtained Henry Clay Wysham's book *The Evolution of the Boehm Flute* (1898) and wrote to Wysham with various observations. Wysham replied in a rambling, idiosyncratic letter:

> I should long since have acknowledged your most cordial and welcome letter and its valuable enclosures respecting the immortal Boehm. Should I issue another edition of that wretched, hastily written and *ill-dressed* pamphlet, I shall make the very important corrections suggested in your esteemed letter.
>
> You must pardon my writing in English, altho' I am quite au fait in the spoken language (French) I have neglected the script—altho' when in Paris in 1851 I wrote the language with much fluency. Mais, il faut d'habitude, and in later years I have had little practice.
>
> My residence in Paris in 1851 was (il va sans dire) most charming. My pension was the Hotel de L'Isle et D'Albion in the Rue St Honoré. At that time I saw Louis Napoleon (then president) and the lovely Empress Eugénie. Ah! "Tempora mutantur, et nos mutamus cum illis [The times are changed, and we with them]." I visited Paris in 1865— just after our Civil War. The "Gay City" seemed very little changed. I should be charmed to meet you my dear Mr. Taffanel—I fancy we should be very congenial![36]

This and the few other surviving letters to Taffanel about the flute in the latter years of his life hint at a much larger ongoing correspondence that he no doubt had with many other players and enthusiasts. He was obviously a focal point, as a letter from an Abbé Tabuteau in Bordeaux demonstrates. Tabuteau was experimenting with rubber pads for flutes, and the first flute of the Grand Théâtre, Feillou, suggested that he inform Taffanel of his invention. Tabuteau offers to pad a flute within eight days for no charge if Taffanel will send him one— and he gives as evidence of trustworthiness his status as a priest.[37]

Taffanel carefully kept some letters, while others were recycled, along with all sorts of other scraps of paper, for notes and lists. The reverse of a letter from Edouard Risler, for example, was used by Taffanel to make a sketch of a section of flute keywork.[38] This was Taffanel's method of planning and recording his research, working usually on quite small sheets of paper that would fit easily into a jacket pocket. Sometimes he would fold several sheets together to make a small booklet. His approach was detailed and enquiring: the smallest reference or idea was noted and annotated with precise comments and often questions to himself for further investigation.

Most entries in his research booklets begin with the name of a source. Some of these are libraries—for example, the archives of the Opéra, Conservatoire, and Société des concerts. Others are instrument collections—in particular the Conservatoire museum and the museum at La Couture just outside Paris, which was the center of French wind instrument making. Then there are references to books, among them the *Histoire de l'instrumentation* (1878) by Lavoix. Taffanel's copy has copious annotations and clearly acted as a stimulus for him to consult many of the original sources. The scope of Taffanel's research encompassed the full range of the history, construction, repertoire, and aesthetics of the flute, as this sequence of entries from one of his *Recherches* booklets demonstrates:

> *Opéra* Make-up of the *orchestra* from the beginnings: look at simultaneous use of *recorders* and *transverse flutes*: discarding of *recorders*? Compare with the *scores* of the period.
>
> *Museum* Is there an *English* 8 keyed transverse flute, old, to see the *largeness* of the *holes*; compare with a French flute for the *Placing* of the holes (Nicholson flute)
>
> *Lavoix* What is the oldest musical work where flutes appear? In which of the most ancient ceremonies is their presence mentioned?
>
> *Laborde* (1780) consult. See if he talks about *Philbert*
>
> *Library S des C.* Review the works of Bach and Handel, look at the use of the flute from the points of view of the instrument and of the music.
>
> Has Monsieur Julliot had the opportunity to conduct experiments on what the influence might be of a *greater* or *lesser* thickness of the tube on timbre and sound quality.
>
> *Quantz* First reread, then mark in the margin everything that I must extract and even copy
>
> *Kastner* Look at his opinions in his various books (Dances of the Dead?)
>
> *House* Everything that I have on the flute.

Sort through works, Musical Gazette
Fétis, everything he has written, etc

No doubt some of these questions were still unanswered when Taffanel died, but the method and clarity of his approach must have made Fleury's task much easier. Among his notes, Taffanel had also made an analysis of the violin article that Narcisse Lefort was writing for the *Encyclopédie*. This gave Fleury an outline and structure that he followed through in the finished flute article.

In one small notebook Taffanel copied out extracts from sources including Hotteterre, Malherbe, Freillon Poncien, Mersenne, and Tromlitz. He took pains all the time to consult the originals and was dismissive of anything else. A note on the outside cover runs: "Hervé is nothing but a straight copy of Chouquet, Mahillon, Grove, Lavoix, Prout." He made notes from the most diverse sources, including Georges Kastner's book *Danse des morts*, which concerns the mythical origins of instruments and their ritualistic uses.

Then there was the music itself: a treasure trove of original editions to consult in the Conservatoire library. "Important collection," he comments on looking through Blavet's flute works, "I think that I am the first to have gone through it." He also pursued the incidence and use of flutes in the orchestral scores of early French operas such as Lully's *Armide* (1686), Campra's *Le Carnaval de Venise* (1699), Marais's *Alcyone* (1705), and Rameau's *Platée* (1749). He was captivated, for example, by an ariette in the prologue to Destouches's *Issé* (1697): "It is accompanied by a transverse flute, viols, and bass continuo. Delightful Ritornello. The whole thing must be delightful—to be copied. The flute is employed well as a soloist. Range in the piece is from C^2 to D^3, the piece is in D. Graceful and agreeable as the words require."

Taffanel did indeed copy out an example of the flute writing in *Issé*, and also an extract from Lully's *Le Triomphe de l'Amour* (1681), and he made line drawings of a renaissance flute, after Virdung, and part of the keywork of a Boehm flute. He also drew up a chart of the life spans of seventeen flutists from Lambert to Devienne.

La Flûte

Fleury finally completed the article "La Flûte" for Lavignac's *Encyclopédie* in 1925 (he refers to the date on page 1503). In his foreword he explains that Taffanel had invited him to collaborate on it just a few months before his death, and that Geneviève Taffanel and Lavignac had then asked him to continue: "The writing of the article had not been started, but I had in my hands all the documents, notes, references that Paul Taffanel had collected throughout a lifetime of research and reflection on a subject which he wished to treat thoroughly."[39] In fact, Taffanel had begun to write up part of his research, albeit still in a semidraft form, in an eight-page manuscript on the early history of the flute and recorder, which he dated 16 September 1906, his sixty-second birthday. In it, he bemoans the fact that Jacques Hotteterre, the man who could have explained most about the crucial remodeling of the transverse flute during his lifetime, chose to say nothing at all. Taffanel is also very forthright about the relative merits of the flute and the recorder. Of the recorder he writes: "It is certain that its design, the means of sound production, its paucity of resources, and total lack of expressivity caused it to be rejected absolutely as an orchestral instrument." And at that point the manuscript breaks off.

Fleury continues the upward story of the flute, and when he arrives at the section on its repertoire he declares his intention to provide "a list of indispensable works which every flutist should possess." Much of this is the repertoire of studies and pieces, old and new, played and taught by Taffanel (and similar to the one compiled by Moyse for Charles DeLaney: see chapter 11). But Fleury also adds the growing number of pieces that had appeared since Taffanel's death, by composers such as Casella, Debussy, Ferroud, Ibert, Koechlin, Milhaud, and Roussel. Fleury, like Taffanel, kept up with the pace of modern music. His comments on the list of study pieces for flute and piano (Tulou, Lindpaintner, Demersseman, Boehm, Andersen, and Langer) also recall Taffanel:

> Whatever our musical preferences, we cannot neglect the works by flute players which are useful for a student to study, without intending later to perform them in public. This observation does not apply to Fr. Kuhlau, all of whose works are worth playing. The three solos (op. 57) are fundamental to the study of the flute.[40]

The voice of Taffanel also echoes through some of the advice in the section on "The Art of Flute Playing." Even the ordering of the five sections recalls Taffanel's priorities in his Conservatoire reports:

> *Tone*: First and foremost a flute player should be concerned with searching for a good quality of tone . . . one must not forget that volume means little and tone quality is everything.
>
> *Intonation*: Being a good flute player is inseparable from being a good musician . . . the lips must obey the ear.
>
> *Breathing*: This is of paramount importance to the art of flute playing . . . the flute player must convince himself, first and foremost, that the aim of breathing is not only to replenish the lungs with air, it is also a means of expression: to make the most of the musical phrases.

Finger Technique: Concern for evenness is more important than speed, and do not forget that all fingering practice which neglects tone quality is disastrous.

Style: The point should be made that the flute is an instrument of limited resources, that the range of its tone is restrained, and that certain effects, or the expression of certain feelings, must be denied it.[41]

Fleury concludes by explaining that flute playing had sunk into decadence under player-composers such as Tulou and Demersseman, and that Taffanel had led the reaction against this style, partly influenced by a return to the eighteenth-century repertoire, "where the flute was used with more discretion and expression . . . In effect, extreme sobriety of style is to be advocated . . . the ideal interpretation is one which puts the instrument at the service of the music, and not the music at that of the virtuoso."[42]

Méthode de flûte

While Taffanel would no doubt have endorsed Fleury's sentiments (tempered perhaps with less harshness toward Tulou and Demersseman), there is no evidence that the preceding text was drafted by him. The same has to be said about much of the text in the *Méthode de flûte*, although Gaubert did use most of Taffanel's material that has survived: a thirteen-page draft document of instructions for posture and tone production. As this breaks off in midsentence it is reasonable to assume that it was originally much longer, and that Gaubert very likely incorporated more of it.

The official version of the *Méthode*'s genesis is given in the preface: the collaboration had been planned long ago and Taffanel had consulted Gaubert regularly as he was drafting exercises and examples. Gaubert therefore knew exactly how everything would fit together: "Documents, pieces of advice, explanations of general theory or of specific rules, lessons written or sketched, drafts of exercises or studies, work completed or simply in outline, numerous musical texts, nearly everything was gathered together.[43]

So far it all sounds perfectly clear—it was just an editing job on Gaubert's part—but then the point is immediately made that Gaubert "contributed a considerable number of new lessons and finished by writing exercises and studies which add up to an entirely new body of work." This thread is picked up again later in the preface, with the description of "a rich collection of practical studies extracted from the works of the great masters, or elegantly composed by Philippe Gaubert." The two major sets of studies (*Vingt-quatre études progressives* and *Douze grandes études de virtuosité*) are therefore by Gaubert. But on the evidence of the detailed extract of Taffanel's text that remains,

Gaubert's general approach throughout the rest of the *Méthode* seems to have been to edit and abbreviate. He therefore laid himself open to the charge that was quickly brought that the *Méthode* progresses too fast and is not methodical enough—a criticism remembered and reiterated independently by four Gaubert students: Fernand Caratgé, Gaston Crunelle, Robert Hériché, and René Le Roy.[44]

Fleury tried to deflect such criticism by maintaining that this was "a method directed above all at advanced study"—which of course it was not.[45] So the problem remained and had to be addressed in a supplementary "Publisher's Note" to the second edition in 1958: "All methods, even the best, are criticized for never being progressive enough at the very beginning . . . " The solution given was to supplement practice in the first stages with the preliminary exercises in *Le Débutant flûtiste* (1935) by Marcel Moyse. It seems likely, however, that Taffanel's original plan and his thoroughness would have rendered supplementary material unnecessary. He may even have been intending to illustrate the *Méthode* with some of the series of eight photographs that show him demonstrating points of embouchure (see fig. 24).[46] These were taken in the back garden of his home in avenue Gourgaud. What they clearly show is the so-called "relaxed embouchure," with the lips loosely turned out and the minimum of muscle effort and facial distortion, unlike the tight, smiling embouchures of English and German players on wooden flutes.

The term "relaxed embouchure," however, was never part of Taffanel's terminology, although much has since been made of it, and its virtues claimed as the hallmark of the modern French school deriving from him.[47] This is a valid point, but it misses the main emphasis in the *Méthode*, and by implication in Taffanel's own playing, on a totally new approach to deep, supple, and expressive *breathing*. Flexibility of the lips should naturally follow from this, but it was the detailed information given in the chapter on breathing ("De la respiration," page 52) that was unique to the French School in the history of flute playing.

The *Méthode* is confused and confusing, however, on the complementary subject of vibrato and has consequently often been quoted out of context to prove or disprove a particular point of view. The edict on page 186 condemning "*vibrato* or wobbling" (the italics are Gaubert's) should be interpreted with great care. An undisciplined wobble in the sound (*chevrotement*) was certainly condemned by Taffanel, as his Conservatoire report sheets testify, but it was a mistake in terminology to use—even in italics—the term *vibrato* for it. The aural evidence of Gaubert's playing on his recordings clearly proves his use of vibrato. The sound is not completely "straight." And according to Moyse (quoted in chapter 11), Taffanel also had vibrato in his sound. The point is that Gaubert and Taffanel controlled it and used it sparingly—and no doubt sometimes not at all, as in the Adagio by J. S. Bach referred to later in this chapter. Like any other means of expression, vibrato could be abused, but it was undeniably part of French flute playing at this period.[48]

By all accounts Gaubert was in a hurry to complete the *Méthode* and get it published. The First World War had already intervened and held him up, so some years had passed since Taffanel's death, and then there had been the Henri Bouillard scandal over the plagiarized *Exercices journaliers* (see chapter 8). That in particular must have put considerable pressure on Gaubert to bring matters to a satisfactory conclusion by publishing the original version of the *Exercices*. But his own impatience as a teacher made him ill-suited to the task of writing a method. Each of the four students quoted earlier had his own story to tell of how Gaubert never taught technique, was impatient with problems, and concentrated solely on musical matters. Robert Hériché had a particularly telling description of Gaubert saying "Listen!" and demonstrating something to him by playing it, then poking him in the ribs and adding, "There you are . . . like that!"—at which point the lesson was over.

Fernand Caratgé observed Gaubert compiling the *Méthode* around 1922 and said that apart from Taffanel's *Exercices journaliers*, there were only "scraps of paper" to go on, and that Gaubert wrote all the studies. He also claimed that Moyse was responsible for part eight, the "Traits Difficiles" (the first time that orchestral extracts had been included in a French flute method), and that other members of the class assisted Gaubert in various ways. Moyse confirmed that he had assisted Gaubert in the editing process and that the choice of orchestral extracts was particularly difficult to make.[49]

Gaubert's great advantage, however, was that he had absorbed better, and for longer than anyone else, Taffanel's basic principles, and whether in his own words, or those of Taffanel, he mainly took care to express them clearly in the text of the *Méthode*. So if Fleury was wrong about the basic intention of the *Méthode*, he was nonetheless right about its usefulness for advanced study. There is more here about the *art* of flute playing than in any previous French method, especially the one by Altès. Ironically, the exhaustive elementary rigor of Altès's *Méthode* has guaranteed it an enduring popularity among French teachers, whereas the Taffanel and Gaubert *Méthode* (apart from the *Exercices journaliers*) has been largely neglected.

Taffanel's annotations throughout the thirteen-page draft text mentioned earlier clearly illustrate his collaboration with Gaubert. References to "Ph" (Philippe) are scattered throughout, and there is also a joking reference to the embouchure problems of Taffanel's friend Lagorsse: "pull the lips back for the very low notes *only!*" But Gaubert suppressed a significant section of the document. This is a detailed exposition of how the flutist should stand and how the instrument should be held and balanced. In essence, Taffanel describes the lever principle, with the chin as the pivot point and the left-hand index finger and right-hand thumb as opposing forces maintaining the flute in a horizontal plane:

> To ensure maximum stability for the flute, the tip of the thumb should be placed at a point on the curvature of the tube where it can not only *support* the flute but also *counterbalance* the support of the index finger, the action of which naturally directs the instrument *from the front to the back*. . . . combined with resting it on the chin.

This is a lucid explanation of the most efficient and natural way to hold the instrument, and its inclusion would have enhanced the *Méthode* as a teaching aid. There is another piece of practical self-help advice that never made it into the published method:

> You should play very often in front of a mirror and scrutinize yourself rigorously. Then you will also notice any facial *tics*, a very frequent fault which is easy to correct early on, but becomes impossible to get rid of if left to develop.

One other element of Taffanel's original text was not so much suppressed as metamorphosed. His key statement that "quality of tone is the most important thing to cultivate on the flute" (*Le son est la qualité principale à obtenir sur la flûte*) becomes, in Gaubert's words, "Nurture the tone quality" (*Soigner la sonorité*), but the intention is the same (see fig. 25):

> When practising each Exercise or Study, whatever the level of difficulty, the student must always have in mind this precept: tone quality, purity of sound, and rigorous accuracy of intonation must take precedent over considerations of finger technique.[50]

The significant opening metaphor in the *Méthode* about tone production—"to make the instrument *speak*"—has already been noted in connection with Taffanel's *Andante pastoral et scherzettino*. A further metaphor, that of spinning a thread, is applied to the flutist's breath.[51] This "thread of breath," variable in thickness, pressure, and direction by the supple action of the lips, informs the distinctive message of the *Méthode*. It is most clearly articulated in the chapter "On Style":

> The breath is the soul of the flute, in other words it is the fundamental principle of the flute player's art . . . It is the life force of the sound, the spirit which animates it, enlivens it and makes it a voice capable of expressing all the emotions. The lips, the tongue, the fingers are only its servants; by it alone can the artist communicate to the world at large, and with the most fleeting nuances, the thousand inflections of musical emotions, with their infinite variety.[52]

Here is the inclusive aesthetic from which everything else in the *Méthode* derives. The flute, "our beautiful instrument," is capable of great musical expressiveness through subtle shadings of tone. The "soul" of this tone is the breath, and all other aspects of technique are subordinate to it. Posture is therefore related to keeping the lungs unrestricted. The aim of embouchure is to attain supple control over modifications of the airstream. The *legato* principle, inspired by bel canto vocal style, demands deep and sustained breathing, so the necessity of marking appropriate places to breathe in the music is also stressed. The ideal of this perfect legato justifies efficiency of fingering, and alternative fingerings are suggested to aid the expressiveness of the sound. Finally, the tongue gives impulse to the sound, and "articulates" the notes.[53]

At this point striking parallels appear between Taffanel's aesthetic values and those of the first French flute school of Jacques Hotteterre and Michel de La Barre. When La Barre wrote the preface to his *Pièces pour la flûte traversière*, the first solo flute music, in 1702, and Hotteterre compiled his *Principes de la flûte traversière*, the first flute method, in 1707, they shared a vision of the nobility of the instrument and the musical expressiveness of all aspects of technique. Taffanel restated that inclusive aesthetic. Meanwhile, his revival of baroque flute music and the growth of a musically significant modern repertoire were at once both the cause and effect of restoring the balance between technique and music.[54]

Given all that is known about what Taffanel played and how he played it, the choice of music and advice on interpretation in the chapter "On Style" appear authentically his. First there is the Adagio from J. S. Bach's Sonata in B minor:

> This piece, one of the most beautiful jewels of flute literature, should be played with sentiments of lofty nobility, with serene purity of line and absolute simplicity.[55]

Then comes the solo from Gluck's *Orphée*:

> This passage is one of the most beautiful ever written for the instrument. The flute is not only capable of brilliant virtuosity, it can also convey the most profound feelings.[56]

Cadenzas for the two Mozart Concertos follow, with characteristic remarks about concentrating on their musical aspects:

> Take care to vary the tone colours, to contrast brilliance with gracefulness, and in a word try hard to achieve that musical atmosphere which will make the audience forget the cadenza's technical dryness.[57]

The *Première Romance* (1897) by Xavier Leroux (mentioned earlier) and the Nocturne (1901) by Georges Hüe—"play this poetic passage with much charm, with an enveloping tone"—stand as models of the modern repertoire.[58] Leroux had been Gaubert's composition teacher, and Gaubert was the dedicatee of both of his *Romances* and also of Georges Hüe's Nocturne and Gigue. The Gigue (1904) and Albert Doyen's *Nymphes et satyres* (1905) are the final two extracts, given for practice in playing "with much lightness and very brilliantly."[59]

It is also worth noting among the orchestral extracts in the final section the inclusion of three that are particularly taxing on expressive breathing: Berlioz's *L'Enfance du Christ*, Debussy's *L'Après-midi d'un faune*, and Mendelssohn's Scherzo from *A Midsummer Night's Dream*.[60]

Henri Rabaud, the grandson of Louis Dorus, was director of the Conservatoire in 1923 when the *Méthode* was published. He gave it an official seal of approval in a letter addressed to Gaubert, reproduced as a frontispiece to the first edition. Rabaud concludes by offering a final perspective on the career of Taffanel and the course of French flute playing before, during, and after him:

> What Taffanel was—the greatest flute player of his time, an equally great musician and a great conductor—you are today. These two names . . . inscribed at the head of this work give it exceptional authority. Allow me to mention a third, and as the grandson of Louis Dorus to tell you how proud he would have been of the work carried out by his dearest student, Paul Taffanel, and by you, who are continuing his teachings today.

When Taffanel died, the critic Pierre Lalo might well have chosen to remain silent, given his antipathy to Taffanel as a conductor. The fact
that Lalo decided to contribute an obituary notice maybe lends his words extra
weight:

> Monsieur Taffanel is dead. Of the conductor he was in the latter years
> of his life, I have nothing left to say. I attacked him often and too vig-
> orously to be able to speak of him today, whether for good or for bad.
> But the flute player that he was before becoming a conductor was an
> incomparable musician. Never has the flute held its own and fulfilled
> its role in the orchestra as it did when Monsieur Taffanel played it;
> never has it had to such an extent, among all the timbres and instru-
> ments, the color which was its alone; never has it had so much poetry,
> so much grace and so much lightness. Those who heard Monsieur
> Taffanel in the Conservatoire orchestra, or at the Opéra, will never
> forget it. And stylistic purity was allied by him to purity of sound. He
> was a wonderful teacher: the class which he directed for twenty years
> has filled our orchestras with excellent instrumentalists who, if they
> have not equaled a matchless master, maintain no less gloriously the
> superiority of French *winds* over those of all other countries. He was
> truly, in a minor artistic realm, a great artist.[1]

Notice the sting in the tail: Lalo allows Taffanel the title of "great artist,"
but only "in a minor artistic realm" — the world of the flute.

Taffanel's significance to that world is certainly evident, and has been the subject of most of this book. There would not have been an influential French flute school in the twentieth century without him, and certainly not one with such a clearly defined aesthetic that imposed itself throughout Europe and beyond. He reintegrated the flute into the mainstream of chamber music and reestablished it as a solo instrument with a flexible, expressive, and evocative character, tapping into its historical and mythical roots. Its immediate emergence, after his career, into the progressive musical worlds of Debussy and Ravel, and the lifelong preoccupation with the flute of a composer like André Jolivet (not himself a flutist), for example, show a continuation of Taffanel's influence. For Jolivet, the instrument had a mystical resonance: "it sings, it cries, it links us to heaven . . . the flute imbues its notes with both the visceral and cosmic in us."[2]

Taffanel occupied himself with every aspect of the flute and its art, but the qualities that informed these activities also led him progressively into wider spheres. First, he spearheaded the renaissance of chamber music for all the wind instruments—and once again his influence was widespread. The results have been conclusive, with wind sonorities established as a vital component of chamber music ever since. Taffanel's own contribution to the genre, his Wind Quintet, the most ambitious of his compositions, stands as a model of its kind. Second, he forged a career as a conductor, something almost unheard of for a non-string player. But it was Taffanel, not a violinist, who guided the fortunes of the Opéra and Société des concerts through a crucial decade. He established Wagner on the French stage, furthered the evolution of orchestral music by contemporary French composers, and won for Paris the world premiere of Verdi's final *Pezzi sacri*.

Louis Fleury regretted the demands made on Taffanel's time by his conducting responsibilities and wanted to claim him just for the flute.[3] Taffanel himself never thought like that. As a *musician*—whether flutist, conductor, composer, teacher, scholar, writer, administrator—he had broad horizons and exercised considerable influence. There were, in fact, few areas of French musical life in which Taffanel did not play a significant role for some fifty years. We may therefore confidently rewrite Pierre Lalo's conclusion: "He was truly, in a *major* artistic realm, a great artist."

Papiers Paul Taffanel

Summary Inventory

A comprehensive inventory of the archive of Paul Taffanel's letters, papers, and other materials—*Papiers Paul Taffanel*—was drawn up as the basis of the original Ph.D. research on which this book is based. A summary is given here, and the references in the notes identify the general subdivision of the *Papiers*, from PPT1 to PPT20, from which each particular source comes. The archive remains in a private collection.

1. Notes biographiques et professionnelles (1844–1907)

Notebook-diary, 85 pages, outlining details of Taffanel's life and professional activities. Includes biographical details, 1844–1907; rehearsal lists for the Société des concerts du Conservatoire and the Paris Opéra, 1871; names of flute pupils, 1871; a brief repertoire list; a rehearsal register for the Société de musique de chambre pour instruments à vent, 1878–79; and details of the Paris Opéra flute section, August to November 1876.

2. Journal professionnel (1866–1867)

Collection of 42 loose sheets of folded notepaper with brief details of Taffanel's daily activities, personal and professional, 22 January 1866 to 25 August 1867.

3. Lettres autographes de Paul Taffanel: copies (1888–1889)

Copybook, 144 pages, and 6 loose copybook sheets of personal and professional letters written by Taffanel, 28 May 1888 to 6 September 1889. Includes an index listing the names of 80 recipients of the letters.

4. Lettres autographes de Paul Taffanel: brouillons

Exercise book, 58 pages, and 24 assorted loose sheets of notepaper with drafts of personal and professional letters written by Taffanel, some dated 1877, 1879, and 1892, others undated.

5. **Lettres autographes de Paul Taffanel à sa fille Marie-Camille**

Collection of 17 letters from Taffanel to his daughter, 1887–1898.

6. **Lettres autographes à Paul Taffanel**

Large collection of correspondence, c. 1000 items, addressed to Taffanel. Most of the letters date from 1890 onward and concern Taffanel's activities as chief conductor at the Paris Opéra and the Société des concerts du Conservatoire.

7. **Lettres autographes de Camille Saint-Saëns à Paul Taffanel, Geneviève Taffanel, et Marie-Camille Taffanel**

Collection of letters and cards from Camille Saint-Saëns to Paul Taffanel, 38 items, 1882–1908; to Geneviève Taffanel, 8 items, 1901–08; and to Marie-Camille Taffanel, 18 items, 1892–1908; plus 2 concert programs and 4 photographs.

8. **Notes diverses: Histoire et technique de la flûte**

Collection of manuscript and printed papers and notes relating to the history and technique of the flute and the art of flute playing. Includes a handwritten draft, 8 pages, of historical information for the projected article on the flute for Albert Lavignac's *Encyclopédie de la musique et dictionnaire du Conservatoire* (1913–31); a draft explanatory text, 13 pages, for the projected *Méthode de flûte*; an incomplete draft translation in 6 notebooks of R. S. Rockstro, *A Treatise on the Flute* (1890); a partial translation, 4 pages, of Theobald Boehm, ed. W. S. Broadwood, *An Essay on the Construction of Flutes* (1882); a partial translation, 63 pages, of Theobald Boehm, *Die Flöte und das Flötenspiel* (1871); a partial translation, 39 pages, of Christopher Welch, *History of the Boehm Flute* (1882/92); 2 booklets, 10 pages and 8 pages, and 39 loose sheets of notes on the history of the flute; 17 loose sheets of notes on flute music; 2 pages of manuscript music examples; 2 pages of pencil sketches of flutes and flute keywork; a chart of the life spans of 17 flutists from Lambert to Devienne; 8 unsigned printed articles, "La Flûte," *Magasin pittoresque* (1868); 12 unsigned printed articles, "La Flûte," *Le Monde orphéonique* (1902); a printed blueprint of a flute by Djalma Julliot, 1901; a printed brochure, 2 pages, of a flute by Pupeschi, 1907; a collection of miscellaneous notes, 11 pages; and a typed sheet of guidelines for contributors to Lavignac's *Encyclopédie*.

9. **Notes diverses: l'Art de diriger**

Large collection of notes, c. 145 pages; a handwritten chart of the life spans of composers from Palestrina to Wagner; a collection of 7 press cuttings; and a draft handwritten copy, 64 pages, of the published article by Taffanel, "L'Art de diriger," *Encyclopédie de la musique et dictionnaire du Conservatoire*, ed. Albert Lavignac and Lionel de La Laurencie. Paris: Delagrave (1913–31), part 2, vol. 4, pp. 2129–34.

10. **Notes diverses: l'Instrumentation**

Incomplete handwritten draft translation, 63 pages, by Taffanel of Ebenezer Prout, *Instrumentation* (1896). Chapters 1–7 complete, and chapter 8 incomplete. (Chapters 9 and 10 and the appendix not begun.)

11. **Notes diverses: Métronome de précision**

Collection of notes, 20 pages, and 5 items of correspondence, 1908, relating to a projected article on the Decastiau-system metronome.

12. **Notes personnelles sur les épreuves des concours et des examens du Conservatoire**

Two sets of official mark sheets for the Paris Conservatoire *examens semestriels* and *concours*, 1873–1907, annotated by Taffanel with comments on the performances. Woodwinds, 52 sheets, 1873–93; piano, 6 sheets, 1882–99; strings, 9 sheets, 1895–1907; brass, 2 sheets, 1897 and 1899; opera, 1 sheet, 1895; voice (female), 1 sheet, 1897.

13. **Programmes de la Société de musique de chambre pour instruments à vent (1879–1893)**

Collection of 90 printed programs for the 15 seasons of the Society's concerts at the Salle Pleyel in Paris. Complete except for the fifth concert of the third season, 14 April 1881. Annotated by Taffanel with alterations as to programs and/or performers, and two sketches of seating plans.

14. **Notes diverses: voyages en Russie (1887, 1889)**

Collection of notes, letters, and papers relating to Taffanel's concert tour to Moscow and St. Petersburg with Camille Saint-Saëns, Georges Gillet, and Charles Turban, April 1887, and his return visit alone to Moscow, February 1889. Includes passports, travel notes, tickets, programs, hotel bills, street maps, general correspondence, and 12 letters to Taffanel from his wife Geneviève, April 1887.

15. **Notes diverses: voyage à Bayreuth (1892)**

Collection of notes, letters, and papers relating to Taffanel's visit to the Bayreuth Festival and tour of Switzerland, Germany, and Italy with his son, Jacques, August 1892. Includes travel notes; train tickets; maps; newspapers; tickets and programs for Wagner's operas *Tannhäuser, Die Meistersinger, Tristan und Isolde,* and *Parsifal* at Bayreuth; tickets for *Lohengrin* at Munich, and Verdi's *Otello* at Genoa; 3 sketches of the layout of the Bayreuth orchestra; general correspondence; and 17 letters to Taffanel from his wife Geneviève.

16. **Notes diverses: voyage à Munich (1893)**

Collection of notes, letters, and papers relating to Taffanel's visit to Munich to see Wagner's operas *Tristan, Tannhäuser, Die Meistersinger, Das Rheingold,* and *Die Walküre,* September 1893. Includes Taffanel's notes, 5 pages, on each of the operas; miscellaneous travel notes; calculations of expenses; train tickets; tickets and programs for the operas (including one for *Götterdämmerung,* which he was unable to see); a newspaper report of the "Viardot Affair," which called him back early to Paris; and 6 items of general correspondence.

17. **Notes diverses: Verdi: Othello (1894), les Pièces sacrées (1898)**

Collection of notes and correspondence relating to the Paris Opéra premiere of Verdi's *Otello,* 12 October 1894; and correspondence relating to the world premiere of the *Sacred Pieces* at the Société des concerts du Conservatoire, 7 April 1898. Includes two notebooks, 12 pages and 8 pages, and 25 loose sheets of rehearsal notes; 25 letters and telegrams from Giuseppe Verdi, Boito, Tito, and Giulio Ricordi; and 10 draft letters and telegrams from Taffanel in reply.

18. **Notes diverses: Wagner: Lohengrin (1891), Tannhäuser (1895), Les Maîtres chanteurs (1897), Tristan et Iseult (1904)**

Collection of notes, papers, and correspondence relating to the Paris Opéra productions of Wagner's *Lohengrin*, 16 September 1891; *Tannhäuser*, 13 May 1895; *Die Meistersinger*, 10 November 1897; and *Tristan und Isolde*, 14 December 1904. Includes a printed rehearsal schedule for *Lohengrin*; for *Tannhäuser*: a notebook, 10 pages, loose sheets of rehearsal notes, and general correspondence; for *Die Meistersinger*: a rehearsal schedule, a printed booklet, the program of the premiere, 5 draft replies to critics, a booklet of manuscript music extracts, 3 dossiers of miscellaneous notes including rehearsal notes, 35 letters from Alfred Ernst, Gustave Fridrich, and Edouard Risler, 3 draft letters from Taffanel in reply, and other general correspondence; for *Tristan und Isolde*: a notebook, 4 pages, 1 loose sheet of rehearsal notes, and general correspondence.

19. **Notes diverses: Exposition 1900**

Large collection of notes, papers, correspondence, and printed material relating to the organization and administration of the official concerts of orchestral and choral music at the 1900 Paris Exhibition. Includes separate dossiers of administrative notes, papers, and correspondence on planning, personnel, and finance; a dossier of notes and correspondence on the inauguration concert, 14 April; programs, notes, and correspondence relating to each of the 10 official concerts, 31 May to 4 October; dossiers on the Swedish concert and prize-giving concert (not conducted by Taffanel); a selection of press cuttings; and a copy of Alfred Bruneau, *Exposition universelle de 1900: Rapport présenté à Monsieur le ministre de l'instruction publique* (1900), inscribed to Taffanel.

20. **Divers: papiers et objets personnels**

Miscellaneous collections of papers and personal items. Includes instruments, books, and scores, portraits and photographs, awards and decorations, conducting batons, miscellaneous legal and family papers, magazines and newspaper cuttings, programs and other memorabilia. Also includes two biographical sketches of Taffanel: a typescript, 4 pages, signed J.J. [Joseph Jemain] and dated 1906, which appears to be the source for the entry in Goldberg (see bibliography); and a manuscript, 7 pages, in the hand of Geneviève Taffanel, which is a modified and expanded version of J.J.

Paul Taffanel Works List

Theoretical Writings

"L'Art de diriger," *Encyclopédie de la musique et dictionnaire du Conservatoire*, ed. Albert Lavignac and Lionel de la Laurencie. Paris: Delagrave (1913–31), part 2, vol. 4, pp. 2129–34. Written by Taffanel c. 1906.

"La Flûte," with Louis Fleury. *Encyclopédie de la musique et dictionnaire du Conservatoire*, ed. Albert Lavignac and Lionel de la Laurencie. Paris: Delagrave (1913–31), part 2, vol. 3, pp. 1483–1526. Completed by Fleury in 1925 and published in 1927.

Méthode complète de flûte, with Philippe Gaubert. 1 vol., 8 parts. Paris: Leduc (1923). 2nd ed., 2 vols., 8 parts, 1958. AL 16588. Compiled and edited by Gaubert, 1922–23.

Original Compositions (published)

Grande fantaisie sur "Mignon," opéra d'Ambroise Thomas for flute and piano. Paris: Heugel (1874). H 5682. "à mon Maître et ami Louis Dorus."

Fantaisie sur "Le Freyschütz" de Ch. M. de Weber for flute and piano. Paris: Mackar (1876). FM 519. (no dedication)

Quintette for flute, oboe, clarinet, horn, and bassoon. Paris: Leduc (1878, comp. 1876). AL 6018. "à Monsieur Henri Reber, Membre de l'Institut."

Fantaisie-transcription sur "Les Indes Galantes," opéra-ballet de J. P. Rameau for flute and piano. Paris: Mackar (1877). FM 581. "à son ami le Docteur B. Coizeau."

Grande fantaisie sur "Jean de Nivelle," opéra de Léo Delibes for flute and piano. Paris: Heugel (1881). H 6869. "à son ami Johannes Donjon."

Fantaisie sur "Françoise de Rimini," opéra d'Ambroise Thomas for flute and piano. Paris: Heugel (1884). H 7990. (no dedication)

Sicilienne-Etude, op. 7 for flute and piano. Paris: Mackar (1885). FM 796. "à Walter Stuart Broadwood Esq." Modern edition, ed. Edward Blakeman. London: Pan Educational Music, 1998.

Trois études (nos. 98–100), in Louis Drouet, *Cent études pour la flûte*, op. 126, vol. 4. Paris: Brandus (1886). B+Cie 657. "Nouvelle édition revue, corrigée, et complétée par Paul Taffanel."

Andantino for cello and piano. Paris: *Le Monde musical*, 1902. MM 56. Sight-reading piece for the Paris Conservatoire *concours*, 1902.

Andante pastoral et scherzettino for flute and piano. Paris: Enoch, 1907. E+Cie 6624. "à Philippe Gaubert." *Morceau de concours*, Paris Conservatoire, 1907.

17 Grands exercices journaliers de mécanisme for flute solo. Paris: Leduc, 1923, 1927. AL 17204. Extracted from the *Méthode complète de flûte*. Exact date of composition unknown, but before 1890.

Cadences pour les concertos en ré et en sol de Mozart for flute solo. Paris: Leduc, 1923. AL 19491, 19492. Extracted from the *Méthode complète de flûte*. Exact date of composition unknown, but after 1883.

Cadence écrite pour Mme Melba (for Donizetti's *Lucia di Lammermoor*), with Mathilde Marchesi, for soprano and flute. In Mathilde Marchesi, *Variantes et Points d'orgue*. Paris: Heugel, 1900, p.51. Composed c. 1886.

Original Compositions (unpublished)

Air varié sur "La Fille du régiment" de Donizetti for flute and piano. Performed from manuscript in Paris, February 1865. Ms lost.

Variations sur un thème allemand for flute and piano. Performed from manuscript in Lille, January 1866. Ms lost

Cadenza for Ferdinand Langer, Flute Concerto (1867). Ms lost.

Morceaux de lecture à vue (sight-reading pieces) for the Paris Conservatoire annual *concours*:

Allegretto grazioso for flute and piano, 1877
[Title unknown] for flute and piano, 1879 (ms lost)
Andantino con moto for flute and piano, 1883
Andante for flute and cello, 1884
Allegro for flute and piano, 1885
[Title unknown] for flute and piano, 1888 (ms lost)
Allegretto for flute and piano, 1890
Allegretto scherzando for flute and piano, 1892
Andante molto espressivo for clarinet and piano, 1891
Andante pastorale for oboe and piano, 1891
Andante espressivo for bassoon and piano, 1892

Modern editions:

Allegretto grazioso, 1877, and Allegretto scherzando, 1892, ed. Edward Blakeman. London: Pan Educational Music, 1986.

Allegro, 1885, and Allegretto, 1890, ed. Edward Blakeman. London: Hunt Edition, 1993.

Andantino con moto, 1883, and Andante, 1884 (originally for flute and cello), arr. and ed. Edward Blakeman. London: Pan Educational Music, 1998.

Original Transcriptions for Flute and Piano

Bach, J. S. *Polonaise et badinerie* (from the B minor Suite). Paris: Mackar (1877). FM 501.

Chopin, Frederic. *Deux nocturnes et une valse* (op. 15, nos. 1 and 2, and op. 64, no. 1). Paris: Mackar (1883). FM 776.

Delibes, Léo. *Valse lente et pizzicati* (from *Sylvia*). Paris: Heugel (1880). H 6801, 6802.

Langer, Curt. *Gavotte d'amour*. Paris: Hamelle (n.d.). J 2005 H.

Massenet, Jules. *Méditation* (from *Thaïs*). Paris: Heugel (1894). H 9626.

Mendelssohn, Felix. *Six romances sans paroles*. Paris: Mackar (1878). 3 vols.: *Doux souvenir* and *Chanson de printemps*. FM 385. *Bonheur perdu* and *L'étoile du soir*. FM 386. *Contemplation* and *Sérénade*. FM 387.

Tchaikovsky, Pyotr. *Arioso* (from *Eugene Onegin*). Paris: Mackar et Noël (1889). M et N 2024.

Transcriptions in Series for Flute and Piano

Souvenirs du Théâtre-Italien, 6 duos très faciles pour piano et flûte, composés pour piano et violon par Charles Dancla, arrangés pour la flûte par Taffanel. Paris: Colombier (1868); and Leipzig: Peters (1868). The score gives the version for violin and piano, and a separate flute part is enclosed, with various differences from the violin part:

1. Bellini. *Norma*. C 2024 (score); C 3260 (part).
2. Bellini. *La Straniera*. C 2025; C 3261.
3. Bellini and Donizetti. *Norma* et *Elisire*. C 2026; C 3262.
4. Donizetti. *Elisire*. C 2027; C 3263.
5. Rossini. *Semiramide*. C 2028; C 3264.
6. Mozart. *Don Juan*. C 2029; C 3265.

Répertoire de la Société des concerts du Conservatoire et des Concerts populaires, 20 transcriptions classiques pour piano et flûte par P. Taffanel d'après A. Berthemet. Paris: Mackar (1873–1876 [1886?]). The series was available for piano and violin, ed. A. Berthemet, and for piano and cello, ed. E. Nathan and F. Demarquette. It was issued in two volumes: *10 Transcriptions . . .* and *20 Transcriptions . . .* Bibliothèque nationale, Paris, gives 1873 for collected vol. 1, 1875 for no. 11, 1877 for no. 14, and 1886 for nos. 15 onward.

1. Mozart. Larghetto (from Quintet in A, op. 108). FM 16.
2. Beethoven. *Thème, variations et marche* (from Serenade, op. 8). FM 314.
3. Haydn. Adagio cantabile (from Symphony no. 5 in D). FM 315.
4. Boccherini. *Minuetto* (from Quintet no. 4 in E). FM 316.
5. Beethoven. Polonaise (from Serenade, op. 8). FM 317.
6. Mozart. *Minuetto* (from Quartet in D minor). FM 318.
7. Haydn. Andante (from Symphony in A, *L'Impériale*). FM 319.
8. Mozart. *Marche turque*. FM 320.
9. Viotti. *Minuetto con variazioni* (from Violin Sonata no. 6). FM 321.
10. Mendelssohn. *Canzonetta* (from Quartet in E flat, op. 12). FM 322.
11. Gluck. *Scène d'Orphée*. FM 488.
12. Haydn. *Sérénade*. FM 489.

13. Leclair (l'aîné). Gavotte (1720). FM 543.

14. Boccherini. *Sicilienne*. FM 588.

15. Beethoven. *Thème et variations* (from Septet, op. 20). FM 844.

16. Haydn. Andante (from Symphony no. 6 in G). FM 845.

17. Mozart. Finale (from Quartet in D minor, ballet music to *Don Giovanni*). FM 846.

18. Beethoven. *Thème varié* (from Quartet in D, op. 18, no. 5). FM 847.

19. Haydn. *Adagio cantabile* (from Quartet in D, op. 65). FM 848.

20. Mozart. Andante (from Quartet in D, op. 18). FM 849.

Album célèbre. Morceaux choisis . . . pour flûte et piano par P. Taffanel. London: Enoch (n.d). Published in Format Litolff, nos. 495 and 498 (1879). V 493:

Gottermann. *Le Rêve*
Gounod. *Sérénade*
Hauser. *Wiegenlied*
Henselt. *Liebeslied*
Raff. *Cavatina*
Rubinstein, A. *Mélodie*
Rubinstein, A. *Romance*
Spohr. Barcarolle
Schumann. *Schlummerlied*

Raff-Album. 6 morceaux op. 85 transcrits pour flûte et piano par P. Taffanel. Paris: Enoch (n.d.). V 496: "Marcia," "Pastorale," "Cavatina," "Scherzino," "Canzona," and "Tarantella."

P. Taffanel, Transcriptions pour flûte avec accompagnement de piano. Paris: Durand (1886–1909). Published in two volumes: *Six transcriptions . . .* (1886), and *Douze transcriptions . . .* (1887).

1. Braga. *La Serenata* (*Légende valaque* for voice). D.S. 2739 (2).

2. Durand, A. *Chaconne*, op. 62. D.S. 1527.

3. Raff. *Cavatine*, op. 85, no. 3. D.S. 1086 (3).

4. Raff. *Tarentelle*, op. 85 no. 6. D.S. 1086.

5. Saint-Saëns. *Pavane* (from *Etienne Marcel*). D et F 3468.

6. Schumann. *Rêverie*, op. 15 (from *Kinderszenen*). D.S. 3941 (2).

7. Durand, A. *Première valse*, op. 83.

8. Saint-Saëns. *Pavane* (from *Proserpine*). D.S. 3809.

9. Saint-Saëns. *Prélude* (from *Le Déluge*). D.S. 3808.

10. Saint-Saëns. *Rêverie du soir* (from *Suite algérienne*, op. 60). D.S. 3745 bis.

11. Saint-Saëns. *Romance*, op. 51 (original for cello). D.S. 2333 bis.

12. Thomé. *Simple aveu*. D.S. 2837 bis.

By 1891 the series had expanded to 17, although the number was no longer used in the title. The additional items were:

Bach, J. S. *Aria en ré* (from Orchestral Suite no. 3, BWV 1068), 1890. D.S. 4273 (score), 4283 (part).

Handel. *Célèbre Largo* (from *Xerxes*), 1891. D.S. 4382 (score), 4384 (part).

Jacquard. *Divertissement*, op. 5, no. 6, pub. 1888. D.S. 3980.

Saint-Saëns. *Le Cygne* (from *Le Carnaval des animaux*), 1888. D et F 3891.

Saint-Saëns. *Airs de ballet* (from *Ascanio*), 1890. D.S. 4211.

P. *Taffanel. Deux transcriptions pour flûte et piano.* Two items (with dedications "à mon ami De Lagorsse") published posthumously. Paris: Durand (1909):

Gluck. *Sicilienne* (from *Armide*). D+F 7367.

Quantz. *Adagio.* D+F 7366.

Miscellaneous Transcriptions

Saint-Saëns. *Feuillet d'album*, op. 81 for flute, oboe, two clarinets, two horns, and two bassoons (original for piano, four hands). Paris: Durand, 1888. D.S. 3893.

Revised Editions

Drouet, L. *Cent études*, op. 126 for solo flute, 4 vols. Paris: Brandus (1887). B+Cie 654, 655, 656, 657. (See above for nos. 98–100, *Trois études*, comp. Taffanel.)

Kuhlau, F. *Six divertissements*, op. 68 for flute solo, or flute and piano. Paris: Collection Litolff no. 2231 (n.d.).

Music Dedicated to Paul Taffanel

This list is necessarily incomplete: Taffanel's library of books and music was dispersed after his death, and therefore the information has been collected piecemeal from libraries and other sources over a number of years. Undoubtedly there are discoveries still to be made.

Flute Solo

Köhler, Ernesto. *Der Fortschritt im Flötenspiel,* op. 33, vol. 3. Leipzig: Zimmerman, n.d. (c. 1888).

Flute and Orchestra

Andersen, Joachim. *Deuxième morceau de concert,* op. 61 (for flute and orchestra or piano). Copenhagen: Hansen, 1895. 11763.

_____. *Moto perpetuo,* op. 8 (for flute and orchestra or piano). Berlin: Ruhle e Wendling, n.d. (1883).

Bernard, Emile. *Romance,* op. 33 (for flute and orchestra or piano). Paris: Mackar, 1885. FM 832.

Borne, François. *Ballade et danse des lutins* (for flute and orchestra or piano). Paris: Durdilly, n.d. (1886). VD 963.

Chaminade, Cécile. Concertino, op. 107 (for flute and orchestra or piano). Paris: Enoch, 1902. E+C 5161.

Gaubert, Philippe. *Nocturne et allegro scherzando* (for flute and orchestra or piano). Paris: Enoch, 1906. E+C 6338.

Godard, Benjamin. *Suite de trois morceaux,* op. 116 (for flute and orchestra or piano). Paris: Durand, 1890. ("Allegretto," "Idylle," and "Valse.") DS 4144 (1–3).

Flute and Piano

Andersen, Joachim. Impromptu, op. 7. Berlin: Ruhle e Wendling, n.d. (1883).

Barrère, Georges. Nocturne. New York: Schirmer, 1913. 24141.

Bériot, Charles de. *Sonate*, op. 64. Paris: Hamelle, n.d.. J 2787 H. Composed c. 1885.

Boisdeffre, René de. *Trois pièces*, op. 31. Paris: Hamelle, n.d. (1885?). ("Prélude," "Orientale," and "Air de ballet.") J 2617 H.

Bruneau, Alfred. *Romance*. Paris: Hamelle, n.d. (1884). J 2333 H.

Busser, Henri. *Prélude et scherzo*, op. 35. Paris: Leduc, 1908. AL 22954.

Catherine, Alphonse. Nocturne. Paris: Durand, n.d. (1900?). D+F 5899.

Damaré, Eugène. *Troisième grand solo, sur le ballet de "Yedda," musique de O. Métra*, op. 103. Paris: Gérard, n.d. (1882). CM 11742.

Donjon, Johannes. *Rêverie*, op. 16. Paris: Lacombe, n.d. (1887). ELD 79.

Durand, Jacques. *Romance*, op. 7. Paris: Durand, n.d. (1888?). D+F 3880.

Duvernoy, Alphonse. Concertino, op. 45. Paris: Durand, n.d. (1899). D+F 5626.

Enesco, Georges. *Cantabile et presto*. Paris: Enoch, 1904. E+C 5888.

Fauré, Gabriel. *Fantaisie*, op. 79. Paris: Hamelle, 1898. J 4283 H.

Fontbonne, Léon. *Chasse aux papillons* (*Sérénade*), op. 30. Paris: Evette et Schaeffer, n.d. (1890). E.S. 207.

Ganne, Louis. *Andante et scherzo*. Paris: Costellat, 1906. C+C 784. Composed 1901.

Gaubert, Philippe. *Sonate*. Paris: Durand, 1918. D+F 9572.

Grandval, Clémence de. Suite. Paris: Richault, n.d. (1876). ("Prélude," "Scherzo," "Menuet," "Romance," and "Final.") 15,831 R (1–5).

Herman, Jules. *Introduction et variations sur "Le Carnaval de Venise,"* op. 23. Paris: Benoit, n.d. (1869). 2731.

Lafleurance, Léopold. *Six études de Chopin* (transcribed for flute and piano), 2 vols. Paris: Durand, n.d. (c. 1895?). D+F 4973 (1–2).

Lalo, Edouard. *Introduction et allegretto* (from *Namouna*). Paris: Hamelle, n.d. (1884). J 2486 H.

Lefèbvre, Charles. *Deux pièces*, op. 72. Paris: Bruneau, n.d. (1889). ("Barcarolle mélancolique" and "Scherzo.") B+Cie 114, 115.

Périlhou, Albert. Ballade (for flute or violin). Paris: Heugel, 1903. H et Cie 21,614.

Pessard, Emile. *Deuxième pièce en mi mineur*, op. 28. Paris: Leduc, n.d. (1886). AL 7566.

Pierné, Gabriel. *Sérénade*, op. 7 (transcribed for flute and piano). Paris: Leduc, n.d. (1887). AL 7785.

Reynaud, Louis. Nocturne (for flute or violin). Paris: Courleux, n.d. (1896). Vve GC 414.

Widor, Charles-Marie. Suite, op. 34. Paris: Heugel, n.d. (1898). ("Moderato," "Scherzo," "Romance," and "Final.") H+C 18909. Composed 1884.

Flute and Harp

Grandval, Clémence de. *Valse mélancolique*. Paris: Heugel, n.d. (1891). GH+Cie 2250.

Mouquet, Jules. *Divertissement grec*, op. 23 (flute and harp or piano). Paris: Lemoine, 1908. 20321 HL.

Flute, Oboe, and Piano

Gaubert, Philippe. *Tarentelle*. Paris: Leduc, 1903. E+C 5791.

Weckerlin, Jean-Baptiste. *Pastorale*. Paris: Heugel, n.d. (1889). H 8549.

Voice, Flute and Piano

Diémer, Louis. *Sérénade*. Paris: Heugel, n.d. (1887). H 4754.

Wind Quintet (flute, oboe, clarinet, horn, bassoon)

Barthe, Adrien. *Aubade*. Paris: Pinatel, n.d. (1888). AP 1893. Composed c. 1879.

Lefèbvre, Charles. Suite, op. 57. Paris: Hamelle, n.d. (1884?). J 2171 H.

Pfeiffer, Georges. *Pastorale*. Paris: L. Grus, n.d. LG 3603. Composed c. 1880.

Wind Octet (flute, oboe, clarinet, cor anglais, two horns, two bassoons)

Lazzari, Sylvio. *Octuor*, op. 20. Paris: Evette et Schaeffer, n.d. (1920). ES 887. Composed 1892.

Wind Nonet (flute, two oboes, two clarinets, two horns, two bassoons)

Gounod, Charles. *Petite symphonie*. Paris: Costellat, 1904. C+C 1000. Composed 1885.

Ten Instruments

Hartmann, Emil. *Sérénade*, op. 43, for flute, oboe, two clarinets, two horns, two bassoons, cello, and double bass. Berlin, Ries & Erler, 1890.

Lalo, Edouard. *Aubade*, for ten instruments or small orchestra (flute, oboe, clarinet, bassoon, horn, two violins, viola, cello, and double bass). Paris: Hartmann, n.d. (1890). ("Allegretto" and "Andantino.") GH et Cie 1826. Composed c. 1872, revised 1884.

Chorus and Orchestra

Saint-Saëns, Camille. *Le Feu céleste*, op. 115. Paris: Durand, 1900 (vocal score only). D+F 5743.

Société classique

Repertoire, 1872–75

No programs have survived for the Société classique concerts, so the list has been compiled from details given in *La Revue et gazette musicale* and *Le Ménestrel*, which regularly reported on the Society's activities.[1] However, no information has been found for the concert on 12 March 1872. See chapter 4 for the history of the Society.

An asterisk denotes an advertised "first performance."

A plus sign denotes a work later played by Taffanel's Société de musique de chambre pour instruments à vent. See chapter 6 and appendix 5.

Works without Wind Instruments

Composer	Title	Date(s) of Performance
Beethoven, Ludwig van	Piano Trio, op. 70 [no further details]	17.02.74
		31.03.75
	Piano Trio, op. 70, no. 1	08.04.73
	Piano Trio, op. 97	27.02.72
		31.03.74
	Sonata for piano, op. 27, no. 2	16.03.75
	Sonata for violin and piano in A [no further details]	16.02.75

---

1. *La Revue et gazette musicale*: 1872, pp. 22, 31, 47, 63, 79, 80, 95, 101. 1873, pp. 22, 46, 54, 62, 79, 86, 95, 101, 111, 118. 1874, pp. 15, 30, 39, 46, 55, 62, 70, 78, 86, 103, 109. 1875, pp. 30, 38, 46, 55, 62, 71, 86, 87, 94, 103, 110, 119, 125.

Le Ménestrel: 1872, pp. 56, 64, 71, 87, 103, 111, 136. 1873, pp. 72, 80, 120, 136, 151. 1874, pp. 47, 71, 87, 104, 119, 136. 1875, pp. 71, 87, 103, 119, 136, 152.

	Sonata, for violin and piano, op. 12 [no further details]	28.02.73
	Sonata for violin and piano, op. 30	30.01.72
	Sonata for violin and piano, op. 69	16.02.75
	String Quartet no. 1, op. 18 no. 1	03.03.74
	String Quartet no. 2, op. 18 no. 2	11.03.73
	String Quartet no. 5, op. 18 no. 5	13.04.75
	String Quartet no. 5, op. 18 no. 5, Andante and Variations	27.02.72
	String Quartet no. 8, op. 59 no. 2	20.01.74
	String Quartet no. 10, op. 74	28.01.73
	String Quartet no. 11, op. 95	02.02.75
	String Quartet no. 13, op. 130, extracts [no further details]	02.03.75
	String Quintet, op. 29	16.01.72
		17.03.74
Castillon, Alexis de	Piano Quintet	26.03.72
David, Félicien	Adagio for string quintet	08.04.73
Gouvy, Théodore	String Quartet, Andante and Variations [no further details]	31.03.75
	*String Quartet no. 3, op. 56, Larghetto	03.03.74
	String Quintet [extracts, no further details]	11.02.73
Handel, Georg Friedrich	Concerto for 2 violins [no further details]	28.01.73
Haydn, Joseph	*Hymne* [no further details]	31.03.75
	String Quartet no. 40, op. 33 no. 4	25.03.73
	String Quartet no. 74, op. 74 no. 3	20.01.74
	String Quartet no. 75, op. 76 no. 1	17.02.72
	String Quartet no. 77, op. 76 no. 3	11.03.73
Mendelssohn, Felix	Octet for strings, op. 20	02.03.75
	Piano Quartet no. 3, op. 3	11.02.73
	Piano Trio no. 1, op. 49	03.03.74
		13.04.75
	Piano Trio no. 2, op. 66	11.03.73
	Sonata for cello and piano, op. 45	16.01.72
	String Quartet [no further details]	16.02.75
	String Quartet no. 2, op. 13	27.02.72
	String Quartet, op. 44 [no further details]	17.02.74
	String Quintet no. 2 in B flat, op. 87	08.04.73
	String Quartet, op. 81, 2 movements [no further details]	25.03.73
	Variations for cello and piano, op. 17	28.01.73

Mozart, Wolfgang Amadeus	Piano Trio, K. 542	16.02.75
	Sonata for violin and piano in A [no further details]	17.03.74
	String Quartet [no further details]	28.02.73
	String Quartet in B flat [no further details]	03.02.74
	String Quartet, Andante con variazioni [no further details]	02.02.75
Rubinstein, Anton	Sonata for cello and piano [no further details]	17.02.74
Schubert, Franz	Piano Trio no. 2, D. 929	02.03.75
	Quintet for piano and strings, D. 667 "Trout"	17.03.74
	String Quartet no. 4, D. 46, Andante and Variations	30.01.72
Schumann, Robert	Piano Quartet, op. 47	25.03.73
		16.03.75
	Piano Quintet, op. 44	17.02.72
		03.02.74
Vieuxtemps, Henri	Sonata for violin and piano, Adagio and Scherzo [no further details]	02.02.75
Weber, Carl Maria von	Piano Quartet	20.01.74

Works with Wind Instruments

Composer	Title	Date(s) of Performance
Bach, Johann Sebastian	Brandenburg Concerto no. 5, for piano, violin, and flute, BWV 1050	17.02.72
	(+) Sonata for flute and piano [no further details]	11.03.73
	Suite no. 2 for flute and strings, BWV 1067	31.03.74
Beethoven, Ludwig van	+ Octet for 2 oboes, 2 clarinets, 2 horns, and 2 bassoons, op. 103	17.02.72
	+ Septet for violin, viola, cello, clarinet, horn, bassoon, and double bass, op. 20	11.02.73 16.03.75
	+ Serenade for flute, violin, and viola, op. 25	26.03.72
	+ Trio for 2 oboes and cor anglais, op. 87	03.02.74
Berlioz, Hector	+ Trio for 2 flutes and harp from *L'Enfance du Christ*	11.02.73 16.03.75
Castillon, Alexis de	*Allegretto for wind quintet and string quintet	25.03.73 17.02.74
Chaine, Eugène	Octet for wind and strings, extract [no further details]	16.02.75
	Wind Quintet, op. 8	17.02.74

Gastinel, Léon	*Andante and Capriccio for wind and strings	03.02.74
	*Sextet for piano and wind, op. 34	02.03.75
Grandval, Clémence de	+ Suite for flute and piano	28.01.73
Handel, Georg Friedrich	Concerto for 2 oboes and strings [no further details]	16.02.75
	(+) Sonata for flute and piano in G [no further details]	03.02.74
Hummel, Johann Nepomuk	+ Septet for piano, flute, oboe, horn, viola, cello, and double bass, op. 74	30.01.72 08.04.73
Kreutzer, Léon	+ Sextet for piano and wind quintet	28.02.73 17.03.74
Lalo, Edouard	*(+) *Intermezzo* for wind quintet and string quintet	26.03.72
	(+) *Andantino* for wind quintet and string quintet	17.02.74
	*(+) *Andantino et intermezzo* for wind quintet and string quintet	11.03.73 13.04.75
Massenet, Jules	*Introduction and Variations for wind quintet and string quintet	26.03.72 08.04.73 02.02.75
Mozart, Wolfgang Amadeus	+ Quintet for clarinet and strings, K. 581	30.01.72 31.03.74 31.03.75
	+ Quintet for piano, oboe, clarinet, horn, and bassoon, K. 452	27.02.72
	*+ Serenade in B flat, for 2 oboes, 2 clarinets, 2 basset horns, 4 horns, 2 bassoons, and double bass, K. 361, "Gran Partita"	28.01.73
	*+ Serenade in C minor for 2 oboes, 2 clarinets, 2 horns, and 2 bassoons, K. 388	03.03.74
	*+ Serenade in E flat for 2 oboes, 2 clarinets, 2 horns, and 2 bassoons	13.04.75
Onslow, Georges	Wind Quintet, 3 movements [no further details]	25.03.73
Rubinstein, Anton	+ Quintet for piano, flute, clarinet, horn, and bassoon, op. 55	20.01.74
Schubert, Franz	+ Octet for 2 violins, viola, cello, double bass, clarinet, horn, and bassoon, D. 803	26.03.72 31.03.74
Schumann, Robert	+ 2 *Fantasiestücke* for clarinet and piano, from op. 73 [no further details]	03.03.74
Spohr, Ludwig	+ Nonet for violin, viola, cello, double bass, and wind quintet, op. 31	16.01.72 28.02.73

	+ Quintet for piano, flute, clarinet, horn, and bassoon, op. 52	02.02.75
Weber,	+ Grand Duo for clarinet and piano, op. 47	31.03.75
Carl Maria von	+ Trio in G minor, op. 63 for piano, flute, and cello	16.01.72

Société de musique de chambre
pour instruments à vent

Personnel and Repertoire, 1879–93

Compiled from Paul Taffanel's set of original, annotated programs for the fifteen seasons of the Society's concerts at the Salle Pleyel in Paris (see appendix 1, PPT13). Only the surnames of players appeared on the programs, so these have been expanded to full names, with dates of birth wherever known. The titles of works appeared on the original programs in a variety of formats, so for ease of identification these have been regularized, and opus numbers and so forth provided where possible. See chapter 6 for the history of the Society.

An asterisk denotes an advertised "first performance."

Personnel

FOUNDER MEMBERS 1879

Instrument	Name	Date of Birth
Flute	Paul Taffanel	1844
Oboe	Georges Gillet	1854
	Auguste Sautet	?
Clarinet	Charles Turban	1847
	Arthur Grisez	1841
Horn	Henri Dupont	1844
	Jean Garigue	1859
Bassoon	Jean Espaignet	1823
	François Villaufret	1833
Piano	Louis Diémer	1843

ADDITIONAL PLAYERS 1879 – 81

Instrument	Name	Date of Birth	Date of First Appearance
Flute	Edouard Lafleurance	1836	1879
	Johannes Donjon	1839	1881
Oboe	Louis Boullard	1852	1879
Clarinet	Louis Mayeur	1837	1879
	Léon Touzard	1837	1879
	Ernest Boutay	1834	1880
	René Bourdin	1854	1881
Horn	Jacques Schlotmann	1825	1879
	Félix Bonnefoy	1831	1879
	François Brémond	1844	1881
Bassoon	Adolphe Bourdeau	1838	1880
Harp	Adolphe Hasselmans	1845	1879
Violin	Martin Marsick	1847	1880
	Alfred Turban	1847	1881
Viola	Charles Trombetta	1834	1880
Cello	Hippolyte Rabaud	1839	1880
	Ermanno Mariotti	1856	1881
Double Bass	Emile de Bailly	?	1879

THE BASIC ENSEMBLE FROM 1882

Instrument	Name
Flute	Paul Taffanel
Oboe	Georges Gillet
	Louis Boullard
Clarinet	Charles Turban
	Arthur Grisez
Bassoon	Jean Espaignet
	Adolphe Bourdeau
Horn	François Brémond
	Jean Garigue

ADDITIONAL PLAYERS 1882 – 93

Instrument	Name	Date of Birth	Date of First Appearance
Flute	Léopold Lafleurance	1865	1886
	Jules Roux	1865	1889
	Adolphe Hennebains	1862	1892

Oboe	Pierre Dorel	1852	1882
	August Triébert	1845	1884
	Georges Longy	1868	1889
	Louis Bas	1863	1889
	Jules Clerc	1862	1891
	François Jean	1869	1893
Clarinet	Prosper Mimart	1859	1885
	Henri Paradis	1861	1886
	Léon Touzard	1837	1889
	Henri Lefèvre	1867	1893
Horn	Fernand Reine	1858	1884
	Jean Penable	1856	1886
	Arthur Delgrange	1858	1892
Bassoon	Lucien Jacot	1852	1888
	Théodore Schubert	1844	1891
	Léon Letellier	1859	1892
Piano	Caroline Montigny-Rémaury	1843	1883
	Camille Saint-Saëns	1835	1885
	Joseph Jemain	1864	1885
	Edouard Risler	1873	1889
	Gabriel Pierné	1863	1890
	Raoul Pugno	1852	1892
	Alphonse Thibaud	1861	1893
Violin	Gustave Fridrich	1850	1882
	Narcisse Lefort	1852	1883
	[?] Guidé	?	1884
	Guillaume Rémy	1856	1884
	Pablo de Sarasate	1844	1885
	Edouard Nadaud	1862	1886
	Théophile Laforge	1863	1886
	Henri Berthelier	1856	1887
	Joseph Joachim	1831	1887
	Eugene Hayot	1862	1887
	Léon Carembat	1861	1888
	Alfred Brun	1864	1889
	Eugène Ysaÿe	1858	1893
Viola	Jean Bernis	1857	1884
	Louis Van Waefelghem	1840	1884
	Elie Prioré	1858	1886
	Victor Balbreck	1862	1893
Cello	Charles Lebouc	1822	1882
	Jules Loëb	1852	1884
	August Gautier	1864	1885

	Léon Jacquard	1826	1885
	Célestin Cros-St-Ange	1855	1886
	André Hekking	1855	1886
	Jules Delsart	1844	1889
	Richard Loys	1841	1889
Double Bass	Frédéric Fischer	?	1882

Repertoire

Composer	Title	Date(s) of Performance
Alary, Georges	*Cavatine et intermezzo* for flute, oboe, 2 clarinets, horn, and bassoon	23.04.91
Bach, Johann Sebastian	Cantabile, Menuetto, and Rondo, for oboe and piano [no further details]	20.03.90
	Concerto for piano, 2 flutes, and strings [Brandenburg Concerto no. 4, BWV 1049]	15.04.80 10.04.84
	Concerto for piano, flute, violin and strings [Brandenburg Concerto no. 5, BWV 1050]	27.04.82 29.03.83 19.03.85 01.03.88 16.02.93
	Sonata in B minor for flute and piano, BWV 1030	06.02.79 28.02.84 31.03.87 26.02.91
	Sonata in E flat for flute and piano, BWV 1031	06.03.79 28.04.81
	Sonata in E minor for flute and piano, BWV 1034	04.03.86 18.02.92 03.03.92
	Sonata in E major for flute and piano, BWV 1035	21.02.89
Barthe, Adrien	*Aubade* for wind quintet	06.02.79 19.02.85
	Pièces for oboe and piano (*Le Berger, Bourrée, Couvre-feu*, and *Scherzo*)	20.02.90
Beethoven, Ludwig van	Octet for 2 oboes, 2 clarinets, 2 horns, and 2 bassoons, op. 103	06.02.79 18.03.80 14.04.81 13.04.82 15.02.83 19.02.85

	29.04.86
	17.02.87
	12.04.88
	18.04.90
	18.02.92
Quintet for piano, oboe, clarinet, horn, and bassoon, op. 16	20.03.79
	17.09.81
	14.02.84
	19.03.85
	14.04.87
	21.03.89
	28.04.92
Rondino for 2 oboes, 2 clarinets, 2 horns, and 2 bassoons, WoO25	19.02.80
	28.04.81
	01.03.83
	18.02.86
	29.03.88
	04.04.89
	08.05.90
Septet for violin, viola, clarinet, horn, bassoon, cello, and double bass, op. 20	27.04.82
	02.04.85
	07.04.87
	03.04.90
	14.04.92
Serenade for flute, violin, and viola, op. 25	15.04.86
	13.04.93
Sextet for 2 clarinets, 2 horns, and 2 bassoons, op. 71	03.04.79
	04.03.80
	16.03.82
	31.03.92
*Sextet for 2 violins, viola, cello, and 2 horns, op. 81b	26.04.88
Sonata for horn and piano, op. 17	20.02.79
	27.03.84
Sonata for violin and piano, op. 47 "Kreutzer"	02.05.89
Trio for piano, clarinet, and cello, op. 11	05.02.80
	16.04.85
	21.02.89
*Trio for piano, flute, and bassoon, WoO37	03.03.92
Trio for 2 oboes and cor anglais, op .87	20.03.79
	16.02.82
	15.03.83
	08.05.84: 2 movs only
	01.04.86

		07.03.89
		26.02.91
		27.04.93
Bériot, Charles de	*Sonata for flute and piano	01.04.86
Berlioz, Hector	Trio for 2 flutes and harp from *L'Enfance du Christ*	03.04.79
Bernard, Emile	*Divertissement* for double wind quintet, op. 36	10.04.84
		16.04.85
		01.04.86
		12.04.88
		20.02.90
		03.03.92
Boccherini, Luigi	Sonata in A for cello and piano	26.03.91
Boisdeffre, René de	*Pièces* for flute and piano (*Prélude, Air de ballet, Orientale,* and *Finale*)	16.04.85
	*Septet for piano, wind quintet, and double bass, op. 29	08.05.84
		18.04.90
	Trois pièces for clarinet and piano	14.04.81
Borne, Fernand Le	*Aquarelles* for wind quintet, trumpet, 2 timpani, and strings, op. 20	13.04.93
Brahms, Johannes	*Quintet for clarinet and strings, op. 115	16.02.93
	Serenade for wind and strings, op. 16	03.03.81
	[14 players]	19.03.85
	Sonata for violin and piano, op. 78	07.04.87
	Trio for horn, violin, and piano, op. 40	04.03.80
Chovan, C.	*Danses hongroises* for 2 pianos	18.04.89
Colomer, Blas-Maria	Andante and Rondo for oboe and piano	13.04.82
	Divertissement for wind and harp from *Les Noces de Fingal*	18.04.90
	*Nonet for flute, 2 oboes, 2 clarinets, 2 horns, and 2 bassoons, op. 52	12.04.83
		13.03.84
Coquard, Arthur	*Deux pièces* for oboe and piano	31.03.92
Deslandres, Adolphe	Scherzo for wind quintet	03.04.79
Diémer, Louis	*Andante and Scherzo for piano and wind quintet	29.04.86
		08.05.90
	Deux pièces for oboe and piano	14.02.84
		19.03.85
		17.03.87
		18.04.89
		16.02.93
	*Sextet for piano and wind quintet	31.03.87
	"Trois solos" for piano [no further details]	14.04.81

Durand, Jacques	*Romance* for flute and piano, op. 7	29.03.88
		23.04.91
Dvořák, Antonin	Serenade for winds, cello, and double bass, op. 44	05.02.80
		02.03.82
		14.02.84
		18.04.89
		14.04.92
Ehrhart, Jacques	*Valses* for piano, flute, oboe, and clarinet	18.02.92
		28.04.92
Fischof, R.	Variations and Fugue for 2 pianos	18.04.89
Gade, Niels	*Fantasiestücke* for clarinet and piano, op. 43	15.03.83
		07.03.89
Godard, Benjamin	*Scènes écossaises* for oboe and piano (*Légende*, *Sérénade* and *Marche*)	04.05.93
	Trois pièces for flute and piano (*Prélude*, *Idylle*, and *Valse*)	06.03.90
Gounod, Charles	*Petite symphonie* for flute, oboe, 2 clarinets, 2 horns, and 2 bassoons	30.04.85
		04.03.86
		17.03.87
		01.03.88
		06.03.90
		03.03.92
Gouvy, Théodore	*Octet for flute, oboe, 2 clarinets, 2 horns, and 2 bassoons, op. 71	28.04.81
		30.03.82
		01.03.83
		27.03.84
		02.04.85
		07.04.87
		16.02.88: 3rd mov only
		20.03.90
	*Octet no. 2	29.04.86
	*Septet for flute, 2 oboes, 2 clarinets, and 2 bassoons	26.04.88
		04.04.89
	Serenade for wind quintet	04.03.80
Grandval, Clémence de	*Deux pieces* for clarinet and piano	13.03.84
	Deux pieces for cor anglais and piano	18.03.80
		31.03.81
		26.04.88
	Suite for flute and piano	18.04.79
	Valse mélancolique for flute and harp	18.04.90

Handel, Georg Friedrich	"Chaconne variée" for piano [no further details]	08.05.84
	Sonata for flute and piano [no further details]	19.02.80
	Sonata for flute and piano [no further details]	17.02.81
	Sonata for oboe and piano [no further details]	16.03.82
	*Sonata for oboe and piano [no further details]	12.04.83
	Sonata in G minor for oboe and piano [no further details]	18.02.86
		21.03.89
		09.04.91
	Sonata in C minor for oboe and piano [no further details]	30.03.93
Hartmann, Emil	*Serenade for flute, oboe, 2 clarinets, 2 horns, 2 bassoons, cello, and double bass, op. 43	26.03.91
Herzogenberg, Heinrich von	*Quintet for piano, oboe, clarinet, horn, and bassoon, op. 43	05.03.85
	*Trio for piano, oboe, and horn, op. 61	18.04.90
Hummel, Johann Nepomuk	Septet for piano, flute, oboe, horn, viola, cello, and double bass, op. 74	18.03.80
		16.03.82
		01.03.83
		19.02.85
		29.03.88
		08.05.90
		26.03.91
		13.04.93
Indy, Vincent d'	Trio for piano, clarinet, and cello	18.04.89
Klughardt, August	*Schilflieder: cinq morceaux de fantaisie for piano, oboe, and viola	09.02.85
		03.04.90
Kreutzer, Léon	Sextet for piano and wind quintet	03.04.79
Lachner, Franz	Octet for flute, oboe, 2 clarinets, 2 horns, and 2 bassoons, op. 156	04.03.80
		03.03.81
		26.04.83
		18.03.86
		15.03.88
		03.04.90
		13.04.93
Lalo, Edouard	*Aubade for wind quintet and string quintet (Allegretto and Andantino)	08.05.84
		26.04.88
		02.05.89
Lassen, Edouard	Deux Fantasiestücke for bassoon and piano, op. 48	16.02.82

Lazzari, Silvio	*Octet for flute, oboe, clarinet, cor anglais, 2 horns, and 2 bassoons, op. 20	16.02.93
Lefèbvre, Charles	*_Intermezzo-Scherzando_ for flute, oboe, 2 clarinets, horn, and bassoon	18.02.92
	*_Méditation_ for flute, oboe, 2 clarinets, 2 horns, and 2 bassoons	03.03.87 16.02.88 20.03.90
	*_Deux pièces_ for wind quintet (_Canon_ and _Scherzo_)	02.03.82 15.02.83
	*_Trois pièces_ for wind quintet (_Canon_, _Scherzo_, and _Allegro_)	13.03.84
	Suite for wind quintet (_Canon_, _Scherzo_, and _Final_)	04.03.86 09.04.91
Liszt, Franz arr. Edouard Lassen	_Trois pièces_ for wind quintet from _Années de pèlerinage_ (_Pastorale_, _Nostalgie_ and _Eglogue_)	20.03.79 30.03.82
Mendelssohn, Felix	_Concertstück_ for clarinet, alto clarinet (basset horn), and piano, op. 114	18.04.79 17.02.81 28.02.84 17.03.87 27.04.93
	Sonata for cello and piano, op. 58	14.04.87
Mozart, Wolfgang Amadeus	"Adagio" for 2 oboes, 2 clarinets, 2 horns, and 2 bassoons [possibly 3rd movement of Serenade, K. 375]	02.05.89 20.02.90
	Adagio for 2 clarinets, and 3 alto clarinets (basset horns), K. 411	01.04.80
	Adagio and Rondo for harmonica, flute, oboe, viola, and cello, K. 617	08.05.90
	*Divertimento for flute, oboe, bassoon, 4 horns, and string quintet, K. 131	14.02.84 18.02.86
	*Quartet for oboe and strings, K. 370/368b	29.03.88
	Quintet for clarinet and strings, K. 581	14.04.87
	*Quintet for horn and strings, K. 407	29.03.83
	Quintet for piano, oboe, clarinet, horn, and bassoon, K. 452	06.03.79 14.04.81 02.03.82 15.02.83 13.03.84 30.04.85 18.03.86 12.04.88 04.04.89 12.03.91 31.03.92

	Serenade in B flat for 2 oboes, 2 clarinets, 2 alto clarinets (basset horns), 4 horns, 2 bassoons, and double bass, K. 361, "Gran Partita" [extracts only: 1879, movs 5–7; 1881–93, movs 1, 3, 4, 6, 7]	18.04.79
		17.03.81
		26.04.83
		05.03.85
		03.03.87
		21.03.89
		23.04.91
		04.05.93
	Serenade in E flat for 2 oboes, 2 clarinets, 2 horns, and 2 bassoons, K. 375	20.02.79
		17.02.81
		12.04.83
		17.03.87
		07.03.89
		09.04.91
		30.03.93
	Serenade in C minor for 2 oboes, 2 clarinets, 2 horns, and 2 bassoons, K. 388	20.03.79
		01.04.80
		31.03.81
		27.04.82
		28.02.84
		15.04.86
		16.02.88
		06.03.90
		17.03.92
	*Symphonia concertante for oboe, clarinet, horn, and bassoon, K. 297b [with piano accompaniment arr. Staub, 1889; arr. Risler, 1893]	21.02.89
		16.03.93
	Trio in E flat for piano, clarinet, and viola, K. 498, "Kegelstatt"	03.03.81
		17.02.87
Nováček, Rudolf	*Sinfonietta for flute, oboe, 2 clarinets, 2 horns, and 2 bassoons, op. 48	21.03.89
O'Kelly, [?]	Menuet de "La Reine" for flute, oboe, clarinet, 2 horns, and 2 bassoons	18.03.80
Onslow, Georges	Sextet for piano, flute, clarinet, horn, bassoon, and double bass, op. 30	05.02.80
		31.03.81
		13.04.82
		28.02.84
		04.03.86
		16.02.88
		17.03.92
Périlhou, Albert	*Divertissement for 2 flutes, 2 oboes, 2 clarinets, 2 bassoons, and 4 horns	26.02.91
		27.04.93
Pessard, Emile	Prélude et menuet for wind quintet	20.02.79

245

Pfeiffer, Georges	*Musette* for oboe, clarinet, and bassoon	03.04.79
		16.03.82
		19.02.85
	Pastorale for wind quintet	15.04.80
		16.03.82
		27.03.84
	*Sextet for piano and wind quintet	18.02.92
Pierné, Gabriel	*Canzonetta* for clarinet and piano	12.03.91
Raff, Joachim	*Romance* for horn and piano	18.03.86
	Sinfonietta for double wind quintet, op. 188	19.02.80
		15.04.80
		16.02.82
		29.03.83
		30.04.85
		31.03.87
		21.02.89
		12.03.91
	Sonata for violin and piano, op. 73	30.03.93
Rameau, Jean-Philippe	*Pièces en concert* for harpsichord, flute, and cello (*Le Vézinet, La Timide, L'Indiscrète,* and *Tambourins*)	08.05.90
Reinecke, Carl	*Octet for flute, oboe, 2 clarinets, 2 horns, and 2 bassoons, op. 216	16.03.93
	*Sonata for flute and piano, op. 167 "Undine"	15.02.83
		04.04.89
		27.04.93
Rheinberger, Josef	*Nonet for wind quintet, violin, viola, cello, and double bass, op. 139	17.02.87
Rietz, Julius	*Concertstück* for piano and wind quintet, op. 41	01.04.80
Röntgen, Julius	Serenade for flute, oboe, clarinet, 2 horns, and 2 bassoons, op. 14	06.03.79
		17.03.81
Rubinstein, Anton	Octet for piano, flute, clarinet, horn, violin, viola, cello, and double bass, op. 9	28.04.81
		15.04.86
	Quintet for piano, flute, clarinet, horn, and bassoon, op. 55	06.02.79
		01.04.80
		16.02.82
		15.03.83
		27.03.84
		18.02.86
		15.03.88
		20.02.90
		30.03.93

Saint-Saëns, Camille	*Caprice sur des airs danois et russes for piano, flute, oboe, and clarinet, op. 79	16.02.88 31.03.92
	Carnaval des animaux for 2 pianos, 2 violins, viola, cello, double bass, flute, clarinet, harmonica, and xylophone	28.04.92
	Rhapsodie d'Auvergne for piano, op. 73	30.04.85
	Romance for horn and piano, op. 36	20.03.79 14.04.87
	Romance for flute and piano, op. 37	05.02.80 14.04.92
	Scherzo for two pianos, op. 87	08.05.90 30.04.91 28.04.92
	Sonata no. 1 for violin and piano, op. 75	30.04.91
	Tarentelle for flute, clarinet and piano, op. 6	06.03.79 31.03.81 13.03.84 02.05.89 12.03.91
	Variations sur un thème de Beethoven for two pianos, op. 35	15.03.83
Saint-Saëns, Camille arr. Paul Taffanel	*Feuillet d'album for flute, oboe, 2 clarinets, 2 horns, and two bassoons [arr. from piano duet, op. 81]	16.02.88 18.04.89
Sarreau, G.	Nonet for piano, flute, clarinet, horn, bassoon, and string quartet	02.05.89
Schubert, Franz	Fantasia for violin and piano, D. 934	02.04.85
	Introduction and Variations on "Trock'ne Blumen," for flute and piano, D. 802	15.04.80 02.03.82 26.04.83 17.02.87 26.04.88
	*Octet for 2 violins, viola, cello, double bass, clarinet, horn, and bassoon, D. 803	01.03.88
	Rondo brillant for violin and piano, D. 895	14.04.92
Schubert, Franz arr. Georges Pfeiffer	Menuet for flute, 2 oboes, 2 clarinets, horn, and 2 bassoons	15.04.80 27.03.84 12.04.88
Schumann, Robert	"Les Veillées" for piano, clarinet, and viola [Märchenerzählungen, op. 132?]	30.03.82 12.04.88
	"Contes des fées" for piano, clarinet, and viola [Märchenerzählungen, op. 132?]	26.03.91
	Fantasiestücke for clarinet and piano, op. 73	15.04.80 29.04.86

		29.03.88
		17.03.92
		16.03.93
	Romances for oboe and piano, op. 94, nos. 2 and 3	20.02.79
		03.03.81
		01.03.83
		30.04.85
		15.04.86
	Romance from *Concertstück* for 4 horns, op. 86	18.02.86
Spohr, Louis	*Nonet for violin, viola, cello, double bass, and wind quintet, op. 31	08.05.84
		30.04.91
	Quintet for piano, flute, clarinet, horn, and bassoon, op. 52	20.02.79
		19.02.80
		30.03.82
		12.04.83
		16.04.85
		01.04.86
		07.03.89
		09.04.91
		04.05.93
Strauss, Richard	*Serenade for 2 flutes, 2 oboes, 2 clarinets, 4 horns, 2 bassoons, and double bass, op. 7	29.03.83
		10.04.84
		15.03.88
		17.03.92
Taffanel, Paul	*Romance et saltarelle* for wind quintet [Quintet, op. 3, movs 2 and 3]	13.04.82
Tchaikovsky, Pyotr arr. Paul Taffanel	*Arioso* for flute and piano from the opera *Eugene Onegin*	15.03.88
Thuille, Ludwig	*Sextet for piano and wind quintet, op. 6	20.03.90
		26.02.91
		16.03.93
Weber, Carl Maria von	Grand Duo for clarinet and piano, op. 47	03.04.79
		17.03.81
		18.03.86
		06.03.90
	Trio for piano, flute, and cello, op. 63	03.03.87
		23.04.91
Widor, Charles-Marie	*Suite for flute and piano, op. 34	10.04.84
		05.03.85
		30.04.91

Paris Conservatoire Flute Class

Registers, Repertoire, Reports, and Awards, 1893–1908

These records are compiled from the manuscript logbooks of the Paris Conservatoire: PAN, AJ37, 162ff (*Tableaux des classes*); 293ff (*Rapports des professeurs*); and 252,3 and 253,3 (*Rapports des concours*); as well as the annually published *Conservatoire national de musique et de déclamation, Distribution des prix*, Paris, Imprimerie nationale, 1893–1909; and Constant Pierre, *Le Conservatoire*, Paris, Imprimerie nationale, 1900.

Paul Taffanel became the flute professor in October 1893 and gave his first lesson on 15 November. He continued as professor until his death in November 1908. See chapter 11 for a commentary on Taffanel's class.

The following information charts the progress of the flute class annually from 1893 to 1908, with names of the students; dates of the twice-yearly examinations (once-yearly from 1906); details of the examination set pieces [note: titles given in the log books are often not precise] and of which students played which pieces (identified by the numbers after their names); a selection of Taffanel's reports; dates of the annual *concours*; names of the jury members; details of the set pieces; and names of the students competing and the prizes awarded.

Year 1893–94

Students	Danis, Leclercq, Deschamps, Barrère, Boyrie, Grenier, Pascal, Leducq, Million, Balleron, Leduc, Stenosse, D. Maquarre, Gaubert [age range 12 years, 7 months (D. Maquarre) to 23 years, 3 months (Grenier)]
Examination	29 Jan. 1894
Set Pieces	1. Kuhlau: Fantaisie
	2. Lindpaintner: Concerto
Selected Reports	Barrère (2) Has made a little progress.

Maquarre (1) Has been ill—has attended only a few classes—
I don't yet know what he is capable of.
Gaubert (1) Good musical aptitude.
Deschamps (2) Tone is rather harsh.
Balleron (1) Is having difficulty improving his tone.

Examination	18 June 1894
Set Pieces	1. Andersen: Concertstück
	2. Briccialdi: Concerto
	3. Briccialdi: Solo de concert
	4. Demersseman: Third Solo
	5. Demersseman: Sixth Solo
	6. Kuhlau: First Divertissement
	7. Kuhlau: Second Divertissement
	8. Kuhlau: Third Divertissement
	9. Kuhlau: Fourth Divertissement
	10. Kuhlau: Third Grand Solo
	11. Mozart: Concerto
Selected Reports	Barrère (11) Making progess in tone quality and finger technique.
	Maquarre (10) Still beginning.
	Gaubert (7) Very talented student.
Concours	30 July 1894
Jury	Thomas (chairman), Jonas, Joncières, Barthe, Montjau, Pugno, Turban, Wettge, Réty (secretary)
Set Pieces	1. Ferdinand Langer: Concerto (extracts)
	2. Paul Vidal: Morceau de lecture à vue
Students Competing	Deschamps, Grenier, Million, Pascal, Leduc, Leclercq, Stenosse, Denis, Gaubert, Barrère.
First Prize	Philippe Gaubert (b. 1879)
	Pierre Joseph Deschamps (b. 1874)
Second Prize	Jules Arthur Leduc (b. 1875)
First Accessit	Jean Louis Grenier (b. 1870)
	Georges Barrère (b. 1876)
Second Accessit	André Hippolyte Stenosse (b. 1874)

Year 1894–95

Students	Leclercq, Barrère, Grenier, Pascal, Million, Leduc, Stenosse, D. Maquarre, Boudier, Blanquart
Examination	28 Jan. 1895
Set Pieces	1. Briccialdi: Concerto
	2. Demersseman: Fantaisie
	3. Demersseman: Sixth Solo

4. Godard: Allegretto
5. Kuhlau: First Solo
6. Kuhlau: Second Solo
7. Pratten: Solo de concert
8. Tulou: Third Solo

Selected Reports	Barrère (4) Very good student—good musician. Maquarre (5) Making a little progress. Blanquart (6) Tone quality defective.
Examination	17 June 1895
Set Pieces	1. Briccialdi: Concerto 2. Demersseman: Sixth Solo 3. Lindpaintner: Concerto in G 4. Mozart: Concerto in D 5. Saint-Saëns: Andante et Allegro 6. Tulou: Fourth Solo
Selected Reports	Barrère (2) Very good student. Maquarre (4) Could have made more progress. Blanquart (4) Has made significant progress.
Concours	29 July 1895
Jury	Thomas (chairman), Jonas, Joncières, Barthe, Lefèbvre, de Vroye, Dupont, Turban, Wettge, Réty (secretary)
Set Pieces	Joachim Andersen: Concertstück, op. 3 Adrien Barthe: Morceau de lecture à vue
Students Competing	Maquarre, Barrère, Pascal, Leduc, Grenier
First Prize	Georges Barrère (b. 1876)
Second Prize	Jean Louis Grenier (b. 1870)
First Accessit	Daniel Maquarre (b. 1881)

Year 1895–96

Students	Grenier, Million, Leduc, D. Maquarre, Boudier, Blanquart, Jurisch, Sorel, Beaudu, Fleury
Examination	27 Jan. 1896
Set Pieces	1. Andersen: Concertstück 2. Demersseman:Second Solo 3. Demersseman: Third Solo 4. Lindpaintner: Concerto in G 5. Lindpaintner: Concerto pathétique 6. Kuhlau: First Solo 7. Kuhlau: Second Solo 8. Kuhlau: Third Solo 9. Mozart: Concerto in D

Selected Reports	Maquarre (3) Making significant progress.
	Blanquart (4) Good student.
	Fleury (7) Quite good aptitude.
Examination	19 June 1896
Set Pieces	1. J. S. Bach: Fourth Sonata
	2. Demersseman: First Solo
	3. Demersseman: Second Solo
	4. Kuhlau: Second Divertissement
	5. Lindpaintner: Concerto
	6. Mozart: Concerto in D
	7. Tulou: Thirteenth Solo
Selected Reports	Maquarre (7) Progress has slowed a little.
	Blanquart (3) Still making progress.
	Fleury (6) Quite good student.
	Million (6) Very good student.
Concours	30 July 1896
Jury	Thomas (chairman), Jonas, Joncières, Pugno, Lefèbvre, de Vroye, Dupont, Turban, Wettge, Réty (secretary)
Set Pieces	Jules Demersseman: Sixth Solo
	Raoul Pugno: Morceau de lecture à vue
Students Competing	Leduc, Maquarre, Million, Blanquart, Boudier, Grenier
First Prize	Daniel Maquarre (b. 1881)
	Jean Louis Grenier (b. 1870)
Second Prize	Antoine Ernest Million (b. 1871)
First Accessit	None awarded
Second Accessit	Charles Boudier (b. 1877)
	Gaston Gustave Alfred Blanquart (b. 1877)
Year 1896–97	
Students	Million, Boudier, Blanquart, Jurisch, Sorel, Beaudu, Fleury, Bladet, Krauss, Monpeurt
Examination	25 Jan. 1897
Set Pieces	1. Demersseman; Second Solo
	2. Demersseman: Sixth Solo
	3. Langer: Concerto
	4. Pratten: Solo de concert
	5. Saint-Saëns: Air de ballet
	6. Tulou: Thirteenth Solo
Selected Reports	Blanquart (3) Very talented: keen worker. Musical—tone quality sometimes defective.
	Fleury (1) Sensitive by nature, but restricted by being so impressionable.

Bladet (2) A serious flutist. Good finger technique, good tone, playing a little cold.

Krauss (6) Conscientious, a worker. Very keen to succeed, good aptitude.

Examination	21 June 1897
Set Pieces	1. Andersen: Concerto
	2. Briccialdi: Solo de concert
	3. Demersseman: First Solo
	4. Demersseman: Third Solo
	5. Langer: Concerto
	6. Lindpaintner: Concerto in G
	7. Mozart: Concerto in D
	8. Mozart: Concerto in G
	9. Tulou: Fifth Solo

Selected Reports   Blanquart (1) Very good student.
Fleury (6) Very impressionable by nature. Good feeling for music.
Bladet (5) Very good student.
Krauss (3) Good qualities—much progress.

Concours	30 July 1897
Jury	Dubois (chairman), Joncières, Lefèbvre, Jonas, Pugno, Marty, Turban, Hennebains, Wettge, Bourgeat (secretary).
Set Pieces	Joachim Andersen: Deuxième Morceau de concert, op. 61
	Alphonse Duvernoy: Morceau de lecture à vue
Students Competing	Jurisch, Blanquart, Million, Bladet, Sorel, Boudier, Fleury
First Prize	Antoine Ernest Million (b. 1871)
Second Prize	Gaston Gustave Alfred Blanquart (b. 1877)
First Accessit	Louis François Fleury (b. 1878)
Second Accessit	Georges Eugène Jurisch (b. 1883)

Year 1897–98

Students	Boudier, Blanquart, Jurisch, Sorel, Fleury, Bladet, Krauss, Monpeurt, Bauduin, Laurent [N.B not Georges Laurent: he did not join the class until 1902]
Examination	24 Jan. 1898
Set Pieces	1. Andersen: Concertstück
	2. J. S. Bach: Fourth Sonata
	3. Briccialdi: Solo de concert
	4. Demersseman: Second Solo
	5. Kuhlau: Second Solo
	6. Kuhlau: Third Solo
	7. Mozart: Concerto in D
	8. Pratten: Solo de concert

Selected Reports Blanquart (8) Very good student.

Fleury (2) Continuous progress. Beginning to have some confidence.

Bladet (1) Very good student.

Krauss (8) Very keen worker. Serious progress.

Laurent (6) A natural flute player. Absolutely no general musical knowledge.

Examination 20 June 1898

Set Pieces
1. Briccialdi: Capriccio
2. Demersseman: Sixth Solo
3. Handel: Third Sonata
4. Langer: Concerto
5. Lindpaintner: Concerto
6. Pratten: Solo de concert
7. Tulou: Third Solo
8. Tulou: Eighth Solo

Selected Reports Blanquart (3) Very good student.

Fleury (3) Attractive personality—too impressionable.

Bladet (6) Very good student.

Krauss (2) Has made great progress. Very good attitude.

Laurent (7) Has some natural aptitude for the flute, but is completely lacking as a musician. No progress.

Jurisch (5) Continuous progress. Tonguing still rather heavy.

Concours 28 July 1898

Jury Dubois (chairman), Paladilhe, Fauré, Widor, Jonas, Pierné, Hennebains, Turban, Wettge, Bourgeat (secretary)

Set Pieces Gabriel Fauré: Fantaisie

Gabriel Fauré: Morceau de lecture à vue

Students Competing Blanquart, Jurisch, Bladet, Monpeurt, Sorel, Krauss, Fleury, Boudier

First Prize Gaston Gustave Alfred Blanquart (b. 1877)

Second Prize Gaston Daniel Bladet (b. 1879)

First Accessit Paul Charles Krauss (b. 1879)

Georges Eugène Jurisch (b. 1883)

Second Accessit Léon Eugène Sorel (b. 1879)

Year 1898–99

Students Jurisch, Sorel, Fleury, Bladet, Krauss, Monpeurt, Bauduin, Laurent, Dusausoy, Cardon

Examination 23 Jan. 1899

Set Pieces
1. J. S. Bach: Sixth Sonata
2. Demersseman: First Solo

3. Demersseman: Second Solo
4. Demersseman: Sixth Solo
5. Kuhlau: Second Divertissement
6. Kuhlau: Second Solo
7. Lindpaintner: Concertino
8. Saint-Saëns: Airs de ballet

Selected Reports

Fleury (1) Good musician. Interesting personality but too impressionable.

Bladet (7) Good student—attractive tone quality. Good finger technique.

Krauss (8) Very good student (often held back by his health).

Bauduin (5) Very diligent student. Embouchure not yet formed. Good finger technique.

Laurent (6) No progress.

Examination   22 June 1899

Set Pieces
   1. Briccialdi: Concerto
   2. Briccialdi: Solo romantique
   3. Demersseman: Sixth Solo
   4. Lindpaintner: Concertino
   5. Mozart: Concerto in G
   6. Pratten: Solo de concert
   7. Saint-Saëns: Airs de ballet
   8. Tulou: First Solo
   9. Tulou: Eighth Solo

Selected Reports

Fleury (3) Beginning to overcome his extreme nervousness. Very interesting student. Good tone.

Bladet (1) Very good student. Finger technique and tone excellent.

Krauss (7) Very good student. Extremely adept.

Laurent (2) I have been unable to do anything with this student for two years.

Bauduin (3) Good student. Constant progress. Good musician.

Concours   27 July 1899

Jury   Dubois (chairman), Duvernoy, Messager, Puget, Fauré, Hennebains, Turban, Wettge, Bourgeat (secretary)

Set Pieces   Alphonse Duvernoy: Concertino
Alphonse Duvernoy: Morceau de lecture à vue

Students Competing   Cardon, Bauduin, Fleury, Bladet, Jurisch, Sorel, Krauss, Dusausoy, Monpeurt

First Prize   None awarded

Second Prize   Louis François Fleury (b. 1878)

First Accessit   None awarded

Second Accessit	Urbain Alexandre Bauduin (b. 1882) Fernand Dusausoy (b. 1882)

Year 1899–1900

Students	Jurisch, Sorel, Fleury, Bladet, Krauss, Bauduin, Dusausoy, Cardon, Delangle, Huet
Examination	26 Jan. 1900
Set Pieces	1. Briccialdi: Capriccio 2. Kuhlau: Air varié in G 3. Kuhlau: Second Solo 4. Langer: Concerto 5. Lindpaintner: Concerto in E minor 6. Mozart: Concerto in G (finale) 7. Tulou: Eighth Solo 8. Tulou: Thirteenth Solo
Selected Reports	No written reports Fleury (6), Bladet (5), Krauss (4), Bauduin (1)
Examination	22 June 1900
Set Pieces	1. Demersseman: Sixth Solo 2. Godard: Allegretto 3. Langer: Concerto 4. Lindpaintner: Concerto, op. 28 5. Lindpaintner: Concertino 6. Mozart: Concerto in G 7. Saint-Saëns: Romance 8. Tulou: First Solo 9. Tulou: Fifth Solo 10. Tulou: Seventh Solo
Selected Reports	Fleury (7, 2) Very marked progress. Refined and musical by nature. Has virtually conquered his nervousness. Excellent student. Bladet (3) His progress this year has been hampered by indolence. Very talented as a flutist; less so as a musician. Could achieve much if he would work. Krauss (6) Very interesting student. A worker. Good finger technique and attractive sound. He has a future. Bauduin (3) Very hard-working student. Constant progress. Dusausoy (9) Attractive personality. Good musician. Has good taste. Tone still imperfect.
Concours	26 July 1900
Jury	Dubois (chairman), Joncières, Gastinel, Jonas, Leroux, Dureau, Turban, Bas, Bourgault-Ducoudray, Bourgeat (secretary)

Set Pieces	Jules Demersseman: Sixth Solo
	Charles-Marie Widor: Morceau de lecture à vue
Students Competing	Dusausoy, Bauduin, Krauss, Cardon, Fleury, Sorel, Bladet, Jurisch ("ill during the concours")
First Prize	Louis François Fleury (b. 1878)
	Gaston Daniel Bladet (b. 1879)
Second Prize	Urbain Alexandre Bauduin (b. 1882)
First Accessit	Fernand Dusausoy (b. 1882)
Second Accessit	Gustave Cardon (b. 1882)

Year 1900–01

Students	Bauduin, Dusausoy, Cardon, Delangle, Huet, Bouillard, Grisard, Puyans, Carvin, Leroux
Examination	29 Jan. 1901
Set Pieces	No details given
Selected Reports	Bauduin. Excellent student, hard-working in class. Good tone, fluent tonguing and finger technique—good taste, is achieving much.
	Bouillard. Has quite an attractive tone . . . [following words unclear]. Has taste. Uneven finger technique. Has ability.
	Grisard. Fluent playing, very adept. Attractive sound, effortless tonguing and finger technique. Has taste.
	Puyans. Has a very fine sound and pleasant playing. Tonguing and fingering a little heavy. Works hard.
Examination	20 June 1901
Set Pieces	1. Briccialdi: Caprice
	2. Briccialdi: Concerto
	3. Demersseman: Second Solo
	4. Lindpaintner: Concerto in E minor
	5. Pratten: Solo de concert
	6. Tulou: Third Solo
	7. Tulou: Eighth Solo
	8. Tulou: Thirteenth Solo
Selected Reports	Bauduin (5) Very good student. Good musician. Constant progress.
	Bouillard (3) Very industrious student. Tone still defective.
	Grisard (8) Very rapid progress. A good feeling for music. Very good student.
	Puyans (7) Very good attitude. Tone not yet developed.
	Leroux (6) Good tone quality. Bad tonguing. Very backward in general musical ability.
Concours	26 July 1901

Jury	Dubois (chairman), Gastinel, Jonas, Busser, Ganne, René, Wettge, Bas, Dureau, Bourgeat (secretary)
Set Pieces	Louis Ganne: Andante et scherzo
	Louis Ganne: Morceau de lecture à vue
Students Competing	Huet, Delangle, Bauduin, Cardon, Grisard, Dusausoy, Bouillard
First Prize	Urbain Alexandre Bauduin (b. 1882)
Second Prize	None awarded
First Accessit	René Charles Grisard (b. 1883)
	Gustave Cardon (b. 1882)
Second Accessit	Georges Louis Delangle (b. 1889)
	Maurice Huet (b. 1884)

Year 1901–02

Students	Dusausoy, Cardon, Delangle, Huet, Bouillard, Grisard, Puyans, Leroux, Hérissé, Laffra, Raonilalao
Examination	29 Jan. 1902
Set Pieces	1. Demersseman: Second Solo
	2. Fürstenau: Ninth Concerto
	3. Kuhlau: Second Solo
	4. Langer: Concerto
	5. Lindpaintner: Concerto in E minor
	6. Lindpaintner: Concerto pathétique
	7. Lindpaintner: Concertino
	8. Mozart: Concerto in G
	9. Tulou: Third Solo
	10. Tulou: Seventh Solo
Selected Reports	Delangle (7) Progress could be more marked.
	Huet (6) Conscientious student, a worker; making progress.
	Bouillard (2) Noticeable progress, very hard-working.
	Grisard (5) Very good student.
	Leroux (1) A student with very little talent. No progress.
	Laffra (3) Tone quality defective. Beginner.
Examination	19 June 1902
Set Pieces	1. Briccialdi: Caprice
	2. Briccialdi: Solo
	3. Demersseman: First Solo
	4. Demersseman: Sixth Solo (Andante and finale)
	5. Demersseman: Le Trémolo
	6. Langer: Concerto
	7. Pratten: Solo de concert
	8. Tulou: Second Solo
	9. Tulou: Eighth Solo
	10. Tulou: Thirteenth Solo

Selected Reports	Bouillard (4) Serious progress. Has taste. Good musician.
	Grisard (7) Excellent student. A natural flutist. Much to learn about reading music.
	Leroux (5) Attends class irregularly. Student with very little talent.
	Raonilalao (10) Very studious. A keen worker. Embouchure not yet formed. Good musician. Mediocre at reading music.
Concours	26 July 1902
Jury	Dubois (chairman), Joncières, Lefèbvre, Dureau, Wettge, Mouquet, Bas, Lafleurance, Letellier, Mimart, Gabriel Marie, Bourgeat (secretary)
Set Pieces	Cécile Chaminade: Concertino
	Cécile Chaminade: Morceau de lecture à vue
Students Competing	Puyans, Grisard, Bouillard, Cardon, Dusausoy, Delangle, Huet
First Prize	Fernand Dusausoy (b. 1882)
Second Prize	Gustave Cardon (b. 1882)
First Accessit	Buenaventura Emilio Puyans (b. 1883)
	Maurice Huet (b. 1884)
Second Accessit	Henri Paul Bouillard (b. 1882)

Year 1902–03

Students	Cardon, Delangle, Bouillard, Grisard, Puyans, Hérissé, Raonilalao, Camus, Guilloteau, Laurent, Joffroy
Examination	28 Jan. 1903
Set Pieces	1. Andersen: Concertstück
	2. J. S. Bach: Sonata in C
	3. Kuhlau: Second Divertissement
	4. Kuhlau: Second Solo
	5. Lindpaintner: Concerto in A minor
	6. Lindpaintner: Concerto in E minor
	7. Mozart: Concerto in G
	8. Tulou: Fifth Solo
Selected Reports	Cardon (1) Very good student, good musician.
	Delangle (6) Working much better this year.
	Bouillard (7) Good musician, constant progress. Very good student.
	Grisard (5) Very good student. A natural flutist.
	Puyans (2) Great progress in terms of tone and finger technique. Very interesting student.
	Camus (4) Has aptitude—too nervous by nature.
	Laurent (8) Natural tone. Has aptitude.
	Joffroy (4) Good tone—has refinement.

Examination	22 June 1903

Set Pieces

1. Andersen: Concertstück
2. Briccialdi: Capriccio
3. Demersseman: Sixth Solo
4. Handel: Fourth Sonata
5. Mozart: Concerto in D
6. Saint-Saëns: Airs de ballet
7. Tulou: Seventh Solo
8. Tulou: Eighth Solo
9. Tulou: Twelfth Solo

Selected Reports Cardon (5) Very good student. Very musical. Tone quality often variable.

Bouillard (4) Very good student. Good musician. Keen and hard-working.

Grisard (6) A really natural flutist. Very good student. Constant progress.

Raonilalao (2) Serious progress. The tone is more refined and the fingering is improving. I am very satisfied with the effort this student is making, very intelligent.

Camus (7) Finger technique still wrong. Tone quite good. Very willing.

Laurent (7) Lovely tone quality. Finger technique still a little heavy, but very well coordinated. Very promising.

Joffroy (8) Refined by nature. Rapid progress. Very promising. Good musician.

Concours 27 July 1903

Jury Dubois (chairman), Lefèbvre, Wettge, Dallier, Périlhou, Hahn, Triébert, Lafleurance, Letellier, Bourgeat (secretary)

Set Pieces Albert Périlhou: Ballade in G minor
Albert Périlhou: Morceau de lecture à vue

Students Competing Raonilalao, Bouillard, Hérissé, Grisard, Delangle, Cardon, Puyans

First Prize Gustave Cardon (b. 1882)
Georges Louis Delangle (b. 1889)

Second Prize Buenaventura Emilio Puyans (b. 1883)
Henri Paul Bouillard (b. 1882)
René Charles Grisard (b. 1883)

First Accessit None awarded

Second Accessit Raonilalao [first name not given] (b. 1884, Madagascar)

Year 1903–04

Students Bouillard, Grisard, Puyans, Hérissé, Raonilalao, Camus, Guilloteau, Laurent, Joffroy, Paul, Cittanova

Examination	27 Jan. 1904
Set Pieces	1. Andersen: Concertstück
	2. J. S. Bach: Fourth Sonata
	3. Demersseman: First Solo
	4. Demersseman: Sixth Solo
	5. Kuhlau: Second Solo
	6. Kuhlau: Ninth Solo
	7. Lindpaintner: Concerto in E minor
	8. Mozart: Concerto in G
	9. Pratten: Solo de concert
	10. Tulou: Eighth Solo

Selected Reports Bouillard (2) Very good student. Often held back by the state of his health.

Grisard (1) Very good student.

Raonilalao (4) Constant progress. Tone quality is not yet perfected.

Camus (10) Too nervous by nature. Faulty finger technique. Very good intentions. Good musician.

Guilloteau (7) Rather timid by nature. Does not yet have command of his instrument.

Laurent (10) Natural tone. Well coordinated fingering. Very good intentions.

Joffroy (4) Good qualities of sensitivity and achievement.

Examination	21 June 1904
Set Pieces	1. Andersen: Concertstück
	2. Andersen: Morceau de concert
	3. Briccialdi: Capriccio
	4. Briccialdi: Concerto
	5. Briccialdi: Solo de concert
	6. Demersseman: Sixth Solo
	7. Handel: Sixth Solo
	8. Lindpaintner: Concerto in E minor
	9. Saint-Saëns: Ascanio

Selected Reports Bouillard (1) Very good student.

Hérissé (9) Has been rather held back by military service. Fine tone quality.

Raonilalao (9) Always progressing. Very interesting student.

Camus (8) Good intentions paralyzed by being too nervous.

Laurent (4) Excellent qualities. Constant progress.

Joffroy (2) Very refined and interesting by nature. Good musician.

Paul (3) Solid qualities. A worker.

Concours	28 July 1904
Jury	Dubois (chairman), Diémer, Pfeiffer, Wettge, Dureau, Enesco, Lafleurance, Mimart, Hamburg, Bourgeat (secretary)

Set Pieces	Georges Enesco: Cantabile et presto
	Paul Hillemacher: Morceau de lecture à vue
Students Competing	Hérissé, Puyans, Raonilalao, Joffroy, Guilloteau, Bouillard, Laurent, Grisard, Camus
First Prize	Henri Paul Bouillard (b. 1882)
	René Charles Grisard (b. 1883)
	Buenaventura Emilio Puyans (b. 1883)
Second Prize	Léon François Joffroy (b. 1886)
	Raonilalao (no first name given) (b. 1884, Madagascar)
First Accessit	None awarded
Second Accessit	Pierre Hérissé (b. 1884)
	Edouard Georges Laurent (b. 1886)

Year 1904–05

Students	Hérissé, Camus, Guilloteau, Laurent, Joffroy, Paul, Cittanova, Bergeon, Cléton, Carivenc
Examination	27 Jan. 1905
Set Pieces	1. Andersen: Concertstück
	2. Demersseman: First Solo
	3. Demersseman: Second Solo
	4. Demersseman: Sixth Solo
	5. Handel: Third Sonata
	6. Lindpaintner: Concerto in A minor
	7. Mozart: Concerto in D
	8. Tulou: Eighth Solo
	9. Tulou: Thirteenth Solo
Selected Reports	Hérissé (1) Beginning to take up work again having been much hindered by military service.
	Camus (5) Good musician. Has taste. Is trying hard to overcome his timidity .
	Laurent (7) Good tone. Finger technique well coordinated. Very good qualities.
	Joffroy (5) Very good student.
	Paul (3) Tone very clear. Attentive and studious.
	Cittanova (4) Tone is still unfocused and harsh. Has little ear for music. Some progress in fingering technique.
Examination	20 June 1905
Set Pieces	1. Andersen: Concertstück
	2. Briccialdi: Capriccio
	3. Briccialdi: Concerto
	4. Briccialdi: Solo de concert
	5. Handel: Third Sonata
	6. Lindpaintner: Concerto in A minor

7. Lindpaintner: Concertino
8. Mozart: Concerto in D
9. Mozart: Concerto in G

Selected Reports Camus (7) Good feeling for music. Very willing, but cannot overcome an overwhelming nervousness which paralyzes him.

Laurent (1) Very good student.

Joffroy (8) Very good student.

Paul (4) Shows potential for the future. Great progress.

Bergeon (6) Excellent natural qualities. Has potential for the future. Very good student.

Concours 27 July 1905 (Salle de l'Opéra-comique)

Jury Dubois (chairman), Lefèbvre, Deslaudrez, Bertelin, Dureau, Gaubert, Letellier, Bleuzet, Paradis, Bourgeat (secretary)

Set Pieces Louis Ganne: Andante et scherzo

Paul Véronge de la Nux: Morceau de lecture à vue

Students Competing Guilloteau, Cittanova, Cléton, Paul, Laurent, Camus, Joffroy, Bergeon, Hérissé

First Prize Léon François Joffroy (b. 1886)

Edouard Georges Laurent (b. 1886)

Second Prize None awarded

First Accessit Pierre Hérissé (b. 1884)

René Bergeon (b. 1887)

Second Accessit Pierre Emile Léon Camus (b. 1885)

Georges Frédéric Auguste Cléton (b. 1888)

Year 1905–06

Students Hérissé, Camus, Paul, Bergeon, Cléton, Chevrot, Lespès, Moyse, Raoul, Castel

Selected Reports: Hérissé. Musical sensitivity could be developed more.

January 1906 Camus. Fine musician by nature, but hindered by extreme nervousness—has made some progress.

Paul. Very keen and willing student.

Bergeon. Often ill. Has nevertheless made progress. Too nervous. Fine tone quality.

Cléton. Very intelligent student, very talented. Rapid progress.

Moyse. Has potential. Very industrious and conscientious student.

Raoul. Tone quality very defective. Heavy playing. Student with very little talent.

Examination 19 June 1906

Set Pieces 1. Briccialdi: Solo de concert

2. Demersseman: Fantaisie

3. Demersseman: Second Solo
4. Demersseman: Sixth Solo
5. Lindpaintner: Concerto in E minor
6. Mozart: Concerto in D
7. Pratten: Morceau de concert
8. Tulou: Eighth Solo
9. Tulou: Thirteenth Solo

Selected Reports Hérissé (1) Very good student. Fine sound. Good finger technique.

Camus (6) Attractive personality. Good musician. Significant progress.

Paul (7) Good student. A worker. Serious.

Bergeon (5) Very talented student. Fine tone quality.

Chevrot (2) Excellent attitude. Very skilled. Much enthusiasm. (As far as I am concerned he could enter the competition if he were not a foreigner.)

Lespès (9) Absolute beginner. Shows some promise.

Moyse (8) Good tone. Good finger technique. Very good attitude. (I think he is ready to enter the competition.)

Raoul (3) Very willing, but that is all. Bad sound. Heavy playing.

Concours 27 July 1906 (Salle de l'Opéra-comique)

Jury Fauré (chairman), de la Nux, Brunel, Ganne, Gaubert, Hess, Brancour, Lafleurance, Bleuzet, Pichard, Bourdeau, Bourgeat (secretary)

Set Pieces Philippe Gaubert: Nocturne et allegro scherzando
Louis Ganne: Morceau de lecture à vue

Students Competing Cléton, Hérissé, Moyse, Bergeon, Camus, Paul

First Prize René Bergeon (b. 1887)
Marcel Joseph Moyse (b. 1889)

Second Prize Auguste Henri Paul (b. 1885)
Georges Frédéric Auguste Cléton (b. 1888)

First Accessit Pierre Emile Léon Camus (b. 1885)

Second Accessit None awarded

Year 1906–07

Students Camus, Paul, Cléton, Chevrot, Lespès, Raoul, Castel, Friscourt, René, Michaux, Dausque, Marchant

Selected Reports: January 1907 Camus. Very good student. Miltary service has hindered his studies. Has only recently begun working again.
Paul. Very good student—same comment as above.
Lespès. Working better this year. Has made some progress.

Raoul. Has been constantly ill since the beginning of the year. Has returned home for the moment to recuperate.

Friscourt. Good musician. A natural player. Very promising.

Examination	12 June 1907
Set Pieces	1. Andersen: Concertstück
	2. Briccialdi: Capriccio
	3. Demersseman: Solo
	4. Demersseman: First Solo
	5. Demersseman: Second Solo
	6. Kuhlau: First Grand Solo
	7. Kuhlau: Second Grand Solo
	8. Langer: Concerto
	9. Pratten: Morceau de concert
	10. Tulou: Eighth Solo

Selected Reports

Camus (8) Very good student. Was seriously ill during recent months. Has valiantly begun working again.

Paul (1) Very good student. Constant progress. Military service has rather hindered his studies.

Chevrot (9) Very talented student. Very capable.

Cléton (9) Very good student. I have only praise for him.

Lespès (10) Making progress. Naturally talented.

Raoul (3) Very keen and willing student. Good finger technique. Embouchure still defective.

Castel (2) Fine sound. Has taste. Rather lazy by nature. Making progress.

Friscourt (10) Has a very good attitude. Natural tone. Good musician.

Michaux (7) Beginner—has everything to learn, no idea about tonguing—tone quite good.

Concours	11 July 1907 (Salle de l'Opéra-comique)
Jury	Fauré (chairman), Messager, Ropartz, Mouquet, Brancour, Parès, Lafleurance, Bleuzet, Bas, Deschamps, Le Bailly, Hess, Vinzentini, Bourgeat (secretary)
Set Pieces	Paul Taffanel: Andante pastoral et scherzettino
	Jules Mouquet: Morceau de lecture à vue
Students Competing	Lespès, Camus, Cléton, Castel, Raoul, Paul, Chevrot
First Prize	Georges Frédéric Auguste Cléton (b. 1888)
	Jules Albert Chevrot (b. 1889)
Second Prize	Pierre Emile Léon Camus (b. 1885)
First Accessit	None awarded
Second Accessit	André Castel (b. 1891)

Year 1907–08

Students Paul, Lespès, Raoul, Castel, Friscourt, René, Michaux, Dausque, Marchant, Clouet, Messier, Brottin

Selected Reports: Paul. Very good student. Military service has hindered his
January 1908 studies a little.

Lespès. Has made some progress, but could improve more.

Raoul. Military student—has not appeared in class since the beginning of the academic year.

Castel. Very good student. Very able.

René. Good student. Good finger technique. Slow tonguing.

Michaux. Military student—numerous absences. Very willing.

Dausque. Military student—numerous absences. Very willing. (These two students have started very late!) [They were aged, respectively, 19 years, 7 months and 19 years, 8 months]

Messier. Useless.

Brattin. Beginner. [Messier and Brattin were aged, respectively, 18 years, 11 months and 18 years, 7 months]

Examination 9 June 1908

Set Pieces 1. Andersen: Concertstück
2. Demersseman: First Solo
3. Demersseman: Second Solo
4. Kuhlau: First Solo
5. Kuhlau: Second Solo
6. Langer: Concerto
7. Lindpaintner: Concertino
8. Lindpaintner: Concerto
9. Pratten: Solo de concert
10. Tulou: Fifth Solo
11. Tulou: Eighth Solo

Selected Reports Paul (6) Very good student.

Lespès (7) Has made serious progress this year.

Raoul (9) Since the beginning of the academic year has only come to the class during the last three weeks (illness or military service).

Castel (8) Very good student. Fine sound. Very fluent playing. Has taste.

Friscourt (1) Good student. Very talented. Good musician.

René (8) Very serious and hard-working student. Good musician.

Michaux (3) Very willing. Little natural aptitude. Tone quite good. Military service hinders his studies.

Dausque (2) Very willing. Limited ability. Same remark as above about military service.

Marchant (10) Serious and hard-working student. Good attitude. Good musician.

Clouet (11) Excellent student. Outstanding and constant
    progress. I think he is ready to enter the competition.

Messier (4) I can do nothing more with this student, who has
    too many ingrained faults, and is too old.

Brottin (5) Some aptitude.

Concours	16 July 1908 (Salle de l'Opéra-comique)
Jury	Fauré (chairman), de la Nux, Busser, Cortot, Mouquet, Brancour, Bloudel, Bas, Lafleurance, Le Bailly, Hamburg, Pichard, Bourgeat (secretary), (Parès ill)
Set Pieces	Henri Busser: Prélude et scherzo Henri Busser: Morceau de lecture à vue
Students Competing	Raoul, Clouet, Castel, Paul, Marchant, Lespès, Dausque, Michaux, René, Friscourt
First Prize	Auguste Henri Paul (b. 1885)
Second Prize	Marcel François Jules Friscourt (b. 1890) Ernest Jean René (b. 1890)
First Accessit	André Castel (b. 1891) Jean André Lespès (b. 1892)
Second Accessit	Julian Ferdinand Clouet (b. 1889) Julien Charles Marchant (b. 1889) Léon Auguste Raoul (b. 1888)

Sources, Abbreviations, and Translations

Full details of all published sources referred to may be found in the bibliography and appendix 2, so the following notes give only the author's name, or name plus short title of the source for authors listed more than once. For unpublished sources, details of the public or private collections are given, with catalog numbers where applicable.

The primary source for this book, the Papiers Paul Taffanel, is indicated by the abbreviation PPT followed by a number from 1 to 20 identifying the subdivision of the archive (see appendix 1 for details).

The following abbreviations are used throughout:
PAN: Paris, Archives nationales
PBN: Paris, Bibliothèque nationale, Départment de la musique
PBO: Paris, Bibliothèque de l'Opéra
M: Le Ménestrel
MM: Le Monde musical
RGM: La Revue et gazette musicale

All material quoted from sources originally in French has been newly translated, unless otherwise indicated.

Introduction

1. Th. Lindenlaub, "La Soirée du 2 juin 1896," in *Le Jubilé de C. Saint-Saëns*, p. 23.

1. Early Life

1. PPT20. Biographical information in this chapter comes from a collection of personal papers kept by Paul Taffanel, relating to his father and other members of the family.

2. PPT1.

3. Bordeaux, Registre des Naissances 1844, 1st section no. 1203.

4. Imbert, *Médaillons*, p. 392.

5. Anon., *Réponse critique*, p. 12.

6. Stendhal, p. 15.

7. Fétis, vol. 4, pp. 441–42, and Supplement, vol. 2, p. 492. See also Riemann, p. 1179.

8. *La Gironde*, 22 Mar. 1861.

9. Taffanel, "L'art de diriger," p. 2130.

10. *MM*, 15 July 1899, leading article on Gaubert by Arthur Dandelot. See also chapter 9.

11. Imbert, *Médaillons*, p. 392.

12. PPT20, typescript of biographical details signed J.J., p. 1. See appendix 1.

13. Quoted in Humblot, p. 82.

14. *La Charente-inférieur*, 27 Aug. 1854; *L'Echo rochelais*, 29 Aug. 1854; J.J., p. 1; and *La Gironde*, 11 Feb. 1854.

15. *L'Echo rochelais*, 1 Sept. 1854.

16. Fallon, pp. 309–25.

17. Archives départmentales de la Gironde (Archives municipales de Bordeaux), Etats de situation des écoles primaires de garçons, 1855–56, 6 T 6.

18. Quoted in Jacobs and Skelton, following the title page.

19. See Burchell for a vivid picture of the political, social, and cultural life of this period.

20. François-Sappey, p. 204.

21. Scudo, *L'Année musicale*, vol. 1, p. 289.

22. Imbert, *Médaillons*, p. 392.

23. Information about the Dorus family kindly communicated by the late Mme. Jacqueline Rabaud, daughter of Henri Rabaud and great-granddaughter of Louis Dorus.

24. PBN, Lettres autographes, Louis Dorus, no. 3.

25. Fétis, vol. 2, pp. 54–55.

26. Boehm, ed. Broadwood, pp. 49–50.

27. *RGM*, 1834, p. 8; 1835, p. 49; *M*, 1843, p. 18; *RGM*, 1845, p. 92; and 1850, p. 66.

28. Pontécoulant, "Des Instruments à vent," p. 30.

29. *RGM*, 24 Mar. 1844, p. 103.

30. *L'Indicateur de Bordeaux*, quoted in *M*, 14 Apr. 1844, p. 4.

31. Fétis, vol. 3, p. 49; and PBN, Ms 10859, variation signed and dated "4 August 1852, L Dorus," and Ms W 24168, "Pièce sans titre," marked "Moderato." This has been edited by the author under the title *Feuillet d'album*. London: Pan Educational Music, 1987.

32. See Fauquet, *Les Sociétés*, pp. 194–98, and a favorable review in *RGM*, 5 Dec. 1847, p. 395.

33. Saint-Saëns, *Ecole buissonnière*, p. 263.

34. *RGM*, 11 Mar. 1877, p. 78.

35. PPT4, draft letter to Firmin Brossa, n.d.

36. Elwart, *Société des concerts*, p. 261.

37. PAN, AJ37 324, Flûte Boehm; and AJ37, 84,7(i), give full reports of the Conservatoire Jury's deliberations. See also Pontécoulant, "Des Instruments à vent," pp. 29, 43, 76, for a trenchant contemporary commentary.

38. See Tulou, Introduction.
39. PAN, AJ37 68,2, Dossier personnel, Victor Coche.
40. PAN, AJ37 72, Dossier personnel, Jean-Louis Tulou.

2. The Conservatoire and After

1. Pierre, *Le Conservatoire* gives full administrative details up to 1900.
2. PAN, AJ37 68,1, letter of appointment; and PAN AJ37 91,4, and AJ37 156, Conservatoire class lists.
3. PAN, AJ37 277, p. 70 (Conservatoire Reports).
4. Elwart, *Concerts populaires*, p. 34.
5. Pontécoulant, "Des Instruments à vent," p. 43.
6. PAN, AJ37 250, 2, p. 401 (Reports on the *concours* 1860–1865).
7. *RGM*, 5 Aug. 1860, p. 276.
8. Pierre, *Les Factures*, pp. 314–16, includes a brief summary of the history and importance of Lot flutes, and Giannini provides a comprehensive modern account of the work of Lot and other French makers.
9. Information kindly supplied by Bernard Duplaix. See also Giannini, pp. 143, 172, and 176–86.
10. Successive editions of the *Annuaire de l'Association des artistes musiciens* indicate that Taffanel served on the committee from 1886, was elected vice president in 1904 and president in 1908.
11. PAN, AJ37 156,3 and 4.
12. PAN, AJ37 72,2, Dossier personnel, Henri Reber.
13. Saint-Saëns, *Harmonie et mélodie*, pp. 295 and 283.
14. Reissued in a modern edition by the author, London: Pan Educational Music, 1987.
15. Massenet, p. 15; and Imbert, *Médaillons*, p. 393.
16. PAN, AJ37 277, pp. 117 (18 Dec. 1860); 196 (16 June 1861); and 269 (9 Dec. 1861).
17. PAN, AJ37 278, p. 97.
18. PAN, AJ37 250,3, p. 62.
19. PAN, AJ37 91,7; AJ37 92,1,2,3,4,5; AJ37 156,5 and 6; AJ37 157,1; and AJ37 250,3.
20. Scudo, *L'Année musicale*, vol. 1, pp. 1, 2, 24, 78, 289, 294, and 397; vol. 2, p. 58; and vol. 3, pp. 108, 132, and 355.
21. PPT1.
22. Bernard gives background details on Pasdeloup's life and career with the Jeunes artistes and the Concerts populaires. Elwart, *Concerts populaires*, p. 23, lists the orchestra personnel of the latter, and pp. 29 ff. give the programs of all the concerts to 1864.
23. Scudo, *L'Année musicale*, vol. 2, p. 161 and vol. 3, p. 164.
24. Letter quoted in Marchesi, *Marchesi and Music*, p. 102.
25. *RGM*, 31 Mar. 1861, p. 98. The precise date and location of the concert are not given.
26. *RGM*, 13 Apr. 1862, p. 121.
27. PPT1.
28. Pontécoulant, "Des instruments à vent," p. 43.
29. Soubies, *L'Opéra-comique* gives detailed information about all aspects of this theater, including two charts of works and dates of performances, p. 30.

30. PPT3, letter to an unnamed addressee (probably a Monsieur Ternisien), 18 Dec. 1888 after the reappearance of Patti in Paris in a revival of Gounod's *Roméo et Juliette*. See also chapter 8.

31. Saint-Saëns writing in *La France*, 29 Nov. 1888, one of his rare newspaper reviews.

32. *RGM*, 23 Nov. 1862, p. 377, article by Paul Smith.

33. Rémusat, p. 8.

34. *RGM*, 29 Mar. 1863, p. 100; PPT1; and *RGM*, 20 Dec. 1863, p. 406. Apart from the unidentified Demersseman work, no repertoire details are given.

35. Fitzgibbon, p. i.

36. Rockstro, p. 603.

3. Advances and Retreats

1. Conati, p. 41; and Saint-Saëns ed. Yves Gérard, p. 201.

2. Among various studies of the Paris Opéra, see in particular Gourret, pp. 11–14 and 141–69 for the administrative and sociological background; and for details of musical organization and repertoire, Soubies, *L'Opéra*; Prod'homme; and Pistone, "L'Opéra de Paris au siècle romantique."

3. The standard histories of the Society, covering all aspects of its activities, are Deldevez, *La Société des concerts*, including a complete list of programs to 1885; Dandelot, *La Société des concerts* (two editions, 1898 and 1923); and the new definitive study by Holoman based on the PBN archives.

4. PPT1.

5. See Terrier; and Pierre, *L'Orchestre de l'Opéra,* for full details. Eustache gives a detailed, but not entirely accurate, list of the members of the flute section from 1835 to 1963, with various other background information. [Note: the entry for Taffanel wrongly states that he joined as third flute in 1861.]

6. See Solum.

7. Giannini, p. 176.

8. Pontécoulant, "Des Instrument à vent," p. 43. Leplus was christened Louis Gabriel Marie but known as Ludovic.

9. Soubies, *L'Opéra*, includes a chart listing fourteen operas and six ballets in the Opéra repertoire in 1864.

10. PAN, AJ13 1010A, Dossier personnel, Taffanel, gives details of his Opéra career. Throughout this period, and up to 1914, five francs were equal to one American dollar, and 25 francs equal to one English pound.

11. PAN, AJ13 1184, Dossier personnel, Donjon. He retired from the Opéra in 1890. Eustache lists him as playing Louis Lot flute no. 541.

12. PBN, D 17345 (1–24), Société des concerts, Comité et assemblées générales, 1828–1966, vol. 6. And see vol. 7 for further elections in 1867 and 1868.

13. Dandelot, *La Société des concerts* (1923), p. 64.

14. *RGM*, 24 Apr. 1864, p. 131.

15. See *M*, 21 Aug. 1864, p. 304; and *RGM*, 14 Aug. 1864, p. 262; 21 Aug. 1864, p. 269; and 4 Sept. 1864, p. 287.

16. *RGM*, 1 Jan. 1865, p. 6; and *L'Art musical*, 29 Dec. 1864, p. 38. Toyon, p. 115, lists the complete program of this concert.

17. PPT14, passport for travel to Russia in 1887.
18. Gaudefroy, pp. 60 and 168.
19. *La Gironde*, 3 Apr. 1865; and *Le Journal de Bordeaux*, 3 Apr. 1865.
20. *M*, 12 Feb. 1865, p. 88.
21. Gaudefroy, p. 174; and see p. 202 for Taffanel's appearance in 1872 playing *fantaisies* by Boehm and Demersseman.
22. Lavignac, *Les Gaietés*, p. 71.
23. PPT2, *Journal professionnel.*
24. PAN, AJ13 1010A, Dossier personnel, Taffanel, includes two doctor's certificates, dated 7 and 8 Dec. 1866, referring to problems with "a boil on the lower lip" since 26 Nov. 1866.
25. PPT3, letter to Johannes Donjon, 8 Oct. 1888; and letter to Joachim Andersen, 28 May 1895 (Duke University Collection, Durham, NC). See chapter 12 for more discussion of these problems.
26. See Decourcelle for details of Taffanel's appearances at this prestigious music society. Fauquet, *Les Sociétés de musique de chambre*, gives various references to Taffanel's involvement in chamber music and details of many of the musicians and societies with whom he is known to have played at this time. See in particular p. 222 for the Cercle des Beaux-Arts, founded by the violinist Georges Jacobi.
27. Sitwell, *La Vie Parisienne*, p. 39.
28. Pontécoulant, *La Musique à l'Exposition*, pp. 5, 105, and 115.
29. Friedrich, p. 145 comments on the vantage point and curious perspectives of Manet's *View of the Universal Exposition.*
30. Quoted in Wysham, pp. 33–34.
31. PAN, AJ37 68,1, Dossier personnel, Louis Dorus; and AJ37 66,16, Dossier personnel, Henri Altès.
32. PBN, D.17345, vol. 7; and Lettres autographes, Henri Altès, no. 6.
33. PAN, AJ13 1010a, Dossier personnel, Edouard Lafleurance. See chapter 8 for details of Léopold Lafleurance.
34. Anon., "La Flûte," p. 295. Copy in PPT8.
35. See appendix 2 for details of this and the many other volumes of transcriptions by Taffanel.
36. Charnacé, *Les Etoiles du chant*, p. 14.
37. Ibid., p. 16.
38. PPT6, letter from Guy de Charnacé, 7 Feb. 1896.
39. *RGM*, 27 Dec. 1868, p. 414; *M*, 18 Apr. 1869, p. 158; and *RGM*, 16 Jan. 1870, p. 22.
40. *M*, 25 Apr. 1869, p. 175. The edition of 20 June 1869, p. 230, notes the departure of the virtuoso flutist Giuseppe Gariboldi for Italy; and 7 Nov. 1869, p. 391, names Génin in passing as flutist of the Théâtre-Italien.
41. See *M*, 13 Dec. 1868, p. 15 (Farrenc Sextet); 14 Feb. 1869, p. 88 (Weber Trio); 19 Dec. 1869, p. 23 (Farrenc Trio); *RGM*, 9 Jan. 1870, p. 12 (Schubert Variations); *M*, 13 Mar. 1870 (Beethoven Serenade).
42. *M*, 19 Sept. 1869, p. 335 (Rouen); and 30 Jan. 1870, p. 72 (Grenoble); and PPT1, June 1870: "Niort. Concerts. Congrès de l'Ouest (return via Chateuneuf–Tours)."
43. See appendix 3 for a list of dedications to Taffanel.

44. PPT20, invoice found among miscellaneous papers.

45. Friedrich, chapter 6, gives a particularly vivid account of this period as it affected artistic life in Paris. See also Labarthe for a near contemporary description; and Cobban, vols. 2 and 3 for general historical background.

46. *M*, 1871, pp. 348, 405, and 414; 1872, pp. 36 and 44. Taffanel's presence is confirmed by the secretary's minutes of meetings of the Société des concerts, 31 Jan. 1871 and 3 Feb. 1871. See PBN, D.17345, vol. 7.

47. PAN, AJ13, 1010A, Dossier personnel, Paul Taffanel.

48. *M*, 3 Sept. 1871, p. 320.

4. New Beginnings

1. PBN, Rés. F 994, archives of the Société nationale.

2. PBN Rés. 2483, and Rés. F 994 F, complete listing of the Société nationale concerts. See also Duchesneau for a history of the Society.

3. Chausson, p. 198. See chapter 7 for discussion of the Bruneau *Romance*.

4. PPT1.

5. *M*, 26 Nov. 1871, p. 416.

6. *M*, 21 Jan. 1872, p. 64.

7. *RGM*, 21 Jan. 1872, p. 22.

8. *RGM*, 12 Mar. 1876, pp. 85 and 101.

9. *RGM*, 25 Jan. 1874, p. 30.

10. Fauquet, *Les Sociétés de musique de chambre*, pp. 148 – 58, analyzes Armingaud's quartet in detail.

11. Imbert, *Médaillons*, p. 393.

12. Ratner, p. 361.

13. Recounted by Caratgé in interview with the author, 5 Sept. 1983.

14. PBN, Lettres autographes, Paul Taffanel, no. 18, 21 Oct. 1872.

15. *RGM*, 3 Mar. 1878, p. 69.

16. Indy, p. 157, letter to Edmond de Pampelonne, 15 Jan. 1872.

17. *RGM*, 9 Feb. 1873, p. 46; and *M*, 5 May 1873, p. 191.

18. *RGM*, 24 Mar. 1878, p. 95. See also 30 June 1878, p. 206; and 27 Apr. 1879, p. 134.

19. *RGM*, 4 Feb. 1872, p. 38; and 26 May 1872, p. 166.

20. *RGM*, 15 Dec. 1872, p. 397; and *L'Art musical*, 12 Dec. 1872, p. 388.

21. Indy, p. 184, letter dated 17 Dec. 1872.

22. *RGM*, 29 Dec. 1872, p. 414.

23. *M*, 3 Jan. 1875, p. 6.

24. Holoman reprints the complete sets of programs for the Société des concerts, with dates of each performance.

25. PAN, AJ37 236,2 (Paris Conservatoire Archives); and Pierre, *Le Conservatoire*, pp. 406 and 373.

26. *RGM*, 3 Aug. 1873, p. 242.

27. PPT12.

28. PAN AJ37 236,2, 26 June 1877.

29. Quoted in Lorenzo, p. 185.

30. PPT6, visiting card from Charles Lebouc, 1873.

31. Information about the Deslignières family and the marriage of Paul and Geneviève Taffanel is drawn from personal papers in PPT20.
32. For details of Lefèbvre's career see Honoré; and Milner, p. 127.
33. Vallas, pp. 146 and 149.
34. Brada, pp. 51, 95–96, and 99.
35. *M*, 19 July 1874, p. 264.
36. *M*, 9 Aug. 1874, p. 288.
37. *M*, 21 June 1874, p. 231.
38. PBN, D 17345 (1–24), Comité et assemblées générales, vol. 9; and D 17341, Rapport des secrétaires, Taffanel; and PBN, D 173–36 (1), Caisse de prévoyance: procès-verbaux. See Holoman, pp. 38–41, on the key role of the secretary of the Society.
39. Massenet, pp. 97–98.
40. Unattributed newspaper obituary notice and other biographical details kindly provided by the late Claude Taffanel, son of Jacques Taffanel.

5. Composing for the Flute

1. Indy, p. 271, letter to Marie d'Indy, 2 June 1874.
2. *RGM*, 28 Dec. 1873, p. 416.
3. See appendix 2, for full details.
4. *RGM*, 20 Aug. 1876, pp. 266 and 270.
5. PPT4, draft letter to Louis Dorus, 26 Sept. 1879.
6. Fauquet, *Les Sociétés de musique de chambre*, pp. 231–32.
7. *M*, 2 May 1880, p. 175.
8. *M*, 26 Dec. 1880, p. 31.
9. *RGM*, 31 Apr. 1874, p. 143; *M*, 11 Apr. 1875, p. 151; 9 May 1875, p. 191; 28 May 1876, p. 206; and 9 May 1875, p. 182.
10. Taffanel and Fleury, p. 1526.
11. *Journal de Monaco*, quoted in *M*, 5 Mar. 1876, p. 70.
12. There is some uncertainty over dating: see appendix 2, Paul Taffanel Works List.
13. *RGM*, 14 May 1876, p. 158.
14. *RGM*, 11 June 1876, p. 190; and 18 June 1876, p. 197.
15. PAN, AJ13, 1010A, Dossier personnel, letter from Deldevez, 20 June 1876.
16. *RGM*, 20 May 1877, p. 158. A copy of this press release is bound into the cover of the Bibliothèque nationale copy of the *Société des compositeurs de musique, Rapport annuel*, 1878. See PBN, Vmc 4293, pp. 17–18 for Taffanel's election to the Society; and p. 27, which notes a debate on the anonymity question and whether the entries should in future be judged by performance. The epigraph on Taffanel's Quintet is not known.
17. PPT6, visiting card from Théodore Dubois, n.d.
18. PPT4, draft letter headed "Bamelier 8 nov 77."
19. The original Leduc edition has individual instrumental parts only, but a score has been reconstructed and edited by Don Stewart, New York: IMC, 1983.
20. *M*, 12 May 1878, p. 190.
21. *M*, 26 May 1878, p. 207.
22. *RGM*, 2 June 1878, p. 174.

23. *RGM*, 7 July 1878, p. 214.

24. Honegger, p. 408. Article from *Le Commoedia*, 1941, no. 18, reporting on a Société des instruments à vent concert on 12 Oct. 1941, in memory of Philippe Gaubert, directed by Fernand Oubradous.

25. PPT20, legal Document of Succession, contracts dated 8 and 10 Jan. 1876. The site where the house stood was later noted in Fouquières, vol. 2, p. 157.

26. Quoted in Ehrlich, pp. 79–80. A brief example of Diémer's playing, in a recording of Chopin's Nocturne in D flat, op. 27, no. 2, dating from 1903, was reissued on LP: Symposium 1020, side 1 band 1.

27. *RGM*, 24 Mar. 1878, p. 45; and 5 May 1878, p. 142.

28. Durand, vol. 1, pp. 35–36. At Jacques Durand's wedding in 1889 the music was supplied by Saint-Saëns, Gigout, Sarasate, Hasselmans, and Taffanel: see p. 62.

29. Quoted in Soriano, p. 36.

30. See appendix 2 for the titles and years of composition of the complete series, and details of the modern editions of the flute pieces.

31. For a complete list of Conservatoire *premier prix* holders, 1860–1950, see Dorgeuille, Eng. trans., pp. 69–76.

32. PPT4. The quotations that follow in this section are from this source.

33. See appendix 2 for details. *M*, 3 Dec. 1878, p. 110, mentions Taffanel playing two of his Mendelssohn transcriptions in a concert with the pianist Caroline Montigny-Rémaury.

34. Fauquet, *Lalo: Correspondance*, p. 269.

35. *RGM*, 3 Mar. 1878, p. 69.

36. *RGM*, 29 Dec. 1878, p. 423.

37. See *RGM*, 16 Feb. 1879, p. 54, for a review of the Mozart Quartet; and *RGM*, 16 Mar. 1879, p. 86; 27 Apr. 1889, p. 134; and *M*, 27 Apr. 1889, p. 176, for the Concerto for Flute and Harp.

38. PPT20 includes Taffanel's copy of the Lavoix and a pass to the reading room of the Bibliothèque nationale, n.d., but with the address 3 rue St Arnaud, where Taffanel lived, 1874–77.

39. Sala, p. xvi. See also Bertaut, p. 52; and Pingeot, which gives a centenary overview of the 1878 Paris Exhibition.

40. PPT20.

41. PPT20 includes a bound copy of the concert program for 11 June 1878; and *M*, 14 July 1878, p. 262, reported the Mendelssohn encore.

42. *RGM*, 9 June 1878, p. 181.

43. Works listed in *RGM*, 19 May 1878, p. 158; 16 June 1878, p. 190; 30 June 1878, p. 206; 18 Aug 1878, p. 261; 25 Aug 1878, p. 270; and 8 Sept. 1878, p. 285.

6. The Wind Society

1. Charnacé, "Musique de chambre," p. 220.

2. Imbert, *Médaillons*, p. 394.

3. Fleury, "Chamber Music for Wind Instruments," p. 114.

4. *M*, 26 Jan. 1879, p. 72. An announcement also appeared in *RGM*, 26 Jan. 1879, p. 30.

5. Chorley, p. 66.
6. PPT4, draft letter to unnamed addressee, n.d.
7. Imbert, *Médaillons*, p. 393.
8. PPT1.
9. *RGM*, 9 Feb. 1879, p. 46; and 23 Feb. 1879, p. 62.
10. See Fourcaud, Poujin, and Pradel for a brief history and an illustration of the Salle Pleyel.
11. Cobbett, vol. 2, p. 310.
12. PPT3, letter to Adrien Barthe, 15 Aug. 1888.
13. *M*, 23 Feb. 1879, p. 103; and 2 Mar. 1879, p. 112. *RGM*, 9 Mar. 1879, p. 77; 23 Mar. 1879, p. 94; and 27 Apr. 1879, p. 134.
14. PPT1.
15. PPT4, draft letter to the Committee of the Société des concerts, 3 Mar. 1879.
16. *RGM*, 16 Mar. 1879, p. 85.
17. In 1886 Vincent d'Indy gained control of the Société nationale, and Saint-Saëns and Bussine resigned. See Bonnerot, p. 128.
18. PPT4, draft letter to Widor, 1880.
19. *RGM*, 4 Apr. 1880, p. 110.
20. *M*, 27 Feb. 1881, p. 104.
21. *M*, 6 Mar. 1881, p. 112.
22. *M*, 17 Mar. 1881, p. 126.
23. Information on Théodore Gouvy kindly communicated by his great-great-niece, Madame Ghylaine Durteste.
24. *M*, 6 Apr. 1890, p. 112.
25. Letter from Taffanel to Théodore Gouvy, 16 Oct. 1887. (Durteste Collection)
26. *Journal d'Amiens*, quoted in *M*, 8 May 1881, p. 183.
27. *M*, 5 Mar. 1882, p. 110.
28. Imbert, *Profils*, p. 77.
29. *M*, 11 Feb. 1883, p. 88; and 29 Apr. 1883, p. 175.
30. PPT4, draft letter, probably to Hug frères in Basel, 1884.
31. PPT4, draft letter to unnamed addressee, 1883.
32. *Le Gaulois* quoted in *M*, 24 Feb. 1884, p. 103.
33. *M*, 6 Mar. 1884, p. 143; and 13 Apr. 1884, p. 157.
34. *M*, 26 Apr. 1885, p. 168; and 4 Mar. 1888, p. 80.
35. *M*, 16 Mar. 1890, p. 85.
36. *M*, 13 Mar. 1892, p. 85.
37. PPT4, draft letter, probably to Gouvy, 1885.
38. PPT4, draft letter to an unnamed director of a Conservatoire, 1885.
39. *M*, 24 Jan. 1886, p. 63.
40. *La Tribune de Genève*, 11 Jan. 1886. See also *Le Genevois*, 11 Jan. 1886; and *Le Journal de Genève*, 12 Jan. and 14 Jan. 1886.
41. *M*, 3 Apr. 1887, p. 144.
42. PPT14, letters from Geneviève Taffanel, 15 Apr. and 17 Apr. 1887.
43. Bellaigue, vol. 1 (1887), pp. 179–80; and vol. 3 (1889), p. 119.

44. *M*, 21 Apr. 1889, p. 135.

45. Lakond, p. 236. The concert was reviewed in *M*, 4 Mar. 1888. See Lakond, pp. 75–88 for Tchaikovsky's diary of his 1886 visit to Paris, and pp. 234–41 for his 1888 visit. [Note: the dates in the diary follow the Russian calendar, twelve days behind the European.]

46. See D. Brown, pp. 77–84 and 138–41.

47. *M*, 4 Mar. 1888, pp. 79–80.

48. *M*, 18 Mar. 1888, p. 95. See chapter 8 for a further meeting between Tchaikovsky and Taffanel in 1889.

49. PPT3, letters to Hermann Wolff, 11 Sept. 1888; n.d. (Sept. 1888); and 9 Oct. 1888.

50. PPT3, letter to George G. Treherne, 15 Jan. 1889.

51. PPT3, letter to Hug frères, 7 Oct. 1888.

52. PPT3, letter to Jules Bordier, 18 Dec. 1888.

53. PPT3, letter to Rudolf Nováček, 23 Mar. 1889.

54. *M*, 13 Jan. 1889, p. 15.

55. Grove, 1st edition (1889), vol. 4, p. 543.

56. *M*, 28 Apr. 1889, p. 135; and 12 May 1889, p. 151.

57. *M*, 3 Nov. 1889, p. 347.

58. *MM*, 28 Feb. 1890, p. 5.

59. *M*, 6 Apr. 1890, p. 112; 2 Mar. 1890, p. 70; 16 Mar. 1890, p. 85; and 20 Apr. 1890, p. 128.

60. PPT6, letter from Marcel Benoit, 2 May 1901. Reviews come from the *Bordeaux-Journal*, 12 Jan. 1891, and *La Gironde*, 13 Jan. 1891.

61. *M*, 1 Mar. 1891, p. 70; 19 Apr. 1891, p. 127; and 3 May 1891, p. 143.

62. PPT5, letter to Marie-Camille Taffanel, 30 Oct. 1891. See chapter 7 for more information on Taffanel's daughter.

63. Théodore Gouvy kept a copy of this program. (Durteste Collection)

64. *M*, 8 Nov. 1891, p. 360.

65. *La Revue* (Lausanne), 2 Nov. 1891, p. 3; and *Nouvelliste vaudois*, 2 Nov. 1891, p. 3.

66. *M*, 28 Feb. 1892, p. 70.

67. *M*, 13 Mar. 1892, p. 85.

68. *M*, 8 May 1892, p. 152. See chapter 7 for details of the premiere of *Carnaval des animaux* in 1886.

69. Quoted in Landormy, *La Musique française après Debussy*, p. 186.

70. Comettant, p. 24.

71. Fourcaud, Pougin, and Pradel, p. 56.

72. See chapter 9 for details of Taffanel's appearance with the Leipzig Gewandhaus Orchestra, conducted by Reinecke.

73. *M*, 19 Mar. 1893, p. 79

74. *M*, 5 Mar. 1893, p. 79.

75. See *The Times*, 14 July 1894; *The Musical Times*, 1 Aug. 1894, p. 535; and *The Musical Opinion and Music Trade Review*, 1 Sept. 1894, p. 765.

76. See chapter 8 for details of Frederic Griffith.

77. Shaw, vol. 2, p. 47.

78. Fleury, "Chamber Music for Wind Instruments," p. 111.

79. *MM*, 28 Feb. 1901. See also *Musica*, April 1904, p. 301, with a photograph of Gaubert's and Mimart's Société de musique de chambre pour instruments à vent.

80. Introduction to the concert program, 12 Oct. 1941, by Fernand Oubradous. A copy was kept by Marie-Camille Taffanel.

81. Quoted in Lorenzo, p. 188.

82. Barrère, *Société moderne d'instruments à vent*, p. 5. See pp. 15 and 12 for the following quotations from Taffanel and Reynaldo Hahn.

83. Fleury, "Chamber Music for Wind Instruments," p. 115.

84. PPT6, letter from Mariano San Miguel, 7 July 1908.

85. See Barrère, *Georges Barrère*; Toff, *Georges Barrère and the Flute in America*; Lorenzo, p. 196; and Whitwell, p. 4.

86. See Whitwell for a history of the Longy Club, including a complete list of repertoire, pp. 193−96.

87. *Annuaire de l'Association des artistes musiciens* (1909), p. 4.

7. The Magic Flute

1. PPT4, draft letter to Joseph Celly, 17 Sept. 1879.

2. PPT4, draft letter to Emmanuel Vaucorbeil, 3 Feb. 1880. The original has not been found.

3. PAN, AJ13, 1010A, letter to Emmanuel Vaucorbeil, 2 June 1880. Draft copy in PPT4.

4. PAN, AJ13 1010A, letter to Emmanuel Vaucorbeil, 8 June 1883. Draft copy in PPT4.

5. The burial plot is described in the deeds as "No.1630 p/1880, 44th division, 2nd line, 12th tomb."

6. PPT20.

7. PPT20, contract dated 18 Oct. 1880.

8. Quoted in Lorenzo, p. 185.

9. Altès, pp. 286, 18, 205, 246, 225, and 428.

10. Letter from Taffanel to Andersen, 5 May 1895 (Duke University Collection, Durham, NC).

11. PBN, lettres autographes, Hennebains to Arthur Dandelot, n.d. Quoted in part in Dandelot, *Petits mémoires musicaux*, p. 34. Taffanel photograph kindly provided by Bernard Duplaix. See Duplaix, "Adolphe Hennebains" for details of his life and career.

12. PPT7, letter to Madame Saint-Saëns, 6 May 1882.

13. PPT7, letter from Saint-Saëns, 7 May 1882, followed by a brief note of congratulations after the birth. See Blakeman, "The Correspondence of Camille Saint-Saëns and Paul Taffanel."

14. Philipp, p. 910.

15. PPT7 includes eighteen letters from Saint-Saëns to Marie-Camille. Thirteen letters and cards from Marie-Camille Taffanel are included in the Saint-Saëns Collection housed in the Musée de Dieppe. The following section quotes from this correspondence.

16. PPT5. The following section quotes from these letters.

17. See Favier, pp. 410−26, for a biography of Charles Samaran.

18. *M*, 20 Feb. 1881, p. 95; 27 Feb. 1881, p. 127; and 27 Mar. 1881, p. 136. See Cossé Brissac; and Chimènes, pp. 114−28, on the Comtesse Greffulhe's musical salon. Taffanel's Wind Society also played there in May 1886.

19. Proust, vol. 1, p. 322.
20. Fauquet, *Edouard Lalo*, p. 236.
21. See appendix 3; and PBO, Dossier d'œuvre, *Namouna*, for a collection of newspaper reports on the production of the ballet.
22. Bordeaux newspaper, *La Guienne*, 20 Feb. 1882.
23. *La Revue du monde musical*, 29 Apr. 1882, p. 268.
24. Gál, pp. 149–51.
25. *M*, 5 Feb. 1882, p. 78; and 19 Mar. 1882, p. 126.
26. *M*, 13 Jan. 1884, p. 55.
27. PPT4, draft letter to unnamed addressee, n.d.
28. *M*, 10 Dec. 1882, p. 15.
29. PPT6, letter from Emma Nevada, 17 Dec. 1900. See also *M*, 6 May 1887, p. 151, for a review of a Marchesi concert in which Nevada and Taffanel performed Mysoli's aria from David's *La Perle de Brésil.*
30. PPT8.
31. PBN, Rés Vma ms 522. Compare in particular the score and solo part in bars 8–9, 18, 39–43, and 61–68. And see chapter 4 for a letter from Chausson to Bruneau about the *Romance.*
32. Bruneau, "Souvenirs inédits," p. 46.
33. *M*, 14 Mar. 1886, p. 120 (concert at the Société de musique française); 9 Jan. 1887, p. 48 (Lebouc matinée); 13 Mar. 1887, p. 119 (concert organized by the violinist Guidé); 3 Mar. 1889, p. 72 (concert organized by Widor); 26 Jan. 1890, p. 30; and *MM*, 30 Jan. 1890, p. 4 (concert organized by the Berthelier Quartet).
34. Thomson, pp. 36–37, quotes a review of the music by Isidor Philipp.
35. Meylan, pp. 93–94.
36. See appendix 3, Music Dedicated to Paul Taffanel.
37. *M*, 24 Jan. 1886, p. 63.
38. *M*, 24 Jan. 1886, p. 63; 7 Feb. 1886, p. 79; and 13 Mar. 1887, p. 118.
39. *M*, 7 May. 1882, p. 183.
40. PPT3, letters to Hug frères, 30 Oct. 1888; and to Paul Martin, 31 Oct. 1888.
41. PPT4, draft letter to François Gevaert, n.d. The pitch of 870 refers to a^2; therefore a^1 would be 435, the pitch at which Louis Lot mainly built his flutes for French players.
42. See Fischer, p. 139.
43. PPT6, letter from Gilbert Gravina, 29 Nov. 1907.
44. PPT4, draft letter to unnamed addressee, "Monday 29/12."
45. *M*, 12 Apr. 1885, p. 150; and 26 Apr. 1885, p. 167.
46. PPT3, letter to Paul Martin, 9 Nov. 1888.
47. Quoted in *M*, 25 Nov. 1888, p. 384. The concert also included Lalo's Symphony in G minor.
48. *Journal de Liège*, 8 Feb. 1887, which is also the source of the quote at the beginning of this chapter.
49. See Dzapo for full biographical details of Andersen.
50. Letter, Taffanel to Andersen, 18 Jan. 1883 (Karl Joachim Andersen Papers, Duke University, Durham, NC). This collection includes ten letters in French from Taffanel to Andersen, 1883–1895, and one in German from Taffanel to an unnamed

addressee (copied in the hand of Betty Prümm, nanny to Marie-Camille Taffanel), and it is the source of the other quotations in this section. Andersen's side of the correspondence has not survived, apart from one unrelated letter in PPT14.

51. Letter, Taffanel to Andersen, 27 Feb. 1883. Also draft copy in PPT4.

52. *M*, 4 Feb. 1883, p. 79. *M*, 29 Apr. 1883, p. 176 reviewed a further performance of the *Concertstück* on 23 April at the last of Lebouc's Monday matinées.

53. PBN, D 17341, Société des concerts: Rapports des secrétaires, 1883, p. 5.

54. Letter, Taffanel to Andersen, 25 July 1883.

55. Letter, Taffanel to Andersen, 11 Nov. 1883.

56. Taffanel and Gaubert, p. 185.

57. PBO, 1900 XV (267).

58. PPT4, draft letter to an unnamed addressee, n.d. (after 1885).

59. David Wainwright (see bibliography) confirms that because of the breach in the family, the whereabouts of any papers relating to W. S. Broadwood are not known; therefore the precise details of his contact with Taffanel cannot be established.

60. *M*, 14 Dec. 1884, p. 14.

61. See Boehm, ed. W. S. Broadwood. The preface is dated April 1882.

62. PPT4, draft letter to unnamed addressee, 8 Dec. 1882.

63. See Welch. The preface is dated November 1882. A second, expanded edition followed in 1892.

64. PPT8.

65. The original plate numbers MS [M. Schlesinger] 654, 655, 656, and 657 become B et Cie [Brandus and Co.] 654, 655, 656, and 657.

66. See PAN, AJ37 293–301, Rapport des professeurs; and appendix 6.

67. *M*, 22 Mar. 1885, p. 128 reviewed two Marchesi concerts.

68. See Mackinlay; and Garcia for background details.

69. Mathilde Marchesi's autobiography, *Marchesi and Music*, chapter 4 gives details of Marchesi's appearance at a Pasdeloup concert in 1862, and there are various references to "the celebrated flutist Taffanel." See pp. 256, 260–62, 269, and 287. See also her *Méthode de chant théorique et pratique*, dedicated to François Gevaert.

70. Marchesi, *Marchesi and Music*, p. 249.

71. *M*, 14 June 1885, p. 223.

72. *M*, 16 May 1886, p. 195.

73. Melba, p. 177. This "cadenza written for Mme Melba" was later included by Marchesi in a book of vocal studies, *Variantes et Points d'orgue*, p. 51.

74. Bellaigue, vol. 4 (1890), p. 38. Also reviewed in *M*, 15 Dec. 1889, p. 395.

75. *M*, 18 Oct. 1891, p. 335.

76. *M*, 5 Apr. 1891, p. 109.

77. See the notes to *Melba: The London Recordings*, HMV RLS 719, box set of LP recordings, 1976. The recordings with Gaubert have also been reissued on Naxos Historical, CD 8.110737 (2002).

78. Melba, op. cit., p. 53.

79. *M*, 7 Mar. 1886, p. 110.

80. *M*, 21 Feb. 1886, p. 96.

81. *M*, 21 Mar. 1886, p. 128.

82. Bonnerot, p. 123. Ratner, pp. 190–92, gives a performance history of *Carnaval des animaux*.

83. PPT4, draft letter to Jules Simon, 14 July (1886).

84. *Le Guide musical belge*, 20 Dec. 1883; also reported in *M*, 30 Dec. 1883, p. 39.

8. From Russia to the Paris Exhibition

1. PPT14. This is the main source of the information that follows on Taffanel's visits to Russia.

2. *M*, 24 Apr. 1887, p. 165.

3. Bonnerot, p. 132.

4. Sitwell, *Valse des fleurs*, p. 9.

5. *Journal de St Petersbourg* quoted in *M*, 8 May 1887, p. 182.

6. PPT3, letter to Ernesto Köhler, 5 Dec. 1888.

7. *M*, 12 June 1887, p. 223.

8. Quoted in *M*, 19 June 1887, p. 230.

9. *The Musical Times*, 1 July 1887, p. 410.

10. Letter, Taffanel to Saint-Saëns, n.d. "Mercredi" (Musée de Dieppe). And see Ratner, pp. 193–95, for publication details and a performance history of the *Caprice*.

11. PPT3. The quotations in the following section are from this source.

12. *M*, 22 Apr. 1888, p. 134 includes an article on this fund.

13. See PAN, AJ13 1010A, Dossier personnel, Léopold Lafleurance; and Duplaix, "Léopold Lafleurance."

14. Fitzgibbon, pp. ii–iii, and 215. See also Griffith, p. 127. His book is dedicated "To John Rutson Esq. of Northallerton."

15. PPT6, letter from Frederic Griffith, 9 Apr. 1900.

16. See Blakeman, "Profiles (2), Geoffrey Gilbert," pp. 8–15; and Floyd, p. 8.

17. Giannini, p. 190.

18. PPT4, draft letter to Djalma Julliot, 5 Nov. 1887.

19. Borne and Julliot, pp. 8 and 41. The letter from Taffanel in the foreword is dated 1895 and accompanied by a signed photograph of him dated 1902.

20. See Toff, *The Development of the Modern Flute*, pp. 131–37 for an interpretation of Julliot's work.

21. Borne and Julliot, p. 115.

22. PPT8.

23. PPT3, letter to François Gevaert, 28 Oct. 1888.

24. Taffanel and Gaubert, part 4, "Note pour le travail."

25. Henri Bouillard, *Exercices journaliers pour flûte*, Lille: Gras, n.d. (1913?), plate number 4897, dedicated "à mes élèves." The late Gaston Crunelle, former professor of the Paris Conservatoire, produced a part copy of these exercises during an interview with the author, 24 Apr. 1982. They were clearly recognizable as adapted from those by Taffanel.

26. PPT20, letter from Philippe Gaubert to Geneviève Taffanel, 3 Dec. 1913; and from Théodore Dubois to Geneviève Taffanel, 1 Dec. 1913.

27. PPT3, letter to Alfred Lorentz, 10 Aug. 1889.

28. PPT3, letter to Friedrich Gernsheim, n.d. (after 29 Nov. 1888).

29. PPT3, letter to Madame J. Heuzay, 17 Jan. 1889. See *M*, 20 Jan. 1889, p. 23 for an enthusiastic review of the concert.
30. PPT3, letter to Marie Jaëll, 4 Jan. 1889.
31. PPT3, letter to Henry Woollett, 5 Apr. 1889.
32. Goldberg, entry for Franz Neuhofer.
33. The Belgian flutist R. Vanderkerkove requested a copy of this cadenza from Taffanel in a letter dated 3 Feb. 1901. PPT6.
34. *M*, 27 Jan. 1889, p. 31.
35. PPT6, visiting card from Edouard Colonne, n.d.
36. Taffanel and Fleury, p. 1524.
37. Taffanel and Gaubert, p. 187.
38. PPT3, letter to Joseph Jemain, 4 Dec. 1888.
39. *RGM*, 14 Feb. 1875, p. 63.
40. *M*, 20 Jan. 1889, p. 23; and see 27 Jan. 1889, p. 31; and 3 Feb. 1889, p. 39 for the following quotes.
41. Julien Tiersot, *Musiques pittoresques*, pp. 9–10. This book was collected from his series of articles, "Promenades musicales à l'Exposition de 1889," published weekly in *M* during the Exhibition.
42. *M*, 6 Dec. 1891, p. 391; and 13 Dec. 1891, p. 397.
43. *M*, 4 Nov. 1888, p. 359, then pp. 363, 371, 382, 387–88 (review of the premiere), 395, 398, 406, and 414; and 1889, pp. 6, 11, 15, and 30.
44. *M*, 28 Nov. 1888, p. 388.
45. Bellaigue, *L'Année musicale*, vol. 3 (1889), p. 19.
46. PPT3, letter to an unnamed addressee (probably a Monsieur Ternisien), 18 Dec. 1888.
47. Patti's complete recordings (22 items) have been remastered and reissued on Pearl GEMM CD 9312 (1988).
48. PPT3, letter to Jules Taffanel, 26 Oct. 1888. The feast day of Saint Simon (Jules Taffanel's given name) was the following day.
49. PPT14, letter from Tchaikovsky, 15 Dec. 1888 (27 Dec. 1888 European calendar).
50. Fédorov, p. 87.
51. PPT3, letters to Jules Simon and Charles Boesch, both 28 Feb. 1889.
52. *M*, 24 Feb. 1889, p. 61.
53. Lakond, p. 269, 27 Mar. 1889 (7 Apr. 1889, European calendar). [Note: the dates in Tchaikovsky's diary follow the Russian calendar, twelve days behind the European.]
54. Fédorov, p. 88, letter to Désirée Artôt, 9 Mar. 1890.
55. Poplavski, p. 311. Also quoted in Poznansky, p. 39.
56. See Harriss, pp. 128–29.
57. The most detailed general source on the Exhibition is the extensively illustrated catalog of the Musée d'Orsay centenary exhibition, *1889: La Tour Eiffel et l'Exposition universelle*. For Debussy, see Devriès, pp. 25–37.
58. PPT20, receipt dated 4 Apr. 1889
59. *Exposition universelle internationale de 1889 à Paris*, p. 86. See also Pierre, *La Facture instrumentale à l'Exposition universelle de 1889*, p. 283, including a useful survey of the development and the present state of the Boehm flute in Europe in 1889.
60. Tiersot, *Musiques pittoresques*, pp. 6–10.

61. PPT5, letter to Marie-Camille Taffanel, 13 Aug. 1889.

62. *M*, 16 June 1889, p. 188.

63. *M*, 24 Nov. 1889, p. 376.

64. See Clark.

65. *L'Art musical*, 15 Nov. 1889, pp. 166–67.

66. *M*, 3 Nov. 1889, p. 347.

9. Toward a New Career

1. Imbert, *Médaillons*, p. 394

2. PAN, AJ13 1010A, Dossier personnel, Taffanel.

3. Lancien was appointed in July 1887 and conducted for the first time on 18 Dec. 1887. See Prod'homme, *L'Opéra*, p. 63; and Wolff, p. 521.

4. *M*, 5 Jan. 1890, p. 7.

5. Busser, pp. 173–74.

6. See PAN, AJ13 1184, Dossier personnel, Donjon; and AJ13 1010A, Dossiers personnels, Hennebains and L. Lafleurance.

7. *MM*, 15 July 1899, leading article by Arthur Dandelot.

8. PAN, AJ37 337,2 (g), Aspirants et demandes d'inscription: flûte, 1892–1924. Gaubert's second application to the class was made on 12 Oct. 1893, when Taffanel became professor.

9. Letter, Taffanel to Philippe Gaubert, 1904. Kindly provided by Madame Yvette Poiré-Gaubert.

10. Philippe Gaubert, "Pourquoi je quitte la direction des Concerts du Conservatoire," cutting from an unidentified newspaper, dated 4 May 1938.

11. Letter from Gaubert to Jacques Taffanel, 20 Nov. 1938, kindly provided by Dominique Taffanel, grandson of Jacques.

12. Poiré-Gaubert Collection; and PPT20.

13. This copy passed to Lafleurance's former student the late Pierre Paubon.

14. Inghelbrecht, p. 231.

15. For general details on Gaubert's life and career see Blakeman, "Philippe Gaubert: A Born Flûtiste;" and Poiré-Gaubert.

16. Five of Gaubert's solo recordings have been remastered and reissued on *The Great Flautists*, vols. 1 and 2, Pearl, GEMM CD 9284 and 9302 (1990), along with examples of the playing of Adolphe Hennebains, Georges Barrère, René Le Roy, and Marcel Moyse.

17. Samazeuilh, p. 261.

18. Communicated to the author in an interview with Robert Hériché, 18 Feb. 1988.

19. PBN, Lettres autographes, Philippe Gaubert no. 54, 1 Aug. 1836; and no. 58, n.d.

20. Program details from *Signale für die musikalische Welt*, vol. 48, 1890, p. 243.

21. See the program listings in Forner.

22. Background information on Schwedler and the Gewandhaus Orchestra kindly communicated by John R. Bailey, including the fact that Schwedler was a pioneer of early performance practice, playing a concerto by Frederick the Great on a one-keyed flute in Vienna: see *M*, 17 July 1892, p. 230. There is no evidence of further contact between Schwedler and Taffanel.

23. Unidentified source from Leipzig quoted in *M*, 23 Feb. 1890, p. 61.

24. *Musikalisches Wochenblatt*, vol. 21, no. 10, 27 Feb. 1890, p. 120.

25. *Signale für die musikalische Welt*, vol. 48, 1890, p. 243, signed E. Bernsdorf.

26. Bellaigue, *L'Année musicale*, vol. 4, 1890, p. 132.

27. *La Liberté*, 24 Mar. 1890. And see PBO, Dossier d'œuvre, *Ascanio* for a collection of other newspaper cuttings from the *Revue d'art dramatique*, *Gil Blas*, *Le Figaro*, and *L'Echo de Paris* citing the extraordinary occurrence of a member of the orchestra being called to take a bow.

28. *La Revue bleue*, 23 Mar. 1890, p. 404.

29. *La Liberté*, 24 Mar. 1890.

30. Malherbe, pp. 25–26.

31. PPT7, letter from Saint-Saëns, 4 June 92. The quotation is from Virgil, *Aeneid*, vi, 143–44 ("Primo avulso . . . " in the original).

32. *M*, 22 Feb. 1891, p. 64.

33. *Gazette de Lausanne*, 14 Feb. 1891, p. 2.; *La Revue*, Lausanne, 16 Feb. 1891, p. 3; and *Feuille d'avis de Lausanne*, 17 Feb. 1891, p. 3.

34. *Le Genevois*, 23 Feb. 1891. See also the *Tribune de Genève*, 21 Feb. 1891.

35. See, for example, *M*, 1 Mar. 1891, p. 67.

36. Benoît, p. 13.

37. Willy, *Bains de sons*, Paris, p. 100, reprint of a review dated 9 Apr. 1891. See also *M*, 12 Apr. 1891, p. 117.

38. Willy, *Soirées perdues*, p. 75, reprint of a review dated 18 Apr. 1891. Paul Fournier's "Allegro" has not been found: it appears not to have been published.

39. PAN, AJ13 1010A, Dossier personnel, Taffanel.

40. PPT18 includes a rehearsal schedule for *Lohengrin*.

41. *M*, 1 Mar. 1891, p. 72; and 22 Mar. 1891, p. 96.

42. PPT6, letter from Gabriel Pierné, n.d. (probably February 1899). Taffanel's letter to Pierné has not survived.

43. PPT20.

44. See Dandelot, *La Société des concerts du Conservatoire, 1828–1923*, pp. 81–82 and 102–03 for further details of Jules Garcin (b. 1830) and Jules Danbé (b. 1840).

45. PBN, Lettres autographes, Paul Taffanel, no. 19, 30 May 1892.

46. PBN, D 17345 (12), Société des concerts: Comité et assemblées générales, 3 June 1892 and 7 June 1892; and voting notes recorded on the reverse of Jules Bordier's biographical note on Taffanel, 4 Jan. 1890: PBN, Fonds Montpensier, Paul Taffanel. Bordier was a composer and the founder of the Association artistique–Concerts populaires at Angers. See also *Le Petit journal*, 4 June 1892; and *M*, 5 June 1892, pp. 182–83 (which wrongly gives the votes as 49 to 36); 12 June 1892, p. 192; and 19 June 1892, p. 198.

47. PPT6, letter from Edouard Risler, 5 June 1892.

48. PPT15.

49. PPT15, letter from Geneviève Taffanel, 13 Aug 1892.

50. PPT5, letter to Marie-Camille Taffanel, 19 Aug 1892.

51. PPT4, draft letter to Charles Lebouc and his wife, n.d. (Aug. 1892).

52. PPT20, printed program of the concert.

53. Imbert, *Médaillons*, pp. 394–95 (quoted from a newspaper review).

54. *M*, 4 Dec. 1892, p. 388.

55. Willy, *Rythmes et rires*, p. 43.

56. Neither letter has been found, but Taffanel refers to both in his reply to Tiersot, PBN, Lettres autographes, Paul Taffanel, no. 12, 28 Dec. 1892, from which the following quotes come.

57. *M*, 5 Mar. 1893, p. 77.

58. *M*, 26 Mar. 1893, p. 104, and 2 Apr. 1893, p. 109.

59. See PBO, Dossier d'œuvre, *Die Walküre* for a selection of newspaper cuttings; and *M*, 14 May 1893, pp. 153–55 and 159; and 21 May 1893, p. 163.

60. PBN, Lettres autographes, Paul Taffanel, no. 5, "Saturday morning," with the envelope stamped 3 June 1893.

61. Imbert, *Médaillons*, p. 395.

62. *Le Figaro*, 30 June 1893, article by Charles Darcours.

63. *L'Univers illustré*, 9 July 1892.

64. *M*, 9 July 1893, p. 222.

65. PPT7, letter from Saint-Saëns to Marie-Camille Taffanel, 11 July 1893 (also quoted in chapter 7).

66. See *M*, 2 Apr. 1893, p. 110; 14 May 1893, p. 155; and 9 July 1893, p. 223, for descriptions of the orchestral layout, and details of the political intrigues at the Opéra during this period.

67. "Silhouettes / Paul Taffanel," *Progrès artistique*, 8 Sept. 1890, signed "P" and reprinted the following year in *MM*, 15 Aug. 1891, p. 3.

68. *La Gironde*, 4 July 1893; and *Musica*, Oct. 1902 and succeeding numbers. See also, for example, *Le Nouvelliste*, 4 July 1893; *L'Univers illustré*, 8 July 1893; and *La Vie illustrée*, 6 Mar. 1903.

69. *M*, 10 Dec. 1893, p. 397.

70. PPT16, which is also the source of the following quotes.

71. PBO, Dossier d'artiste, Paul Viardot, doctor's certificates dated 21 Sept. 1893 and 25 Sept. 1893. Blanche Marchesi was an eyewitness to Viardot's breakdown, see *The Singer's Catechism and Creed*, p. 111. Viardot later modified his story, see *Souvenirs d'un artiste*, pp. 281–84. His niece, Madame Michèle Beaulieu, revealed in an interview with the author, 28 May 1986, that it was common knowledge that Viardot had a drinking problem.

72. *M*, 24 Sept. 1893, p. 311; and 1 Oct. 1893, p. 319.

10. Wielding the Baton

1. Dancla, pp. 34–35.

2. Samazeuilh, pp. 369–70.

3. Lynch, pp. 127, 130, 142, and 146.

4. Carse, chapters 6 and 7, surveys the rise of the conductor; and Bamberger presents an anthology of writings on conducting from Weber onward, including a translation of the seminal French text Hector Berlioz's *L'Art du chef d'orchestre* (1855).

5. Rohozinski, vol. 2, p. 283.

6. Inghelbrecht, p. 225.

7. Quoted in Wye, p. 85.

8. Lalo, *La Musique*, pp. 81, 177, and 345 (reprints of reviews from *Le Temps*).

9. Mendès in *Le Journal*, 26 Nov. 1899; and Lalo, *La Musique*, p. 288.

10. *Le Temps*, 9 May 1905. See Nichols, *Ravel*, p. 13; and Darras for a collection of essays illuminating the many sides of Pierre Lalo's character and his obsessions.

11. Willy, *La Mouche des croches*, p. 250. See also, for example, *Entre deux airs* (1895), p. 140, a review of the Bach B minor Mass; *Notes sans portées* (1896), pp. 147 and 239, reviews of Berlioz's *Roméo et Juliette* and Beethoven's *Missa Solemnis*; and *Garçon l'audition* (1899), p. 73, a review of Raoul Pugno playing a Mozart piano concerto.

12. Dukas, p. 261. See also pp. 255, 269, and 457 for other reviews of Taffanel's conducting.

13. PPT7, letters from Saint-Saëns to Taffanel, 24 Dec. 1895 and 24 Dec. 1900.

14. PPT20, letter from Francis Planté to Geneviève Taffanel, 26 Oct. 1907.

15. *MM*, 15 May 1897, review signed "E.M."

16. *MM*, 26 Apr. 1899, p. 175. See also Dandelot's leading feature article on Taffanel in *MM*, 30 Dec. 1897.

17. Letter from Taffanel to Joachim Andersen, 5 May 1895 (Duke University, Durham, NC).

18. See PBO, Dossier d'œuvre, *Tannhäuser*, for reviews of the premiere.

19. Harcourt, p. 17.

20. *MM*, 30 May 1895, p. 32. See also PBN, Lettres autographes, Paul Taffanel, no. 4, to Hugues Imbert, 11 Oct. 1894.

21. *Le Charivari*, 11 Feb. 1896, cartoon by Henriot.

22. Wolff, pp. 521–23; and Busser, pp. 155–72.

23. Inghelbrecht, p. 225.

24. PPT18 includes dossiers Taffanel kept for the Wagner operas he conducted. And see Curzon for details of Wagner productions conducted by Taffanel; and Bruneau, *Musiques d'hier et demain* for studies of these and other works at the Opéra in 1890s.

25. PPT16, Taffanel's notes on Wagner's operas in Munich.

26. See PBO, Dossier d'œuvre, *Les Maîtres chanteurs*, for reviews of the premiere.

27. Grovlez, p. 711.

28. PPT17 includes dossiers Taffanel kept for *Otello* and the *Pezzi sacri*, also correspondence with Verdi and Boito. The following section quotes from this correspondence, with dates of letters given in the text.

29. Quoted in Osborne, p. 198.

30. See PBO, Dossier d'œuvre, *Othello*, for reviews of the premiere.

31. *Revue musicale*, 1898, p. 702; and *M*, 10 Apr. 1898, p. 116.

32. The list has been compiled from information in PPT1; Wolff; and the Paris Opéra Archives.

33. PPT6, letter from Jules Massenet, 20 Mar. 1894.

34. Chabrier, p. 1115.

35. PBN, D 17341, Société des concerts, Assemblées générales, Rapports des secrétaires, 18 May 1881; 28 May 1890; 29 May 1891.

36. In the list only the first date of each pair of concerts is given. See Blakeman, "The Correspondence of Camille Saint-Saëns and Paul Taffanel," for letters concerning some of these works.

37. Rohozinski, vol. 2, p. 283.
38. Holoman lists the complete programs from the archive in PBN, and also surveys Taffanel's career at the Society: see especially pp. 294–311. See also Dandelot, *La Société des concerts du Conservatoire de 1828 à 1897*, pp. 122–56, and the 2nd edition, pp. 109–44, for comment and listings of highlights across the repertoire.
39. PBN, Lettres autographes, Paul Taffanel, no. 4, 11 Oct. 1894.
40. Dukas, p. 255.
41. PPT6, letter from Vincent d'Indy, 10 Mar. 1896.
42. PPT6, letter from Raoul Pugno, 4 Jan. 1899. Pugno also appeared at the Société des concerts in April 1896, March 1899, and February 1900.
43. PPT6, letter from Raoul Pugno, 20 Dec. 1899 (1 Jan. 1900 European calendar).
44. Busser, pp. 68–69. And see, for example, *M*, 16 Apr. 1893, p. 126; and 26 Nov. 1893, p. 384 for details of two prizewinners' concerts for the 1893 *Concours Rossini*.
45. *Musica*, Dec. 1903, p. 249. See also *M*, 26 Feb. 1893, p. 71; and 30 Apr. 1893, p. 143.
46. Maurat, *Souvenirs musicaux et littéraires*, pp. 25–26. See also Maurat's obituary article, "Paul Taffanel," *SIM*, 15 Dec. 1908.
47. PPT19 includes all the material that Taffanel collected about the Exhibition. For general background see Jullian; *MM*, 15 Oct. 1900, a special issue on all aspects of the Exposition; and Pistone, "La Musique à Paris en 1900."
48. Bruneau, *Rapport*, pp. 7 and 55. The copy in PPT19 is inscribed by Bruneau "to Paul Taffanel in memory of our concerts, with friendship and gratitude."
49. Taffanel recorded the various awards in his *Notes biographiques*, PPT1.
50. Letter from Taffanel to Saint-Saëns, 26 Mar. 1900. (Musée de Dieppe).
51. PPT6, letter from Louis Bourgault-Ducoudray, 16 Dec. 1900.
52. Busser, p. 118; and PPT20, copy of a letter from Taffanel to Henri Busser, 11 May 1902.
53. PPT6, letter from Claude Debussy, 7 Aug. 1900.
54. PPT6, letter from Claude Debussy, n.d.
55. *Le Figaro*, 24 Aug. 1900.
56. *MM*, 30 Aug. 1900, p. 259.
57. Lesure, pp. 198–99 quotes extracts from press reviews, including Lalo's, and a letter from Debussy to Blanche Marot after the performance.
58. *Gil Blas*, 7 Mar. 1903.
59. PBN, Lettres autographes, Paul Taffanel, no. 16, 4 Feb. 1901.
60. Waël-Munk, p. 47.
61. PBN, Lettres autographes, Paul Taffanel, no. 20, 29 Apr. 1901.
62. PBN, D 17345, Société des concerts, Comités et assemblées générales, vol. 14, pp. 136 and 141. See PBN, Lettres autographes, Paul Taffanel, nos. 21 and 22, for a letter of thanks from Taffanel, and a further letter resigning as Secretary of the Caisse de prévoyance. *M*, 12 May 1901, and *MM*, 15 May 1901, carried articles on Taffanel's retirement.
63. PBN, D 17342, Société des concerts, Procès-verbaux des Assemblées générales, vol. 1, pp. 103–29.
64. PPT10.
65. PPT11. Joseph Jemain published his own article in *MM*, 30 Sept. 1908, pp. 274–76.
66. PPT9. The quotes in the following section are translated from the published version: see appendix 2.

11. Teaching the Flute

1. PAN, AJ37 66,16, Dossier personnel, Henri Altès, letters dated 3 June 1893 and 25 June 1893. Also included is a copy of the invitation to his funeral in 1895.

2. PAN, AJ37 65,1, Conservatoire, Candidats, 1820–1923.

3. PAN, AJ37 72,2, Conservatoire, Dossier personnel, Paul Taffanel.

4. *M*, 12 Nov. 1893, p. 368.

5. Letter from Taffanel to Joachim Andersen, 5 May 1895 (Duke University Collection, Durham, NC).

6. PAN, AJ37, 293, pp. 127, 285, 435, and 577.

7. Quoted in Lorenzo, p. 185. An abbreviated and slightly modified version of this story is included in Barrère, *Georges Barrère*.

8. Fleury, "Souvenirs d'un flûtiste," June 1925, p. 220.

9. See Anon., *The Platinum Flute and Georges Barrère*; and a forthcoming definitive account of Barrère's life and career by Nancy Toff.

10. Fleury gives further autobiographical information in "The Flute in Paris," pp. 176–77. See also Duplaix, "Louis Fleury"; and obituary notices by Robert Brussel, *Le Figaro*, 12 June 1926; Louis Vuillemin, *Paris Soir*, 12 June 1926; and Darius Milhaud, *The Chesterian*, 1926, pp. 264–65.

11. Fleury, "The Flute and Its Powers of Expression," pp. 384 and 393.

12. See Doret, pp. 94–97 for an account of the premiere of *L'Après-midi d'un faune*, which he conducted; and Orledge, *Debussy and the Theatre*, pp. 253–56 for an explanation of the genesis and structure of *Syrinx*.

13. Fleury, "The Flute and Its Powers of Expression," p. 384.

14. Willy, *Notes sans portées*, p. 7, reprint of review dated 14 Oct. 1895. The orchestra is not named.

15. See Rohozinski, vol. 2, pp. 187 ff., for a general description of the evolution of the Conservatoire during this period; and Orledge, *Gabriel Fauré*, pp. 21–22 for Fauré's specific reforms.

16. Rohozinski, vol. 2, p. 352; and Fleury, "Souvenirs d'un flûtiste," p. 220.

17. See Goldberg, p. 66; and Lorenzo, p. 252.

18. See Dorgeuille, Eng. trans., pp. 35–37; and Duplaix, "Gaston Blanquart."

19. See Lorenzo, pp. 197–202; Collis; and Mather. Dorgeuille, Eng. trans., pp. 77–106 includes articles by Barrère, Fleury, Laurent, and Moyse; and pp. 107–31 provide a complete discography of all Taffanel's pupils, compiled by Christopher Steward.

20. See Wye; and McCutchan for studies of Moyse's life and art. Some of the material for Wye's book came from a series of interviews with Moyse's pupils recorded by the author for a BBC Radio 3 documentary program, *Pan and Syrinx*, 1985.

21. Fleury, "Souvenirs d'un flûtiste," p. 220.

22. Information given by Marcel Moyse in an interview with the author, 28 Aug. 1983.

23. Information given by Fernand Caratgé in an interview with the author, 5 Sept. 1983.

24. Information given by Gaston Crunelle in an interview with the author, 24 Apr. 1982. See chapter 8 for the genesis of the *Exercices journaliers*.

25. For details of the new wind and brass works, 1897–1900, see Pierre, *Le Conservatoire*, pp. 629 (oboe), 633 (clarinet), 637 (bassoon), 641 (horn), and 647–60 (brass). The piano, organ, strings, and voice were not involved in the commissioning process.

26. Letter from Taffanel to Joachim Andersen, 5 May 1895 (Duke University).
27. Letter from Taffanel to Joachim Andersen, 28 May 1895 (Duke University).
28. Letter from Taffanel to Joachim Andersen, 6 June 1895 (Duke University). This is the final letter to have survived.
29. From the transcript of an interview with Marcel Moyse for a film on his life, given to the author by Moyse during a series of interviews, March 1984.
30. Fischer, p. 34.
31. PAN, AJ37, 69, letter from Gabriel Fauré to Théodore Dubois, n.d., but annotated "June 98."
32. Fauré's sightreading piece was edited and published by Anabel Hulme Brieff under the misleading title *Morceau de concours* (New York: Bourne, 1977) and extended with an inauthentic repetition of bars 1 to 14.
33. PPT6, Letter from Fauré, n.d., annotated by Taffanel, "London June 98."
34. PPT6, Letter from Alphonse Duvernoy, n.d. (1899).
35. PPT6, Letter from Alphonse Duvernoy, n.d. ("Saturday 3;" "June" added in another hand).
36. PPT6, Letter from Cécile Chaminade, n.d. (1902).
37. PPT6, Letter from Cécile Chaminade, 26 July 1902.
38. Colette, p. 143. The name given as Racnilaleo should be Raonilaleo. He was originally from Madagascar.
39. PPT8.
40. Information given by Moyse in an interview with the author, 28 Aug. 1983.
41. The Conservatoire "Album photographique" was announced in *MM*, 15 June 1895, ed. E. Mangeot and published as a supplement to the journal.
42. *Conservatoire . . . Distribution des prix*, 1895 and 1902.
43. *L'Europe artiste*, 1 Sept. 1895.
44. *MM*, 15 Aug. 1896, p. 123.
45. PAN AJ37 72,2, letters from Taffanel to the Conservatoire director, Théodore Dubois, 6 Apr. 1903 and 10 Apr. 1906. PPT18 includes a note on the back of a rehearsal booklet for *Tristan* (1904): "My class by Hennebains. Monday 26/Nov."
46. Wysham, p. 33.
47. PPT6, Letter from F. Sanchis, 29 Apr. 1899; and from Auguste Giroud, 27 Nov. 1900. Giroud had success as a player and also became professor of flute at the Lausanne Conservatoire. See Goldberg.
48. PPT6, Letter from Eugène Crosti, 6 Nov. 1902, annotated by Taffanel: "recommend Gaubert."
49. PPT20 includes a membership card for the Association des anciens élèves du Conservatoire, dated 3 June 1907.
50. Waël-Munk, p. 47. Compare the version by Fernand Bourgeat, secretary general of the Conservatoire, quoted in the chapter heading and taken from his speech at Taffanel's graveside, 24 Nov. 1908.
51. PPT20, letter from the ministère de l'instruction publique, 6 Nov. 1908.
52. Quoted in Lorenzo, pp. 187–88.
53. Barrère, *Georges Barrère*, p. 5.
54. Quoted in Lorenzo, p. 187.

55. Barrère, *Georges Barrère*, p. 11; and Lorenzo, pp. 187 and 194.
56. Fleury, "Souvenirs d'un flûtiste," p. 220.
57. Ibid.
58. Taffanel and Fleury, "La Flûte," p. 1526.
59. Letter from Fernand Dusausoy to Jeanne Samaran, 28 June 1949.
60. Letter from René Bergeon to Jeanne Samaran, 28 Oct. 1949.
61. "Biographie Taffanel: projet," unpublished ms page by Marcel Moyse given to the author during a series of interviews, March 1984.
62. Letter from Marcel Moyse to Jeanne Samaran, 27 Jan.1970.
63. Information given by Marcel Moyse in interview with the author, 28 Aug. 1983.
64. Moyse, "A Paris Conservatory Course of Study," pp. 2–5.
65. Quoted in Wye, p. 85.
66. Information given by Robert Hériché in interview with the author, 18 Feb. 1988.
67. See Moyse, "The Unsolvable Problem: Considerations on Flute Vibrato;" and *The Flute and its Problems*, pp. 9–11.
68. "Vibrato," unpublished ms page by Marcel Moyse given to the author during a series of interviews, March 1984. The translation retains the layout and grammatical style of Moyse's original in French.

12. Last Words on the Flute

1. PPT20, Giraud, no. 30.
2. PPT7, letter from Camille Saint-Saëns to Taffanel, 17 Apr. 1899.
3. *M*, 19 Feb. 1893, p. 61; Commettant, p. 170; *M*, 9 Apr. 1893, p. 118; 18 Apr. 1893, p. 127; and 23 Apr. 1893, p. 135.
4. See, for example, *M*, 8 Jan. 1893, p. 15; 19 Mar. 1893, p. 95; and 12 Jan. 1896, p. 31.
5. PBN, Lettres autographes, Paul Taffanel, no. 2, 17 Apr. 1896.
6. PPT1, 1894; and *M*, 11 Feb. 1894, p. 47.
7. PPT6, letter of introduction from Jules Massenet, 26 June 1894.
8. Letter from Taffanel to Joachim Andersen, 28 May 1895. (Duke University Collection, Durham, NC).
9. PPT6, letter from Raoul Pugno, n.d., annotated by Taffanel 4 Jan. 1899 with a draft reply enclosed.
10. PPT20, program for the Rouen concert, 11 Feb. 1899. The Rameau movements played were *La Livri*, *La Pouplinière*, and *Tambourins*.
11. *Le Jubilé de C. Saint-Saëns*, following p. 11.
12. Dukas, p. 337; and *MM*, 15 June 1896, p. 51. See the introduction for the quote from Th. Lindenlaub on this concert.
13. PPT7, letter from Saint-Saëns to Taffanel, n.d. (1896), with an explanatory note enclosed from Marie-Camille Taffanel.
14. Lemoine recounted the history of La Trompette in *La Revue musicale*, 15 Oct. 1903. See Augé de Lassus, pp. 48, 73, 82, 92, 101, and 158 for Taffanel's appearances with the Society.
15. PPT6, three letters from Emile Lemoine, 2 Feb. 1897; 12 Feb. 1897; and 8 Mar. 1897.
16. PPT6, letter from Emile Lemoine, 28 Mar. 1897.
17. See appendix 3, Music Dedicated to Paul Taffanel.

18. Date recorded in PPT1.

19. Fleury, "Song and the Flute," pp. 110–11.

20. Taffanel and Gaubert, p. 194. Page number references are to the 1958 second edition of the *Méthode* (see appendix 2, Paul Taffanel Works List).

21. Information given by William Bennett in conversation with the author, 1985. See *Taffanel: Works for Flute and Piano* (originally issued on LP and cassette, Bravura Records, BVA 8612, 1985; reissued on CD, Beep Records, BP27, 1996).

22. Taffanel and Gaubert, p. 5.

23. Details from Taffanel's death certificate dated 23 Nov. 1908: *GY 79328 / Préfecture du Département de la Seine / Extrait des minutes des actes de décès du 17e Arrondissement de Paris* . . .

24. PPT7, Letter from Saint-Saëns to Geneviève Taffanel, 25 Nov. 1908.

25. Letter from Geneviève Taffanel to Saint-Saëns, 3 Dec. 1908. (Musée de Dieppe)

26. Waël-Munk, p. 49.

27. The most detailed obituary notices appeared in *Comoedia*, 23 Nov. 1908, signed L. Vuillemin; *La Petite Gironde* (Bordeaux), 24 Nov. 1908, unsigned; *Le Ménestrel*, 25 Nov. 1908, signed Arthur Pougin; *Le Monde illustré*, 28 Nov. 1908, signed L. De M.; *Le Monde musical*, 30 Nov. 1908, two notices, one signed A. Mangeot, the other unsigned; *Le Courrier musical*, 1 Dec. 1908, signed D.R.; *SIM Bulletin*, 15 Dec. 1908, signed Edmond Maurat; *La Revue musicale*, Dec. 1908, signed B.; *La Revue musicale de Lyon*, Dec. 1908, signed Pierre Lalo; and *Musica*, Jan. 1909, unsigned.

28. PPT20, Letter from Juliette Rabaud Dorus to Geneviève Taffanel, 2 Dec. 1908.

29. PPT20, Letter from Nadia Boulanger to Geneviève Taffanel, 23 Nov. 1908.

30. Legal document, "Partage de la succession de M. Taffanel," retained by Taffanel's Paris lawyer, Albert Père.

31. See the inventory to PPT8, appendix 1, for a listing of the materials described and quoted in the following sections.

32. This copy of the book was shown to the author during an interview with Le Roy, 24 Apr. 1982.

33. Taffanel and Gaubert, "Préface des Editeurs."

34. Information communicated to the author in a series of interviews with Gaubert's stepdaughter, Madame Yvette Poiré-Gaubert, 1981.

35. PPT6, letters from Zimmermann, 15 Nov. 1898; 11 Jan. 1899; 10 Mar. 1899; and 19 Apr. 1899.

36. PPT6, letter from Henry Clay Wysham, 17 Oct. 1898. Wysham's book includes an appreciation of Taffanel, p. 33.

37. PPT6, letter from Abbé Tabuteau, 16 Jan. 1899.

38. PPT6, letter from Edouard Risler, 18 Sept. 1907.

39. Taffanel and Fleury, p. 1483.

40. Taffanel and Fleury, p. 1525.

41. Taffanel and Fleury, p. 1523–25.

42. Taffanel and Fleury, p. 1525.

43. Taffanel and Gaubert, "Préface des Editeurs."

44. Information given to the author in interviews with Fernand Caratgé, 5 Sept. 1983; Gaston Crunelle, 24 Apr. 1982; Robert Hériché, 18 Feb. 1988; and René Le Roy, 24 Apr. 1982.

45. Taffanel and Fleury, p. 1525.

46. The eight photographs are undated, but 1906 or later seems likely, based on comparisons with earlier photographs (e.g. in *Musica*, 1904) that show Taffanel looking much younger.

47. See, for example, Baines, p. 56; and Bate, p. 239.

48. See Philip, pp. 109–18 for further (unresolved) discussion of flute vibrato, and of Taffanel's influence.

49. Fischer, pp. 117 and 141. Fischer discusses the *Méthode* on the assumption that all the material was by Taffanel, based on claims made by Marcel Moyse in interviews with her and Michel Debost in 1982: see pp. 118, 146, and 243.

50. Taffanel and Gaubert, p. 3.

51. PPT8, draft text, p. 13; and Taffanel and Gaubert, page 8.

52. Taffanel and Gaubert, p. 185.

53. Taffanel and Gaubert, Avant Propos; and pp. 5–9; 14–16; 49; 52–54; 58–59; 90–92; and 184.

54. See Blakeman, *The French Flute Schools of the Baroque and Late-Romantic Periods*, which explores the many aspects and implications of the parallels between Taffanel and the first French flute school.

55. Taffanel and Gaubert, p. 185.

56. Taffanel and Gaubert, p. 187.

57. Taffanel and Gaubert, p. 189.

58. Taffanel and Gaubert, pp. 194 and 196.

59. Taffanel and Gaubert, pp. 198 and 201.

60. Taffanel and Gaubert, pp. 207, 208, and 215.

Conclusion

1. Lalo, "Mort de Taffanel."

2. Quoted in the booklet notes to Pierre-André Valade's CD set of Jolivet's complete works for flute: *André Jolivet, L'Œuvre pour flûte*, Accord 202292 (1993).

3. Fleury, "Souvenirs d'un flûtiste," p. 220.

Books and Articles with References to Paul Taffanel

The main obituary and feature notices from journals and newspapers are listed here, but in addition there were frequent press reviews of Taffanel throughout his career in *Le Courrier musical, Le Figaro, Le Ménestrel, Le Monde musical, Musica, La Revue et gazette musicale, Le Temps,* and other publications. These are not listed separately, but the most significant ones are referred to in the main text.

Alvin, H., and R. Prieur. *Métronomie expérimentale.* Paris: Fischbacher, 1895.

Andrew, Nancy. *The Music of Paul Taffanel.* D.M.A. diss., Peabody Institute, Johns Hopkins University, Baltimore, MD, 1993.

Anon. "Nécrologie: Paul Taffanel." *Musica,* January 1909, p. 16.

Anon. "Société des concerts." *Musical Courier,* New York, 17 March 1897.

Astruc, Gabriel. *Le Pavillon des fantômes.* Paris: Grasset, 1929.

Augé de Lassus, L. *La Trompette: un demi-siècle de musique de chambre.* Paris: Delagrave, 1911.

"B." "Paul Taffanel: la carrière d'un artiste." *La Révue musicale,* vol. 8, December 1908, p. 656.

Baines, Anthony. *Woodwind Instruments and Their History.* London: Faber, 1967.

Barrère, Georges. *Georges Barrère.* New York, 1928.

———. *Société moderne d'instruments à vent, 1895–1905.* Paris, 1905.

Bate, Philip. *The Flute.* 2nd ed. London: Benn, 1979.

Bellaigue, Camille. *L'Année musicale.* 7 vols., 1886–93. Paris: Delagrave, 1887–94.

Benoît, Camille. *La Grande messe en si mineur de Jean-Sébastien Bach.* Paris: Imprimerie de l'Art, 1891.

Bertrand, Paul. *Le Monde de la musique.* Geneva: La Palatine, 1947.

Bessand-Massenet, Pierre. *Massenet.* Paris: Julliard, 1979.

Blakeman, Edward. "The Correspondence of Camille Saint-Saëns and Paul Taffanel, 1880–1906." *Music and Letters*, vol. 63, nos. 1–2, January–April 1982, pp. 44–58.

———. *The French Flute Schools of the Baroque and Late-Romantic Periods.* M.Litt. thesis, University of Lancaster, 1979.

———. "Paul Taffanel: The Father of Modern Flute Playing." *Pan* (Journal of the British Flute Society), vol. 1, no. 1, April 1983, pp. 7–9.

———. "Philippe Gaubert: A Born Flûtiste." *Pan*, vol. 2, no. 1, March 1984, pp. 10–14.

———. *Paul Taffanel (1844–1908) and His Significance in French Musical Life.* Ph.D. thesis, University of Birmingham, 1994.

Blanchard, Roger, and Roland de Candé. *Dieux et divas de l'Opéra de 1800 à 1950.* Paris: Plon, 1987.

Bonnerot, Jean. *C. Saint-Saëns (1835–1921), sa vie et son œuvre.* Paris: Durand, 1921.

Borne, François, and Djalma Julliot. *Notice concernant les améliorations apportées à la flûte de Théobald Boehm.* Paçy-sur-Eure: E. Grateau, 1905.

Brett, Adrian. "300 Years of the French Style;" "The French Style in England;" "The French Style in America;" and "The Other French Players." *The Flute Worker*, November 1982, pp. 1–5; May 1983, pp. 1, 5, 7; December 1983, pp. 1, 5; Winter 1985, pp. 1, 6, 8.

Brody, Elaine. *Paris, the Musical Kaleidoscope, 1870–1925.* London: Robson Books, 1988.

Brown, David. *Tchaikovsky: The Final Years (1885–1893).* London: Gollancz, 1991.

Brown, Rachel. *The Early Flute: A Practical Guide.* Cambridge: Cambridge University Press, 2002.

Bruneau, Alfred. *Musiques de Russie et musiciens de France.* Paris: Charpentier, 1903.

———. *Rapport . . . des grandes auditions musicales de l'Exposition Universelle de 1900.* Paris: Imprimerie Nationale, 1900.

———, ed. D. Pistone. "Souvenirs inédits." *Revue internationale de musique française*, no. 7, February 1982, p. 8.

Busser, Henri. *De Pelléas aux Indes galantes.* Paris: Fayard, 1955.

Casella, Alfredo, trans. and ed. Spencer Norton. *Music in My Time.* Norman: University of Oklahoma Press, 1955. 1st ed., Florence, 1941.

Cesari, Gaetano, and Alessandro Luzio. *I Copialettere di Giuseppe Verdi.* Milan: 1913.

Chabrier, Emmanuel, ed. Roger Delage and Frans Durif. *Correspondance.* Paris: Klincksieck, 1994.

Chantavoine, Jean. *Camille Saint-Saëns.* Paris: Richard-Masse, 1947.

Charnacé, Guy de. "Musique de chambre." *La Grande dame*, no. 4, April 1893, pp. 219–20.

Chausson, Ernest, ed. Jean Gallois and Isabelle Bretaudeau. *Ecrits inédits.* Paris: Editions du Rocher, 1999.

Chimènes, Myriam. *Mécènes et musiciens: Du salon au concert à Paris sous la IIIe république.* Paris: Fayard, 2004.

Cobbett, W., ed. *Cyclopedic Survey of Chamber Music.* 2 vols. London: Oxford University Press, 1929–30.

Colette, ed. Alain Galliari. *Au concert.* Paris: Le Castor Astral, 1992.

Collis, James. "On Flute Legato: An Interview with Georges Laurent." *Woodwind World*, no. 2, February 1958, p. 14.

Comettant, Oscar. *La Musique de chambre 1893.* Paris: Gautherin, n.d. (1893).

(Conservatoire). *Distribution des prix, Conservatoire national de musique et de déclamation*. Paris: Imprimerie nationale, 1860– (annual).

Cooper, Jeffrey. *The Rise of Instrumental and Concert Series in Paris, 1828–1871*. Michigan: UMI Research Press, 1983.

Cordey, Jean. *La Société des concerts du Conservatoire*. Paris, 1941.

Curzon, Henri de. *L'Œuvre de Richard Wagner à Paris et ses interprètes, 1850–1914*. Paris: Senart, n.d.

Dandelot, Arthur. *Petits mémoires musicaux*. Paris: Editions de la Nouvelle Revue, 1936.

———. *La Société des concerts du Conservatoire de 1828 à 1897*. Paris: Havard, 1898.

———. *La Société des concerts du Conservatoire, 1828–1923*. Paris: Delagrave, 1923.

———. *La Vie et l'œuvre de Saint-Saëns*. Paris: Dandelot, 1930.

Decourcelle, Maurice. *La Société académique des Enfants d'Apollon, 1741–1880*. Paris: Durand, 1881.

Deldevez, E. *La Société des concerts, 1860 à 1885*. Paris: Firmin-Didot, 1887.

Doret, Gustave. *Temps et contretemps*. Fribourg: Editions de la Librairie de l'Université, 1942.

Dorgeuille, Claude. *L'Ecole française de flûte, 1860–1950*. Paris: Coderg, 1983.

———, trans. and ed. Edward Blakeman. *The French Flute School, 1860–1950*. London: Tony Bingham, 1986.

"D.R." "M. Paul Taffanel." *Le Courrier musical*, 1 December 1908.

Duchesneau, Michel. *L'Avant-garde musicale à Paris de 1871 à 1939*. Liège: Mardaga, 1997.

Dukas, Paul. *Les Ecrits de Paul Dukas sur la musique*. Paris: Société d'Editions Françaises et Internationales, 1948.

Dumesnil, René. *La Musique en France entre les deux guerres, 1919–1939*. Paris: Editions du milieu du monde, 1946.

Dupêchez, Charles. *Histoire de l'Opéra de Paris, 1875–1980*. Paris: Perrin, 1984.

Duplaix, Bernard. "Adolphe Hennebains: le bien-aimé." *La Traversière* (Journal of the French Flute Society), October 1995, pp. 56–64.

———. "Gaston Blanquart: un saint homme," *La Traversière*, April 1994, pp. 42–50.

———. "Léopold Lafleurance: un hérisson au cœur tendre." *La Traversière*, January 1994, pp. 52–61.

———. "Louis Fleury: un homme pressé." *La Traversière*, July 1994, pp. 46–52.

Durand, Jacques. *Quelques souvenirs d'un éditeur de musique*. 2 vols. Paris: Durand, 1924, 1925.

Dzapo, Kyle J. *Joachim Andersen: A Bio-Bibliography*. Westport, CT: Greenwood Press, 1999.

Ehrlich, David. *The History of the Flute from Ancient Times to Boehm's Invention*. New York: Ehrlich, 1921.

Elwart, A. *Histoire des Concerts populaires de musique classique*. 2nd ed. Paris: Librairie Castel, 1864.

Eustache, Jean-Pierre. *Tableau des flûtistes ayant appartenu aux orchestres de l'Opéra*. Ms. Paris: Bibliothèque de l'Opéra, B. Pièce 615.

Exposition universelle internationale de 1889 à Paris, Catalogue général officiel, Section II: Arts libéraux. Lille: L. Danel, 1889.

Fauquet, Joël-Marie. *César Franck*. Paris: Fayard, 1999.

————. *Edouard Lalo: correspondance réunie et présentée.* Paris: Aux Amateurs de Livres, 1989.

————. *Les Sociétés de musique de chambre à Paris de la Restauration à 1870.* Paris: Aux Amateurs de Livres, 1986.

————, ed. *Dictionnaire de la musique en France au XIXe siècle.* Paris: Fayard, 2003.

Favier, Jean. *Charles Samaran.* Paris: Bibliothèque de l'Ecole des Chartes, vol. 141, 1983.

Fédorov, Vladimir. "Cajkovskij et la France." *Revue de musicologie*, vol. 54, no. 1, 1968, pp. 16–95.

Fischer, Penelope. *Philippe Gaubert, 1879–1941.* D.M.A. thesis, University of Maryland, College Park, MD, 1982.

Fitzgibbon, Henry. *The Story of the Flute.* 2nd. ed. London: Reeves, 1928.

Fleury, Louis. "Chamber Music for Wind Instruments." *The Chesterian*, January/February 1924, pp. 111–14, and 144–48.

————. "The Flute and Its Powers of Expression." *Music and Letters*, vol. 3, 1922, p. 383.

————. "The Flute in Paris." *The Flutist*, August 1921, pp. 176–77.

————. "The Flute in Modern Chamber Music." *Cyclopedic Survey of Chamber Music*, ed. Cobbett, vol. 1, p. 402 (see above).

————. "Souvenirs d'un flûtiste." *Le Monde musical*, vols. 35 and 36, 8 parts, September 1924–June 1925.

Forner, Johannes. *Die Gewandhausorchester zu Leipzig, 1781–1981.* Leipzig: VEB Deutscher Verlag für Musik, 1981.

Fouquières, André de. *Mon Paris et ses parisiens.* Vols. 1 and 2. Paris: Horlay, 1953, 1954.

Fourcaud, Louis de, Arthur Pougin, and Léon Pradel. *La Salle Pleyel.* Paris: Librairies Imprimeries Réunies, 1893.

Frémiot, Marcel. "Paul Taffanel." *MGG*, ed. F. Blume, vol. 13, p. 46. Kassel: Bärenreiter, 1949–66.

Friedland, Bea. *Louise Farrenc, 1804–1875: Composer, Performer, Scholar.* Michigan: UMI Research Press, 1980.

Galleras, Roger. *Histoire de la flûte.* Pau: Imprimerie Moderne, 1977.

Gärtner, Jochen, trans. E. W. Anderson. *The Vibrato.* Regensburg: Gustav Bosse, 1981. Original German edition, 1974.

Gatti, Carlo, trans. E. Abbott. *Verdi.* London: Gollancz, 1955. Original Italian edition, 1931.

Gaudefroy, A. *Les Concerts du cercle du Nord de Lille.* Lille, 1892.

Giannini, Tula. *Great Flute Makers of France, the Lot and Godfroy Families, 1650–1900.* London: Tony Bingham, 1993.

Girard, Adrien. *Histoire et richesses de la flûte.* Paris: Librairie Grund, 1953.

Giraud, Charles. *Caricatures de personnes avant des rapports avec le Théâtre de l'Opéra.* 50 plates, copy in Paris: Bibliothèque de l'Opéra, C. 250.

Goldberg, Adolph. *Biographieen zur Porträts-Sammlung hervorragender Flöten-Virtuosen, Dilettanten und Komponisten.* Berlin, 1906. Reprinted in facsimile. Celle: Moeck, 1987.

Goubault, Christian. *La Critique musicale dans la presse française de 1870 à 1914.* Geneva: Slatkine, 1984.

Griffith, Frederic, ed. *Notable Welsh Musicians of Today.* London: Francis Goodman, 1896.

Grove, George, ed. *Grove's Dictionary of Music and Musicians.* 1st ed., London: Macmillan, 1890.

Grovlez, Gabriel. "Le chef d'orchestre au théâtre." *Le Courrier musical*, 25 December 1928, p. 711.

Gut, Serge, and Danièle Pistone. *La Musique de chambre en France de 1870 à 1918.* Paris: Honoré Champion, 1978.

Harcourt, Eugène d'. *Quelques remarques sur l'exécution du Tannhaeuser de Richard Wagner à l'Opéra de Paris (Mai 1895).* Paris: Fischbacher, 1895.

Harding, James. *Gounod.* London: Allen and Unwin, 1973.

Henriot. "Attaquons l'ouverture musiciens." Cartoon. *Le Charivari*, 11 February 1896, p. 30.

Hériché, Robert. *A Propos de la flûte.* Paris: Billaudot, 1985.

Hervé, A. "La Flûte." *Le Monde orphéonique*, nos. 36–47, July–Dec. 1902 (series of twelve articles).

Holoman, D. Kern. *La Société des concerts du Conservatoire (1828–1967).* Berkeley and Los Angeles: University of California Press, 2004.

Honegger, Arthur, ed. Huguette Calmel. *Ecrits.* Paris: Honoré Champion, 1992.

Humblot, Emile. *François Devienne, 1759–1803.* Paris: Brulliard, 1909.

Imbert, Hugues. *Médaillons contemporains.* Paris: Fischbacher, 1902.

Indy, Vincent d', ed. Marie d'Indy. *Ma vie: Journal de jeunesse, correspondance familiale et intime, 1851–1931.* Paris: Séguier, 2001.

Inghelbrecht, Désiré-Emile. *Le Chef d'orchestre et son équipe.* Paris: Julliard, 1949.

Joly, Charles. *Les Maîtres-chanteurs de Richard Wagner.* Paris: Fischbacher, 1898.

Le Jubilé de C. Saint-Saëns, à l'occasion du cinquantenaire de son premier concert, Salle Pleyel, en 1846. Paris: Librairies-Imprimeries Réunies, 1896. Includes articles by Louis de Fourcaud and Th. Lindenlaub.

Jullian, Philippe, trans. S. Hardman. *The Triumph of Art Nouveau, Paris Exhibition 1900.* London: Phaidon, 1974.

Kahane, Martine, and Nicole Wild. *Wagner et la France.* Paris: BN/TNOP/Herscher, 1983.

Lakond, Wladimir, trans. and ed. *The Diaries of Tchaikovsky.* New York: Norton, 1945.

Lalo, Pierre. "Mort de Taffanel." *Revue musicale de Lyon*, December 1908, p. 247.

———. *La Musique, 1898–1899.* Paris: Rouart Lerolle, 1900.

Landormy, Paul. *La Musique française après Debussy.* Paris: Gallimard, 1943.

Lavignac, Albert. *Les Gaietés du Conservatoire.* Paris: 1899. Reprint. Hayen, Belgium: Mardaga, 2002.

———. *Le Voyage artistique à Bayreuth.* Paris: Delagrave, 1897.

———, and Lionel de La Laurencie. *Encyclopédie de la musique et dictionnaire du Conservatoire.* 11 vols. Paris: Delagrave, 1913–31.

Lenski, Karl, and Karl Ventske. *Das goldene Zeitalter der Flöte, Frankreich 1832–1932.* Celle: Moeck, 1992.

Lesure, François. *Debussy.* New edition. Paris: Fayard, 2003.

Lorenzo, Leonardo de. *My Complete Story of the Flute.* New York: Citadel Press, 1951.

Lynch, Hannah. *French Life in Town and Country.* London: George Newnes, 1901.

McCutchan, Ann. *Marcel Moyse: Voice of the Flute.* Portland, OR: Amadeus Press, 1994.

Mangeot, A. "M. Philippe Gaubert." *Le Monde musical*, vol. 23, no. 4, 28 February 1911, p. 53.

———, and Anon. "Paul Taffanel." *Le Monde musical*, vol. 20, no. 22, 30 November 1908, p. 334.

Manuel, Roland, and Nadia Tagrine. *Plaisir de la musique.* Paris: Editions du Seuil, 1947.

Marchesi, Blanche. *The Singer's Catechism and Creed.* London: Dent, 1932.

Marchesi, Mathilde. *Marchesi and Music.* London: Harper, 1897.

Martinet, André. *Histoire anecdotique du Conservatoire de musique et de déclamation.* Paris: Ernest Kolb, 1893.

Massenet, Jules. *Mes souvenirs.* Paris: Lafitte, 1912.

Mather, Roger. "The Flute Sound of Georges Laurent." *Woodwind World*, Brass and Percussion, vol. 15, March 1976, p. 12, and May 1976, p. 30.

Maurat, Edmond. "Paul Taffanel." *SIM*, vol. 4, no. 12, 15 December 1908, p. 1317.

———, ed. L. Roux. *Souvenirs musicaux et littéraires.* Saint Etienne: Université de Saint-Etienne, 1977.

Melba, Nellie. *Melodies and Memories.* New York: Liberty, 1926.

Meylan, Raymond. *La Flûte.* Lausanne: Payot, 1974.

Moran, William R. *Nellie Melba, a Contemporary Review.* Westport, CT: Greenwood Press, 1986.

Moyse, Marcel. *The Flute and Its Problems: Tone Development Through Interpretation for the Flute.* Tokyo: Muramatsu, 1973.

———. "A Paris Conservatory Course of Study." (Letter to Charles DeLaney.) *The Marcel Moyse Society Newsletter*, vol. 3, no. 1, April 1992, pp. 2–5.

———. "The Unsolvable Problem: Considerations on Flute Vibrato." *Woodwind World*, March, April, May 1950, and February 1952 (4 parts).

Nectoux, Jean-Michel. *Gabriel Fauré, correspondance présentée et annotée.* Paris: Flammarion, 1980.

———, trans. Roger Nichols. *Gabriel Fauré, a Musical Life.* Cambridge: Cambridge University Press, 1991.

Nichols, Roger, and Richard Langham Smith. *Claude Debussy: Pelléas et Mélisande.* Cambridge: Cambridge University Press, 1989.

Orledge, Robert. *Debussy and the Theatre.* Cambridge: Cambridge University Press, 1982.

———. *Gabriel Fauré.* London: Eulenburg, 1979.

Philip, Robert. *Early Recordings and Musical Style.* Cambridge: Cambridge University Press, 1992.

Pierre, Constant. *Le Conservatoire national de musique et de déclamation, documents historiques et administratifs.* Paris: Imprimerie Nationale, 1900.

———. *La Facture instrumentale à l'Exposition Universelle de 1889.* Paris: Librairie de l'Art Indépendant, 1890.

Pincherle, Marc. "French Performing Organizations." In *Cyclopedic Survey of Chamber Music*, ed. Cobbett, vol. 1, pp. 434–36 (see above).

———. *Musiciens peints par eux-mêmes.* Paris: Cornuau, 1939.

Pistone, Danièle. *La Musique en France de la révolution à 1900.* Paris: Champion, 1979.

———, ed. "La Musique à Paris en 1900." *Revue internationale de musique française*, no. 12, November 1983, pp. 5–120.

Poiré-Gaubert, Yvette. *Philippe Gaubert.* Garches, France: Société IDJ, 2001.

Poplavski, J. I. "La Dernière journée de Tchaikovsky à Kline." In *Piotr Tchaikovsky, Ecrits critiques, lettres, souvenirs de contemporains.* Moscow: Radouga, 1985.

Pougin, Arthur. Obituary for Taffanel (untitled). *Le Ménestrel*, 28 November 1908, p. 383.

Powell, Ardal. *The Flute*. New Haven, CT: Yale University Press, 2002.

Poznansky, Alexander. *Tchaikovsky's Last Days: A Documentary Study*. Oxford: Oxford University Press, 1996.

Prochasson, Christophe. *Paris 1900: essai d'histoire culturelle*. Paris: Calman-Lévy, 1999.

Prod'homme, J. G. *L'Opéra, 1669–1925*. Paris: Delagrave, 1925.

Prunières, Henri. "French Chamber Music Since the Revolution." In *Cyclopedic Survey of Chamber Music*, ed. Cobbett, vol. 1, pp. 430–34 (see above).

Ratner, Sabina Teller. *Camille Saint-Saëns, 1835–1921, A Thematic Catalogue of His Complete Works. Vol. 1: The Instrumental Works*. Oxford: Oxford University Press, 2002.

Rockstro, R. S. *A Treatise on the Construction, the History and the Practice of the Flute*. London: Rudall Carte, 1890, 2nd ed. 1928.

Rohozinski, L., ed. *Cinquante ans de musique française de 1874 à 1925*. 2 vols. Paris: Editions Musicales de la Librairie de France, 1925.

Rolland, Romain. *Musiciens d'aujourd'hui*. Paris: Hachette, 1908.

Samazeuilh, Gustave. *Musiciens de mon temps*. Paris: Daubin, 1947.

Scheck, Gustav. *Die Flöte und ihre Musik*. Mainz: Schott, 1975.

Schonberg, Harold. *The Great Conductors*. New York: Simon and Schuster, 1967.

Servières, Georges. *Edouard Lalo*. Paris: Laurens, 1925.

Soriano, Marc, ed. *Les Secrets du violon, souvenirs de Jules Boucherit, 1877–1962*. Paris: Edition des Cendres, 1993.

Stockhem, Michel. *Eugène Ysaÿe*. Liège: Pierre Mardaga, 1990.

Storch, Laila. "Georges Gillet: Master Performer and Teacher." *Journal of the International Double Reed Society*, no. 5, June 1977, pp. 1–19.

Terrier, Agnès. *L'Orchestre de l'Opéra de Paris de 1669 à nos jours*. Paris: Editions de la Martinière, 2003.

Tiersot, Julien. *Musiques pittoresques*. Paris: Fischbacher, 1889.

———. "Taffanel (Claude-Paul)." *La Grande encyclopédie*, vol. 30, p. 867. Paris: Société anonyme de la grande encyclopédie, 1901.

Toff, Nancy. *The Development of the Modern Flute*. New York: Taplinger, 1979.

———. *The Flute Book*. New York: Scribner, 1985.

———. *Georges Barrère and the Flute in America*. New York: New York Flute Club, 1994.

Verroust, Denis. "La Flûte à Paris en 1900." *Revue internationale de musique française*, no. 12, November 1983, pp. 69–74.

———. "Les Flûtistes romantiques françaises." *Revue internationale de musique française*, no. 13, February 1984, pp. 7–32.

Viardot, Paul. *Souvenirs d'un artiste*. Paris: Fischbacher, 1910.

Vidal, E., and A. Hervé. "La flûte à travers les âges." *Musica*, vol. 8, no. 84, September 1909, p. 140.

Vuillemin, L. "Paul Taffanel est mort." *Comoedia*, 23 November 1908.

Waël-Munk, Francis. "Compte rendu des travaux du comité." *Annuaire de l'Association des artistes musiciens*. Paris, 1909.

Wetzger, Paul. *Die Flöte*. Heilbron: Schmidt, 1905.

Whitwell, David. *The Longy Club, a Professional Wind Ensemble in Boston, 1900–1917*. Northridge, CA: CA Winds, 1988.

Willy (Henry Gauthier-Villars). "Lettres de l'ouvreuse." Newspaper reviews collected in

9 vols. Paris: Léon Vanier: *Bains de sons* (1891), *Soirées perdues* (1892), *Rythmes et rires* (1893), *La Mouche des croches* (1894), *Entre deux airs* (1895), *Notes sans portées* (1896), *Accords perdus* (1897), *La Colle aux quintes* (1898), *Garçon l'audition* (1899).

Wolff, Stéphane. *L'Opéra au Palais Garnier, 1875–1961.* Paris: L'Entr'acte, 1962.

Wye, Trevor. *Marcel Moyse, an Extraordinary Man.* Cedar Falls, IA: Winzer Press, 1993.

Wysham, Henry Clay. *The Evolution of the Boehm Flute.* New York: Conn, 1898.

General Books and Articles

Altès, Henri. *Méthode pour flûte système Boehm.* Paris: Millerau, 1880.

Anon. "La Flûte." *Magasin pittoresque*, vol. 36, 1868. (Six articles.)

Anon. *The Platinum Flute and Georges Barrère.* New York, 1935.

Anon. *Réponse critique à l'auteur des Bordelais en 1845.* Bordeaux: Causserouge, 1845.

Bailey, John. "The Elusive Mr. Andersen." *Flute Talk*, vol. 1, no. 9, May 1982, p. 1.

Baillot, Pierre. *L'Art du violon.* Paris: Dépôt central de la musique, 1834.

Bamberger, Carl, ed. *The Conductor's Art.* New York: McGraw-Hill, 1965.

Barrère, Georges. "Expression Unconfined." *Musical Quarterly*, vol. 30, April 1944, pp. 192–7.

———. *The Flautist's Formulae, Six Basic Exercises.* London: Schirmer, 1935.

Berlioz, Hector, trans. and ed. Jacques Barzun. *Evenings with the Orchestra.* New York: Alfred Knopf, 1956.

———. *Grande traité d'instrumentation et d'orchestration modernes.* Paris: Schonenberger, 1843. 2nd ed. 1856, including "Le Chef d'orchestre: théorie de son art."

Bernard, Elisabeth. "Jules Pasdeloup et les Concerts populaires." *Revue de musicologie*, vol. 57, 1971, pp. 150–78.

Bertaud, Jules, trans. R. Millar, rev. John Bell. *Paris, 1870–1935.* London: Eyre and Spottiswoode, 1936.

Blakeman, Edward. "Profiles (2), Geoffrey Gilbert." *Pan* (Journal of the British Flute Society), vol. 2, no. 3, September 1984, pp. 8–15.

Bloch, Jean-Jacques, and Marianne Delort. *Quand Paris allait "à l'Expo."* Paris: Fayard, 1980.

Boehm, Theobald, ed. Walter Stewart Broadwood. *An Essay on the Construction of Flutes* (1847). London: Rudall Carte, 1882.

———, trans. Dayton C. Miller. *The Flute and Flute Playing.* New York: Dover 1922.

Brada (Contessa di Puliga). *Souvenirs d'une petite second empire.* Paris: Calman-Lévy, 1921.

Bruneau, Alfred. *Musiques d'hier et de demain.* Paris: Charpentier, 1900.

Burchell, S. C. *Upstart Empire.* London: Macdonald, 1971.

Burnand, Robert. *La Vie quotidienne en France de 1870 à 1900.* Paris: Hachette, 1947.

Busch, Hans, trans. and ed. *Verdi's Otello and Simon Boccanegra in Letters and Documents.* Oxford: Clarendon Press, 1988.

Carse, Adam. *The Orchestra from Beethoven to Berlioz.* Cambridge: Heffer, 1945.

Charnacé, Guy de. *Les Etoiles du chant.* 3 vols. Paris: Plon, 1868–69.

———. *Musique et musiciens.* Paris: Pottier de Lalaine, 1873.

Chorley, Henry. *Music and Manners in France and Germany.* London: Longman, 1844.

Clark, (?), ed. *Appréciations sur le gramophone, Paris, Gramophone.* Paris: ?, 1893.

Cobban, Alfred. *A History of Modern France*. Vol. 2, 1799–1871, and vol. 3, 1871–1962. London: Penguin, 1961 and 1965.

Conati, Marcello, ed. *Interviews and Encounters with Verdi*. Trans. Richard Stokes. London: Gollancz, 1984.

Cooper, Martin. *French Music from the Death of Berlioz to the Death of Fauré*. London: Oxford University Press, 1951.

———. "Charles Louis Ambroise Thomas." In *The Music Masters*, ed. A. A. Bacharach. London: Cassell, 1952.

Cossart, Michel de. *The Food of Love, Princesse Edmond de Polignac (1865–1943) and Her Salon*. London: Hamish Hamilton, 1978.

Cossé Brissac, Anne de. *La Comtesse Greffulhe*. Paris: Perrin, 1991.

Cronin, Vincent. *Paris on the Eve, 1900–1914*. London: Collins, 1989.

Curzon, Henri de. "History and Glory of the Concert Hall of the Paris Conservatory." *Musical Quarterly*, vol. 3, 1917, pp. 304–18.

Dancla, Charles. *Notes et souvenirs*. Paris: Delamotte, 1893.

Dandelot, Arthur. *Evolution de la musique de théâtre depuis Meyerbeer jusqu'à nos jours*. Paris: Flammarion, 1927.

———. *Petits côtés amusants de la vie musicale*. Paris: Dandelot, 1929.

Darras, Jacques, ed. *Hommage à Pierre Lalo*. Paris: Imprimerie R.O., n.d.

Debussy, Claude, ed. François Lesure. *Monsieur Croche et autres écrits*. Paris: Gallimard, 1971. New edition, 1987.

Deldevez, Edouard. *Mes mémoires*. Le Puy: Marchessou fils, 1890.

———. *La Société des concerts, 1860–1885*. Paris: Firmin-Didot, 1887.

Devriès, Anik. "Les Musiques d'Extrême-Orient à l'Exposition universelle de 1889." In *Cahiers Debussy*, new series, no. 1. Paris: Minkoff, 1977, pp. 25–37.

Dorus, Louis. *L'Etude de la nouvelle flûte, méthode progressive arrangée d'après Devienne*. Paris: Schonenberger, 1845.

Duteurtre, Benoît, ed. *150 Ans de musique française: 1789–1939*. Lyon: Actes Sud, 1991.

Duvergès, Marie Joseph. *Nouvelle méthode complète de flûte*. Paris: Escudier, 1873.

Ehrlich, A. *Celebrated Pianists of the Past and Present Time*. London: E. Donajowski, 1895.

Elwart, A. *Histoire de la Société des concerts du Conservatoire impériale de musique*. Paris: S. Castel, 1860.

Escudier, Léon. "Mme Dorus Gras." *La France musicale*, 8 March 1840, pp. 101–3.

Exposition universelle internationale de 1889. *1889: La Tour Eiffel et l'Exposition universelle*. Paris: Réunion des Musées nationaux, 1989.

(Exposition 1889). *Japonisme: Japanese Influences on French Art, 1785–1910*. Cleveland, OH: Cleveland Museum of Art, 1975, 1978.

Fallon, Daniel. "Saint-Saëns and the Concours de composition musicale in Bordeaux." *Journal of the American Musicological Society*, vol. 31, 1978, pp. 309–25.

Fétis, François. *Biographie universelle des musiciens*. 2nd ed. Paris: Firmin-Didot, 1861–65.

Fitzlyon, April. *The Price of Genius: A Life of Pauline Viardot*. London: Calder, 1964.

Fleury, Louis. "The Evolution of Musical Habits." *The Chesterian*, December 1921, pp. 70–75.

————. "The Flute and British Composers." *The Chesterian*, December 1919, pp. 79–82 and 115–17.

————. "The Flute and Flutists in the French Art of the 17th and 18th Centuries." *Musical Quarterly*, vol. 11, no. 4, October 1923, pp. 515–37.

————. "Music for Two Flutes without Bass." *Music and Letters*, vol. 6, no. 2, April 1925, pp. 110–18.

————. "Song and the Flute." *The Chesterian*, January–February 1926, pp. 109–13 and 161–65.

Floyd, Angelita. *The Gilbert Legacy*. Cedar Falls, IA: Winzer Press, 1992.

François-Sappey, Brigitte. "La Vie musicale à Paris à travers les Mémoires d'Eugène Sauzay, 1809–1901." *Revue de musicologie*, vol. 60, nos. 1–2, 1974, pp. 159–210.

Friedrich, Otto. *Olympia, Paris in the Age of Manet*. London: Aurum Press, 1992.

Gál, Hans. *Franz Schubert and the Essence of Melody*. London: Gollancz, 1974.

Garcia, Manuel, trans. Beata Garcia. *Hints on Singing*. Ed. Hermann Klein. London: Ascherberg, Hopwood and Crew, 1911.

Gaubert, Philippe, ed. *Célèbre méthode complète de flûte système Boehm et ordinaire par Devienne*. Paris: Leduc, 1909.

Gevaert, François. *Nouveau traité d'instrumentation*. Paris: Lemoine, 1885.

————. *Cours méthodique d'instrumentation*. Paris: Lemoine 1890.

Giroux, Paul H. "The History of the Flute and Its Music in the United States." *Journal of Research in Music Education*, vol. 1, Spring 1953, pp. 68–73.

Goncourt, Jules, and Edmond de Goncourt, trans. and ed. George J. Becker and Edith Philips. *Paris and the Arts, 1851–1896, from the Goncourt Journal*. Ithaca, NY: Cornell University Press, 1971.

————, trans. and ed. George J. Becker. *Paris Under Siege, 1870–1871, from the Goncourt Journal*. Ithaca, NY: Cornell University Press, 1969.

Gosling, Nigel. *Paris 1900–1914, the Miraculous Years*. London: Weidenfeld and Nicholson, 1978.

Gourret, Jean. *Histoire des salles de l'Opéra de Paris*. Paris: Trédaniel, 1985.

Grubb, Thomas. *Singing in French*. New York: Schirmer, 1979.

Guest, Ivor. *The Ballet of the Second Empire*. London: Pitman, 1974.

Guiral, Pierre. *La Vie quotidienne en France à l'âge d'or du capitalisme, 1852–1879*. Paris: Hachette, 1976.

Guiraud, Ernest. *Traité pratique d'instrumentation*. Paris: Durand, 1890.

Hahn, Reynaldo. *Du Chant*. Paris: Gallimard, 1957.

Harriss, Joseph. *The Tallest Tower*. Boston: Houghton Mifflin, 1975.

Hartford, Robert, ed. *Bayreuth, the Early Years*. Cambridge: Cambridge University Press, 1980.

Hervey, Arthur. *French Music in the XIXth Century*. London: Grant Richards, 1903.

Higonnet, Patrice, trans. Arthur Goldhammer. *Paris: Capital of the World*. Cambridge, MA: Belknap Press/Harvard, 2002.

Hill, Edward Burlingame. *Modern French Music*. London: Allen and Unwin, 1924.

Honoré, Léopold. "Jules Lefèbvre." *Revue régionale Brie et Gatinais*, 15 July 1911, pp. 217–19.

Horne, Alistair. *Seven Ages of Paris*. London: Macmillan, 2002.

Hurst, P. G. *The Golden Age Recorded*. Rev. ed. London: Oakwood Press, 1963.

Imbert, Hugues. *Profils d'artistes contemporains.* Paris: Fischbacher, 1897.

Jacobs, Robert, and Geoffrey Skelton. *Wagner Writes from Paris.* London: Allen and Unwin, 1973.

James, W. N. *A Word or Two on the Flute.* London: Cocks and Co., 1826. 3rd ed., London: Tony Bingham, 1982.

Jarociński, Stefan, trans. Rollo Myers. *Debussy, Impressionism and Symbolism.* London: Eulenburg, 1976.

Jean-Aubry, G., trans. Edwin Evans. *French Music of Today.* London: Kegan Paul, 1919.

Jemain, Joseph. "Un Métronomie rationnel, Le Métronome de précision à pendule normal." *Le Monde musical,* 30 September 1908, pp. 274–76.

Kastner, Georges. *Les Danses des morts.* Paris: Brandus, 1852.

Klauwell, Otto. *Théodore Gouvy, sein Leben und seine Werke.* Berlin: Harmonie, 1902.

Klein, Hermann. *The Reign of Patti.* London: Fisher and Unwin, 1920.

Labarthe, Gustave. *Le Théâtre pendant les jours du siège et de la commune.* Paris: Fischbacher, 1910.

Lalo, Pierre. *De Rameau à Ravel.* Paris: Albin Michel, 1947.

Landormy, Paul. "La Musique de chambre en France de 1850 à 1871." *Société internationale de musicologie,* August–September 1911.

———. *La Musique française de Franck à Debussy.* Paris: Gallimard, 1943.

———. *La Musique française de la marseillaise à la mort de Berlioz.* Paris: Gallimard, 1944.

Laurencie, Lionel de la. *Le Goût musical en France.* Paris: Joanin, 1905.

Lauw, Louisa, trans. J. Loder. *Fourteen Years with Adelina Patti.* New York: Munro, 1884.

Lavoix (Henri-Marie Tallement). *Histoire de l'instrumentation.* Paris: Firmin-Didot, 1878.

Lesle, Lutz. "Liebesklagen aus Arkadien, Kleiner Versuch einer Ästhetik der Flöte." *Das Orchester,* vol. 23, no. 5, 1974, pp. 294–99.

Lockspeiser, Edward. *Debussy, His Life and Mind.* 2 vols. London: Cassell, 1962, 1965.

Loquin, A. *La Musique à Bordeaux.* Bordeaux: Feret, 1879.

Lough, John and Muriel. *An Introduction to Nineteenth-Century France.* London: Longman, 1978.

Mackinlay, M. Sterling. *Garcia the Centenarian and His Times.* London: Blackwood, 1908.

Magnusson, Magnus, ed. *Chambers Biographical Dictionary.* 5th ed. London: Chambers, 1990.

Malherbe, Charles. *Notice sur Ascanio, opéra de Camille Saint-Saëns.* Paris: Fischbacher, 1890.

Marchesi, Blanche. *Singer's Pilgrimage.* London: Grant Richards, 1923.

Marchesi, Mathilde. *Méthode de chant théorique et pratique, Op. 31.* Paris: Grus, 1886.

Maréchal, Henri. *Paris, souvenirs d'un musicien, 1850–1870.* Paris: Hachette, 1907.

Martin, J. *Nos artistes des théâtres et des concerts.* Paris: Flammarion, 1898.

———. *Nos auteurs et compositeurs dramatiques.* Paris: Flammarion, 1897.

Martin-Fugier, Anne. *Les Salons de la troisième république.* Paris: Perrin, 2003.

Merlin, Olivier. *L'Opéra de Paris.* Fribourg: Hatier, 1975.

Milhaud, Darius. "Louis Fleury." *The Chesterian,* 1926, pp. 264–65 (obituary notice).

Milner, John. *The Studios of Paris.* New Haven, CT: Yale University Press, 1988.

Nectoux, Jean-Michel. *Camille Saint-Saëns et Gabriel Fauré, Correspondance.* Paris: Société française de musicologie/Heugel, 1973.

Nichols, Roger. *Debussy Remembered.* London: Faber, 1992.

———. *Ravel.* London: Dent, 1977.

Noël, Edouard, and Edmond Stoullig. *Les Annales du théâtre et de la musique.* Paris: Charpentier, 1875– (annual).

Ory, Pascal. *Les Expositions universelles de Paris.* Paris: Editions Ramsay, 1982.

Osborne, Charles, trans. and ed. *Letters of Giuseppe Verdi.* London: Gollancz, 1971.

Pasler, Jann. "Paris: Conflicting Notions of Progress." In *Man and Music: The Late Romantic Era,* ed. Jim Samson. London: Macmillan, 1991.

Paul, Charles B. "Rameau, d'Indy, and French Nationalism." *Musical Quarterly,* vol. 58, part 1, 1972, pp. 46–56.

Philipp, Isidor. "Souvenirs sur Anton Rubinstein, Camille Saint-Saëns et Busoni." *Revue internationale de musique,* special number, April 1939, pp. 907–12.

Pierre, Constant. *B. Sarrette et les origines du Conservatoire national de musique et de déclamation.* Paris: Librairie Delalain, 1895.

———. *Les Factures d'instruments de musique.* Paris: Sagot, 1893.

———. *Histoire de la composition de l'orchestre de l'Opéra.* Ms., unpublished. Paris: Bibliothèque nationale (Music Department), Rés Vmc 53.

Pierreuse, Bernard. *Flute Literature.* Paris: Editions Jobert et Musicales transatlantiques, 1982.

Pingeot, Anne. *1878: La 1ère Exposition universelle de la république.* Carnet parcours du Musée d'Orsay, no. 14, Paris: Editions de la Réunion des Musées nationaux, 1988.

Pistone, Danièle. "Musique et société à Paris sous la deuxième république, 1848–1852." *Revue internationale de musique française,* no. 3, November 1980, pp. 313–401.

———. *L'Opéra italien au XIXᵉ siècle de Rossini à Puccini.* Paris: Honoré Champion, 1986.

———. "L'Opéra de Paris au siècle romantique." *Revue internationale de musique française,* no. 4, January 1981, pp. 5–55.

———. "Paris et la musique, 1890–1900." *Revue internationale de musique francaise,* no. 28, February 1981, pp. 5–55.

———. "Wagner à Paris." *Revue internationale de musique française,* no. 1, February 1980, pp. 7–84.

Pontécoulant, Adolphe de. "Des Instruments à vent et leur construction." *La France musicale,* 1840, pp. 3–143. Six articles, including "M. Coche et la nouvelle flûte," p. 76.

———. *La Musique à l'Exposition universelle de 1867.* Paris: L'Art musical, 1868.

Pougin, Arthur. "Tablettes artistiques." *Le Ménestrel,* 1870, pp. 339 ff. (nine articles).

Prill, Emil. *Führer durch die Flöten-Literatur.* 2 vols. Leipzig: Zimmermann, 1899, 1913.

Prod'homme, J. G. "La Musique et les musiciens en 1848." *Sammelbände der Internationalen Musik-Gesellschaft,* 1912–13, pp. 155–82.

Proust, Marcel. *A la recherche du temps perdu.* Paris: Gallimard (Bibliothèque de la Pléiade), 2001.

Prout, Ebenezer. *Instrumentation.* London: Novello, n.d. (1896).

Rearick, Charles. *Pleasures of the Belle Epoque.* New Haven, CT: Yale University Press, 1985.

Rémusat, Jean. *Méthode pour la flûte ordinaire et Boehm.* Paris: Leduc, 1862.

Riemann, Hugo. *Musik-Lexikon.* Leipzig: 1882.

Robert, Gustave. *La Musique à Paris*. Paris: Fischbacher, 1895– (annual to 1900).

Rocheguide, Marquis de. *Promenades dans toutes les rues de Paris*. Paris: Hachette, 1910.

Rudorff, Raymond. *Belle Epoque, Paris in the Nineties*. London: Hamish Hamilton, 1972.

Saint-Saëns, Camille. *Ecole buissonnière*. Paris: Pierre Lafitte, 1913.

———. *Harmonie et mélodie*. Paris: Calman-Lévy, 1885.

———. *Portraits et souvenirs*. Paris: Calman-Lévy, 1909.

———, ed. Yves Gérard. *Regards sur mes contemporains*. Paris: Coutaz, 1990.

Sala, George Augustus. *Paris Herself Again*. London: Vitzetelly, 1879.

Schmid, Manfred Hermann. *Die Revolution der Flöte, Theobald Boehm (1794–1881)*. Tutzing: Hans Schneider, 1981.

Schwarz, Boris. *French Instrumental Music Between the Revolutions, 1789–1830*. New York: Da Capo, 1987.

Scott, Michael. *The Record of Singing*. Vol. 1 (to 1914). London: Duckworth, 1977.

Scudo, Paul. *L'Année musicale*. 3 vols. Paris: Hachette, 1860, 1861, 1862.

———. *La Musique en l'année 1862*. Paris: J. Hetzel, 1863.

Shaw, George Bernard. *Music in London, 1890–94*. 3 vols. London: Constable, 1932.

Sitwell, Sacheverell. *Valse des fleurs*. London: Faber, 1941.

———. *La Vie parisienne*. London: Faber, 1937.

Solum, John. "Degas' Portrait of the Flautist Altès." *Pan* (Journal of the British Flute Society), vol. 3, no. 1, March 1985, p. 24.

Sordet, Dominique. *Douze chefs d'orchestre*. Paris: Fischbacher, 1924.

Soubies, Albert. *Soixante-neuf ans à l'Opéra-comique en deux pages, 1825–1894*. Paris: Fischbacher, 1894.

———. *Soixante-sept ans à l'Opéra en une page, 1826–1893*. Paris: Fischbacher, 1893.

———. *Le Théâtre-Italien de 1801 à 1913*. Paris: Fischbacher, 1913.

———, and Charles Malherbe. *Histoire de l'Opéra-comique*. Paris: Flammarion, 1893.

Steane, J. B. *The Great Tradition, Seventy Years of Singing on Record, 1900–1970*. London: Duckworth, 1974.

Stendhal. *Mémoires d'un touriste, Paris, 1838*. Reprinted. Paris: Maspero, 1981.

Stonequist, Martha E. *The Musical Entente Cordial, 1905–1916*. Ph.D. thesis, University of Colorado at Boulder, 1972 (University Microfilms 73–18,597).

Strakosch, Maurice. *Souvenirs d'un impressario*. Paris: Ollendorf, 1887.

Tellier, Michelle. *Jean-Louis Tulou, flûtiste, professeur, facteur, compositeur, 1786–1865*. Thèse de musicologie, Paris Conservatoire, Spring 1981.

Thomson, Andrew. *Widor*. London: Oxford University Press, 1987.

Tiersot, Julien. *Un Demi-siècle de musique française, 1870–1919*. 2nd ed. Paris: Alcan, 1924.

Toyon, Paul de. *La Musique en 1864*. Paris: Arnauld de Vresse, 1866.

Tulou, Jean-Louis. *Méthode de flûte*. Paris: Brandus, 1851.

Vallas, Léon. *La Véritable histoire de César Franck*. Paris: Flammarion, 1955.

Ventzke, Karl, and Dietrich Hilenbach. *Boehm-Instrument*. Frankfurt: Verlag das Musikinstrument, 1982.

Vester, Frans. *Flute Repertoire Catalogue*. London: Musica Rara, 1967.

Vuillermoz, Jean, trans. and ed. Edward Blakeman. "Marcel Moyse on His Method of Learning the Flute." *Pan* (Journal of the British Flute Society), vol. 3, no. 4, December 1985, pp. 10–12.

Wainwright, David. *Broadwood by Appointment.* London: Quilter Press, 1982.

Walsh, Tom J. *Second Empire Opera, the Théâtre-lyrique Paris, 1851–1871.* London: John Calder, 1981.

Ward, Cornelius. *The Flute Explained.* London, 1844.

Weber, Eugen. *France, Fin de Siècle.* Cambridge, MA: Harvard University Press, 1986.

Welch, Christopher. *History of the Boehm Flute.* London: Rudall Carte, 1882; 2nd ed., 1892. Reprinted in facsimile. New York: McGinnis and Marx, 1961.

Widor, Charles-Marie *Technique de l'orchestre moderne.* Paris: Lemoine, 1904.

Zeldin, Theodore. *France, 1848–1945.* 2 vols. Oxford: Clarendon Press, 1973, 1977.